THE AFFECTIVE TURN

The Affective Turn

THEORIZING THE SOCIAL

Edited by PATRICIA TICINETO CLOUGH,

with JEAN HALLEY

FOREWORD BY MICHAEL HARDT

Duke University Press
Durham and London
2007

© 2007 DUKE UNIVERSITY PRESS

ALL RIGHTS RESERVED

PRINTED IN THE UNITED STATES OF

AMERICA ON ACID-FREE PAPER ∞

DESIGNED BY AMY RUTH BUCHANAN

TYPESET IN MINION BY KEYSTONE

TYPESETTING, INC.

LIBRARY OF CONGRESS CATALOGING-

IN-PUBLICATION DATA APPEAR ON THE

LAST PRINTED PAGE OF THIS BOOK.

CONTENTS

ACKNOWLEDGMENTS

The Affective Turn is a collection of essays whose authors have been participants in projects supported by the Center for the Study of Women and Society at the Graduate Center of the City University of New York from 1999 to 2006: the Conviction Seminar and The CLEAR Project dedicated to the study of mass incarceration and the conditions of life for women and men living with criminal convictions; The Future Matters Project dedicated to the study of culture, technoscience, and governance; and the Rockefeller Foundation funded project on global capitalism, human rights, and human securing, Facing Global Capitalism/Finding Human Security: A Gendered Critique. I want to thank the administrators at the Graduate Center for their support of the Center for the Study of Women and Society and its projects, especially Frances Degan Horowitz, William Kelly, Steve Brier, and Brian Swartz. I want to thank the Ph.D. program in Sociology and the Women's Studies program at the Graduate Center and the faculty of the Sociology department at Queens College who generously gave me time to be Director of the Center for the Study of Women and Society over the past six years. I want to thank those of the larger intellectual community beyond CUNY who also participated in the projects of the Center for the Study of Women and Society: Jonathan Cutler, Norman Denzin, Richard Dienst, Michelle Fine, Stephano Harney, Janet Jakobsen, Michael Hardt, Jill Herbert, Anne Hoffman Anahid Kassabian, David Kassanjian, Charles Lemert, Michal McCall, Randy Martin, Barbara Martinsons, Brian Massumi, Mary Jo Neitz, Jackie Orr, Luciana Parisi, Jasbir Puar, Amitabh Rai, Joseph Schneider, Joan W. Scott, Steven Seidman, Charles Shepherdson, Catherine Silver, Tiziana Terranova, Judith Wittner, and Angela Zito. I want to thank all my colleagues and fast-made friends at the Institute for Advanced Study at Princeton for their support while I was a member there and to all those at Duke University Press, especially J. Reynolds Smith who has done so much to make this book project come to completion. My warmest appreciation to Jean Halley for her patient support throughout and to Una Chung for her assistance in the final stages of this manuscript and so much more. And to my family, especially my sister Virginia, my son Christopher, and the newest member of the family, Elizabeth.

Last but not least, I thank all the members of "the book group," those whose writings are presented here, as well as those whose writings are not. The many hours that I have spent as your teacher and the hours we have spent together reading and writing are memorable. Filled with the joy, laughter, and occasional tears that make for fresh thought, our time together has been for me an experience of excellence in teaching and learning. It is to you that I dedicate this book.

The essays in this volume are evidence of what Patricia Clough identifies as an "affective turn" in the humanities and social sciences. Like the other "turns" that academic fields have undergone in recent decades— the linguistic turn, the cultural turn, and so forth—this focus on affects consolidates and extends some of the most productive existing trends in research. Specifically, the two primary precursors to the affective turn I see in U.S. academic work are the focus on the body, which has been most extensively advanced in feminist theory, and the exploration of emotions, conducted predominantly in queer theory.[1] Like the other turns, too, however, while extending previous research, this affective turn also opens new avenues for study, casts previous work in a fresh light, and indicates novel possibilities for politics. It might be useful, then, to take this opportunity to reflect briefly on what affects are good for.

A focus on affects certainly does draw attention to the body and emotions, but it also introduces an important shift. The challenge of the perspective of the affects resides primarily in the syntheses it requires. This is, in the first place, because affects refer equally to the body and the mind; and, in the second, because they involve both reason and the passions. Affects require us, as the term suggests, to enter the realm of causality, but they offer a complex view of causality because the affects belong simultaneously to both sides of the causal relationship. They illuminate, in other words, both our power to affect the world around us and our power to be affected by it, along with the relationship between these two powers.

Baruch Spinoza, the philosopher who has advanced furthest the theory of the affects and whose thought is the source, either directly or indirectly, of most of the contemporary work in this field, grasps the powers of the affects in terms of two sets of parallel developments or correspondences.[2] First, the mind's power to think and its developments are, he proposes, parallel to the body's power to act. This does not mean that the mind can determine the body to act, or that the body can determine the mind to think. On the contrary,

Spinoza maintains that mind and body are autonomous but that they none-theless proceed or develop in parallel. Such a claim does not in any way resolve the question of the relation of body and mind; rather, it poses it as a problem or mandate for research: each time we consider the mind's power to think, we must try to recognize how the body's power to act corresponds to it—and the notion of correspondence here is importantly open and indefinite. An affect straddles this relationship insofar as it indicates at once the current state of the mind and the body. The perspective of the affects, in short, forces us constantly to pose the problem of the relationship between mind and body with the assumption that their powers constantly correspond in some way.

Spinoza also, secondly, proposes a correspondence between the power to act and the power to be affected. This applies equally to the mind and the body: the mind's power to think corresponds to its receptivity to external ideas; and the body's power to act corresponds to its sensitivity to other bodies. The greater our power to be affected, he posits, the greater our power to act. Once again, Spinoza proposes a correspondence but does not fix what determinate form it will take. And in this case, too, the notion of affect straddles the divide. In his terms, affects can be actions, that is, determined by internal causes, or passions, determined by external causes. On the one side we have reason, actions of the mind, along with actions of the body, which one might call provocatively corporeal reason; on the other side are the passions both of the mind and the body. The perspective of the affects does not assume that reason and passion are the same, but rather poses them together on a continuum. For Spinoza, the ethical and political project involves a constant effort to transform passions into actions, to replace encounters that result from external causes, which may be joyful or sad, with encounters determined by internal causes, which are necessarily joyful. And yet we need to remember that Spinoza's preference for internal causes does not lead to an isolation of any sort since every increase of the power to act and think corresponds to an increased power to be affected—the increased autonomy of the subject, in other words, always corresponds to its increased receptivity. One way of understanding this com-plex set of propositions, then, is simply to say that the perspective of the affects requires us constantly to pose as a problem the relation between actions and passions, between reason and the emotions. We do not know in advance what a body can do, what a mind can think—what affects they are capable of. The perspective of the affects requires an exploration of these as yet unknown powers. Spinoza thus gives us a new ontology of the human or, rather, an ontology of the human that is constantly open and renewed.

One of the central challenges for research posed by this Spinozian perspective of the affects, then, resides in the fact that the affects straddle these two divides: between the mind and body, and between actions and passions. The affects pose a problematic correspondence across each of the divides: between the mind's power to think and the body's power to act, and between the power to act and the power to be affected. These are some of the primary theoretical challenges that the texts in this volume, and indeed all those that would constitute the affective turn, must address.

To give one example of how the perspective of the affects, which I have thus far articulated only in philosophical terms, can be useful for social science research, allow me to explain briefly my own effort to employ it in order to understand recent changes in the dominant forms of labor and production. I use the term *affective labor* as a way to build on two rather disparate streams of research. The first stream is composed of work developed by U.S. feminists about gendered forms of labor that involve the affects in a central way—such as emotional labor, care, kin work, or maternal work—and that consider the nature and value of such activity both in the waged and unwaged economies.[3] The second stream primarily involves writings by French and Italian economists and labor sociologists who try to grasp the increasingly intellectual character of productive practices and the labor market as a whole, employing terms such as cognitive labor and the new cognitariat.[4] The term *affective labor* is meant to bring together elements from these two different streams and grasp simultaneously the corporeal and intellectual aspects of the new forms of production, recognizing that such labor engages at once with rational intelligence and with the passions or feeling.

Consider, for example, just to indicate the range of activities identified by this category, health care workers, flight attendants, fast food workers, and sex workers—all strongly gendered activities that, to a large degree, produce affects. Identifying these as forms of affective labor highlights not only the common qualities their products share but also the fact that in all these activities the body and the mind are simultaneously engaged, and that similarly reason and passion, intelligence and feeling, are employed together. The perspective of the affects requires, as I said earlier, that with respect to these forms of labor we pose as a problem the relations that bridge across the two divides, between the mind and body, and between reason and passion. Furthermore, the identification of a category of labor such as this that brings together conceptually a range of productive activities can be useful in a variety of ways— by clarifying, for example, the differences of this category of labor with respect to others, and for illuminating the divisions and hierarchies within this category. Finally, identifying the category of affective labor allows one further step:

to consider it together with the various other forms of labor whose products are in large part immaterial, that is, to think together the production of affects with the production of code, information, ideas, images, and the like. This analytical recognition suggests new political possibilities, bringing to light new and intensified forms of exploitation that are shared among a range of laboring activities and, most important, opening up avenues for political organizing and collective practices of refusal and liberation.[5] The purpose of my example about the concept of affective labor is simply to indicate the potential utility of the perspective of the affects in one field of study, demonstrating how it forces us to focus on the problematic correspondences that extend across its two primary divides—between the mind and body, and between reason and the passions—and how the new ontology of the human it reveals has direct implications for politics.

The innovative essays in this volume offer a series of other examples, demonstrating the potential of the perspective of the affects in a wide range of fields and with a variety of methodological approaches. Some of the essays, for example, use fieldwork to investigate the functions of affects—among organized sex workers, health care workers, and in the modeling industry. Others employ the discourses of microbiology, thermodynamics, information sciences, and cinema studies to rethink the body and the affects in terms of technology. Still others explore the affects of trauma in the context of immigration and war. And throughout all the essays run serious theoretical reflections on the powers of the affects and the political possibilities they pose for research and practice. The originality of these essays thus opens up several avenues for future work, and as a whole they furnish ample reason to believe that there exists a significant trend in academic research worthy of being called the affective turn.

Michael Hardt

NOTES

1. Some of the classic examples of feminist theory that focuses on the body as a central problematic are Judith Butler, *Bodies That Matter: On the Discursive Limits of "Sex"* (New York: Routledge, 1993); and Elizabeth Grosz, *Volatile Bodies: Toward a Corporeal Feminism* (Bloomington: Indiana University Press, 1994). For work in queer theory on the emotions, in addition to Eve Kosofsky Sedgwick and Adam Frank, eds., *Shame and Its Sisters: A Silvan Tomkins Reader* (Durham, NC: Duke University Press, 1995), which several essays in this volume cite, see the two collections edited by Lauren Berlant: *Intimacy* (Chicago: University of Chicago Press, 2000); and *Compassion: The Culture and Politics of an Emotion* (New York: Routledge, 2004).

2. See Baruch Spinoza, *Ethics*, in *Complete Works*, ed. Edwin Curley (Princeton, NJ: Princeton University Press, 1985), esp. part 3, 1. Gilles Deleuze's interpretation gives the most complete and innovative reading of the affects in Spinoza. See his *Expressionism in Philosophy: Spinoza*, trans. Martin Joughin (New York: Zone, 1990). For an excellent example of contemporary work that draws creatively on Spinoza's theory of the affects and Deleuze's interpretation of it, see Brian Massumi, *Parables of the Virtual: Movement, Affect, Sensation* (Durham, NC: Duke University Press, 2002).

3. See, for example, Arlie Russell Hochschild, *The Managed Heart: Commercialization of Human Feeling* (Berkeley: University of California Press, 1983); Joan Tronto, *Moral Boundaries: A Political Argument for an Ethic of Care* (New York: Routledge, 1993); and Robin Leidner, *Fast Food, Fast Talk: Service Work and the Routinization of Everyday Life* (Berkeley: University of California Press, 1993).

4. See, for example, Maurizio Lazzarato, "Immaterial Labor," in *Radical Thought in Italy: A Potential Politics*, ed. Paolo Virno and Michael Hardt, 133–47 (Minneapolis: University of Minnesota Press, 1996); and Carlo Vercellone, ed., *Sommes-nous sortis du capitalisme industriel?* (Paris: La Dispute, 2002).

5. See Michael Hardt, "Affective Labor," *Boundary 2* 26.2 (1999): 89–100; as well as Michael Hardt and Antonio Negri, *Empire* (Cambridge, MA: Harvard University Press, 2000), 289–294; and Michael Hardt and Antonio Negri, *Multitude: War and Democracy in the Age of Empire* (New York: Penguin, 2004), 103–115.

PATRICIA TICINETO CLOUGH

> Each self-reproducing system in this generalized production of order out of chaos combines modulations of what could be called, broadly, the "political" dimension . . . the "economic" dimension . . . , and contributes in a way that could be called "cultural" . . . . For lack of a better word, the chaotic cofunctioning of the political, economic and cultural dimensions could be dubbed the "social"—although all of these designations are fairly arbitrary at this point.
> —Brian Massumi, "Requiem for Our Prospective Dead (Toward a Participatory Critique of Capitalist Power)"

The increasing significance of affect as a focus of analysis across a number of disciplinary and interdisciplinary discourses is occurring at a time when critical theory is facing the analytic challenges of ongoing war, trauma, torture, massacre, and counter/terrorism. If these world events can be said to be symptomatic of ongoing political, economic, and cultural transformations, the turn to affect may be registering a change in the cofunctioning of the political, economic, and cultural, or what Brian Massumi in the epigraph to this introduction dubs the "social." The essays collected in *The Affective Turn: Theorizing the Social* explore these political, economic, and cultural tendencies and investigate how they are being rendered as a shift in thought—captured in critical theory's turn to affect.

The essays collected in *The Affective Turn*—written when their authors were completing doctoral work in sociology, women's studies, and cultural studies—explore the recent turn in critical theory to affect, especially the conceptualization of affect that draws on the line of thought from Gilles Deleuze and Félix Guattari back through Baruch Spinoza and Henri Bergson.[1] The essays engage the insights of scholars presently working in this line of thought and who treat affectivity as a substrate of potential bodily responses, often autonomic responses, in excess of consciousness. For these scholars, affect refers generally to bodily capacities to affect and be affected or the augmentation or diminution of a body's capacity to act, to engage, and to connect, such that autoaffection is linked to the self-feeling of being alive—that is, aliveness or vitality.[2] Yet affect is not "presocial," as Massumi argues. There is a reflux back from conscious experience to affect, which is registered, however, as affect, such that "past action and contexts are conserved and repeated, autonomically reactivated but not accomplished; begun but not completed."[3] Affect constitutes a nonlinear complexity out of which the narration of conscious states such as emotion are subtracted, but always with "a never-to-be-conscious autonomic remainder."[4]

In this conceptualization, affect is not only theorized in terms of the human body. Affect is also theorized in relation to the technologies that are allowing us both to "see" affect and to produce affective bodily capacities beyond the body's organic-physiological constraints. The technoscientific experimentation with affect not only traverses the opposition of the organic and the nonorganic; it also inserts the technical into felt vitality, the felt aliveness given in the preindividual bodily capacities to act, engage, and connect—to affect and be affected. The affective turn, therefore, expresses a new configuration of bodies, technology, and matter instigating a shift in thought in critical theory. It is this shift in thought that the following essays engage. Taken together, the essays explore the movement in critical theory from a psychoanalytically informed criticism of subject identity, representation, and trauma to an engagement with information and affect; from privileging the organic body to exploring nonorganic life; from the presumption of equilibrium-seeking closed systems to engaging the complexity of open systems under far-from-equilibrium conditions of metastability; from focusing on an economy of production and consumption to focusing on the economic circulation of pre-individual bodily capacities or affects in the domain of biopolitical control. Taken together, the essays suggest that attending to the affective turn is necessary to theorizing the social.

This not only means thinking about affect in terms of the historical changes in Western capitalist industrial societies but also recognizing that politics, economy, and culture always have been and are presently being reconfigured differently across various regions of the world. This recognition comes not so much from a comparative but rather from a geopolitical analysis of the ongoing transformation of relations of power across international organizations, regions, nations, states, economies, and private and public spheres. *The*

Affective Turn especially marks the way these historical changes are indicative of the changing global processes of accumulating capital and employing labor power through the deployment of technoscience to reach beyond the limitations of the human in experimentation with the structure and organization of the human body, or what is called "life itself."[5] The affective turn throws thought back to the disavowals constitutive of Western industrial capitalist societies, bringing forth ghosted bodies and the traumatized remains of erased histories. It also sends thought to the future—to the bodily matter and biotechnologies of technoscientific experimentation.

The affective turn invites a transdisciplinary approach to theory and method that necessarily invites experimentation in capturing the changing cofunctioning of the political, the economic, and the cultural, rendering it affectively as change in the deployment of affective capacity. The authors of the essays collected in *The Affective Turn* have made use of theory and method both to grasp the changes that constitute the social and to explore them as changes in ourselves, circulating through our bodies, our subjectivities, yet irreducible to the individual, the personal, or the psychological. Irreducible because the shift in thought that *The Affective Turn* elaborates might itself be described as marking an intensification of self-reflexivity (processes turning back on themselves to act on themselves) in information/communication systems, including the human body; in archiving machines, including all forms of media technologies and human memory; in capital flows, including the circulation of value through human labor and technology; and in biopolitical networks of disciplining, surveillance, and control.

As self-reflexivity becomes internal to these systems, an ongoing and readily available feature of their functioning, it is increasingly realized in feedback loops, which shoot off with varying speeds, in multiple directions, and in multiple temporalities, emerging by chance and out of control—the chaos that, as Massumi proposes, is at this time the condition of possibility for the social. System self-reflexivity shifts from seeking homeostasis and equilibrium to seeking control and freedom in complexity in systems under far-from-equilibrium conditions.[6] In introducing the essays, then, I want to give some sense of the chaotic processes that presently constitute the social. I also want to revisit the various intellectual discourses that the authors and I explored together in order to refind the capacities of critical theory to address the reconfiguration of technology, matter, and bodies—captured in the affective turn.

In 1999, I taught a course entitled "Psychoanalysis and Social Theory," which I organized around a list of readings meant to move us through psychoanalytic discourses on trauma, melancholy, and loss and allow us then to turn to Gilles Deleuze's work on time, bodies, images, and memory. I wanted students to examine the ways bodies are thought in relationship both to trauma and to technoscientific productions of bodily capacities beyond the human body's organic-physiological constraints.

.....

A number of the essays that follow might be described as experimental and autoethnographic as each essay reflects the subjectivity of the writer. But what is more important is the way the essays render changes in processes of embodiment, that is, employ new writing/methods for grasping the materialities and temporalities of bodies. On the one hand, the essays touch on a psychoanalytically oriented account of trauma in order to welcome bodies haunted by memories of times lost and places left. On the other hand, the essays engage technoscientific experimentation in exploring the disjointed temporalities of experiences that cannot be known for certain, cannot be placed once and for all, but which repeatedly pressure the subject with bodily effects.

.....

Grace M. Cho's essay, "Voices from the *Teum*: Synesthetic Trauma and the Ghosts of the Korean Diaspora" is a performed movement from a psychoanalytic understanding of trauma to Deleuze's notion of machinic assemblage. Cho's essay focuses on the traumatic history of Korean women from Japanese colonization to the U.S. diaspora. She treats the diasporic body as an effect of a transgenerational haunting and as a composed machinic assemblage. Diasporic bodies, she proposes, carry a vision, a machinic vision, of what they did not see and what an earlier generation saw but could not say they saw. Cho shows the diasporic body as it acts out being haunted, repetitively and melancholically, in a constant movement toward the traumatic experience of an earlier generation, her mother's. Hosu Kim's essay, "The Parched Tongue," focuses on the production of trauma in terms of a body without organs, a body that does not privilege the organism, and thereby lets loose body parts for a machinic assemblage. One body part in particular constitutes the focus of Kim's "Parched Tongue": the mouth, its ability or failure to shape words. In the aftermath of the move from Korea to the United States, the mouth of the diasporic body holds a cracked tongue, having become parched with envy in an economy of English. It is made to gather all sensations, the effects of the history of the American Dream gone nightmarish, the textualization of which invents: a broken English gone poetic.

.....

It is not surprising that students and I first began to engage the shift in thought in critical theory and the attendant intensification of self-reflexivity through a discussion of psychoanalysis—the self-reflective methodology of choice of critical theory just before the turn of the century. Nor is it so surprising that this engagement would lead us to move through trauma studies, and the queering of melancholy and loss, in order eventually to think about technoscience and rethink technology, time, and the ontology of bodily matter. After all, in the last years of the twentieth century, critical theory came to focus on trauma, loss, and melancholy borrowing from psychoanalytic discourse. That it did so at the turn of the century might well be expected, but what is nonetheless important to notice is how psychoanalytic discourse about trauma could so ably serve as a summary rendition of the epistemological crisis in Western thought, which critical theory instigated, at the same time that psychoanalysis could offer an opening to the future of thought in the ontology it proposes for bodies, temporality, memory, and materiality.

Even before the turn of the century, critical theory had been engaged with psychoanalysis, especially with a Lacanian understanding of the subject, which emphasized the human being's entrance into subjectivity and language through a subjugation to the symbolic law of the father—the oedipal law that demands that the infant-child submit to symbolic castration, to a loss of wholeness, a loss of what Jacques Lacan had referred to as the imaginary wholeness of the mirror stage. While the subject does submit to the law, as Lacan argued, there also is a refusal of the law, so that the subject is shaped around a lack in being, a castration both avowed and disavowed in the unconscious, which sends unconscious desire along a chain of signifiers in a blind search to recapture what is lacking. The subject is shaped around a void, a real that is always already lost and only leaves traces of its loss as traumatic effects.

It is in the Lacanian understanding of the subject that trauma is linked to the "Real," which is equated with the "unassimilable," presenting itself in analysis, as Lacan put it, "in the form of the trauma, determining all that follows, and imposing on it an apparently accidental origin."[7] For Lacan, the Real is unassimilable because it is nonsymbolizable. It is that which is in excess of the symbolic, an exclusion or void interior to the symbolic but not reducible to the symbolic or the imaginary. Rather, this interior exclusion or void in the symbolic constitutes the very condition of possibility of the symbolic, what will surface seemingly accidentally as an origin of subjectivity, identity, meaning, and materiality.

Critical theory was not only influenced by Lacan's understanding of the subject and unconscious desire. The Lacanian understanding of the interrelationship of the real, the imaginary, and the symbolic also took hold in critical theory as it explored a more general treatment of the unassimilable. Critical theory turned psychoanalysis into a provocative and productive way of thinking politically about subjectivity, identity, meaning, bodies, and reality. For one, it retraced the unassimilable presenting itself in thought, finding the traces of the unthought of authorized knowledge. It did so often on behalf of those excluded from authorship or the authority of knowledge.

In taking up trauma, critical theory was able to transition from the deconstruction of the Subject of Western modernity to the production of multiple subjectivities and multiple modernities expressed in new forms of history, often presented at first in autobiographical experimental writings by diasporic subjects. These experimental forms of writing render the traumatic effect of the long exclusion from writing, which haunts the writing as a motive force. These writings are traumatizing as they call into question the truth of representation, the certainty of memory, if not the very possibility of knowledge of the past.

Just as experimentation in autoethnographic writing was being elaborated in critical theory and cultural criticism, trauma was being discussed in terms of its effects on memory, its producing in the subject the incapacity to retrieve the past, or to speak truth about it. In her take on various debates over the effects of trauma, Ruth Leys proposed that trauma is a forgetting without memory, so that traumatic effects are a symptomology substituting for what was never experienced as such. It cannot be said that there is repression of what is experienced. There is no repression and therefore no possibility of projection or displacement onto the other. Instead, trauma is drawn back into the ego. The ego is overrun by the object or event, fixating the ego.

The ego is put into something like a trance state, what Leys has referred to as the ego's "mesmerized immersion in the object," a "fascinated attention" to the object or the event. There is a coalescence of the ego with the object or event of fascination, such that it might be said that there is no ego, surely not one distinguishable from the object.[8] Trauma is the engulfment of the ego in memory. But memory might better be understood not as unconscious memory so much as memory without consciousness and therefore, incorporated memory, body memory, or cellular memory. As a surfacing of a difficulty in remembering or in being certain about the truth of memory, the body becomes a memorial, a ghosted bodily matter.

Although there are efforts to work out trauma, more commonly trauma is acted out or compulsively repeated, a seemingly wasteful but actually productive repetition. The effort to overcome the repetition fails and fails to put an end to forgetting. Not surprisingly, the experimental forms of writing that mean to capture trauma often present the subject in blanks or hesitations—a topographic formulation of forgetting, loss, uncertainty, disavowal, and defensiveness. Moreover, the loss and the forgetting might not be those of the writing subject per se. As Nicolas Abraham and Maria Torok suggest, in an elaboration of what they refer to as "transgenerational haunting," the forgetting of trauma is passed down from one generation to another, mesmerizing multiple egos, putting all in a transgenerational bodily trance.[9] Not only does one generation act out the trauma of the generation before it. There also can be a haunting across different groups of one generation, in different places, "creating a monstrous family of reluctant belonging," as Jacqueline Rose puts it in her treatment of the transgenerational haunting joining Palestinians and Israeli Jews.[10] One lives in the unconscious fantasy of the other, not unfamiliar to each other, but, rather, all too familiar. There is what Petar Ramadanovic calls "an entanglement," "where, instead of the we-that-will-have-been, there is an entanglement beyond all possibility of disengagement."[11]

But what kind of body is the body of entanglement? What is the ontological status of a ghosted body, of a haunted materiality? Of course, critical theory of the late twentieth century had drawn on a psychoanalytic account of trauma to rethink bodily matter. Judith Butler had introduced queer theory with her notion of "melancholic heterosexuality"; she had argued that with the imposition of the cultural norm, or regulatory ideal, of heterosexuality, what she referred to as "heteronormativity," the love for the same-sexed parent is not merely repressed but foreclosed. As such, the loss is never actually experienced and, therefore, cannot be mourned. The loss is, however, melancholically incorporated and lived in the body as compulsively repeated traumatic effects, giving form to the matter of the body, giving the body the sexed morphology of a melancholic heterosexuality.[12] As such, the body is materialized as ghosted or haunted by a loss that is endlessly repeated, performed albeit with a possibility of difference (*différance*) in the interval between repetitions. Butler's queer theory makes bodily matter dynamic with an incorporated haunted/haunting imaginary, the materialization of a foreclosed unconscious desire. In recognizing the material effects of the imaginary or haunted body, Butler begins to move theorization of the body beyond Lacanian semiotics and opens up the possibility of rethinking bodies, matter, and technology.

However, while for Butler the matter of the body is dynamic, its dynamism is the effect of the productivity of a cultural form imposed on the body. The nature of bodily matter is culturally or unnaturally formed, so that while neither form nor matter preexist each other, only form is productive, what in his critique of Butler Pheng Cheah has described as the "hypertrophic productivity" of a historicized or politicized notion of form.[13] Cheah concludes that for Butler, "matter is invested with dynamism and said to be open to contestation only because the matter concerned is the product of sociohistorical forms of power, that is, of the human realm."[14] Matter remains undifferentiated. The social, too, remains undifferentiated, serving only as a site for the deployment of power in the imposition of a cultural form. In this, matter and form are opposed in an ahistorical way, in a way unreflective of the changing relation of matter and form elaborated in the technologies that give a body and a sociality to such relations. Butler's treatment of the body therefore does not open up to rethinking bodily matter or matter generally beyond the human body. She inevitably reproduces the distinction, if not opposition, between matter and form, nature and culture.

Refusing to think the dynamism of the body as only the product of cultural form or the effect of the performativity of language, Cheah raises the possibility that form inheres in matter as the potential capacity for self-organization out of which bodies, and not only human bodies, arise. Cheah wonders "if *tekhne* is *physis* deferred, then must there not be another nonanthropologistic level of dynamism subtending these different orders (of culture and nature), irreducible to mechanical laws of causality and naturalist teleology, of which the performativity of language would only be a case?"[15] Such questioning not only opens to the thought of matter as dynamic or alive, necessarily reconfiguring the relationship of bodies, matter, and technology. It also opens to rethinking the form of the human body, the relationship of the human body to its environment. To engage in such rethinking requires contending with the idea of compulsive repetition that is central to the psychoanalytic discourse on trauma linked to the Freudian death drive.

FROM THE BODY AS ORGANISM TO NONORGANIC LIFE

In his use of the term *nonorganic life*, Manuel DeLanda points to chemical clocks, solitons, and cloud patterns as examples. These examples, he argues, show matter's capacity for self-organization and emergence. However, what "has allowed us to 'see' matter as self-organizing," DeLanda argues, "is the advance in technology that materially supports (nonlinear) mathematics, and with it mathematical technology."[16] I suggested to students that the thought of a dynamism inherent to matter troubles the body-as-organism, the body presumed in theories of trauma. And thus, with the thought of nonorganic life, the autoethnographic writing about trauma is called to go beyond itself, beyond speaking of the incapacity to speak, beyond a compulsive repetition of memory that fails to master traumatic effects. I proposed that we rethink the repetition central to psychoanalytic discourse on trauma in the context of technoscientific experimentation and the reconfiguration of bodies, technology, and matter.

·····

For me, the shock of Keith Ansell Pearson's *Germinal Life: The Difference and Repetition of Deleuze* was the critique it offered of Humberto Maturana and Francisco Varela's concept of autopoiesis, a critique that Pearson drew from Deleuze's biophilosophical criticism of Freud's death drive.[17] Maturana had been my teacher years earlier and had interested me in neurophysiology, information theory, and the field of cybernetics to which Maturana and Varela's thinking about autopoiesis is deeply indebted. Exploring the relation of Deleuzian biophilosophy to autopoiesis in the context of a reconfiguration of bodies, matter, and technology was challenging, but discomforting as well. In 2000, I taught a course entitled "Feminism and Science Studies," with the intention of exploring more deeply the ongoing transformations in science, or what would be better referred to as technoscience. Just before the course began, it was announced that the mapping of the human genome was completed.

·····

A number of the essays that follow are engaged in rethinking the subject of trauma as something more like an assemblage of body memories and pre-individual affective capacities. Trauma is made to open up to a new ontology of bodily matter, beyond the autopoiesis of the human organism, making it possible to rethink heredity, repetition, and time in terms of the virtual and the crack in time. Jean Halley's "The Wire" is a moiré patterning of times and places, where the distinction between past and present, here and there, as well as human and animal, life and death cannot be made. For Halley, the autoethnographic form cannot be used for telling a story of self-development, as is often now the case with autoethnographic writing. For her, the autoethnographic form cannot be given over to producing the truth of a self (re)discovered because of the difficulty of being able to know, especially to know oneself. In this recognition, strangely, hopefully, Halley's scripting of the desire for suicide as a release unto life sits alongside the becoming of a new life form in the thought of a machinic assemblage. Jonathan Wynn's essay, "Haunting Orpheus: Problems of Space and Time in the Desert," maps the space of arriving and leaving, of separation deferred and displaced onto a juxtaposition of real places, Las Vegas and Rhyolite, the former in constant reconstruction, the latter long a ghost town. Producing a wild oscillation around the architectural tension between construction and destruction, Wynn manipulates the tempo of creation and decay, even life and death. Deborah Gamb's "Myocellular Transduction: When My Cells Trained My Body-Mind" explores social bodies below the level of the human organism through movement and transformation at the cellular/muscular level. "Myocellular Transduction" reacts to the crossing of body mind/mind body in the process of physical training. It explores the affects and sensations of movement in a way that complicates the relations of bodies, power and cultures as they become for a human-body-becoming-runner.

．．．．．

In *Beyond the Pleasure Principle*, Sigmund Freud takes up repetition and memory in discussing the war neuroses of men who suffer from repeated reminiscences of what had threatened them with death.[18] Freud connects this unpleasurable repetition, this threat to the subject's unity or integrity, to the death drive, which he also calls the "drive for mastery." The repetition of the death drive functions at the limit of the subject's identity, where there is a contest within subjectivity between mastery and disintegration: repeating near disintegration over and over again seemingly in order to regain integration and restore equilibrium. Freud's theorization of the death drive is folded into his discussion of trauma as the excess of in-flowing energy and of traumatic repetition as a curative rebinding of energy that tends toward the preservation of the equilibrium or homeostasis of the bodily ego. As such, Freud's theorization of the death drive moves psychoanalysis from its focus on sexual libido and the repression of sexual desire to anxiety and the disavowal or management of the threat to the ego's definition or boundaries, a threat that, for Freud, comes from the environment.

Not only does Freud concern himself with threats to the boundary of the bodily ego in terms of energy flows; he also treats these threats in relationship to the evolution of the species. Arguing that ontogeny recapitulates phylogeny, Freud suggests that in seeking homeostasis and equilibrium, the repetitions of the death drive function in order to return the ego to nonorganic matter, the primitive, the infantile, and the instinctual. In a defense against disequilibrium or death, there is a repetition of the development of the human organism, which is a repetition of the development of the species. Thus the boundedness of the ego, the human body, and the species are reproduced. What never evolves is the organism's desire to regress or return to homeostasis and equilibrium. For Freud, as for Butler and for theorists of trauma generally, the body is the body as organism, a closed system, seeking homeostasis and equilibrium. To think the body differently is to rethink matter and the dynamism inherent to it. It is to rethink the evolution of the species as well.

In rethinking evolution, Pearson takes up Deleuze's critique of Freud's death drive in relation to Maturana and Varela's treatment of autopoiesis. Deleuze refuses to think, as Freud did, that the only force of evolutionary change comes from the environment outside the human organism. Instead, a coevolution of organism and environment is posited. Maturana and Varela agree, but for them, coevolution occurs in terms of the organism's autopoiesis, or its being informationally closed to the environment. This means that in its relationship to the environment, the organism's functional organization of its components, their interaction, is maintained. Closed to information, the organism can not merely be determined from without by the environment; instead, the organism engages the environment, autopoietically. The organism selects the environment in ways that allows it to self-make itself as a self–reproducing organism. In other words, while relating to its environment, the organism seeks homeostasis and equilibrium for itself; it is in terms of or on behalf of its homeostasis and equilibrium that the organism selects its environment. Therefore, the environment's effect on the organism is, in part, selected by the organism. For Maturana and Varela, this is what constitutes the coevolution between the autopoietic organism and the environment.[19]

Pearson suggests that a Deleuzian biophilosophy offers a criticism of autopoiesis and therefore a different view of the organism. Autopoiesis, as Pearson sees it, does not offer enough in the way of elaborating the potential for the coevolution of organism and environment because autopoiesis takes disturbances to the organism's equilibrium and homeostasis as destructive. The closure of the organism to information is questioned by Pearson. Autopoiesis, he argues, places "the stress on operational closure, which can only conserve the boundaries of the organism," and therefore presents the organism with "a stark choice between either entropy or maximum performance." What Maturana and Varela do not see is, in his eyes, "that living systems and their boundaries are caught up in machinic assemblages that involve modes of transversal becoming," that is, communication across species and genus, across the evolution of phyletic lineages.

Deleuzian biophilosophy suggests that the organism must be rethought as open to information, where information is understood in terms of the event or chance occurrence arising out of the complexity of open systems under far-from-equilibrium conditions of metastability, that is, where microstates that make up the metastability are neither in a linear nor deterministic relationship to it. As such the organism is opened to the possibility of change in its organization and structure and is better understood as a machinic assemblage, which, at this time, is approaching a "techno-ontological threshold," such that "the human is implicated in a postbiological evolution as part of its very definition."[20]

Pearson defines a machinic assemblage in relationship to such a threshold: "A machinic assemblage connects and convolutes the disparate in terms of potential fields and virtual elements and crosses techno-ontological thresholds without fidelity to relationships of genus or species." Neither organic nor mechanical, the machinic assemblage arises out of the machinic heterogeneity of dynamic matter and as such introduces into autopoiesis the far-from-equilibrium conditions "required for a truly creative model of evolution, in which evolution does not simply involve self-reproduction through the dissipation of outside forces and nullification of dimensions of alterity."[21] For Pearson, the thought of a machinic assemblage is linked to the thought of an "artificial evolution" of a "machinic evolution," which not only is resonant with the potential of postbiological evolution; it is also resonant with a way of thinking about evolution that differs from Darwin's.[22] Here Pearson draws on the contentious rethinking of evolution in the work of Lynn Margulis and Dorian Sagan, who point to the parasitic and symbiotic relations that precede the appearance of reproduction through nucleic DNA, a process called endosymbiosis that challenges the model of evolution based on linear or filiative evolution. Whereas the Darwinian treatment of evolution proposes that natural selection ensures common descent through a regulated transmission of variations, Margulis and Sagan point to mitochondrial transmission, which like bacteria, transmits information just through contact, reengineering the genetic material of each lineage it moves through without fidelity to genus or species.[23]

For Pearson, endosymbiosis points to a virtual multiplicity out of which novelty emerges. This move away from privileging homeostasis to thinking evolution in terms of information, complexity, and open systems under far-from-equilibrium conditions of metastability undoes the opposition between the organism and the environment, as well as the opposition between the organic and the nonorganic. Rather than presuming matter or the nonorganic to be inert, such that form is imposed on it, matter is understood to be in-formational, that is, form arises out of matter's capacity for self-organization out of complexity.

In his reading of Deleuze's biophilosophy, Pearson points to Deleuze's thinking about heredity and time as the measure of an increase of disorder and disequilibrium, and the possibility of chance. Here, time is no longer the narrative time of human subjectivity, that is, human development linked to historical development, or to Darwinian thought of the evolution of species. Instead, time is thought of in terms of "the virtual," which Deleuze, following Bergson, contrasts with "the actual."[24] The virtual is not the possible that is to be realized; instead, the virtual calls forth actualizations that have no resemblance to the virtual. Actualization is not a specification of a prior generality. Actualization out of virtuality is creation out of heterogeneity. Actualization is an experiment in virtuality, an affecting or materializing of a virtual series.

For Deleuze, the virtual is linked to what he refers to as the "time-image." The time-image gives a direct image of time and therefore differs from what he refers to as "the movement-image," the most important variant of which is "the action-image." The action-image is fixed to the movement of a human "sensory-motor schema," which fixes time to the unfolding movement of a linear narrative, typical of classical cinematic representation. Unlike the movement-image, the time-image is no longer deployed to make something seen or to make a viewer see something. It is not a matter of representation, but rather a matter of images moving in conjunction with each other at different angles and speeds. The time-image makes time visible in its own movement and without appearing as a movement aberrant to narrative.[25] As such, the time-image points to the productivity of time, the movement of time outside the subject, and suggests a different sort of memory, or storage, which is readily linked to electronic imaging or digital technologies.

In this context, Deleuze's notion of "the crack" offers an invitation to think memory, image, and time differently, and therefore to think differently about trauma and writing about trauma.[26] In psychoanalytic terms, trauma makes the past and future meet without there being a present. The future is collapsed into the past as the past overwhelms the present—all this usually taken as pathological in the psychological sense. For Deleuze, however, the crack of heredity is not about what is being passed down, something being passed from the past to the present, as for example, in the passing on an addiction to alcohol. The crack is rather the potential for a swerving in terms of inheritance, the potential for swerving to the future. As a result, the past does not overcome the present because the past in general is ontologically present. The crack arises in the present out of the past as a virtuality, as a chance of repetition veering off from what is, off from what is a passing to the past from the present.

The crack of time, in which the actualization of the virtual is made possible, is like the imaginary of psychoanalysis, where it is unclear whether one is in the past or the present, resulting in a haunting in time, of time, a folding of time. But the imaginary of psychoanalysis haunts the individual's time through the displacement of loss or lack in being, in the being of the subject, as well as through the incorporation of others' displaced losses or lack, especially those of the parents. Memory is often the memory of childhood to which one regresses. For Deleuze, the imaginary should not be reduced to the individual subject's unconscious. The imaginary does not just belong to the subject or even to the subject's body. The imaginary is part of a machinic assemblage, which may include the subject, but does not do so necessarily. As Pearson argues, Deleuze treats memory not as regressive but as creative, a shift "from its function as a psychological faculty of recollection."[27] Rather, memory is conceived "as the membrane that allows for correspondence between 'sheets of past and layers of reality,' making insides and outsides communicate," with the potential to swerve to the future.[28] Memory intervenes and intensifies, opening up new paths.

Memories become a block, a "block of becoming" that allows lines of flight, of inventiveness, through transversal communication, that is, communication without any fidelity to genus or species, or a hierarchy of forms. There is a creation that involves deterritorialization, which, however, is not regression; it does not presume loss or a lack in the being in the subject, as the psychoanalytic treatment of trauma does. Even the thought of childhood memories must be rethought. As Deleuze (and Guattari) put it: "We write not with childhood memories but through blocs of childhood that are the becoming-child of the present."[29] This writing block of childhood calls forth experimental writing that constitutes not merely an experiment with a given form, such as experimenting with the ethnographic form. It is rather an invention that strives to capture a shift in thought happening to the writer and which the writer is inviting. Each writer is thrown backward and forward to find the self that is turned into parts, turned around parts of a new assemblage: an autobiographical-techno-ontological writing block.

FROM DISCIPLINE AND REPRESENTATION
TO CONTROL AND INFORMATION

Following Deleuzian biophilosophy, we were moving away from thinking of bodies only in terms of the human organism and rethinking the relationship of life, information, and technology. We retraced the crossing of information theory from physics to biology.[30] This allowed us to think of both matter and the human body (linked to genetics and recombinant DNA) as informational, where information, as Eugene Thacker writes, "is seen as constitutive of the very development of our understanding of life at the molecular level—not the external appropriation of a metaphor, but the epistemological internalization and the technical autonomization of information as constitutive of DNA."[31]

.....

We read Martin Heidegger's "The Question Concerning Technology" and John Johnston's "Machinic Vision"[32] and wondered about scientific self-reflexivity in the production of knowledge, at a time when science had become a primary agency of power. We concluded that it would matter what we thought about technoscience or technological development in the late twentieth century. It would matter if we thought, as Heidegger did, that there is a fall from nature into technology that, in relationship to a history of the capitalist development of technology, means the increasing displacement of the human laborer by the machine, taken to be a detriment to humanity. Or, if instead, the natural and the technological are indistinguishable, as Johnson proposes, what question should we raise about the relationship of information, labor, and bodily matter? What should be the nature of criticism? Donna Haraway suggests that the object of study is inextricable from the apparatus or the technology of both its production and further elaboration. Each object/event, or what Haraway refers to as "a material semiotic entity," is dynamic and generative. Each object/event is like a temporary knot in a field of moving forces and requires a form of criticism different from a scientist's self-reflection or the critic's reflexivity.[33] It requires, at least, understanding the field of moving forces.

.....

A number of the essays are engaged with technology's reach to affective bodily capacities and in rethinking representation in terms of these technologies. The essays also treat the shift in governance from discipline to control in which these technologies play a part. In "Slowness: Notes toward an Economy of Différancial Rates of Being," Karen Wendy Gilbert ironically speeds through studies in physics and biology, writing fast, trying to capture the very speed of thought coming from the future. In doing so, Gilbert argues that there are two complementary systems within living entities: one a rule-following unidirectional mode of being subject to entropy understood in nineteenth-century terms of thermodynamics, the other a mode of being, arising in a field of flows and phase shifting, which Gilbert takes up in terms of quantum theory. Jamie "Skye" Bianco's "Techno-Cinema: Image Matters in the Affective Unfoldings of Analog Cinema and New Media" treats technoscientific experimentation as a literary genre in order to draw out an ethical approach to film criticism. In taking up *Requiem for a Dream*'s television world explosion, *Lola Rennt*'s body-clocked repetitions, and *Memento*'s sheets of reversing time, Bianco registers a shift from a politicized aesthetics of desire and subject identity to an ethics of capture (and flight) in response to biopolitical control. She explores time and writing about time, writing in time "in a prompt language . . . equal to the moment,"[34] as Walter Benjamin might put it, or when "the end of the game is before the game," as Bianco puts it. In their essay, "Losses and Returns: The Soldier in Trauma," Greg Goldberg and Craig Willse focus on the soldier-body both in terms of the technoscientific preparation of a body made ready for war and in terms of media accounts of the damaged bodies of soldiers returning from the war in Iraq. Goldberg and Willse argue that the soldier-body, both as the production of highly technologized war training and as the object of medical-scientific practices reveals an organization of bodily matter and its capacities that exceeds the treatment of the body in trauma studies because the latter fails to grasp the way in which trauma (studies) presumes the body as organism.

. . . . .

What the body is thought to be, Luciana Parisi and Tizina Terranova argue, is a matter of a historically specific organization of forces brought into being by capital and discursive investments. For example, Parisi and Terranova point to the late nineteenth century and the becoming of the body as organism that was not so much produced but "reinforced and given strength by the disciplinary society (of industrial capitalism) so that it could become the ultimate definition of what a body is."[35] Following Michel Foucault, Parisi and Terranova point to the enclosures of civil society—the family, the school, the labor union—as sites of ideological interpellation, as well as of the enforcement of social and cultural practices that constitute a regime of representation.

Making an organism into a human subject, this regime of representation centers on the perception of the body mirrored, from a distance, as a whole. The investment in the body as organism makes the body a closed system drawing energy from the outside, thus drawing the body back into homeostasis and equilibrium, which leads inevitably to entropic heat-death. As Parisi and Terranova put it: "The great confinement was essential to this process of reorganization of power in the interests of an emerging industrial capitalism. Thus, the fluids which were circulating outside and between bodies, are folded onto themselves in order to be channeled within the solid walls of the organism/self/subject."[36]

In this context, "the body becomes abstracted and organized so that it can be trained: trained to reproduction within a thermodynamic cycle of accumulation and expenditure; and trained to work."[37] However, with the further expansion of capitalism in the late twentieth century and its disorganization pressured by globalization, structural adjustment, and flexibilization, Parisi and Terranova argue that there is a shift in biopolitics, a shift from disciplinary societies to what Deleuze refers to as "societies of control."[38] Control is the effect and the condition of possibility of an investment in the reorganization of material forces, of bodily matter.

Parisi and Terranova suggest that to understand the extension of biopolitics in the passage from discipline to control, it is necessary to understand the changing relationship of information to bodies, labor, and energy, from industrial capitalism to the present globalization of finance capitalism, from the nineteenth-century elaboration of the first and second laws of thermodynamics to the late-twentieth-century elaboration of complexity theory. This movement in the theorization of information begins with a closed mechanical system, where, as the second law of thermodynamics states, the increase in entropy is inevitable as an irreversible process of heat-death. Here entropy is defined as energy that can no longer be put to work, no longer organized to do something, having become chaotic, like microparticles moving out of order, without aim or purpose. Entropy is the measure of turbulence or disorder in a closed system.

It is this idea of entropy that would undergo a change with the theorization of information by Claude Shannon in the late 1940s who defined information mathematically as positively correlated with entropy or noise.[39] For Shannon, information is the measure of the (im)probability of a message going through a channel from sender to receiver. Information, in the mathematical account, Terranova suggests, "represents an uncertain and probabilistic milieu by reducing it to sets of alternatives that determine more or less likely sets of possibilities on the basis of a given distribution of probabilities as determined by the relation between channel and code."[40] As such, meaning is secondary to information; information is primarily a matter of contact and connectibility, a modulation of affectivity and attention by fashioning or reducing the real through the exclusion of possibilities.

In contrast to Shannon's theorization of information in the late 1940s, Norbert Wiener's theorization of information at around the same time was more directly linked to biology and life itself. Wiener conceived of information differently than Shannon did. Shannon had theorized information as positively correlated with entropy such that the more entropy, the more improbable the message being sent, and, therefore, the more information. Wiener proposed that information was an organization or an ordering in the indifferent differences of entropy or noise, and thus was to be understood to decrease entropy. For Wiener, information is a local organization against entropy, a temporary deferral of entropy—that is, life. Even as entropy increases in the universe as a whole, information can prevent entropic collapse temporarily as extrinsic resources of informational order or energy arise.[41] If we take Shannon's definition of information to hold at the point of sending the message and Wiener's at the point of receiving the message, these definitions are not as contradictory as they first seem; both fit the mathematical definition of information.

But when Wiener's understanding of information as a negentropic decrease of entropy is put alongside Shannon's understanding of information as positively correlated with entropy, a retheorization of information is once again invited. This time, in the latter part of the twentieth century, information is theorized in terms of open systems under far-from-equilibrium conditions of metastability. Here, irreversibility, or the passing of time, is disconnected from heat-death or the entropic closed system and is understood instead in terms of the movement from disorder to order and from order to disorder in the metastability of an open system, where microstates are ontologically probabilistic; they are in a nondeterministic, nonlinear relationship with the metastability they constitute. As such, the negentropic decrease of entropy can be understood to decrease information (or to increase the probability of the range of microstates that make up a metastability), while at the same time an increase of complexity or turbulence can emerge at another level, thus increasing information (or the improbability of any particular microstate at this level). This is what Ilya Prigogine and Isabelle Stengers capture in theorizing dissipative structures that emerge by chance in open systems under far-from-equilibrium conditions of metastability and dissipate the dissipation of entropy or temporarily reverse it. Order turns to disorder turns to order across various levels of microstates.[42] To "see" matter as informational is to recognize matter's inherent capacity for self-organizing out of complexity, or to see "the imperceptible speed of matter."[43]

It is in these terms that it becomes possible to think the body as an open system, beyond the containment of the organism, and therefore to think of preindividual bodily capacities or affectivity in relation to the passage from discipline to control. In control societies, the body, as Parisi and Terranova argue, "no longer corresponds to the fleshy representation or phenomenon of the human subject, but rather is opened up to particles, waves and attractors, which constitute it as a far-from-equilibrium system."[44] What is perceived as the body "is the movement of forces, the process of composition of differential elements which defines the origin of life as turbulent rather than derived from entropic collapse. In contemporary technoscience, lethal entropy becomes vital turbulence."[45] It is in these terms that bodily matter is conceived as infinitely productive and control becomes a matter of strategizing an optimized reproduction.

The bodies of a control society are a composition of dynamic matter invested into being, an investment of capital and technoscientific experimentation. This investment of bodies for control is part of a reconfiguration of state and economy, the nation and civil society, the public and private spheres. As Foucault argued, in disciplinary societies, the "governmentalization of the state" enables the state to extend its disciplinary practices through institutions such as the church, the school, the prison, the family, and the union, what he called "the enclosures of civil society."[46] Foucault's revision of Hegelian thought about socializing laborers to the ideology of the nation-state explores the way the state moves deeply into the lives of individual subjects through disciplining, through complex strategies of socialization that the institutions of civil society deploy in managing individuals subjected to the moral order. Disciplining engages a politics of representation; it forms part of a cinematic regime of representation by which familial and national ideological apparatuses function to constitute subject identities, and wherein resistance to these identities and the transgression of the institutional norms that support them is possible, at times even enabled, by the instability of the strategies of disciplining.

The target of control is not the production of subjects whose behaviors express internalized social norms; rather, control aims at a never-ending modulation of moods, capacities, affects, and potentialities, assembled in genetic codes, identification numbers, ratings profiles, and preference listings, that is to say, in bodies of data and information (including the human body as information and data). Control is an extension of what Foucault referred to as biopolitics, where the individual body is not so much the focus as the species body and the regularities of the aggregate effects of individual bodies that institute a politics of population. Control is a biopolitics that works at the molecular level of bodies, at the informational substrate of matter.

The production of normalization is no longer simply entrusted to the family, kin groups, or other institutions of civil society; it also involves the investment in and regulation of a market-driven circulation of affect and attention. No longer captured in the disciplined body, the subject's desire passes beyond the enclosed spaces of the home, the school, and the labor union, beyond the opposition of normal and deviant. As Massumi puts it: "The normative undergoes rapid inflation, as classificatory and regulative mechanisms are elaborated for every socially recognizable state of being . . . .

'Normal' is now free-standing, no longer the opposite and necessary complement of 'abnormal,' 'deviant,' or 'dysfunctional,' as it was under disciplinary power, except in limited cases." The meaning of normative is changing,
having become more about a group's "collective visibility and social oper-
ativity," about their practices for increased self-control in self-effacing or self-
aggrandizing programs meant to modulate illness and health, limitation and
freedom, life and death.[47]

Rather than an ideological interpellation of the subject, there is the deployment of "generic figures of affective capture," which provide a "gravitational
pull around which competing orbits of affect and thought are organized."
Generic figures, Massumi argues, do not indicate an absence of determination,
"but the continuity and coexistence of determinabilities." A figure can be
determined when needed, and when it is so determined, it brings forth "competing bureaucratic bodies of control procedure and political command centers."[48] And all of this plays its part in the production of value. For Massumi,
who follows Deleuze's thinking about control, control is linked to the tendency
in capitalism toward what Marx referred to as real subsumption, where capital
shifts its domain of accumulation to life itself, to preindividual bodily capacities, so that value is produced through modulating affect. All of this is inseparable from technoscientific experimentation.

Control societies call into question the politics of representation and subject
identity, even as a method for achieving representation for those who had not
been subjects of representation or who had been traumatically excluded from
voice. The shift to control calls into question autobiographical experimental
writing; it calls into question the political effectiveness of self-reflexivity in the
production of knowledge. Instead, an experimental writing is called forth that
shifts from critically responding to discipline to critically responding to control, moving as well from privileging the organism as the figure of life to
considering preindividual bodily capacities or affect. Experimental writing
veers toward affectivity and control by way of rethinking materialism, memory,
bodies, time, and repetition. Experimental writing assembles with information
technologies and something passes into the writing from the outside, another
technological flow, reassembling images, sounds, languages, and bodies.

Thinking in terms of control societies is itself an experiment, a theoretical
experimental response to the turbulence of a global capitalist economy arising
in the late 1960s and early 1970s, near and around the 1973 oil crisis. There is at
that time an intensification of the flexibilization of capital and labor, structural
adjustment around the world, and the ongoing investment in a postcybernetic
understanding of energy, information, labor, and technology. These political,

economic, and cultural transformations pressure a shift in capitalist accumulation to the domain of affect or preindividual bodily capacities—to life itself. That is to say, there is a putting into play something like a primitive accumulation for the reorganization of value around bodily capacities. Preindividual bodily capacities are made the site of capital investment for the realization of profit—not only in terms of biotechnology, biomedicalization, and genetics but also in terms of a technologically dispersed education/training in self-actualization and self-control at the preindividual, individual, communal, national, and transnational levels.

FROM PRODUCTION AND CONSUMPTION TO THE CIRCULATION OF AFFECT

Just a week before September 11 and the attacks on the World Trade Center, my course "The Sociology of Bodies" began. I had assigned for our first meeting two readings: George Caffentzis's 1980 "The Work Energy Crisis and the Apocalypse" and Antonio Negri's 1999 "Value and Affect."[49] I intended to use the readings as a way to get students to think about the postcybernetic bodies of the early twenty-first century by means of reconsidering the relationship of energy, entropy, work, information, and capital. Following September 11, the class discussion of this relationship continued, but frenetically, as we set out to explore the U.S. response to the events. As we thought about an affect economy conjoined with biopolitical control, we also began to focus on two social issues: mass incarceration and postprison experience, and the deployment of human rights/human security frameworks in the context of counter/terrorism, massacre, and war.[50] As our interest in control, information, and affect was stretched from U.S. mass imprisonment to the transnational concern with security in relationship to global capital, we began to think that the horrifying point of contact between the two, or the switching point from one to the other, is the growing numbers of persons who have been categorized as "human waste," to use Zygmunt Bauman's term, and in the intensification of the operation of "necropolitics," as Achille Mbembe would describe it.[51]

.....

A number of the essays focus on affective labor and rethink capitalism as it moves from the formal to the real subsumption of "life itself." The essays take up paid and unpaid affective labor, both in relationship to nationally based and global economies in the age of structural adjustment. In his "Women's Work and the Ambivalent Gift of Entropy," David Staples rethinks 1970s Marxist feminist studies of women's housework and their unpaid labor. He argues that these studies function within the limits of "a restricted political economy," rather than "a general political economy." He takes this distinction from Georges Bataille, which serves Staples in his elaboration of what Gayatri Chakravorty Spivak calls "an expanded textuality of value."[52] Staples takes up the general economy of the gift in the figure of home-based labor and traces the tendency of home-based laborers to go outside the operation of a closed system of the restricted economy of orthodox Marxian and neoclassical political economics as well. Taking note of Jacques Derrida's reflection on the gift, Staples finally finds a way to address the postthermodynamic speculations appropriate to unpaid reproductive labor in the era of structural adjustment. In "Always on Display: Affective Production in the Modeling Industry," Elizabeth Wissinger focuses on the work of fashion models. Arguing that understanding the body in terms of affective capacities proves a more effective model for researching postmodern bodies, Wissinger traces links between the growth of imaging technologies, the growth of the modeling industry, and increased investment in the means of modulating affective flow between bodies. Wissinger points to the socialization of affect or affective capacity in late-twentieth-century capitalism as a way to think beyond the subjectivist bent of traditional critiques of consumer culture. Melissa Ditmore's "In Calcutta, Sex Workers Organize" takes up labor in an affective economy in order to understand prostitution as sex work and to argue that abuses connected to prostitution and trafficking, which policy and law mean to legislate, would be better treated as labor issues aimed at the empowerment of sex workers. In "More Than a Job: Meaning, Affect, and Training Health Care Workers," Ariel Ducey focuses on allied health care workers—nursing assistants, technicians, and other paraprofessional workers— and on the educational and training industry that enrolls these workers into schooling for most of their careers as workers. While meeting the desires of workers to make their work "more than a job," the job training and education industry not only prospers. It invests in the health care workers' affect, strongly contributing to the generalization of service work for an affect economy.

.....

George Caffentzis discusses the energy crisis of 1973 and the investment in technoscience around that time in the context of the changing relationship of profits and wages. Focusing on the movements beginning in the late sixties— which were linked to the identity politics of gender, sexuality, race, ethnicity, and nation—Caffentzis argues that these movements forced a breakup of the Keynesian-Fordist regime of accumulation. In the Keynesian-Fordist development of a welfare state, along with the extension of mass consumption, the reproduction of the laborer is drawn into the market. There is a formal subsumption of labor to capital, and mass consumption becomes a force of production. At the same time, there is an intensifying of the productivity of labor power given the expansion of work-saving technologies. As a result, an imbalance between wages and profit arises, intensified by the movements of liberation and the refusal of their participants to produce or reproduce. Capitalists respond by readjusting the organic composition of capital investment and accumulation.

For Caffentzis, what this means is that starting in the early 1970s, there is an increased investment in the high investment end of capital, in the capital-intensive industries of information and communication, resulting in the increase in the prices of these commodities but without real increases in labor's productivity. As profits diverge from the production of surplus value, a break occurs with the Keynesian link of wage, profit, and increases in productivity. Wages become disconnected from production and from the use value of labor so that the wage and increases in the wage become political; wages must be fought for politically through management-labor union agreement as laborers seek wage hikes based on demands for schooling for themselves and their children, for health care, for therapy, for leadership training, and more. In such circumstances, it is not the wage that the capitalist has to manipulate in order to increase profit, but the prices of commodities generally.

To manipulate all commodity prices, capitalists in the early 1970s manipulated the price of a basic commodity, one that could affect all others, that is, the price of energy. Thus the oil crisis! But how was it possible to increase the price of energy, an increase that demanded as well an increase of capital investment in the already capitalist-intensive or high-investment sector of energy production? From where did the surplus for investment come from? As Caffentzis sees it, the surplus available for investment came from the surplus value of labor extracted from the profoundly expanded low-investment sector of the service economy, an expansion that would bring women into the labor market as the tasks of social reproduction, which women once performed without wage, would become waged. As such, reproductive services became commodified and globalized, all this pointing to the subsumption into capital of global reproduction. It is from this low-end sector of labor, expanding all around the world, that surplus value is extracted from long hours of work, often done by women from all over the world, and is transferred for investment in the high-end sector of energy, along with investment in information and information technologies.

But how, Caffentzis asks, did the investment in energy become an investment in information? He answers by pointing to a number of ways in which technoscientific development is needed in relationship to the investment in energy in late-twentieth-century capitalism. First, the service industry is intensely decentralized and requires information and communication technologies to make it work. Second, information and communication technologies are also needed in the transfer of surplus value extracted from the low investment sector of the service industry to the high investment sector of high priced commodities, the sector of information and communication. Third, there is a need to self-police constant capital; the investment of technoscience must be protected from accident and sabotage, even to the point of waging war. Surveillance technologies are central to an economy dependent on information and communication technologies.

So while there is an ongoing need for research and development as science and technology become more apparently inextricable from each other, part of this research and development is geared toward technological protections of the constant capital of technoscience itself. In this situation, the need for hypersimulation of risk translates into control mechanisms being made immanent to information and communication flows; information and communication technologies subsume or internalize self-reflexivity. The need to discipline labor by interpellating laborers to the ideology of nation and family is surpassed or brought into capital so fully that a shift to direct control is made possible.

Thus the shift to control does not mean that the labor of service workers and low-end factory workers all around the world does not produce surplus value. Yet in pointing to the drive toward control—and its becoming immanent to information and communication technologies, central to capital accumulation—Caffentzis's analysis also suggests rethinking the organic body, machinic assemblages, and information in relationship to work, energy, and the tendency to the real subsumption of labor, or life itself to capital. After all, while it has been in the interests of capitalists to displace laborers with technology, this has been done only up to a certain threshold, that is, without risking the reproduction of the lives of human laborers. With the real subsumption of labor into capital, it not only is the reproduction of the life of human laborers but of life itself that is set to an economy of risk. Life is risked where the risk is estimated to be worth it. To rethink the importance of human labor in this context is to rethink the relationship of bodies and value, the body as organism and labor.

Negri suggests that the relationship of labor, the body as organism, and value has changed because the use value of labor cannot be measured; it is no longer outside capital, as in feudalism, for example. Nor is it simply inside of capital because labor's reproduction, having been subsumed by capital, has become a force of production and therefore is not simply a nonwaged reproduction of the laborer, added to labor's use value. With real subsumption, labor is situated in a "nonplace" in relationship to capital—no place and all-over-the-place, where work goes on all of the time, such that "labor finds its value in affect, if affect is defined as 'the power to act.' "[53] As such, capital produces its own outside from inside the viscera of life, accumulating at the level of preindividual bodily capacities and putting preindividual bodily capacities to work. On the one hand, biotechnology seeks to make possible and profitable the control of the "labor performed routinely by cells, proteins, and DNA."[54] On the other hand, the processes of laboring, socializing, and entertaining are changed as they become directly engaged in modulating affectivity.

In an affect economy, value is sought in the expansion or contraction of affective capacity. In this sense, affect is a power or potential that cannot be limited. Power or potential face obstacles to expansion rather than limitation. As such, labor power becomes itself "a subset of attention, one of the many kinds of possible attention potentially productive of value."[55] It is in this context that education turns into a profitable biopolitical control, or what Massumi refers to as the "powering-up—or the powering-away—of potential."[56] Institutions of social reproduction become nodes of control in a network of economic flows, where capitalism "usurps" "the very expression of potential. The movement of relationality. Becoming-together. Belonging."[57] Institutions like the school, the labor union, the hospital, and the prison function as switch points for circulating bodies, along with information and capital, through channels, not with the aim of arrival, but with the aim of keeping the flows moving at different speeds. In this circulation, new channels also can be opened, however, creating new possibilities inside capital for making an outside for capital, and the potential for change.

While affective labor is not the primary form of labor worldwide (agriculture still is), there is nonetheless a worldwide meshing of biopolitics with an affective economy. There is a marking of populations—some as valuable life and others as without value. Increasingly it is in these terms that differences such as those of ethnicity, race, gender, class, sexuality, and nation become materialized. Some bodies or bodily capacities are derogated, making their affectivity superexploitable or exhaustible unto death, while other bodies or body capacities collect the value produced through this derogation and exploitation.[58] This can be seen in the relationship made between victimized, terrorized, and hated bodies brought forth for the discourse and practices of counter/terrorism, surveillance, and unending war.[59] There also are examples to be drawn from the worldwide treatment of HIV/AIDS, the trafficking in persons, the drug trade, or intercountry adoption, which point not only to a global affect economy but also to the shift in governmentality toward bio-political control at a global level, where as João Biehl puts it, there is an intensifying "contradiction between a generalized culture of human rights and emergent exclusive structures through which these rights are realized, biologi-cally speaking, but only on a selective basis—who, for how long, and at what cost? In this context, "letting die" is a political action, continuous with the biomedical and political power that 'makes live.' "[60]

It would seem that one of the often unintended consequences of organiza-tions of social management engaged in all sorts of relief work, including human rights work at the national, regional, and global levels, is to open up channels for economic flows, also contributing to the expansion of informa-tion technologies and biotechnologies all around the globe. These organiza-tions lend themselves to the extension of a political economy of security and control. As they function in the wake of the imposed structural adjustment of economies of debt, they are asked to manage the devastating effects. Assisting in making debt more productive by treating it with a microfinanced affect economy shaped in the demand for human rights and human security policy commitments, these organizations come to play a part in tilting the world-political economy to affect and the deployment of biopolitical control. These organizations can also serve to provide the moral justification for "excep-tional" political intervention, if not (para)military intervention, overriding national sovereignty.[61]

The shift from discipline to biopolitical control in a global affect economy harkens back to the rise of the modern state, where, as Giorgio Agamben puts it, the demand for "the free life," "the good life," resulted in drawing biological life or "bare life" under the control of the state's calculations.[62] But comment-ing on Agamben's take on biopolitics, Mbembe argues that colonialism played an important role in the development of biopolitics, such that, in neocolonial-ism, biopolitical control only becomes intensified, so that politics (state and nonstate politics) has become the deployment of the right to kill on the basis of enmity within systems that can only function in the turbulence or complexity of a state of emergency. In this context, a new machinic assemblage emerges out of turbulence and complexity in which necropolitics intensifies biopolitics, that is, in which politics constitutes a form of war, provoking the ongoing activity of what Deleuze and Guattari describe as "a war-machine."[63] As a military power that is bought and sold, the war machine arrives in part with the failure of the state to maintain an economic infrastructure of political authority, such that war can be waged by those who have no state but who have gained control over a given territory.

With this form of war, a question is raised as to how bodies, life, and death are related to power. This question is raised not only because the technologies of destruction are now "more tactile, more anatomical and sensorial." The question also is raised because the practices of necropolitics, as Mbembe sees it, "are less concerned with inscribing bodies within disciplinary apparatuses as inscribing them, when the time comes, within the order of the maximal economy now represented by the 'massacre.' "[64] The war machine not only kills outright but it also takes possession of the resources for life in a given territory, an economic function of the war machine that either disperses populations or immobilizes them, leaving them to a life of living death.

Under these conditions, Bauman argues, there can be no security. Rather, there are situations of "unalloyed contingency" and "unaccountable accidents," where any attempt to govern faces "ad hoc alliances of powers held together or dismantled by bribery or blackmail."[65] There is a generalization of criminality mixed with governance posing as legitimate. Everyone is at risk of arrest, even as this risk is in fact differently borne by different populations, different bodies. Indeed, as Massumi suggests, "crime is itself the figure of the limit-case (particularly 'crimes against community' and 'against humanity,' which by their generic nature tend to subsume all other varieties)."[66] In this situation, Bauman argues, "one can possibly avoid being a victim, but nothing can be done to escape the fate of being a collateral casualty." For Bauman, this is the "sinister dimension" of turbulence and complexity.[67]

IN CONCLUSION

Michael Taussig writes: "What if it is not a system but 'a nervous system,' in which order becomes disorder the moment it is perceived?"[68] Deleuze writes: "Chaos and catastrophe imply the collapse of all the figurative givens, and thus they already entail a fight, the fight against the cliché, the preparatory work (all the more necessary in that we are no longer 'innocent'). It is out of the chaos that the 'stubborn geometry' or 'geologic lines' first emerge and this geometry or geology must in turn pass through the catastrophe in order for colors to arise, for the earth to rise toward the sun."[69]

Returning to Colombia in May 2001, Michael Taussig keeps a diary. He will publish diary entries from the two weeks he spent there in a town under a paramilitary control imposed by "law and order through selective assassinations." The term *paramilitary* is an elusive one, Taussig proposes, since it points to soldiers who are not really soldiers, "but more like ghosts flitting between the visible and the invisible between the regular army and the criminal underworld of killers and torturers that all states seem to have no trouble recruiting when their backs are up against the wall."[70] Ghostly soldiers drain the potential of honoring the ghosted, the haunted, as a form of social criticism: violence comes too easily, too quickly, and without legitimacy, but also without much resistance.

But there still are honorable ghosts just as representation, discipline, ideology, subject identity, and the extraction of surplus value from human bodies conceived as organic all still matter. There still are traumatized subjects who matter. But there is something else, something about the sociality of a system, a nervous system, that pulls us to complexity, to turbulence, to far-from-equilibrium conditions—pulling us to critically engage the sinister side of the system, as well as its potential for freedom. We are drawn as well to and beyond a techno-ontological threshold and asked to think preindividual affectivity, where the politics of mourning ghosted bodies is too slow to engage preindividual affective capacities that a capitalist political economy already maps and mines.

So we take Deleuze's words as a motto for critical theory, although it might seem obscene. It is after all difficult to see the sun with which he lights up the collapse of all the figurative givens and energizes the preparation to fight the cliché in order to find in chaos colors arising. It is difficult when the changes that are rendered in the affective turn are those brought about by, or at least along with, great violence and the disinterest and the arrogance of those who control, no matter for how brief a time and over whatever rigged-up geopolitical arrangement, often with the support of what Fred Moten and Stefano Harney have named the "negligence" of the professionalization of the academic disciplines.[71]

Against the turn to this professionalization of know-how for administering the world (away), Moten and Harney propose "stepping out of this skeptical of the known into an inadequate confrontation with what exceeds it and oneself."[72] Inadequate confrontation: it is this because the disciplines, having gone professional, can only judge what is not already marked for their easy assimilation as inadequate, unprofessional, even unethical or criminal. The essays that follow go right ahead and step out into an inadequate confrontation with the social, changed and changing, which exceeds all efforts to contain it, even our efforts to contain its thought in the affective turn. So we have what is left, the remains of learning together, encouraging us to be braver, more creative and even less adequate next time. So we leave you not only with our honored ghosts but with bodies, and bodily capacities, affective capacities to act, to attend, to feel, to feel alive.

NOTES

1. All of the authors of the following essays have studied with me. They have taken classes with me, and I have mentored them in their dissertation work. They have also been part of what we refer to as the "book group," which met to prepare the essays for this collection.

2. I am paraphrasing slightly a definition of affect offered by Brian Massumi in his notes on the translation of Gilles Deleuze and Félix Guattari's *A Thousand Plateaus: Capitalism and Schizophrenia*, trans. Brian Massumi (Minneapolis: University of Minnesota Press, 1987), xvi. I am also drawing on Mark Hansen for his treatment of autoaffection, see his "The Time of Affect; or, Bearing Witness to Life," *Critical Inquiry* 30.3 (2004): 584–626. Also see my *Autoaffection: Unconscious Thought in the Age of Teletechnology* (Minneapolis: University of Minnesota Press, 2000). While I have been interested for some time in autoaffection, my earlier interest focused on the critique of autoaffection as that which allowed for the presence of the selfsame subject of Western discourse, a critique linked to Jacques Derrida's work. The rethinking of autoaffection in this work and in my work with students forms part of my engagement with the different approach to affect in Deleuze's work, which only had begun to have an influence on my thinking as represented in *Autoaffection*. Beside the conceptualization of affect I am pursuing here, there have been a number of disciplines that have taken up a discussion of affect in which the meaning of affect varies. In literary studies, discussion perhaps began with the publication of Eve Kosofsky Sedgwick and Adam Frank, eds., *Shame and Its Sisters: A Silvan Tomkins Reader* (Durham, NC: Duke University Press, 1995). Also see Sianne Ngai, *Ugly Feelings* (Cambridge, MA: Harvard University Press, 2005); and Elizabeth A. Wilson's treatment of affect, including her review of neurological and psychological treatments of affect in *Psychosomatic: Feminism and the Neurological Body* (Durham, NC: Duke University Press, 2004).

3. Brian Massumi, *Parables for the Virtual: Movement, Affect, Sensation* (Durham, NC: Duke University Press, 2002), 30.

4. Ibid., 25.

5. Eugene Thacker argues for maintaining scare quotes around the term *life itself* to guard against any concurrence with the idea that an essence is discoverable—as life itself. But since the term has been used by molecular biologists since the 1950s, Thacker keeps it. See his *The Global Genome: Biotechnology, Politics, and Culture* (Cambridge, MA: MIT Press, 2005), 60–61.

6. For an interesting discussion of the social in relation to complexity and far-from-equilibrium conditions, see Immanuel Wallerstein, *The Uncertainties of Knowledge* (Philadelphia: Temple University Press, 2004).

7. Jacques Lacan, *The Four Fundamental Concepts of Psycho-analysis*, trans. Alan Sheridan, ed. Jacques-Alain Miller (New York: Norton, 1978), 55.

8. Ruth Leys, "Death Masks: Kardiner and Ferenczi on Psychic Trauma," *Representa-*

tions 53 (1996): 44–73. In this essay, Leys summarizes psychoanalytic approaches to trauma, drawing on the works by Sigmund Freud, Sandor Ferenczi and Abram Kardiner. In her more recent work, *Trauma: A Genealogy* (Chicago: University of Chicago Press, 2000), Leys points out that there are various approaches to trauma within psychoanalytic discourse, but in treating these, she focuses especially on the indefinite oscillation across various authors' works and within various individual authors' works between a mimetic and an antimimetic approach to trauma. The mimetic approach suggests that the traumatized subject has identified with, indeed is fixated on, the object or event of trauma, therefore making the representation of trauma impossible, although the symptoms suffered in place of the re-presentation of trauma may be narrated. The antimimetic approach, according to Leys, does not recognize identification and therefore imagines that the trauma comes from outside of the subject and can eventually be represented, even if the process of doing so takes a great deal of time and is difficult to accomplish. In the work students and I did on trauma, we leaned toward the mimetic view. But as Leys points out, it is easy to be drawn toward the antimimetic view, especially when writing about subjects of trauma. In her later work on trauma, Leys also makes reference to Mikkel Borsch-Jacobsen who engages Freud's writing on trauma and the ways in which Freud (at least in some of his writings) links trauma to affective bonds. The description of affective bonds offered by Borch-Jacobsen is interesting given the shift being made by students and me from a psychoanalytic approach to desire to affect. According to Borch-Jacobsen, for Freud, affect is an early form of identification, which is not "a question of optical representation (not an 'ideal,' 'objectivizing' and 'spatial' identification)." Before the identification of the mirror stage, affective identification "gives birth to the ego." Even for Lacan, Borch-Jacobsen argues, there is at times an understanding of the proprioceptive sensations that constitute affective relationships prior to the identification of the mirror stage. See Mikkel Borch-Jacobsen, *Lacan: The Absolute Master*, trans. Douglas Brick (Stanford, CA: Stanford University Press, 1991), 65–71.

9. Nicolas Abraham, "The Notes on the Phantom: A Complement to Freud's Metapsychology," in *The Shell and the Kernel: Renewals of Psychoanalysis*, ed. Abraham and Maria Torok (Chicago: University of Chicago Press, 1994), 171–86.

10. Jacqueline Rose, *States of Fantasy* (Oxford: Clarendon, 1996), 30–31.

11. Petar Ramadanovic, "When 'To Die in Freedom' Is Written in English," *Diacritics* 28.4 (1998): 62.

12. Judith Butler, *Gender Trouble: Feminism and the Subversion of Identity* (New York: Routledge, 1990). For a provocative engagement with Butler's work, along with other work on trauma and embodiment, also see David L. Eng and David Kazanjian, eds., *Loss: The Politics of Mourning* (Berkeley: University of California Press, 2003).

13. Pheng Cheah, "Mattering," *Diacritics* 26 (1996): 108–39.

14. Ibid., 113.

15. Ibid., 120.

16. Manuel DeLanda, "Nonorganic Life," in *Incorporations*, ed. Jonathan Crary and Sanford Kwinter (New York: Zone, 1992), 134.

17. Keith Ansell Pearson, *Germinal Life: The Difference and Repetition of Deleuze* (New York: Routledge, 1999), 139–85.

18. Sigmund Freud, *Beyond the Pleasure Principle*, trans. James Strachey (New York: Norton, 1961).

19. Humberto R. Maturana and Francisco G. Varela. *Autopoiesis and Cognition: The Realization of the Living* (Boston: D. Reidel, 1980).

20. Pearson, *Germinal Life*, 170, 216.

21. Ibid., 170.

22. Ibid., 216.

23. Following Pearson, I am drawing on Lynn Margulis, *Symbiosis in Cell Evolution* (San Francisco: W. H. Freeman, 1981); and Lynn Margulis and Dorion Sagan, *Microcosmos: Four Billion Years of Evolution from Our Microbial Ancestors* (New York: Summit, 1986). Also see, Luciana Parisi, "Information Trading and Symbiotic Micropolitics," in "Technoscience," ed. Patricia Ticineto Clough, special issue, *Social Text* 80 (2004): 25–50.

24. For a discussion of Deleuze's treatment of the virtual and the actual see Gilles Deleuze, *Bergsonism*, trans. Hugh Tomlinson and Barbara Habberjam (New York: Zone, 1991).

25. For the discussion of the time-image in contrast to the movement image, I am referring to Deleuze's *Cinema 2: The Time-Image*, trans. Hugh Tomlinson and Robert Galeta (Minneapolis: University of Minnesota Press, 1989). For an insightful treatment of the time-image as electronic, see Richard Dienst, *Still Life in Real Time: Theory after Television* (Durham, NC: Duke University Press: 1994), 144–69.

26. For a discussion of the crack, see Gilles Deleuze, *The Logic of Sense* trans. Mark Lester with Charles Stivale, ed. Constantin V. Boundas (London: Athlone, 1990).

27. Pearson, *Germinal Life*, 196.

28. Ibid.

29. Gilles Deleuze and Félix Guattari, *What is Philosophy?* trans. Hugh Tomlinson and Graham Burchell (London: Verso, 1994).

30. See N. Katherine Hayles, *How We Became Posthuman: Virtual Bodies in Cybernetics, Literature, and Informatics* (Chicago: University of Chicago Press, 1999).

31. Eugene Thacker, *Biomedia* (Minneapolis: University of Minnesota Press, 2004), 40.

32. Martin Heidegger, *The Question Concerning Technology and Other Essays*, trans. William Lovitt (New York: Harper and Row, 1969); and John Johnston, "Machinic Vision," *Critical Inquiry* 26 (1999) 27–48.

33. Donna J. Haraway, *Modest_Witness@second_Millennium. FemaleMan_Meets_OncoMouse_* (New York: Routledge, 1997).

34. Walter Benjamin, "One-Way Street," *Reflections: Essays, Aphorisms, Autobiographical Writings*, trans. Edmund Jephcott, ed. Peter Demetz (New York: Harcourt Brace Jovanovich, 1978), 61.

35. Luciana Parisi and Tiziana Terranova, "Heat-Death: Emergence and Control in Genetic Engineering and Artificial Life," *CTheory*, 5, www.ctheory.com/article/a84.html.

36. Ibid., 4.

37. Ibid., 5.

38. Gilles Deleuze, "Postscript on the Societies of Control," *October* 59 (1991): 3–7. See also Michael Hardt, "The Withering of Civil Society," *Social Text* 45 (1995): 27–44.

39. See Claude Elwood Shannon and Warren Weaver, *The Mathematical Theory of Communication* (Urbana: University of Illinois Press, 1949). While Shannon published his theory in 1948, in 1949 this larger work was published, including Shannon's theory with a commentary by Warren Weaver.

40. Tiziana Terranova, *Network Culture: Politics for the Information Age* (London: Pluto, 2004), 24.

41. See Norbert Wiener, *The Human Use of Human Beings* (Boston: Houghton Mifflin, 1950).

42. Ilya Prigogine and Isabelle Stingers, *Order out of Chaos: Man's New Dialogue with Nature* (New York: Bantam, 1984).

43. Terranova, *Network Culture*, 33.

44. Parisi and Terranova, "Heat-Death," 9.

45. Ibid., 8–9.

46. Michel Foucault, "Governmentality," in *The Foucault Effect: Studies in Governmentality; with Two Lectures by and an Interview with Michel Foucault,* ed. Graham Burchell, Colin Gordon, and Peter Miller (Chicago: University of Chicago Press, 1991), 87–104.

47. Brian Massumi, "Requiem for Our Prospective Dead (Toward a Participatory Critique of Capitalist Power)," in *Deleuze and Guattari: New Mappings in Politics, Philosophy, and Culture,* ed. Eleanor Kaufman and Kevin Jon Heller (Minneapolis: University of Minnesota Press, 1998), 57.

48. Ibid., 54.

49. George Caffentzis, "The Work Energy Crisis and the Apocalypse," in *Midnight Oil: Work, Energy, War, 1973–1992* (Brooklyn: Autonomedia, 1992); and Antonio Negri, "Value and Affect," *boundary 2* 26. (1999): 77–88.

50. Nearly all of the authors have been participants in two projects I organized as the director of the Center for the Study of Women and Society at the Graduate Center CUNY. The projects have involved two seminars: "The Conviction Project Seminar" and the Rockefeller Foundation–funded seminar entitled "Facing Global Capital, Finding Human Security: A Gendered Critique," which were respectively focused on issues of mass incarceration and postprison experience and the evaluation of the effectiveness for women of the human rights/human security frameworks in the context of global capitalism, counter/terrorism, and war. The two seminars offered an opportunity to further develop our thinking about biopolitical control, information, affect, and non-organic life in relationship to politics, policy, and activism.

51. Zygmunt Bauman, *Wasted Lives: Modernity and Its Outcasts* (London: Polity, 2004); Achille Mbembe, "Necropolitics," trans. Libby Meintjes *Public Culture* 15.1 (2003): 11–40.

52. Gayatri Spivak, "Scattered Speculations on the Question of Value," in *In Other Worlds* (New York: Routledge, 1988), 154–175.

53. Negri, "Value and Affect," 79.

54. Thacker, *Global Genome*, 201.

55. Jonathan Beller, "Capital/Cinema," in *Deleuze and Guattari: New Mappings in Politics, Philosophy, and Culture,* ed. Eleanor Kaufman and Kevin Jon Heller (Minneapolis: University of Minnesota Press, 1998), 91.

56. Massumi, *Parables for the Virtual*, 88.

57. Ibid., 88.

58. Ann Anagnost, "The Corporeal Politics of Quality (Suzhi)," *Public Culture* 16.2 (2004): 189–208.

59. Sara Ahmed, "Affective Economies," *Social Text* 79 (2004): 117–39; also see

Jasbir K. Puar, "Abu Ghraib: Arguing against Exceptionalism," *Feminist Studies* 30.2 (2004): 1–14.

60. João Biehl, "Vita: Life in Zone of Social Abandonment," *Social Text* 68 (2001): 138.

61. Michael Hardt and Antonio Negri, *Empire* (Cambridge, MA: Harvard University Press, 2000), 34–41.

62. Giorgio Agamben, *Homo Sacer: Sovereign Power and Bare Life*, trans. Daniel Heller-Roazen (Stanford, CA: Stanford University Press, 1998).

63. Deleuze and Guattari, *A Thousand Plateaus*, 351–423.

64. Mbembe, "Necropolitics," 23.

65. Bauman, *Wasted Lives*, 89.

66. Massumi, "Requiem for Our Prospective Dead," 57–58.

67. Bauman, *Wasted Lives*, 89.

68. Michael Taussig, *Law in a Lawless Land* (New York: New Press, 2003), xi.

69. Gilles Deleuze, *Francis Bacon: The Logic of Sensation*, trans. Daniel W. Smith (Minneapolis: University of Minnesota Press, 2003), 91.

70. Taussig, *Law in a Lawless Land*, 17–18.

71. Fred Moten and Stefano Harney, "The University and the Undercommons: Seven Theses," *Social Text* 79 (2004): 108.

72. Ibid., 109.

HOSU KIM

> What is passed on, finally, is not just the meaning of the words
> but their performance: a performance that . . . takes place in
> the movement—in the repetition and the gap.
> —Cathy Caruth, *Unclaimed Experience:*
> *Trauma, Narrative, and History*

> "The ghostly emptiness of a lost other" will constitute the
> speaking subjects.
> —Anne Anlin Cheng, *The Melancholy of Race:*
> *Psychoanalysis, Assimilation, and Hidden Grief*

A foreign student's lack of command in English awakens her to unclaimed experiences and to the bodies of Koreans and diasporic subjects at different temporalities. The broken tongue not only denotes the political economy of language in English, of the dominant society, but also makes claims to many different, unrecognized tongues, bodies, and memories. This experience transmits the awakening to the other. "In the face of both the urgency and the impossibility of performing one type of mouth-work—speaking to someone about what we have lost—another type of mouth-work is utilized."[1] My awakening: a Korean foreign student's loss of verbal capacity in words, a mother's memory of the Korean War, and a mother's loss of memory about the baby she left behind, juxtaposed in the form of craving for foods—binge eating and American chocolate bars. These narratives may suggest the conditions for reconciling the traumatic pasts by acknowledging the impossibility of knowing the losses and pains in displaced tongues and disjointed bodies.[2] At the very time of choosing a dissertation topic, international adoption from Korea, a birth mother's unclaimed grief for her lost child is heard in the form of an incomprehensible sobbing sound on a Korean foreign student's parched tongue.

When I first learned the Korean alphabet at my age of six.
Sitting with a mother grabbing a whip
Swallow swallow the fear the sweat
I knelt down and began to write and pronounce
the Korean alphabet from *kiuk, niun, digut, . . .*
I knew I would not be able to get through all the letters
Jiut-chee-ut, khiyuk, khiyuk, khiyuk, . . .
Um-ma hit my palm.[3]
"Hosu-ya! What is the next character? How many times I had to
    tell you? Are you stupid or what? Why you did not memorize
    this yet?" Shouted at me, "Write *tee-ut* a hundred times!"
Even before I mastered the Korean alphabet . . .

I can hear the ABC song
Ei bee shee dee ee eh-puh jwee ei-che a-ee jei kei el em en oh pee
kyu al es tee yoo bee duh-bool-yoo ek-shuh wai jee[4]

A	B	C	D	E	F	G
H	I	J	K	L	M	N
O	P	Q	R	S	T	U
V	W	X	Y	Z		

SCENE 1. KOREAN TONGUE CANNOT TELL *L* FROM *R*, *B* FROM *V*, *G* FROM *Z*

Native speaker L—R; Korean tongue repeats el / ahl 앨—알
Native speaker B—V; Korean tongue repeats bee / bee 비—비
Native speaker G—Z; Korean tongue repeats jwee / jee 쥐—지

SCENE 2. LANGUAGE OF THE CENTER

One time in my early school-hood in Korea,
We learned that we should speak standard Korean *ppyo-joon-
    mal,*[5] 표준말
Living in a southern part, we all have Jeolla accent
Every time, our regional accent comes out accidentally
You got 혼나 (disciplined) by 선생님 (teacher)
But, every time, the standard Korean accent is too foreign to us

Moving from Jeolla to Kyungsang province[6]
We learned that we should not speak Jeolla accent

Because these two provinces traditionally are not getting along
So people don't like each other
I hided Jeolla accent with my trying standard Korean
Which I never belong to
Which I never live in
So many friends asking me I am from Seoul
Too many
Too afraid to say I am not
I get known as from Seoul, from center
Which I never belong to
Which I never live in

SCENE 3. A-EE EM AH BO-EE

Four days a week, six years of middle and high school,
we learn English.
Before a class, a student reads the dialogue for today's lesson out loud.

"A-ee em ah bo-ee." (I am a boy.)
"Yoo al ah geuh-rul." (You are a girl.)
"Mai nae-eem is tom."
"Your nae-eem is min-ho."
"Glad too mee choo."
"Aah dare maenee students in da classroom?" (Are there many students in the classroom?)

A classmate sitting by laugh at me trying English
Got blushed and stopped
A word of English couldn't get out of my mouth quite a while
    afterwards
Although I couldn't figure out what I did wrong
I felt ashamed of my tongue
I felt ashamed of my shame

And yet, I heard her speaking english sounds much smoother,
    and tender
Like her smell with floral soap breeze
Like the precious banana taste we occasionally had in our
    childhood

Her English never felt with my breathed-like kimchee-smell
   english.
We all adore her
We all want to become a friend to her
Sheepishly wanting, passionately resisting
My tongue chasing after her sound back and forth

Every day coming back home,
I tried to remember the shape of her lip
Tried to locate her tongue on mine
making "beautiful" and "correct" sounds of English
Every day coming back home,
I mimicked secretly her sound of English
"Are there many students in the classroom?"
"Are there many students in the classroom?"

To bite the tongue.
Swallow. Deep. Deeper.[7]

As if I could incorporate the perfect tongue into my body.

Later, I learned that she was living with missionaries from the United States.

Later, I learned that she spent some time in the United States.

In the 1970s, when I was growing up in Korea, there were two kinds of children who went to the United States. One came mostly from well-to-do families. The other were the orphans that I went to school with. Ironically, those orphans could also go to America. I heard American people would take them in, and they would live with American parents. Whenever a classmate moved to America, the whole class wrote a card and wished the orphaned classmate a good life in the United States. I thought, "Americans must not only be superrich but also kind, caring, and benevolent people." Like everyone in our class, I wished I could go to America and maybe live with Americans.

SCENE 4. THE PAST IS NOT DEAD; IT IS NOT EVEN PAST[8]

It was 1945 when Japan was defeated by a new power, the United States in Korea. The Japanese language, once a symbol of power and civilization, was replaced by English, a "global" language connected with prosperity and modernity. "Ever since then, countless South Koreans have been driven to learn

English as a means of economic survival and upward mobility."[9] "Her childhood dream of Japan was replaced by [my] dream of America."[10]

> my grandmother did not have a formal education
> she could have known Japanese if she went to school
> where her mother tongue was forbidden under Japanese colonial
>   rule
> but she couldn't afford to learn the powerful language, Japanese,
>   nor learn to read Korean, her national language. Thus, she had
>   a difficult life until the last day of her life.

> my mother went to only the second year of high school
> but she knew how to survive after the war—working as an Avon
>   lady for a black market in a neighboring U.S. military base in
>   her hometown
> she felt proud of herself being able to offer the decent and rare
>   American food to her children[11]

> I grew up with my mother's leftover sales products from the base
> Once I realized that I have nothing to sell,
> I murmur to myself maybe I should master English fluently
> Then nobody treats me as if I am nothing here
> Maybe I can go over there and study
> The power of English is a guarantor for your success
> The ability to speak English is directly tied to the power of
>   America
> Gazing on the West thinking someday I will be there
> Dusky blue sky held a hope for many days bruised with envy for
>   American life
> I started to go back to my painful mimicry English once again.
>   One more time.

In search of a conversational partner to practice English, I sought the opportunity to meet Americans from private English institutes and the uso,[12] through which I tasted America on the soil of Korea. Located in the center of a crowded city, Camp Hialeah had everything. Everywhere was filled with green grass, big, huge buildings, an excess of Mountain Dews, hot dogs, and those Korean women, whom I remembered as my mother's sales partners, hanging out with U.S. gis at bars.

Nobody dared to question why I wanted to learn English so bad
    like that
Nobody asked why I wanted to study in the United States
Agreed silence may connote the shame and the pain interlaced
    with U.S.-Korean relations
Instead I was told that we are living in a global society and
    English is the global language

Thought that English gave me a power that I can't reach
Hoped that English would be the language that I can master
Carefully chosen, meticulously practiced
Yet my unruly Korean accent in English disclosed soon
After passing a few seconds
My accented tongue sticking out of its own will against my
    arduous efforts
too much foreign touch, translated into *untamable and
    uncivilized—*
grocery, nail salon, fish market English in the United States.[13]

Korean tongue with English treated differently from those European tongues in English. Korean-accented English does not invite the same curious gazes and envy as European-accented English does. Instead, disapproving looks and outlandish racial slurs.

Hey, gooks; ching chang chong
I often felt
puzzled and pondered.
Then maybe not a matter of fluency or mastery in English.
My tongue already and always surfaces the other
Re-membering our tongue has been embodiment of shame, pain,
    violence
Our grandmothers speaking with Japanese words here and there
In boasting speech implying, "I am civilized and modernized"
Our mothers' memory of tongue indulged by and succumbing to
M&M's, candy bars, Skippy peanut butter, powdered milk,
    caramels,
All sweets from C-ration box of *mi-goon-boo-dae*[14]
and a song that I never learn but know how to sing

hello, hello
chocolate do giboo me
hello, hello
mok-dun-gut-do jo-a-yo
hello, hello
cigarreto giboo me
hello, hello
pidyun gut do jo-a-yo[15]

SCENE 5. TODAY'S THE FIRST CLASS OF THE SEMESTER

Once again i
breathe in to keep composure allowing me to have clear ears
After twenty minutes my efforts to focus all my energies on ears
   defeated
In American classroom i learned you are supposed to say
   something in order to prove you read, you understood, you
   have opinions
Students are competing each other to hold the appropriate
   moment their voices get in
not showing interference in other people's speech often people
   are not
listening but
waiting
listening ears gone while speaking tongues floated filled in the air
   then nothing heard

once again i
breathe in to keep composure allowing me to have clear ears

my turn is coming coming, my throat gets drier and drier, and
my tongue sucking all my breathe, then my parched sound of
English translated from even unformed Korean

I do not remember how many times i have to write something
down before i say something out loud Sometimes i hear my heart
pounding louder than my voice ringing i feel always sweaty
wobbly almost falling from the edge of my second tongue in the
midst of heated discussion, subject matter gets more complicated
and multiplied and my second tongue gets too restless to grasp

the right moment instead evaporated with its heavy weight i
found myself being caught up with a simultaneous translation of
multiple sets of vocabulary, syntax, and logic of thoughts with
different cultural frameworks between English and Korean

time passed like this
speechless always belated
sigh
breathlessly

> bodies without words
> words emptied of bodies
> when words fail to fill her bodies
> she seeks to fill the word in her mouth
> an imaginary thing is inserted into the mouth
> she craves for the food, American food
> becomes her *shameful secret and love object*[16]

> Swallow. Deep. Deeper
> Swallow. Again even more.[17]

the shame of my inadequate English
the shame of being silenced and voiceless along with other
        women
the shame of *hal-mo-ni* who could not to go back to hometown
        after serving sexual slavery[18]
the shame of *o-mo-ni* who utterly evacuated her mind including
        the memory of her baby who was left behind for adoption[19]
those shameful memories are surfaced through my parched
        tongue
echoing the pains of unclaimed experiences

**SCENE 6. PARCHED TONGUE: DISSERTATION TOPIC,
INTERCOUNTRY ADOPTION**

There are numerous people whose first languages had to be given up for their
bare condition of survival. Even after colonialism has ceased to exist in official
history, this tradition of displacement in exchange for survival has continued.
Mother tongues became a fossil or an obsolete cultural artifact stored away
within those displaced bodies.

Of many displaced bodies:

Korea-born adoptees were never allowed to learn nor retain their
　　mother tongues.

Instead they speak English, although not everyone. Some French,
　　some Swedish.

They returned before Koreans had a chance to remember their
　　existence.

To the land in which they were never allowed to live

To the land in which they might now be secured often only with
　　their displaced tongues

English fever has simmered in South Korea for the past fifty years

From preschoolers and to university students

America, Canada, Australia, and Philippines according to their
　　economic strata

to learn English, to gain a better bargaining power in a
　　competitive global market.

Many Americans, Canadians, British, Australians and other diasporic Koreans
with these powerful tongues become UN (United Nations) forces as their
predecessors during the Korean War formed to "protect democracy" from
North Korea's invasion. They flock into South Korea to promote (se-kwe-hwa)
세계화 by disciplining tongues in Korea.[20]

The Korean adoptees' return renders more complex the narrative of a better
life in adoption, which corroborates the American Dream. The American
Dream is actively promoted by the Korean national government's aggressive
development plan and was collectively dreamed by its faithful citizens after the
war, in the name of upward social mobility. From my mother to myself as
유학생, a foreign student in America. From the unknown number of birth
mothers to two hundred thousand adoptees.

Korean-born adoptees' returns invoke the shame of nation and of
　　mothers.

South Korea known as the country offered its own children to
　　Westerners

150,000 children to America and another 50,000 to Europe over
　　the past fifty years

Displaced bodies, diasporic tongues demanding their addresses
Where did they come from?
Whose bodies are they born of?

Um-ma, bogosipuh yo[21]
To search for their birth mothers, fathers, any family members
who might not know how to remember their children who have
    been adopted
who sacrificed one child to save another
who had to hide there was another child to the rest of her family
A baby who was once buried in a woman's heart returned alive.

UNKNOWN ADDRESSES

> *I have this memory so faded that I can no longer tell whether it is*
> *real or not*
> *My mother talking with the aunt about my twin sisters with an*
> *angry voice*
> *I thought to myself, maybe in my dream, "we must have done some*
> *stupid things again"*
> *That's why my mother got mad at us*
> *I fear her whipping again*
> Um-ma *said, "I should have placed them in adoption."*
> *I did not know what it meant at that time, but my heart ached*

It took long time for me to learn about the path that my younger sisters and my mother could have lived.[22]

On TV, another *um-ma* in her fifties, dressed in a worn-out purple sweater, held a young woman's hand, who was identified as her daughter by her Korean name. Her Korean name may sound authentic to many Koreans but utterly foreign to herself. The old woman started to say in her sobbing voice, "내가 죄인이지, 내가 죄인이야 . . . 그때는 너무 가난했고. 여자가, 남편도 없이, 아이를 혼자 잘 키울수가 없었어. 아니 키우는 거는 키운다고 쳐 도 학교도 못보냈을 거고 . . . (울음)—"I am a sinner. We were devastated at that time, too poor. I, as a woman with no husband, could not raise you well. That's why I sent you to the States. For a better life, to eat well and to get a better education." The *um-ma*'s eyes became flooded with tears. A translator intervened and translated. The daughter looked down and a tear dropped to the floor. She looked at the translator and said to her *um-ma*: "Tell her that I am okay. Tell her that I am happy to meet her again." And she embraced the mother's emptied breasts.

The birth mother came into being as a figure embodying personal shame and guilt where Korean national shame could easily be relegated. Through public testimonials of their irresponsible motherings, they themselves are recognized as the mothers, and thus Korea is reconciled with the losses and pains in adoption. Birth mothers' wishes, dreams, anguish, pain, guilt, anger, *han*,[23] and the shame of poverty and il/legitimate pregnancy—which visibly indicates women's sexual conduct—could not find a regular channel of communication, thus spilling through porous body lines and being left disjointed from its original sources. It floats and passes into different discrete bodies and matter.

> To *Um-ma*
> Did you ever notice that I despise your curse?
> Did you ever notice that I felt embarrassed because of your tongue?
> I have been running away from your swearing and devouring
>   tongue
> Far farther farthest
> Time arrested
> for the moment my envy to perfect English halted
> The voice heard
> Which is not from me
> Which has never lived in, but through me
> My loss in words filled with your memory and someone else's
>   memory
> It slams back to my own experience, which has never been fully
>   experienced
>
> Running away from you, *um-ma*
> Running from your impoverished tongue
> I met different *ummas* through my blushed skin
> Many untold stories without a body
> Passing through my broken tongues
> Other mothers' unacknowledged sobbings
> Joined my bruised tongue with many injured bodies
> in the American dream for *a better life*

Um ma,
My tongue always accidentally configured
My tongue always in between
My tongue always dreaming
My tongue always unsealing
For the stories yet to be told

EPILOGUE

She couldn't wake up by herself, maybe she decided not to, instead subjecting herself to sleep by the ABC lullaby.

Ei bee shee dee ee eh-puh jwee ei-che a-ee jei kei el em en oh pee kyu al es tee yoo bee duh-bool-yoo ek-shuh wai jee

A	B	C	D	E	F	G
H	I	J	K	L	M	N
O	P	Q	R	S	T	U
V	W	X	Y	Z		

NOTES

1. Nicolas Abraham and Maria Torok, *The Shell and the Kernel: The Renewals of Psychoanalysis* (Chicago: University of Chicago Press, 1994), 129.

2. See Sara Ahmed, *The Cultural Politics of Emotion* (Edinburgh: Edinburgh University Press, 2004), 39.

3. *Um-ma* (엄마) means "mother" in Korean; it is often used by children.

4. This is a transliteration of the Korean pronunciation of the English alphabet. In several sections throughout this piece, the author makes use of Korean words, pronunciations, transliteration, syntax, grammar, and cadences of the Korean language.

5. The standard Korean accent commonly spoken in Seoul, the capital of South Korea; those who speak this standard are thought of as respectable and contemporary.

6. A province in the southwestern region of Korea, Jeolla was historically known as the land of political exiles during the Cho-sun dynasty. In contemporary Korean history, Kwang-ju, the capital city of Jeolla Province, is known as the site of people's resistance against the Korean military dictatorship. Kyungsang is a province in the southeastern region of Korea; there has been an ongoing tension between Kyungsang and Jeolla provinces; this regional division has been, to a great extent, institutionalized in Korean society—people from Jeolla Province are often discriminated against and looked down on.

7. Theresa Hak Kyung Cha, *Dictée* (New York: Tanam, 1982), 69.

8. William Faulkner, *Requiem for a Nun* (1951; New York: Vintage, 1975).

9. Ji-Yeon Yuh, *Beyond the Shadow of Camptown: Korean Military Brides in America* (New York: New York University Press, 2002), 80.

10. Ibid., 45.

11. The underground economy thrived in Korea until the 1980s. "In most marketplaces in Seoul, [one can see] piles of black market American goods obtained from PXs and commissaries, as well as by occasional newspaper reports of the arrest of black marketers" (ibid., 247 n. 8).

12. The acronym USO stands for United Services Organization, chartered by the U.S Congress as a nonprofit, charitable corporation. The USO's mission is to provide morale, welfare, and recreational services to uniformed military personnel. The USO currently operates 121 centers, including overseas centers located in Germany, Italy, France, the United Arab Emirates, Bahrain, Iceland, Bosnia, Japan, Korea, Kuwait and the U.S. Virgin Islands. I volunteered for the USO in Busan, Korea, which allowed me entry into a U.S. military base. For the USO Web site, see www.uso.org.

13. Most Korean immigrants in the United States operate small businesses in service industries due to language barriers and racial discrimination in the primary labor market. The ones mentioned here are some of the common service industries in which Korean immigrants work.

14. This translated as "U.S. military base."

15. "Give me chocolate; even left-over chocolate, I'll take. Give me cigarettes; even leftover butts, I'll take."

16. Abraham and Torok, *The Shell and the Kernel*, 129.

17. Cha, *Dictée*, 69.

18. This literally means "grandmother"; it connotes a generation of comfort women who were forced to work as sexual slaves to maintain high morale among soldiers in the Japanese imperial army.

19. This literally means "mother"; it connotes birth mothers who have sent their babies away for adoption to other countries due to poverty, war, and the stigma of unwed motherhood. South Korea has been known as the first sending country in intercountry adoption between the mid-1950s and the late 1980s. The stories of the birth mothers have only recently been disclosed to the public in Korea.

20. This literally means "worldization" (as opposed to globalization). It is a concept introduced and supported by the Korean government, particularly by the Kim Young-sam administration since the mid-1990s' age of neoliberal globalization. *Sekewha* means to promote Korea's national agenda globally to become a leading economic force.

21. "I miss you, mother."

22. There is a high prevalence of twins, particularly female ones, among Korean-born adoptees. A strong association between prejudice against female twins and adoption is found in many anecdotal accounts.

23. This is an untranslatable term; it may be approximated as "unresolved grief."

TECHNO-CINEMA:

IMAGE MATTERS IN THE AFFECTIVE UNFOLDINGS

OF ANALOG CINEMA AND NEW MEDIA

JAMIE "SKYE" BIANCO

CONTROL: "VOR DEM SPIEL IST NACH DEM SPIEL"

Matter, in our view, is an aggregate of "images." And by "image" we mean a certain existence which is more than that which the idealist calls a representation, but less than that which the realist calls a thing.

—Henri Bergson, *Matter and Memory*

Representation is perceived as ultimately ineffectual not because it necessarily establishes a gap between referent and signs, reality and images, but because it is an intrinsic misunderstanding of the nature of perception and matter.

—Tiziana Terranova, "Cybernetics Surplus Value: Embodiment and Perception in Informational Capitalism"

"Vor dem Spiel ist nach dem Spiel," or "the end of the game is before the game": tracing this paradoxical second epigraph to Tom Tykwer's *Lola rennt* (1999) and inverting Eve Kosofsky Sedgwick's useful notion of "thick description,"[1] a "thin," or affective, description of *Lola*'s opening sequence follows.[2]

Foucault's pendulum violently swipes the screen, strung up to an oddly gothic wall clock sporting a fast-moving Chronos that then swallows its own image. Time emerging from the belly of time, the image movement of *Lola* unfolds in a massive and meandering flow of human bodies across which a "mystery of unanswered" (*Lola*) onto-epistemological questions are posed, along with their indeterminate grounds and topoi: "Who are we? Where do we come from? Where are we going? How do we know what we think we know? Why do we believe anything at all? Countless questions in search of an answer, an answer that will give rise to a new question and the next answer will give rise to the next question and so on. But in the end, isn't it always the same question? And always the same answer?"[3] The movement swirls to a rest, an interval, in which the rules of the game are stated by a security guard, "The ball is round. The game lasts ninety minutes. That's a fact. Everything else is pure theory."[4] At this point, a soccer ball is kicked into the sky, becoming both the viewer's trajectory and movement, and as we and the ball fall back to earth, the meandering bodies on the ground organize themselves into the main title, with the ball coming down onto the forming multitude, opening up as the *o* in the word *Lola*. The ball falls into the *o*, swallowing the image once again and becoming a now-animated Lola already running. Falling, swallowing, and emerging transmogrified, the image and we are always running, always movement in play, and always opening onto the emergent.

And Lola runs in three experiments or twenty-minute rounds—all in an attempt at continuity. In "theory," she must find 100,000 DM with which to save her boyfriend, Manni, who in his attempt to prove himself to several members of organized crime, acts as a courier for their cash and then proceeds to lose it on Berlin's subway, the *U-Bahn*.

And Lola runs. She runs in three twenty-minute cycles or rounds. In each, the endings are changed even though she encounters the same bodies and forces along the way; however, in this play on the butterfly effect,[5] each round reaches out to several virtual futures because of the slightest temporal modulations or swerves from run to run. The game is rebooted, but this game of close-circulating and materializing images remembers as well. And so, "the end of the game is before the game."

The source of the second epigraph is Sepp Herberger, the 1954 World Cup–winning "German soccer coach."[6] The film's first epigraph, though slightly bent, is taken from "Little Gidding" by T. S. Eliot, which reads, "Wir lassen nie vom Suchen ab, / und doch, am Endt allen unseren Suchen, / sind wir am Ausgangpunkt zurück / und warden diesen ort zum ersten Mal enfassen" (And the end of all our exploring / will be to arrive where we started / and know the place for the first time). Coach Herberger's tactical comment, however unintentionally,[7] emphasizes the intensive temporality and feedback loop of the game as play and movement itself. And though Eliot's quotation might be read as a metaphoric motif of the cyclical human voyage, or perhaps as the representational processes of psychoanalytic trauma and forgetting, I would argue that given *Lola*'s insistent kinesthesia, Eliot here might instead be read through dynamism or through the time and movement that it takes to accomplish the exploring. Our arrival at the same coordinates "where we started" carries the active accumulation of a familiar but new material condition.

"The end of the game is before the game" summons the cinematic event (film and spectator) to the end/s of a game, one in which controlling or configuring the conditions and movement of play and the playing field itself constitutes the game. Winning consists only of the continuation of play, and continuity necessitates a learning curve of losing through movement first— similar to that found in any form of digital gaming. By these constraints, whereby losing as incompletion allows for the continuity of play, Lola (and we) must lose the first round of the game in order to continue to the second round and likewise on to the third round. Productive continuity becomes the process and object of play, and losing then becomes winning more time(s) to play. And even in the incompletion of play as losing, the loss here cannot be read as the equivalent to psychoanalytic lack. Quite to the contrary, losing becomes the fullness of memory in movement, as well as in that which has already happened—that which is both materially and perceptually present as actuality and that which is virtually to come. Losing is also a desiring force by which Lola and we become the continuously subjectivized avatars of close-circuiting movement. The game continues as movement and therefore as avatars at play. By extension, once a successful navigation of the objects in the temporal circuit is achieved, the game discharges play and movement and extinguishes the avatars of movement and the desiring forces of continuity. This is precisely what occurs in Lola's successful navigation of the third round of the film. Lola's and *Lola*'s respective game ends only when she, we, and the images stop running together. Lola's and our running is ultimately constrained by the running time of *Lola*, and when the dynamic movement of *Lola*'s image world is run out—a close-circuited world materialized in the film, its viewing, and its viewers—a dematerializing of the movements circulating between the film and the viewers comes to a true end that is constituent of a material and permanent loss.

Following David Kazanjian and David Eng's use of loss in *Loss: The Politics of Mourning*,[8] I intend both senses in which I have discussed loss to indicate inertial, dynamic, and material remains, and in the case of *Lola*, the material remains of movement as an energized and embodying memory. Therefore during the run of the film, the end/s of a round of the game that is incomplete or lost also become the possibility of the game continuing, and as Eliot's lines tell us, a game that is both the same and new with each round. The lost game has an accumulated temporality and play, a *history for the future* that finds itself at the same initial material coordinates but not at the same initial material conditions as the prior round. The same game becomes new, and we "know the place for the first time" as repetition with difference.

Keeping in mind the first epigraph of this essay, in which Henri Bergson asserts that images are matter and matter is imaged, consider what *Lola*'s director, Tom Tykwer, offers as the articulation of his compositional process: "I always start with the image. I get an image in my head and I start wanting to get it moving . . . because the film is really fast moving and you have to have time . . . . The time-space continuum gets taken right off its hinges without anyone really noticing . . . in a synthetic, artificial world."[9] Not unlike Siegfried Kracauer's notion of "the cinematic significance of the reveling in speed,"[10] the "synthetic" world that Tykwer describes is one in which experiments with images in nonhuman time and space are made. Using Bergson's ontology, these experiments might be described as experiments with matter in *nonhuman* durations and extensions. Let this experimentation be part of a definition for technoscience, new mediated digital objects, and techno-cinematics.

Techno-cinema and my reading of *Lola* are movements in a larger project that tracks the designed technoscientific and new mediated capture and release of temporalities, force, and complex matters in order to produce affect, extra-anthropocentric perceptual speeds, and modular control.[11] Gilles Deleuze in "Postscript on Societies of Control" briefly outlines the function of control following Michel Foucault's sociopolitical account of regimes of disciplined and segmented movements. Antonio Negri in "Value and Affect" makes the connections and notes disjunctions between traditional Marxist models of political economy and an affective, technologized economy.[12] This project takes together the practices and productions of new media and technoscience and cultural, critical, and literary productions, studies, and theories. I have suggested that, in part, technoscience might be thought of as experimentation with matter in nonhuman time and space. Technoscience and new mediated digital environments are reality-by-design, as well as reality-in-the-making. Technoscience and new mediated digital ecologies make futures without loyalty to any past(s), all while charging themselves on the affects of histories.[13] As methodology, technoscience is (1) instrumentality, know-how, systematic treatment, or *techné*; and (2) epistemes, the fields, states, or facts of knowing, or *scienza* in mutual constitution.[14] The powers of technoscience are the captured forces of transhuman or beyond human temporalities and materialities occurring by design, but also in excess of their designs, and new mediated digital objects live in this ecology of transposition. Therefore what begs examination in humanities and social science theory is what Ronald Bogue has called the "aesthetics of force."[15] Force operates through energy, matter, and time as materializing affect. And such affect can be programmed, designed, and modulated by control parameters and thresholds, as well as culturally interfaced with new media. Technoscience brings the body and the body brings technoscience to resonate across a multitude of material and energetic scales wherein macroscopic and microscopic, complex and virtual dynamics operate. And despite mechanized production, the sheer power of controlled affective forces—as well as the presence, puissance, and accelerated potentials of new mediated environments and technoscientific dynamics—demand a political aesthetics that might engage these faster and more intensive material and energetic dynamisms. Critical and constructive engagements with force, its capture as power, its affects, and the control functions that deploy, modulate, and threshold time, matter, and energy are vital. Technoscience and new media offer critical experimentation by which designed incursions might intensify or capture energy in systems of material power, or bifurcate onto emergent aesthetic and political open systems.

Creative though not necessarily controlled open-systems experimentation captures a set of initial tempo-material conditions for a technoscientific flow, digital image world, or that which I am calling a "techno-cinematic event" in the case of the three prescient analog films under consideration in this article, *Lola rennt*, *Memento* (2000), and *Requiem for a Dream* (2000). However, these three objects are indeed analog films and not digital or integrated media, or digital cinematics such as soft cinema, microcinema, or DV (digital video). Yet as techno-cinematic experiments, they express affective aesthetic and compositional processes of new media objects. In fact, they both anticipate and arrive with the complex, distributed temporal and materializing affects and aesthetics of new mediated digital worlds. They are constructed not simply as representational narratives but more primarily as designed distributions of movement and affect. The admixture of any material capture, design, program, or plan operates as an "abstract machine," a force function staging the capture of matter and force into affective power.[16] Gilles Deleuze and Félix Guattari define an abstract machine as a "matter-function" over and against a "substance-form." An abstract machine functions as an attractor, as the virtual counterpart to emergent structure, or as an open system's gross material tendencies. This matter-function, or capture and control of force, are the function and constitution of fields of modular power, of volatile bodies,[17] of reterritorializations, and of becoming affectively and therefore materially new.

Territorialization is a term for particular physical phenomena taken from Deleuze and Guattari's *A Thousand Plateaus*. Along with deterritorializations and reterritorializations, territorializations are movements in which material vectors are captured and constituted within the "plane of consistency" or a generalized, heterogeneous, material topography. A territorialization is a specific stratification and temporality of a particular material vector. Given these open, material capacities and tendencies in movement across variegated spatial and temporal domains, technoscientific and techno-cinematic experimentation operates via assemblages, and from e-bombs to biochemistry to digital media, they operate beyond the particular extensive and durational scales and capacities of the human sensorium. And given their dynamism or tempo-material flux, these experiments can also exceed their designs and controls.

We can think of *Lola*, then, as a technoscientific or techno-cinematic film wherein the mattering of images constituting the filmic experience in the body of the perceiver operates across a modulated space-time continuum. Following Bergson, if we take the perceiver as the mattering of bodily images capable of engaging affectively with other mattered images, then there are multiple scales or interplays of movement, image/matters and body/images. This assemblage of technoscientific matterings of film and perceiver constitute the techno-cinematic event. Given the energetics and affectivity of image/matters, technoscientific cinematic events are able to "jump scales" of matter,[18] space, and time to the techno-cinematic, "synthetic, artificial world" that Tykwer describes in *Lola*. The techno-cinematic event, which runs together analog imaged bodies, rhythms, colors, and light at different speeds and intensities, is the synergistic flow of energies and matters that constitute the affective bodies of the perceiver and the film. We are a new, mobile entity, and our running game of *Lola* ends with the third run when the event has optimized and extinguished the energies and motion of running. This event is a noncausal repetition game, a reterritorializing, recoding game modulating its temporal loops and durations for the optimization of its forces and energetics across the topographies of the image/matters and body/matters that constitute it.

With technoscience, new mediated digital worlds and techno-cinematic events, the affects of multiple scaled time and space prove far more *sensible*, and the thresholding and induction of designed affects (catastrophe,[19] capture, and control) prove far more *possible*, impinging on the body/bodies directly. We are made faster, slower, livelier, deader, more nonorganic, more narrowly centering, and far too loosely centrifugal; we are in the being-made. It is to this morphogenetic making that the virtual capacities of integrated digital media or new media tend explicitly. And in techno-cinematics we are made, but in new mediated ecologies we are making as well as being made in the controllable activations and user interfaces that charge body/matters with the extensive powers to modulate the image/matters in real time.[20] Agency, power, and force are not lacking; they are programmatically and randomly distributed, modulated, captured, and controlled across multiple topographies and temporalities. Techno-cinema, like television, modulates speeds and forces, but it constrains movement to a single trajectory, moving from image/matters to body/matters. In this speedy material constructivism that opens to new media's capacities for modular, interfaced, technosociality (and not the reverse), how do we engage the deadly productions emerging in the new mediated and technoscientific opening up of slow and rigid liberal humanisms onto variable, distributed, and controlled transhuman ecologies?

CAPTURE: "REMEMBER TO FORGET"

> Memory . . . is just the intersection of mind and matter.
> —Henri Bergson, *Matter and Memory*

Christopher Nolan's *Memento* counts backward, but the numbers begin to change scale and duration before we reach zero. *Memento* opens with photographic image capture. A Polaroid of a man's head blown off undevelops, returns to the Instamatic camera as the gun leaps into the hand that once held the snapshot, and pulls both the bullet back into the gun's body and the man's head back onto his body. The gun has saved this man's life by unshooting him in the causal chain of the opening flow of images. Clearly, causality and linear, irreversible temporality come unhinged in this game. Leonard (Guy Pierce): "So where are you? You're in some motel room. You just, you just wake up and you're in . . . in a motel room. There's the key. It feels like, maybe, it's just the first time you've been there, but perhaps, you've been there for a week, three months. It's kinda hard to say. I don't know. It's just an anonymous room." Leonard's spatial and temporal dislocation echoes the image/matters of Leonard sitting on the bed in one such nondescript, black-and-white motel room. Contrary to the prior scene, he tracks through the motions of the voice-over chronologically. Of extra-bodily environs, Bergson argues, "the objects which surround my body reflect its possible action upon them."[21] If this is so, these objects in Leonard's motel room and the montage of the film evoke paralysis, not movement but its suspension or capture, for both Leonard and the observer. *Memento* as a techno-cinematic event breaks away from the observer at the end of each sequence. Leonard and the observer must actively trace the reflections of the surroundings with concerted force and limited mobility, something that constitutes their captured possibility or intensive energy for action. In this game of concentration, and in order for these mementos and memory to act rationally on these images, Leonard goes about matching Polaroids and tattoos to faces, places, and actions much as does the observer, matching and significantly mismatching segments and sequences that unfold in narrative, nonnarrative, proactive, and retroactive temporalities.

This techno-cinematic game does not run, as *Lola* does, but rather contracts and dilates. Sequence endings are segmented against every other preceding sequence, such that each beginning does not remind of or parse together the image/matters of *Memento* passively or rationally. This force of disarticulation in place and time actively undoes suturing in what is an active symbolic *dis*ordering. Rather than subjectivizing the observer, the disorder brings the movements of the film affectively to the captured observing body and auto-affectively to the film in its own captured movements. Exposures are produced constantly, extending that which is intensively behind the current image, making staid, analog images (the Polaroids, maps, and tattoos) particularly resonant and dynamic. With nothing missing or lacking and yet under constraint, we begin the constant effort, like Leonard, of parsing and matching the unfolding and unmatched pieces. And yet because we are dealing with a techno-cinematic event rather than inter*active* new media, there is no user interface that allows us to access, retrieve, and composite these disordered and sometimes corrupted memory images. And yet like new media, *Memento* produces a past through the production of unmatched futures, genealogies of a thinking forward rather than a thinking back.[22]

In Leonard's voice-over heard in the "here" of the black-and-white sequences but produced or coming from elsewhere, we learn the techniques of knowing out of time or place, from the here that is also somewhere else, both in and out of chronological memory. According to Bergson's definition of memory, mind and matter are always out of joint, but this occurs differentially in *Memento*. In *Memento*, mind out of joint is matter of a particular dysfunction that "interrupt[s] the current which goes from the periphery by way of the center, and, consequently, to make it impossible for [a] body to extract, from among all the things which surround it, the quantity and quality of movement necessary in order to act."[23] Leonard's overlaid topography of tattoos—mnemonic traces carved and inked in Leonard's flesh—reads as an overabundance of correspondences between memory traces, Freud's *Wunderblock* writ too large and overexposed. Leonard's mind has unfolded from its encased bodily matter onto all the visible surfaces of the surrounding matter. His environments become activated and hypertextual, but at the same time function as corrupted external memory storage. And thus perception and memory, for Leonard, are one and the same, yet productive of enormous noise in their cohabitation.

Bergson argues that the centering of the human image by itself (autopoiesis) occurs in that most perception is already memory of the sensible and of the flesh. In *Matter and Memory*, Bergson writes of this centering, "My body, an object destined to move other objects, is, then, a center of action; it cannot give birth to a representation."[24] The present then constitutes an amalgamation of the sensate or affectively embodied image/matters of the past and the perceived present, as well as of the virtual energies unfolding in action in "compassable" futures. The compassable futures in Bergson and Deleuze are futures that probabilistically could happen, but do not once a specific future actualizes. Their attractions remain with the present and coming futures as the virtual. For Leonard, though, the center through which the extraction of necessary movement can circulate is spread out across the surface of the visible and merged with noisy perception and sensation. Leonard traces the distanciation and differentials of speed, matter, and space across surfaces of the visible, including his own affectively charged body, and the techno-cinematic observer must do the same. However, unlike Leonard, the observer's perceptions meet with more distinguishable, sensate memories in the flesh. Therefore Leonard's surfaces are not memories but activating mementos. For Leonard, the multi-scaled dynamics or virtualities of surfaces trigger a noisy and tilted "quantity and quality of movement necessary in order to act." For example, the injunction inscribed on the Polaroid of Teddy (Joe Pantoliano), "Don't believe his lies," becomes a generalized "don't believe Teddy" since there can be no distinction made between writing and the writer of the text, perception and memory, the image/text of the Polaroid of Teddy and Teddy, and, ultimately, Teddy and his lies. And this prompts Leonard to act. Leonard's mementos are intensive affects—image/matters made in advance not to be remembered but made to activate bodily affect to prompt to do the next.

With this collapse of mind and memory, *Memento*'s techno-cinematic image/matters tilt the centralizing observer out of her centering by disrupting the temporality and direction of the current of images. In some sequences, a possible precedent follows that which happens at the end of a sequence. In other sequences, chronological flashbacks of Leonard engaged on the telephone are undercut by chromatic and spatial disjuncture with other images. The telephone/voice-over sequences are shot in black-and-white and on a reverse (180-degree) angle, appearing inverted as mirror or negative-lensed images. The current of images is broken up into tributaries, an open system or a rhizome, in which all are resonant but also tilted, noisy, and unable to fit together. The mobile constraints centering the matter/images of the observer are forced to return constantly to the discontinuous surfaces of *Memento* without the capacity to interface with them as Leonard does. More important, we are paralyzed and inhibited in our narrative, chronological, and cinematic memories. The image/matters of *Memento* affectively force actions of forgetting: forgetting how we have conditioned sensation, thought, and action; forgetting chronology and the structures of narrative genres; and forgetting our acts of centering. From both the mobile constraints and active acts of forgetting, we may then engage in the navigable resonance of the image field.

Cut to: Leonard in full color, leaving a cheap motel room, with no necessary trace of correspondence to where we have been before. He moves into the world through the gate of the motel's front desk, tracking telephonic traces, messages received and held, and a Polaroid of Teddy, the resurrected dead, exceeds itself as the moving image Teddy opens the door to the world of "Lenny!" Our linear narrative tendencies privileging accumulation are unhinged like Leonard's when the formulaic temporality of the cinematic event is generically disordered, but we are also not in sync with Leonard's temporalities, which are fleeting, simultaneous, multiple, and perpetual presents. Deleuze notes this quality as "voluntary memory proceed[ing] by snapshots (*instantanées*)."[25] For Leonard and for us, the seeming function of the game of *Memento* is to feel out the affect of traces, the mnemonics for lost time. But like those in *Lola*, even if temporalities and forces are intensified to constrain the movement to one direction or mobility, the image times of *Memento* are not human-clocked and can never be lost, but nor can they be found. This game is more intensive in a tempo-material sense. A slippage of discreet and random moments are cut out and marked in Leonard's biotechnical record of tattoos, Polaroids, maps, police reports, directions, and topographies of identity and direction. The events of *Memento* and Leonard (as a gerund) have no beginnings or endings, but rather roll a vertiginous summoning of inserts without any sense or presence of an antecedent master shot. The centering observer diverts the images through a forced master shot chronology only to lose her or his sense of location by the end of the interval. The intervals overlap, multiply, and thicken. And the afterburners of sensation and revelation are an affective rhythm, a jagged undulation, the flush of losing what comes next but happened before, and the practice of what already remains in the future. But again, loss and losing here are not lack, but rather processes or even floods of accumulation opening onto something else—the determination of the necessary or pertinent and the capture of remnant value in the present generating a protected eddy in the current, the remains or the actual undeveloping against the virtual.

However, the end/s of *Memento* and Deleuze in the following articulation adds dynamic refinement and virtual dynamism to Bergson's oddly static sense of surface or surroundings:[26] "What is essential is not to remember, but to *learn*. For memory is valid only as a faculty capable of interpreting certain signs; time is valid only as the substance or type of this or that truth. And memory, whether voluntary or involuntary, intervenes only at specific moments of the apprenticeship, in order to concentrate its effect or to open a new path."[27] Deleuze suggests that the contingencies of space-time and substance are radically dynamic and agential. The time of *Memento* will validate only the substance of Leonard's manufactured signs, collected and made to prompt and to forget. In order to play at the techno-cinematic game of *Memento*, we must *learn* to remember to forget, to become perceptively transversal and to become forgetting transitively, as a gerund, in order to be prompted to continue and to act anew. This play is marked in the many recursive, unrecorded, and differentiated repetitions of Leonard's, "So where are you? You're in some motel room. You just, you just wake up and you're in . . . in some anonymous motel room." *Memento* is a rhythm and a repetition of thrown attempts to set or sediment the grounds of memory on which an epistemology of chronological continuity in knowing might be, but never will be, found. Instead, Leonard and we are made to feel vertigo atop mountains of signs inside and outside of streaming but disjunctive times.

Continuity in *Memento* is losing without winning the game, but as in *Lola*, continuity is necessary to the play. And our attempts at remembering what came before but happened afterward leave us blank when we are sent through yet another before sequence that swipes the board of the game and demands yet another futile strategy of sense and memory. Leonard articulates "memory is unreliable," but with no ability to form new memories that might dynamically reterritorialize his older memories, he is then also caught in the melancholy evoked by affective, material remains embodying past times: "I can't remember to forget you [his dead wife]." How can we let go, go on, or know if we cannot expect a consistent strategy of sense, a contiguous remembered cinematic form and formula? "Remember Sammy Jenkis," as Leonard's tattoo prompts; remember that as constrained matter/images with and among other matter/images we are not and cannot be memory, but, rather, that memory *becomes* us. We cannot safely circulate as a sedimented and centered being of memory or thought, but we might remember just long enough to forget in order to open to the virtual multiplicities held in the present out of which will arrive an actualization of the future. Remember that the future will learn us, or as Patricia Clough insists, that we might "give thought over to a future that [we] have not always fully grasped . . . as [we] are drawn to the future by it."[28] *Memento* is a game that insists against the sedimentation of memory but instead demands active learning. We might forget enough to allow thought its affect on our centralizing memories and to allow thinking to act anew. To go on, we can learn to trace the summoning of the future, that is, we might be the *conditioning of sensation and affect.*

Whereas chronological rescripting might seem a sensible strategy to capture and control the affects of the techno-cinematic event's image/matters, *Memento* offers the Sammy Jenkis prompt. Leonard develops techniques "to concentrate [memory's] effect" differentially given the more obvious tendencies of his short-term memory loss: the remains of his sensible memory, on the surface, discontinuous, merged with perception and the energies of affect. He learns to act, affect, and swerve the future, "to open a new path" onto the *unknown* or unthought by the fluid matters of visible and corporeal scripts. In *Memento*, Nolan plays around the slowly looping cinematic formula as a processual threshold or the limit of a function, wherein the *known* is a function of storage, repetition, and time, a past that arrives in the present as the already determined future. The capacities for the material storage of the cinematic event are modulated using our conditioning to the known affects of narrative, genre, and the visible. Narrative filmmaking captures and striates the cinematic event in a singular threshold or a tightly looped, closed trajectory—mobile constraints multiply across the filmmaking, distribution, and spectatorship. These design parameters execute control functions that slow movement to meet the capacities of the human sensorium and modulate image/matters to a cinematic biocircuit. This generates a designed affect, a retracing of the already familiar, the already experienced, and the symbolically familiar and known. What is most salient for the striated narrative, as for all closed systems and methodologies, are the machinics of repetition and re-cognition, with little or preferably no difference, working with the machinics of synchronization, in which time binds and captures movement. The capacity or force function to capture time in a closed system allowing for control and repetition machined to design.

CATASTROPHE: BODIES ~~AT REST AND~~ IN MOTION

> There are then, in short, divers tones of mental life, or, in other words, our psychic life may be lived at different heights, now nearer to action, now further removed from it, according to the degree of our *attention to life.*
> —Henri Bergson, *Matter and Memory*

Darren Aronofsky's *Requiem for a Dream* (2000) takes capture seriously as a techno-cinematic event that becomes an increasingly tight-looped trajectory played to a centering or centrifugal extreme. Control functions with such suffocating forces and speeds that this *Requiem* summons multiple forms of death. From the opening, the acinematic dirge is relentless and synced to televisual temporalities in *Requiem*'s opening television commercial for self-help videos: WEeeeeeeeee've gotta winner! WEEEEeeeeee've gotta winner! WEEEEEEEEEE've gotta winner! . . . BE excited! BE, BE excited! . . . Three things is [*sic*] all I did to change my life. ~~RED MEAT. REFINED SUGAR~~. . . . Juice by you! Juice by you! . . . Join us in creating energy! . . . Tappy Tibbons' 'Month of Fury' will revolutionize your life in just thirty days or your money back!" This interactive revolution ends life. Tappy Tibbons promises the attractions of a dream, the American Dream, but what becomes of the embodied matters of the human dreamers at the death of the image world dream, especially an extinguishing dream that does not happen with sleep but with eyes wide open? Take Bergson's construction of a centering image among images—light with differing speeds and some at the speed of light. At what point does the composition of forces and image/matters blended through contraction and flux compose a system, haecceity,[29] or bodily matters? What are the forces and speeds of centrifugal attraction that allow the body to coalesce, or the centripetal forces and speeds that dissipate the body? Can an autopoetic, entropic, organic body open up enough to admit image world dreams of futurities, and what happens if the body opens up to too many, to too much, or only opens up to the quickening pursuit of the receding dream? Chasing dreams that are composed of image/matters in excess of the temporal, spatial, and material capacities and mobile constraints of human body/matters means that these dreams never could come true, and yet the body will be hacked. Hacking the body with nonorganic dreams and matters is the game of *Requiem*, and it plays the games of death.

From *Lola* and *Memento* we learn that memory is simply continuity in the agglomeration of sense memories in bodily matters. Therefore disjuncture in time and multiple temporalities begin to swerve the forces of material centering and centrifugal attraction. These force-filled breaks bifurcate matter/images onto new matter/images. In the human assemblage, this is both necessary and dangerous. Programming a change, in this case, an imag(in)ed televisual dream, constitutes an opening onto new sensate matters and temporalities. When the surface tensions of body/matter do not hold, these catastrophic breaks effusively extend biomatter out of which our slow, macroscopic human bodies give way to death and extend into what Deleuze and Guattari call "the body without organs."[30] Deleuze and Guattari use this term to designate undifferentiated matter and forces. As autopoetic *and* entropic organisms, humans remain open to the movements of unstriated images from the body without organs, and we are able to experiment with our degree of openness. Surface tension is one facet that maintains a bodily assemblage and that allows the body the necessary volumaic folding around which it can conceive of its own wholeness or center. And this centering is itself a process of programming ourselves as living matter/images in distinction to, but among, the dead. But Manuel DeLanda argues that given their material dynamism, nonorganics are very much "alive,"[31] yet live across different degrees or scales of extension, intension, and duration.

Requiem is a programming or design experiment with the forces of organic and nonorganic life in which the intensification of the folds or centering through the use of drugs causes a sliding of the sensate and centering scales of the striated matter of human bodies away from organismic durations and extensions tending toward the nonorganic. In *Requiem*, the biological/organic temporalities that heavily threshold the image/matters of narrative and montage are also overcome by the affects of chemical/nonorganic life, becoming what Kracauer in *Theory of Film* called "the transient," or fleeting images; "blind spots in the mind," or images beyond our habitus; and "special modes of reality."[32] Reading Kracauer's subjective description of *representational* affect through Bergson's deployment of a *material* affect and embodied perception, we sense a great irony at play in the plosive collisions of sound and image/matters in the techno-cinematic event of *Requiem*. We *sense* and *feel drugged* in this explosion of intensive powers and control that normally bind the apparatus to the organic clock. The game that *Requiem* plays out is the relentless organization of nonorganic rhythms, temporalities, diffractions, and affects decentering the capacities of the observer.

Prelude: *Requiem* rolls the biotechnics of television into the biochemics of heroin and love; Harry (Jared Leto) steals his mother Sarah's (Ellen Burstyn) television set, pawns it for heroin, and shoots up the proceeds with his best friend, Tyrone (Marlon Wayans), and his girlfriend, Marion (Jennifer Connelly). The nonorganic life values and capacities of teletechnological and biochemical affects are exchanged. In a 180-degree series of Harry moving about the living room, Harry steals the television in a split screen with point-of-view shots from Sarah through a keyhole in the closet, and the accelerating and disorienting impact of images continues to modulate as Harry meets Tyrone in the hallway, followed by long tracking image/matters across the front of the building as they roll the TV down the street. When they reach the pawnbroker, a low-angle, handheld, fish-eye lens captures them and begins to transform the image/matters until we find them back in Marion's apartment with speedy time-lapse jump shots and insert shots of the processes of cooking, shooting, and absorbing heroin in the flesh. The hallway and the front of Sarah's building are the only two images that align with organic human perceptive parameters or thresholds of detectable temporalities, spatialities, and light refraction. This mix of image/matters offer a techno-cinematic event wherein *we* are jonesing for a fix, rushing ahead to get it, getting high, and becoming chemical in the vein. First round of the game, and we are captured by the forces of nonorganic play.

First movement: "Tappy's inspiration series is not available in any stores and is 100% money back, satisfaction guaranteed!" The television circulates back through Sarah once she retrieves the black box from the pawnbroker. She hops up and plops back into the easy chair, frustrated by the lack of televisual transmission and/or affection. A substitution occurs. The telephone reaches out to her and pulls her into the television set through the telephone lines and the mail service—an offer to be a contestant. She dreams of being ON TV, interfacing with the image/matters of her own past embodiments, looking thin, young, svelte, happy, never widowed, and never lonely. But in the present, as she is hurtling into a futurity that holds death, becoming thin is the only real possibility. The image/matters of Sarah are captured in the flesh of our matter/images, and Sarah begins to program herself and us "thin" with diet pills and tranquilizers. Sarah dreams through her television double and television family but must settle for dieting on grapefruit and, eventually, bottles of uppers and downers in the company of a terribly vindictive refrigerator. Second round of the game and the nonorganic life force of speedy, dieting, and lonely Sarah forcibly transverses us.

Second movement: "Get the juice now! Dial 1-900-976-JUICE! . . . Dial the last 'E' for excitement!" Harry dreams himself becoming Prince Charming for the beautiful Maid Marion. Their love is like no other, but these image/matters are something less than human. The image movements of Harry and Marion "in love" are chronically and bodily dismembered. We find Harry and Marion in time-lapse gaps and mismatched split screens, particularly provocative because they reach out to touch one another and the image movements of bodily segments do not parse together. The body parts are detachable and do not fit. They are both slowly transformed into disposable limbs with necessary holes and accessible to penetration, Harry's gangrenous injection site and Marion's mouth, vagina, and anus. Third round of the game and bodies are becoming mismatched and penetrated body parts.

Third movement: "All major credit cards are accepted!" Tyrone dreams of being his dead mother's perfect son but must settle for failing the perfect score and heroin withdrawal in prison. The image/matters of Tyrone, an African

American, are suspiciously chromatic and fleshy. As with those of Harry and Marion, image movements of Tyrone's love are dismembered and dehumanized. Unlike Harry and Marion's, Tyrone's play in the newly purchased mirrors cuts up the bodies of him and his girlfriend Alice (Aliya Campbell) when they are at a distance, but in proximity, the bodies become effusively organic, chromatically reflective, and nearly metallic in their swirling and undulatory movements. Hanging over the bed and capturing symmetrical, spooning sex, the image begins to spin, not unpleasantly, and is then shockingly arrested by another flattened static image. Tyrone and our sexual high are cut short. This trajectory will be repeated with the image/matters of Tyrone in the car with a successful dealer, Brody (Bryan Chattoo) swelling and metallic, to the gunshot, and again, getting high on the road trip to Florida, to the Georgia prison work crew, and bedtime withdrawals. Fourth round of the game: undulation and disruption.

Fourth movement: "More passion for living than you ever imagined!" Marion dreams of becoming a famous fashion designer and a beautiful body, but must settle for becoming a junky and a prostitute. The image/matters of Marion naked in the mirror repeat Tyrone's naked body in the mirror, but with such difference. Marion's image is nearly nonorganic, pale, deathly gray, and still, and as with Tyrone, the image cuts away sharply. Unlike with the image/matters of Tyrone, a cut back to Marion in the mirror occurs. The interval marks the possible qualities of Marion's "divers tones of mental life"—lacking and later suffused with heroin—producing a divers repetition of the body in the mirror but with a different "degree of *our* attention to life." Attention here means attending as well as concentration. And the image/matters of Marion are produced repeatedly as those of the flesh that differ in degrees of attention to livingness and that "oscillate wildly," to use Peter Hitchcock's eponymous title and description of millennial bodies.[33] We see urbane and lovely Marion at the dinner table, prostituting herself to her shrink, and radically break into an image movement in which she stabs the back of his hand. Later, she is static and floating in the tub, and the image breaks into an underwater shriek of horror. Marion, most intensely, is a haecceity of an affective *aesthetic* of force, for the oscillating *feel* of beauty and horror—made harsh and palpable when in the final sequence the elegant fragility of her makeup and dress, chromatically metallic in this scene only—shatter into a bludgeoning series of pornographic image/matters in Big Tim's (Keith David) sex show. Fifth round of the game: the body is a shifting topography.

Coda: "Juice it up!" Our addiction for *Requiem* is a force of attraction, of gravity and of intensity, cycling periodically as movement and rest, as suction and expulsion, of radical change and compensation for these losses/remains. And we become this movement in this techno-cinematic game as the affects of Sarah, Harry, Tyrone, and Marion's off-kilter bodily assemblages strike us. Transversed by the continuous forces of nonorganic motion and plosive modulation, how many speeds or oscillations can be sustained before spinning out onto the body without organs? *Requiem*'s game ends with a relentless hip-hop montage of bodies-come-undone to an erratic and crashing techno-aural rhythm during which these image/matters, coalesced as bodies, open onto the body without organs. Aronofsky, quoted on the DVD's "Anatomy of a Scene," describes these montages as "sharp sounds with sharp images and [composing] them one after the other and basically form[ing] almost a musical piece." This construction of montage is provocatively sensate, rhythmic, and affective, rather than ideological along the lines of Eisenstein's montages of contrasted content and meaning, a more analogic, allegorical, sociopolitical practice of montage. Sarah and the television become monstrous together, and Marion fucks herself into becoming Little John's spectral sex show.

Taking our gains from being played by *Lola*—continuity in running, and from being played by *Memento*—continuity in a memory that must be actively forgotten to continue—*Requiem* would seem to be more direct, excessively programmable in its play. Deleuze and Guattari famously query, "How to make a body without organs?" But how might we open onto the new without rupturing the organismic rhizome when we need to forget in order to experiment, to run, to learn, and to become? The image/matters of *Requiem* are autocatalyzed, self-programmed, and recursively designed to dismantle organicism through the forces of attraction to nonorganic image/matter assemblages, and in *Requiem*, they are catalyzed, programmed, and designed to do so across our flesh, a becoming dismembered, dehumanized, drugged, gangrenous, penetrated, withdrawing, and dead. As a game, *Requiem* is a flash grenade of "subjective" filmmaking, as the DVD insert states, a term reminiscent of Kracauer's 'subjective' [cinematic] movements"—movements, that is, "which the spectator is invited to execute."[34] And this execution, flowing across our flesh in the cinematic event, this rhizome of accelerating and bifurcating image/matters, does not die but rather becomes our sense perception and our sense memory. The play of *Requiem* suggests that organic continuity in an ecology of techno-scientific nonorganics and new mediated digital ecologies requires designed buffers, interfaces, thresholds, and control. Nonorganic life can be both too fast and too slow when organic life encounters it. Perhaps organic life and human life have such a terribly narrow threshold for continuity that control and capture, especially new mediated and technoscientific control and capture, provide small machines, designs, and programs for the ordering of times and space.

Requiem for a Dream offers a techno-cinematic vision too fast, a biotechnic montage overly sensible and affective for the body/matters to process the forces. Yet without the active discharge (again, we are entropic and autopoetic, a fatal combination), the movement and energies of such a circulating bombardment of affect are still in the flesh. *Requiem* is a game of coming together in attraction and coming undone through intensively folded centering and extensively unfolded dissipation occurring simultaneously. Charged by the affects of our dreams—our autopoetic moving sound images violently capturing and centralizing us into a controlled, contained, and individualized scope—we disallow any other future. The American Dream in Aronofsky's tale of four Brooklynites is a funereal procession whereby desiring images are captured into a repetition pattern, hardened and slow images moving in an accelerating stream, wherein affective capacities are thresholded into a constrained capacity for action unto death and dispersal. Each of the four characters attempts to compensate for entropic (energetic and material) loss and also attempts to construct through what remains. By chemically altering their rhizomatic fields, the rhythmic and resonant centrifugal attraction that keeps bodies assembled is put out of sync and loosened from their organic thresholds. They and we are caught up in an unbalancing sensation of forces, in the deterritorialization of the human body by nonorganic image/matters and body/matters.

Furthermore, if our needs are programmed by dreams, and in the case of *Requiem*, The American Dream, and these dreams are not probable or even possible, we will experience withdrawal. Withdrawal itself is an affective energetic consisting in variegated sense memories of affective pleasures across a bodily topography. Withdrawal is the body's forcible attempt to remember a prior sensate balance. These "abstract machines" called dreams can kill us, then, in their ever-receding retreat and in our ever-constant pursuit. The forces and attractions of the dream and the American Dream constrain and threshold our bodily memories to their pursuit at all cost. What psychic "height," to use Bergson's phrase, does the dream offer, and at what distanciation from its pursuant action? These abstract machines that become dreams render our bodies desiring machines and are affections of power moved into sensate actualization. These image/matters as abstract machines, and ultimately fleshed out as desiring machines, seek out transformative and forceful encounters. Sarah's television (regardless of the content, although the Tappy Tibbons infomercial self-help regime adds yet another abstract force function to the televisual flow) reaches out into her living room with the force of transformative transmission and toward reception or encounter. Sarah, with her bodily memory of smooth rhythms of fullness, becomes a jagged loneliness, amped in chocolate, schizoid on uppers and downers, and terrorized by a mean-spirited and ravenous refrigerator. For Tyrone, Marion, and Harry, heroin begs the vein and the opening of skin and vessel, in return offering a rhizomatic perceptive, affective, and active shift. But begging becomes demand becomes command becomes death, as with the accumulated sense memory of Harry's gangrenous shooting arm. The game: forget compensating for loss such that we might go on and become new. Harry never forgot the black hole in his arm, and we all fell through its vortex. Game over.

TECHNO-CINEMATIC EVENTS

> The brain is the screen. I don't believe that linguistics and psychoanalysis offer a great deal to the cinema. On the contrary, the biology of the brain—molecular biology—does. Thought is molecular. Molecular speeds make up the slow beings that we are.
>
> —Gilles Deleuze and Gregory Flaxman, "The Brain Is the Screen: An Interview with Gilles Deleuze"

The challenge of a critical reading of techno-cinematic events is that they ask us to think in terms of processual and heterogeneous assemblages of materializing bodies rather than in discreet subjectivization, explicitly symbolic objects and object interactions, film and perceiver. There are three force functions in motion in the dynamic reading of techno-cinematic events. Techno-cinema pursues (1) the play or game of *affect-by-design* and the catastrophic and recursive reterritorialization of tempo-materiality in the process; (2) the *thresholding* or *capture* of the material attentions and intentions of the image/matters constituting the body/matters of the observer across variegated organic and nonorganic speeds; and (3) the *control* of these thresholds across the observer/techno-cinematic event-in-progress in order to modulate material affectivity—"like the monster, like the spiral, they are reborn from their metamorphoses."[35] We are running the *Lola* spiral, remembering to forget *Memento*, and becoming monstrous, transhuman, or, perhaps, the necessary death for the *Requiem*. The techno-cinematic event becomes one of *captured and controlled* energetics and dynamics suffusing embodied matter as expressed in transhumanist practices.[36] Techno-cinematic events are material processes shot through with the energetic capacity to autoaffect their own material constituencies and to affect a constellation of bodies *by design*. New media makes these processes interactive by interfacing the affective capacities of the variegated body/matters to modulate the event as well.

New media, technoscience fictions in general, and the techno-cinematic events discussed here are deterritorializing events at the critical threshold of reterritorializations: reterritorializations that include and constrain our organic, biocircuited vision machines,[37] and more intensively, our sensation machines along with the perceptive and receptive bodily distributions becoming together these techno-cinematic events. The multiple-scaled physics of these image/matters and image systems are neither organismic nor the rhythmic composition of living assemblages. This collision and admixture of micromatters, variable speeds, and nonorganic and biorhythms signal a germinal unfolding of "the *age* of mechanical reproduction,"[38] as well as the interactive materializations of the "precession of realist simulation,"[39] and calls for a mixed-media aesthetics that is also a *bio*aesthetics of force. The humanist game is no longer running solo in *Lola*, no longer the only temporality of memory in *Memento*, and no longer privileging the anthropologized livingness of the human being in *Requiem*, where the dying dream of naturalized humanizations becomes the entropic, spinning death of the bodily matters of the dreamers. Given the irreversibility of this constructivist onto-epistemology of affective becoming over stabilized being, copies and originals are only modulations of programmed interfaces, ever-evolving matters in dynamic constellations and affective auras and attractors. We biocircuited image systems or techno-cinematic bodies are the sum movement of this running, forgetting, and spinning, pulsing splatter in *Lola*, *Memento*, and *Requiem*. Ultimately, recursive techno-cinematic events are volatile systems captured, summoned by the virtual, unfolding the possible futures of a particular image system as a volatile but rhythmic material event, as cinematic technoscience fictions.

As *Lola*, *Memento*, and *Requiem* move across the patterns of rhythm and vibrations to which their soundtracks beat, techno-cinema is an involution of what John Johnston calls "machinic vision,"[40] in which the initial conditions of these cinematic systems unfold through a tempo-material flux in which perceptive simultaneity meets multiple nonhuman sensations, as in *Requiem*'s television world explosion and hip-hop montage, *Lola*'s body-clocked spirals and repetitions, and *Memento*'s sheets of reversing time and erased memory. The perpetually produced present continues in and splits off from its relationship to organicism, linear historicism, and narrative temporalities, extensions and dimensionalities. We follow the differential play of technoscientific forces and the modulations of intensities and haecceities that flow across these techno-cinematic experiments, tracing these sensate and affective image systems. Biocircuited by design, inhuman or perhaps transhuman in their material conduction, these events are a confluence of organic and nonorganic life forces. But the dynamics of multiscaled materialities and temporalities produce the most voracious and differentiated forces in terms of the modulation of organic sensation.

As I have argued earlier, these techno-cinematic events are controlled productions of affect *by design* as well. It is the thresholding of force, temporality, and matter through intention and the intension of affect, capture, and recursion by design, a design that is always exceeded in its very recursion, that makes technoscience the open-ended "reality studio."[41] In addition, critical experimentation—and in these particular cases, the techno-cinematic experiments of Tykwer, Nolan, and Aronofsky—may also, by design or capture, *induce* bifurcation and work through the powers of capture beyond bifurcation. Technoscientific, new mediated, and techno-cinematic experimentation exceed their initial parameters or initial conditions in a given open system at a point where control meets catastrophe and capture.

AFFECT AND THE APPARATUS: THE DYNAMISM
OF FORCE, MATTER, AND SENSATION

> The cinema doesn't reproduce bodies, it produces them with grains that are the grains of time.
> —Gilles Deleuze and Gregory Flaxman, "The Brain Is the Screen: An Interview with Gilles Deleuze"

What of these sumptuous physicalities through which the cinematic experience strikes us, captures our attentions and perhaps intentions, and, at certain times, throws us for a loop? These chills, rhythms, and sensations cannot *simply* be articulated as the three-part representational metaphors deployed in readings of cinema through spectatorship, its libidinal economies, or ideological apparatus, though apparatus theory is perhaps the most approximate materialism to techno-cinematics. Jean-Louis Baudry's articulation of the apparatus of cinema in "The Ideological Effects of the Cinematographic Apparatus" expresses a remarkable similarity to Bergson's idea that the human image/matter centers itself in relation to other images, producing a subject that is a process. For Baudry, though, the filmic complex centers the human body and produces a static viewing subjectivity. This subjectivity is a material function that has become strangely disembodied and immobilized by a material apparatus capturing "the eye which moves [and] is no longer fettered by the body."[42] This removable, cyclopean eye stripped of its stereoscopy and purified of any astigmatic or myopic defects becomes an unchallenged and coherent processor of image/matters. And these image/matters that are shot in temporal and spatial correspondence to this culturally void eye's positionality in space analogically become a correspondence between organic temporality and the supposed real time of narrative film. Subsequently, the eye's position and temporal correspondences to narrative cinema establish a subjectivity of uncontested meanings emanating from the flow of image/matters produced by the filmic apparatus. The subject for Baudry comes to be defined through the symbolic construction of these meanings. This concept of meaning as subjectivity assumes real time in continuity, an analogue to narrative cinema in his view, necessitating the machinics of memory, which of course do not occur in real or continuous time.

Baudry and other apparatus critics, as well as aspects of some semiotic and psychoanalytic critical engagements, do offer openings onto a fully material encounter with the cinematic, techno-cinematic, and new media. However, memory and thought have been forced into a rigid spatio-temporality and taken out of the body and even out of matter itself in order to stabilize the production of meanings, ideology, and subjectivity. The energetic body and its dynamic positioning become an undifferentiated totality that has been replaced by a subjective analogue with one cognizing eye. In addition, memory has only come to serve the continuity of the eye as it serves to register and rewind ideas, much like a playback machine. This is strange mix for a materialist theory of film. Selected bits and processes of body, memory, time, space, and the apparatus are parsed and imbricated together in highly particularized combinations, which exclude many other affective, bodily, and tempo-spatial movements, processes, rhythms, saturations, positions, and partial incursions out of which the dynamism and agency of biomatter, presubjective bodily matters, and the nonhuman, nonorganic elements of the apparatus are taken to pieces or utterly eliminated. Indeed, there are serious critical problems raised by cutting the eye out of its body and plastering it across a passive, centered, and abstracted subject possessing no capacity for material or energetic sensation or affect.

Baudry has inverted Bergson's thought, but their mutual concern for the centering movement produced in humans is important for cinematic theory. However, Bergson's construction remains a complex, material *process* wherein the human, ideology, and meaning are image/matters and body/matters in circulation among others. That the actual physico-material encounter of the cinematic event is left unattended means to miss much of the affect (ideological and otherwise) of techno-cinematic events and new media. How is it possible for the materialist critic to stand outside of time, matter, and force in both the cinematic and critical events? The temporalities of *Lola, Memento,* and *Requiem* do not only offer a continuous narrative subjectivity but also, rather, a disjunctive and affective continuity that is resonant, rhythmic, repetitious, tonal, and sensate. And though an ideological narrative might certainly be produced, the effects of affect, sensation, and force are left behind—matter left out of a materialist reading of cinema. In addition, if we take Baudry's emphasis on the production of subjectivity by cinematic meanings, we must go back to this plethora of denaturalizations, substitutions, analogues, and metaphoric correspondences. Here, the engaging creativity of the analytic or interpretive narrative begins to capture a variety of disparate and descriptive image/matters, centering them, disembodying, and capturing them together in a controlled, contracted, and closed network. These practices can be productive, but they also exclude or cannot account for the material encounters between and imbrications of image/matters and body/matters as ecologies of materialization. Baudry suggests that the disembodied eye functions "*as if*" the body is "defective" and the subject "unable . . . to account for his own situation."[43] The necessarily hidden instrumentation of the apparatus must then *substitute* "ideological formations" for the actual matter and assemblages suspending and constituting the eye (354). I would suggest that the unaccounted analogy of formal, bodily defect and the substitutional metaphor of content offer us little or nothing about the "objective reality" (346) of the techno-cinematic event and new media and the physico-material impact of image/matters of varying speeds, saturations, densities, volumes, dynamisms, and rhythms interacting or more interfaced with organic body/matters. Baudry himself exclaims, "To seize movement is to become movement, to follow a trajectory is to become a trajectory, to choose a direction is to have the possibility of choosing one, to determine a meaning is to give oneself a meaning" (350), and yet this disallows bodies for the very material and affective conditions he describes. Deleuze, in *Cinema 2*, offers a more interesting and not unrelated construction of spatio-temporal subjectivity that remains physico-material, "the only subjectivity is time, non-chronological time grasped in its foundation, and it is we who are internal to time, not the other way round."[44] We, in this context, are biomaterial assemblages. Aesthetics of force, affect, speed, and control are required to engage our cultural ecology critically.

FORCE-FILLED AESTHETICS OF SENSATION,
AFFECT, CAPTURE, AND CONTROL

> Beauty, here, is not perceived in relation to good form, but
> to a temporal element, or process, movement, dynamism—a
> "haecceity" . . . . The beautiful, in this new definition, is a
> processuality, a continual movement. The determination of
> beauty becomes temporal, not reflective: an open-ended pro-
> cess, a feeling of flowing, rhythm, or "becoming." Indeed, a re-
> freshing concern with sensation, rather than desire or pleasure,
> requires us to think about sensation as a rhythmical experience.
> —Barbara Kennedy, *Deleuze and Cinema: The Aesthetics of
> Sensation*

Filmic image/matters are engaged with human matter/images such that the
milieu of the techno-cinematic event is constituted by its own affects and not
simply phenomenologically produced by the passive materiality of the isolated
observer as a historical or psychoanalytic "floating eye" or point of view, abstractly unfurling an ideological filmic montage in real time and space across
our dematerialized consciousness. The capture of attentions, intentions, intensities, and saturations demands further attention, as these are in-tensions,
forces, force fields, and tempo-material vectors that cannot be fully accounted
for in ideological, semiotic, or psychoanalytic critiques, all of which share a
dematerializing tendency to drain off the respective affects, energies, motions,
interactions, and powers. Caught in the centering actions occurring at the
affective register of the human image and processing at organismic speed,
techno-cinematic events stage openings, bifurcations, and catastrophic breaks
in order to threshold the workings of image/material capture and control.
These new mediated, technoscientific, cinematic images produce fluctuating
speeds and worlds in excess of the perceptual capacities of the optical complex
of the organism and beyond humanist or realist scales of time and space. The
simultaneity of human and nonhuman temporalities and organic and nonorganic matters makes for contemporaneous worlds that technoscientific cinematic events make visible through affection and speed.

   This exploration of the technoscientific cinematic event intends to add
to the small body of work that has begun to elaborate and construct aesthetics
of force and, certainly, an understanding of the interfaced activations of new
media. In the quotation heading this section, Barbara Kennedy also articulates
the need for a material and political aesthetics of sensation of the cinematic

event. Her emphases on the processual, affect, and materialities beyond ana-logic meanings, libidinal excitations, and the form of subjectivized organisms or organismic subjects are Deleuzian modalities, suggesting that resonance, movement, and rhythms are tempo-material modulations. What of the tin-gling socius we become as a cinematic body, the vibrancy and vibrations, the creeps and revulsions, and the micromaterial and corporeal experience of the cinematic as a biotechnological process? I have argued that the techno-cinematic event can be thought and sensed through an affective game of several bodies: movement and sound image/matters of the cinema and the moving matter/images of the perceiver.[45] The striking forces of the techno-cinematic, as well as the new mediated, videographic, televisual, and "techno-textual,"[46] should be pursued in terms of materializing sensations and af-fects, and with few exceptions—such as the affect of horror or pornography, studies on carpal tunnel syndrome, and the forces of evil that Marilyn Manson or Osama bin Laden apparently deploy through videos—affect has received sparse attention despite the cultural deluge of affective production. The meet-ings of force-filled sensations becoming affect undergo additional forces of critical capture, organization, striation, and control, and thus affective criti-cism faces the complexity of reflexive recursion as well.

The capture of attentions, intentions, and intensities, the thresholding of temporal scales and speeds, and the control of the scales and speeds of matter are precisely those virtual attractors around which the material of a haecceity, composition, assemblage, organization, structure, or institution tends and becomes. In this manner, *Lola* sets into motion a force function, an attraction, whereby the tendencies of the techno-cinematic event are strongly drawn to reboot. The game is restarted three times, always with a difference tending toward an optimization. Conscious of the processes of capturing attention and intensity, *Lola* is programmed to "grab the viewers and drag them along" to the play and pull of repetition with a difference, set by the modulation constitutive of "the sheer unadorned pleasure of speed." *Memento* externalizes memory onto an activated set of surfaces in the environment. And *Requiem* hacks into bodies with nonorganic information, speeds, and forces, suggestive of the morbidity produced in our new mediated, technoscientific moment.

The present is not at all a natural given of the image.

—Gilles Deleuze and Gregory Flaxman, "The Brain Is the Screen: An Interview with Gilles Deleuze"

In each of these techno-cinematic events, multiple tempo-materialities play in multiple spatio-materialities. Aronofsky pursues a line of slipping bodily detection, bodies that escape the threshold of human sensibility and legibility. Nolan, in *Memento*, traces a similar line of departure in terms of human memory. The traces of memory on Leonard's body reset the world with each erased episode. Likewise, Tykwer allows his film to chase the clinamen, the moment of divergence and bifurcation, such that the ends of these lines of flight are irreconcilable as possible futures, such that "each sheet of the past is a continuum . . . of variable speed."[47] *Requiem*'s organic hyperbodies pulse too fast for their organizational striations. In the confluence of all three of these techno-cinematic events, *Lola rennt*, *Memento*, and *Requiem for a Dream*, pulsing, spinning resonators, Harry, Sarah, Marion, Tyrone, Leonard, Lola, and *we* become sped up and transversed by sensation and immanent trans-human affections. And the physics of nonlinear dynamism and grasping from within time seem provocative motions in the aesthetics of force, techno-cinematics, and the emergent critical engagement with technoscience and new media.

NOTES

1. Eve Kosofsky Sedgwick, *Touching Feeling: Affect, Pedagogy, Performativity* (Durham, NC: Duke University Press, 2003), 21. She elaborates Clifford Geertz's term of a thick description to an affectively tuned close reading. By contrast, what follows is a wide-tracking affective description of the opening sequence of *Lola rennt*. Clifford Geertz, *The Interpretation of Culture* (New York: Basic Books, 1973), 14.

2. This sentence is presented as the second epigraph to the film *Lola rennt* (1999), distributed as *Run, Lola, Run* in English-speaking countries. I will comment on its source in what follows. For my purposes, the game is synonymous to a controlled experiment, be it a video game or gene splicing.

3. Indeed, we discover that the answers are not all the same even if the procedures applied to answer the questions are.

4. Proximate extension and duration of space-time are controlled. "Everything else" is an experiment in probabilities.

5. The butterfly effect is a popularized example of complexity theory. A butterfly flapping its wings on one side of the planet initiates a minute disturbance in the

immediate environment that ripples across the atmosphere. Ultimately, the climactic turbulence probabilistically accumulates into a huge weather phenomenon on the other side of the planet.

6. Tom Whalen, "*Run Lola Run*," *Film Quarterly* 53.3 (2000): 33.

7. Herberger's tactic of pregame mapping was an attempt at the scientific rationalization of the game of soccer. Thanks to Peter Hitchcock for this insight.

8. David Kazanjian and David Eng, eds., *Loss: The Politics of Mourning* (Berkeley: University of California Press, 2003).

9. *Lola rennt*, DVD insert.

10. Siegfried Kracauer, *Theory of Film: The Redemption of Physical Reality* (New York: Oxford University Press, 1960), 42.

11. Patricia Ticineto Clough, "Affect and Control: Rethinking the Body 'Beyond Sex and Gender,'" *Feminist Theory* 4.3 (2003): 381–86. This brief essay, as well as Manuel DeLanda's "Nonorganic Life," in *Incorporations*, ed. Jonathan Crary and Sanford Kwinter (New York: Zone, 1992), 128–67, are present in my thinking here, and I read these texts more fully in Jamie Skye Bianco, "Virtual Theories: Virtualities, Actualities, Affection, and Bodies of Information," unpublished manuscript, 2005.

12. Gilles Deleuze, "Postscript on the Societies of Control," *October* 59 (1991): 3–7; Michel Foucault, *Discipline and Punish: The Birth of the Prison*, trans. Alan Sheridan (New York: Vintage, 1977); and Antonio Negri, "Value and Affect," *boundary 2* 26 (1999): 77–88.

13. Manuel DeLanda, *Intensive Science and Virtual Philosophy* (New York: Continuum, 2002). DeLanda furthers the work from his *A Thousand Years of Non-linear History* (New York: Swerve, 2000) in a critique of chronological, causal, and evolutionary fictions, operating on trajectories akin to thermodynamic systems wherein, "optimal design or optimal distribution of energy represented an *end* of history" (13–14; italics added). In *Lola*'s epigraphs, and as demonstrated in Patricia Clough's *The End(s) of Ethnography: From Realism to Social Criticism*, 2d ed. (New York: Peter Lang, 1998) ends suggest both aims and closure. While the flattening of temporalities and materialities into linear ends and systemic closure produce the narrative fictions of History, world-producing technoscience fictions produce open, self-organizing systems. As such, these emergent entities cannot be expressed simply as an effect of a linear history, but rather as the movements of an intensive and unfolding material world. Given technoscientific involutions or "folds" of space-time and matter, relations of power and matter cannot be determined by a linear past or by an evolutionary history either. On the technoscientific plane, causal evolution, history, and "the" past can only exist as energetic capture. And as Gilles Deleuze, Manuel DeLanda, and Patricia Clough insist, the making of history and the capture of power occur as thresholds designed to control the flow of bodies, matter, and space-time itself. See Gilles Deleuze, "Postscript on the Societies of Control," *October* 59 (1991): 3–7. They reach through many possible futures-as-now, in other words, from and through the virtual. When the past is *narrated* as history, it is a forceful movement of matter and energy *made* to swerve the *present* toward a specific future designed within parameters of capture and control. They argue that technoscientific practice shares the practice of critical experimentation with virtuality, dynamic space-time, and affective relations of force and energy. I elaborate this issue in greater detail in Bianco, "Virtual Theories."

A note on open systems: An open system is an ecology or material circuit open to receive energy and matter/information. This is usually contrasted by a closed system, which is only open to energy. Open systems are also referred to as far-from-equilibrium systems, while closed systems are also called equilibrium systems. Grégoire Nicolis and Ilya Prigogine in *Exploring Complexity: An Introduction* (New York: W. H. Freeman, 1989), a controversial elaboration of nonlinear dynamics in far-from-equilibrium systems, suggest that at a "critical threshold" (59), dynamic systems successively reach Borgesian "forking paths" (see Jorge Luis Borges, *Labyrinths: Selected Stories and Other Writings*, ed. Donald A. Yates and James E. Irby [New York: New Directions, 1962], 19), so that tempo-material "bifurcation" occurs (*Exploring Complexity* 72). As Nicolis and Prigogine point out, "We can easily understand why this phenomenon should be associated with catastrophic changes and conflicts" (ibid). Therefore, all open, self-organizing systems, including open techno-cinematic events and technoscientific fictions, are open systems of bifurcating emergence. As such, they are experimental universes unfolding nonlinear, multidimensional, and durational, complex, chaotic, if not catastrophic, realities that register affectively. For an excellent critique of the work of Nicolis and Prigogine, see N. Katherine Hayles, "From Epilogue to Prologue: Chaos and the Arrow of Time," in *Chaos Bound: Orderly Disorder in Contemporary Literature and Science* (Ithaca, NY: Cornell University Press, 1999), 91–114. I am struck by the resonance of her chapter title and *Lola*'s second epigraph, "The end of the game is before the game."

14. The Oxford English Dictionary (OED) defines technoscience as "technology and science viewed as mutually interacting disciplines, or as two components of a single discipline; reliance on science for solving technical problems; the application of technological knowledge to solve scientific problems." Not surprisingly, the first use of this term could be found in 1960 in the *American Political Science Review* in an essay entitled "American Government and Politics" describing emergent military policy. Paul Virilio's definition of technoscience in *The Information Bomb*, trans. Chris Turner (New York: Verso, 2000), is worth noting: "Technoscience—the product of the fatal confusion between the operational instrument and exploratory research" (1). My larger project questions the possibility of separating know-how from knowing in the production of the operation, instrument, and research that make up Virilio's notion.

15. Ronald Bogue, "Gilles Deleuze: The Aesthetics of Force," in *Deleuze: A Critical Reader*, ed. Paul Patton (Oxford: Blackwell, 1996), 257–69.

16. Gilles Deleuze and Félix Guattari, *A Thousand Plateaus: Capitalism and Schizophrenia*, trans. Brian Massumi (Minneapolis: University of Minnesota Press, 1987), 141.

17. Elizabeth Grosz, *Volatile Bodies: Toward a Corporeal Feminism* (Bloomington: Indiana University Press, 1994).

18. On jumping scales, see Neil Smith, "Contours of a Spatialized Politics: Homeless Vehicles and the Production of Geographical Scale," *Social Text* 33 (1992): 54–81; and Patricia Ticineto Clough and Joseph Schneider, "Donna Haraway," in *Profiles in Contemporary Social Theory*, ed. Anthony Elliott and Brian S. Turner (London: Sage, 2001), 340.

19. Catastrophe opens up relative stability to the emergent, whereas control thresholds or captures the emergent to achieve a modular stability.

20. Bianco, "Virtual Theories."

21. Henri Bergson, *Matter and Memory*, trans. N. M. Paul and W. S. Palmer (New York: Zone, 1991), 21.

22. Walter Benjamin, "Theses on the Philosophy of History," in *Illuminations: Essays and Reflections*, trans. Harry Zohn, ed. Hannah Arendt (New York: Schocken, 1969), 257–58. In his famous parable of the angel of history facing away from the oncoming future is a critical image of thought pulled from the past while the body is exposed to the future, an implicit inference that we might consider allowing thought to be pulled to the future. Thanks to Peter Hitchcock for the mementos.

23. Bergson, *Matter and Memory*, 21.

24. Ibid., 20.

25. Gilles Deleuze, *Proust and Signs*, trans. Richard Howard (Minneapolis: University of Minnesota Press, 2000), 57.

26. Again picking up on Henri Bergson in *Matter and Memory*, the disjunction can be read in the fact that matter and images are described dynamically except in the context of the centering matter/image of the mind. As Bergson writes, "The objects which surround my body reflect its possible action upon them" (21), and here, Bergson suggests that the matter/images described as objects do not have the same circuitous power of centering and extraction that the matter/image of the human does. In part this may be due to Bergson's lack of interest in futurity.

27. Deleuze, *Proust and Signs*, 91; emphasis added.

28. Patricia Ticineto Clough, *Autoaffection: Unconscious Thought in the Age of Teletechnology* (Minneapolis: University of Minnesota Press, 2000), 2.

29. This is a term from Deleuze, imported from John Duns Scotus. *Haecceity* indicates the "thisness" rather than "is-ness" of a material conglomeration, designating a dynamic process of what becomes an entity versus the demarcation of being.

30. Deleuze and Guattari, *A Thousand Plateaus*, 150.

31. De Landa, "Non-Organic Life," 133. For example, the half-life of uranium is 240,000 years.

32. Kracauer, *Theory of Film*, 52–59.

33. Peter Hitchcock, *Oscillate Wildly: Space, Body, and Spirit of Millennial Materialism* (Minneapolis: University of Minneapolis, 1999), 2.

34. Kracauer, *Theory of Film*, 34.

35. Deleuze, *Proust and Signs*, 86.

36. Jamie "Skye" Bianco, "Fertility and the Quantum Matrix: Hacking Bodies; or, Death Is a Fashion Accessory in Chuck Palahniuk's *Survivor* and Richard Calder's *Dead Girls*," unpublished manuscript, 2005.

37. Paul Virilio, *The Vision Machine*, trans. Julie Rose (Bloomington: Indiana University Press, 1994).

38. Benjamin, *Illuminations*, 242. His beautiful essay offers that "the destructiveness of war furnishes proof that society has not been mature enough to incorporate technology as its organ, that technology has not been sufficiently developed to cope with the elemental forces of society" (242). Two interesting analogues—human maturity next to mechanico-technological development, and cyborgian incorporation of the machine offset by the elemental forces of the social—articulate the very transversal of tempo-materiality and control that is the technoscientific.

39. Jean Baudrillard, *Simulacra and Simulation*, trans. Sheila Faria Glaser (Ann Arbor: University of Michigan Press, 1994). See the copy machine precariously and unsuccessfully reinscribe the authentic while dismantling Platonic idealism.

40. John Johnston, "Machinic Vision," *Critical Inquiry* 26.1 (1999): 27–48.

41. Larry McCaffery, introduction to *Storming the Reality Studio: A Casebook of Cyberpunk and Postmodern Fiction*, ed. McCaffery (Durham, NC: Duke University Press, 1991). This reference is taken from McCaffery's guiding metaphor, one that opens similar connections to cyberpunk's conception of technoscientific world-making capacities. For an extended critique, see Bianco, "Fertility and the Quantum Matrix."

42. Jean-Louis Baudry, "The Ideological Effects of the Cinematographic Apparatus," in *Film Criticism and Theory: Introductory Readings*, ed. Leo Braudy and Marshall Cohen, 5th ed. (New York: Oxford University Press, 1999), 350.

43. Ibid., 354.

44. Gilles Deleuze, *Cinema 2: The Time-Image*, trans. Hugh Tomlinson and Robert Galeta (Minneapolis: University of Minnesota Press, 1989), 82.

45. Deleuze writes in *Proust and Signs*, "Neither things nor minds exist, there are only bodies: astral bodies, vegetal bodies" (92).

46. N. Katherine Hayles, *Writing Machines* (Cambridge, MA: MIT Press, 2002), 25.

47. Deleuze, *Cinema 2*, 119.

SLOWNESS: NOTES TOWARD AN ECONOMY

OF DIFFÉRANCIAL RATES OF BEING

KAREN WENDY GILBERT

The Industrial Revolution and the age of thermodynamic machines created its concomitant body. This body, the thermodynamic body, replaced the earlier body of the age of water, wind, and muscle power, which had been enshrined nostalgically in an almost edenic natural history. This seventeenth-century body governed by humors and tempers gave way, by the nineteenth century, to the thermodynamic body composed of standing reserves and regulated by pumps and siphons, tariffs and degradations. By the twentieth century, the discourse on the body had already imported all the metaphors of contemporary warfare. Thus we have the "friendly fire" of *méconnaissance* in the autoimmune system's attacks on its own body, and the skillful camouflage and penetration of our model of cancer. Even the language of computer technology has permeated our discourse on genetics. Replacing the homunculus of earlier times, a highly automated black box "reads" the genetic "code" as if it were a printout.

Our earliest computers, room-sized UNIVAC and ENIACs, evolved into small, slippery, cyborgian devices that are nothing in themselves but constitute portals into an electronic/photonic slipstream of information. What is the material formation of this in-formation? What body does it call forth in a far-from-equilibrium economy of turbulence and homeorrhesis? With what discourse can we discuss it? The work of Michel Serres and that of Gilles Deleuze writing with Félix Guattari offer theories with which I explore what constitutes a body and its component parts. I also draw on Mae-Wan Ho's work on whole system bioenergetics, Gerald Pollack's work on the phase-state shifting of cells, and Lynn Margulis and Dorian Sagan's work of symbiogenesis.[1] These works constitute a discourse in which it is presumed that matter and time are two aspects of the same thing, what might be usefully designated as "dynamic matter." But here, *time* does not connote the unit of measurement by which we determine the interval between two events, that is, clock time. Instead, *time* means that quality immanent in consciousness that Henri Bergson referred to as *durée*, or duration. The universe is composed of duration made manifest, that is, dynamic matter. All matter exists at a unique frequency, at a rate of being. The question of speed, then, is a question of rate; that is, the rate of being. Actor-network theory provides a suitable methodology to explore the matter of bodies—including the human body—in terms of rates of being; and the concept of the gift economy provides a way to differ with the thought of exchange elaborated in relationship to capitalism.

THE SHIFT FROM A THERMODYNAMIC TO A TURBULENT BODY

Luciana Parisi and Tiziana Terranova locate "the shift from a thermodynamic to a turbulent body" in a space of "postindustrial capital . . . held together by the circulation of decoded flows (flows of money, flows of culture, flows of people)."[2] Thus they remind us that it "is important not to confuse a body with the organism." The body-as-organism was established as part of a certain "biopolitical apparatus of meaning and order," where "the organization of the organs responded to a centralized movement towards balance and equilibrium" —a disciplinary formation of the body.

Rediscovering the distinction between bodies and organisms requires rethinking the distinction between equilibrium and fluency (i.e., flowing), a distinction informed by the history of thermodynamics and the later development of cybernetics, where, as Parisi and Terranova argue, entropy is separated "from its . . . relation with heat engines and thermodynamic systems" to the point where, as Lynn Margulis and Dorion Sagan phrased it in *What Is Sex?*, "non-equilibrium thermodynamics studies entities, including living beings, which increase their complexity and gain a capacity for work."[3] This move to the "fluid and turbulent order" of nonequilibrium thermodynamics is a move to a system of bricolage where, as Serres puts it, "nothing gets lost or wasted, but everything becomes useful." This move is possible as soon as we go submolar or molecular, leaving the organism for the affective body. "This molecular order . . . operates beyond the thermodynamic logic of the industrial apparatus," such that the "uncertainty of flows . . . no longer drive the self-reproduction cycle to finitude, but open up possibilities of infinite production." Parisi and Terranova go on to describe this bodily matter in terms of "a relation of forces *between* bodies, and a dynamic capacity of affecting and being affected," and, in Deleuzean and Guattarian terms, where "on the plane of consistency, *a body is defined only by a longitude and a latitude. . . .* Nothing but affects and local movements, differential speeds."[4]

If we give up the metaphor of the body as a thermodynamic machine in favor of a body that seems more like an aggregate of microscopic marine creatures subject to the lunar tides, we are in need of methodologies with which to approach the economies of these bodies. These economies are those of information and of emergent complexity. We might ask: How does the turbulent body operate?

THE SYMBIOTIC UNION OF FASTER AND SLOWER CODWELLERS

The nineteenth-century model of work and time was based on two laws of thermodynamics: Energy can neither be gained nor lost—only transformed from more to less useful forms (*useful* in this case meaning for productive work); things at rest (or in motion) tend to stay at rest (or in motion) unless acted on by an outside force, so that additional energy (or force) is needed to effect a change of state. Each accomplishment required overcoming inertia, and it was this additional effort—the effort of starting and stopping—that tipped the balance. Each endeavor used more energy than it produced in the transformed form. Eventually, all the residue of work, all the leftover inertia, gummed up the works, and the engine (of a car, or of life) ground to a halt. It was this gumming of the works with inertial residue that prevented the creation of a perpetual motion machine or immortality. This model was applied to both factory and organism. In a thermodynamic model of life, life is no different from work. Work, or the use of calories (heat), is that which organisms do to survive. Hunting for food, digesting food, circulating blood, circulating oxygen, preparing and making use of germ cells to procreate all require the expenditure of energy. In a closed system such as an engine or a body, each application of work exacts a price of wear and tear on the parts. Even if there was an infinite supply of energy (steam, food), eventually things fall apart.

This model of the body engine was expanded on and eventually upset by the development of cybernetics and the concept of the Turing box. The development of cybernetics depended on two different ways of looking at thermodynamic systems. First, the translation of the notion of "noise" from the random residue of inertia gumming up the works into a useful source of information. And second, the notion of information as something equivalent to a form of energy. The very inertia that eventually ground the system to a halt could be translated into a new source of energy. Alan Turing's notion of a conscious machine (or of a human as an organic conscious machine) involved the ability to recognize and extract information when it appeared within a stream of noise.

There are two models of recognizing and extracting information—for organizing information to be available to create and/or maintain systems. The top-down model requires replication and recreation. One must have the instructions for assembly (of a molecule, an amino acid, an organ, etc.), and then one must actually assemble it from appropriate materials. Much of the current work on how DNA tells RNA to tell mitochondria to produce amino acids and make proteins follows this model. On the other hand, the bottom-up model has proven more useful for understanding the work of complex systems of many variables that are robust with regard to adaptability (i.e., living systems and systems with intelligence). It consists of simple directives to respond to base conditions. This model relies on qualities of emergent complexity that exist in synergistic systems. A molecule is "smarter" (i.e., better organized) than an atom; atom-plus-organization (i.e., information, or energy equivalent) equals molecule. Amino acids supersede molecules, proteins amino acids, and so on up the food chain until Turing's black box (consciousness, followed by self-consciousness) appears.

The latter model is one of entities that move and link, and as they do so, create, or exhibit, difference. They differ from each other in both configuration and rates of moving—that is, different rates of being. And they defer, postponing results until critical masses are achieved. They can do this because they can store energy and/or information, and also because complexity emerges synergistically. What then, are the mechanisms of these linkages, this storage, and this synergy? This model takes us beyond nineteenth-century thermodynamics and raises the question of thermodynamics in terms of an organized complexity.

THERMODYNAMICS OF ORGANIZED COMPLEXITY

Commenting on Deleuze and Guattari's concept of the "body without organs," Keith Ansell Pearson argues that in the production of the disciplined body-as-organism, "the 'organism' is always extracted from the flows, intensities, and pre-vital singularities of pre-stratified, non-organic life."[5] The organism is given a certain state-sanctioned organization. What is contained in this organization are temporal differences, the varying rates of being. As Deleuze puts it, "beneath species and parts, we find only these times, these rates of growth, these paces of development, these decelerations or accelerations, and these durations of gestation. It is not wrong to say that time alone provides the response to a question, and space alone provides the solution to a problem."[6]

In her understanding of the organized complexity of living systems, Mae-

Wan Ho echoes Deleuze. She argues that unlike closed systems, which tend toward thermodynamic equilibrium, living systems are better understood as making use of a multiphasic metabolism that stores energy (in chemical or electrical form) in many parts of the cell and distributes it throughout the entire (neuronal or circulatory) system.[7] Thus "energy flow organizes the system which in turn organizes the energy flow."[8] The more coherent ([literally, patterned in synchrony, i.e., same-timeness) a dynamic subsystem is, the higher an amount of energy (i.e., heat) it can operate at without melting down the surrounding metabolic environment. Like a giant time-release energy capsule, the organized subsystems of the living being store, and use, heat at differential rates. It is as if the very hot bits (i.e., energy intensive) were of a substance that dissolved more slowly, that is, were in a slower time. This allows the more intense energy not to be expended before all the components of the system are in place and receptive. Of course, we only have metaphors for a temporal system that yet lacks description in much of contemporary science writing.

Ho uses the term *system* for processes better described by the term *network*. *System* usually means a linkage of differing members and channels (passages), such as cars on highways, or blood in veins; whereas *network*, as used in actor-network theory, implies a virtual relation of the coconstitution between the actor and the linkages. The network only exists when the actor is in transit through it; the actor only exists as a point particle of the network. *Point particle* is a term from quantum electrodynamics (QED) field theory, where subatomic particles such as the electron or photon only exist as temporary actualizations of permanent virtual fields of electromagnetic energy. Point particles are subject to Werner Heisenberg's Law of Indeterminacy.[9] The car or the blood cell can be separated from the highway or the vein (although it may cease to function, it will not cease to exist as an ontic being), whereas the actor does not exist outside of the network, and the presence of a network always implies an actor, or, in this case, "stored energy is explicitly dependent on the *space-time structure of the system*."[10] The capacity of the system to store, and then to access stored energy, is intrinsic to the *structure* of the system rather than an attribute of that which is stored (matter or energy). Neither is it an attribute of the physical/chemical composition of the storage structure (nerves, veins, capillaries, etc.).[11]

The significance of this ontology of becoming lies in the distinction that Ho makes between free energy and stored energy.[12] Thermodynamic theory is based on a model of free energy. It is the ratio of free to already used (and thus degraded and more highly entropic) energy in a system that matters. The capacity to store energy in fossil fuel–powered mechanical devices, for example, was so minimal as to be energetically insignificant. But living organisms constitute a different mode of matter because energy storage happens across all scales of the body, from the single molecule to entire systems (muscular/skeletal, etc.): "Indeed, stored energy has meaning with respect to single molecules in processes involving quantum molecular machines as much as it has with respect to the whole organism."[13] Ho suggests that what we need to understand about living systems is a *"thermodynamics of organized complexity."* Free energy was never free, but was paid for in entropy. Expressed thus, it formed part of the nineteenth-century thermodynamic metaphor of capitalism.

Ho is building a case for moving beyond issues of entropy to issues of coherence, a special kind of coherence that, as we will see, is characteristic of macroscopic quantum systems and concerns not function and structure but rates of being. The absolute energy in a system, therefore, is less important, in Ho's belief, than in what way(s) the energy is available, that is, stored. The organism's economy, therefore, depends on issues of liquidity. In order to address these economic issues, Ho first conceptualizes energy in living systems as "stored not only as electronic bond energies, but also in the structure of the system: in gradients, fields and flow patterns, compartments and organelles, cells and tissues. All this in turn enables organisms to mobilize their energies *coherently* and hence make available the entire spectrum of stored energies."[14]

The differing physical shapes and states of cells and molecules, whether they are twinned, folded, compressed, or shaped otherwise, and the transition from one to the other become important, allowing for a more complex definition of energy. Rather than being based on movement through space (as the mechanical assembly line moved goods), it is based on movement within time (as mighty oaks from acorns grow). One can study the economy of this temporal organization; however, the marketplace model of exchange, left over from nineteenth-century capitalism, does not afford the appropriate methodology.

THE GIFT AS QUASI OBJECT

While the exchangist economy has been presumed to seek equilibrium (homeostasis), the gift economy seeks something else: a stability in motion, or the homeorrhesis of an open system.[15] It is not the nature of the thing/service-in-itself that distinguishes a gift from a commodity, but its ontology.[16] A gift can best be conceived as a quasi object, or actor network, something that has a virtual value that actualizes as the gift object/service materializes in the gift circuit.

In theorizing the quasi object, Serres likens it to the *furet*,[17] or ferret, the object used for games such as hot potato. Neither the ferret-in-itself nor the player-in-him(her)self nor the circuit (circle of players) is of any significance; they are all only the background or field on which the play transpires. Serres writes of the ferret, "This quasi-object is not an object, but it is one nevertheless, since it is not a subject" (225). Furthermore, "it is also a quasi-subject, since it marks or designates a subject who, without, wouldn't be a subject" (225).

The ferret confers identity not by any quality of its own materiality, but by its possession or location: "This quasi-object, when being passed, makes the collective, if it stops, it makes the individual. . . . The moving furet weaves the 'we,' the collective; if it stops, it marks the 'I'" (225). However, the possession is always only temporary, for the ferret's ontology is a thing-in-motion: "The ball circulates just like the furet. . . . The ball is the subject of circulation; the players are only the stations and relays" (226). If it ceases to circulate, the play ceases and the players become nothing—they, too, cease to exist.

It is not the object itself that confers ontic status to the holder, but the speed of its motion within the circuit; too fast or too slow and the subject is not called into being: "The speed of passing accelerates him and causes [he who holds the quasi-object] to exist" (228). But, in the *beingness* of the circuit, there is only the beingness *of the circuit*. There is always the risk of "the abandon of . . . my being in a quasi-object that is there only to be circulated" (228). As Serres points out, "It is . . . the transubstantiation of being in relation. Being is abolished for the relation" (228). The value of this mode of being is "collective ecstasy [of] the abandon of the 'I's' on the tissue of relations" (228). But, "this movement is an extremely dangerous one. Every one is on the edge of his or her inexistence" (228).

Can the circulation of the gift apply to the energy dynamic of the living organism? If in the gift economy the quasi object comes close to being the *perpetuum mobile*, what in the body could operate in this way? Furthermore, what within the body is parallel to the coconstitutive calling into being of the circuit and the quasi object?

CIRCULATION OF THE GIFT AND PHASE SHIFTING OF THE CELL

Gerald Pollack's reconceptualization of the cell allows it to be thought of as a quasi object with a gift economy of phase shifts (a physical form of virtual-to-actual transition) rather than a commodity.[18] Offering a brief history of the cell's conceptualization, Pollack suggests that when the cell is conceived as a bounded liquid regulated by valves and pumps allowing the passage of sodium (which must be excluded) and potassium (which must be retained), it functions as part of an exchangist economy. The chemicals that saturate, or must be leached from the cytoplasm, must be kept at proscribed levels in order to regulate the cell's worth (i.e., its ability to function properly). The potassium or sodium is "paid" into or out from the cell into the surrounding environment. While Pollack does not question the presence of pumps and channels, he does question their function as equilibrium governors for membrane-bounded liquid cells. Therefore he prefers the concept of phase shifting, which includes defining the cell as both a contracted entity, with certain properties, and an extended entity, with other properties. The cell does not transform once and for all, from one state to the other; rather, it alternates. Unlike a bought and sold object that is either mine or yours, the cell is both mine and yours depending on its state, which is always temporary. For Pollack, the cell is a gel: "Consider the cytoplasm as a gel instead of an . . . aqueous solution, . . . gels don't . . . disintegrate when sliced . . . The focus . . . shifts from statics to dynamics. . . . gels are not inert. . . . polymer gels undergo structural transitions that can be as profound as the change from ice to water, which is why they are classified as phase-transitions."[19] In the cell, "the long configuration [of polymers] is stable.[20] The short state is also stable."[21] Two stable states, which nevertheless are highly sensitive to abrupt change.[22] In just such a way, "equilibrium for the gift is to be found in the tension of the reciprocal debt. . . . To make its laws explicit mathematically would require . . . a long temporal series . . . on a statistical scale, like the series . . . used to develop the theory of fractal objects.[23] Thus the fractal is both one and many, the cell is both compressed and expanded, the value of the gift inheres in both the giver and receiver.[24]

It is not the cell-as-such that is of interest in this new model of an energy economy. Both the compressed state and the expanded state are merely descriptions. It is the nature of the cell as dynamic, as that-which-shifts-states, that is significant. In particular, it is the notion of the cell as shifting space in response to its environment that offers itself as a mechanism for an economy of différancial rates of being. The boundary has moved from the edge of the cell to the time within which the cell-and-its-environment is in the compressed or expanded form. It is the dynamics of this time-space that we must explore, the time of transition.

WHAT'S PHASE SPACE GOT TO DO WITH IT?

The argument for heat-death in thermodynamics as an inevitable outcome is predicated on a closed system. The question of whether the human organism is vulnerable to dissolution via entropy is, likewise, based on whether or not it is classified as a closed or open system. Cybernetics broached this question, moving from the closed-system models of the first wave of cybernetics to a more open second-wave model.[25] However, the question still remains within a finite universe: how open can we ultimately be? The human organism may be considered open vis-à-vis its physical/corporeal or cultural/consciousness-and-language-inducing environment, but is not the organism-plus-environment system ultimately closed? On both a physical/ecological level (e.g., global warming, death of the rain forests) and a cultural level (e.g., "Hollywood will be the death of us"; "no one reads anymore") Cassandras daily warn us that our human-planet biosphere is rapidly approaching the death state of universal lukewarmness.

But the openness I am engaging has to do with time rather than space. Those familiar with the notion of time travel recall that the traveler shall go from today in her or his desk chair to tomorrow (or yesterday) in her or his desk chair—yesterday, today, or tomorrow, one remains in the desk chair.[26] But rather than time being located in a (spatialized) past or future, I am writing of time as rivers of different rates of flow. What happens (in terms of open systems) if one steps from a river moving at one mile per hour into one moving at ten miles per hour? And back again? Surely, like the energy used or released when electrons jump from inner to outer shells, there will be energy—used or gained. I am suggesting that like the clever day trader, one could come out with a net gain of energy, an energy profit that would exactly offset the rate of entropy. Here is the dream of the perpetual motion machine in a living automaton composed of a human organism, where organism is viewed as a collective assemblage of organic and nonorganic (including information in various forms) component parts.[27] Each part is a sovereign entity-unto-itself, transiently and/or permanently (or perhaps both at once in superimposition) linked—an assemblage, a bricolage. And each bit exists at its own proper rate of being (ontic rate). Each linkage between different rates of being requires a translation like a lock in a canal. Each intersection performs as a phase shift. And the surplus, the residue—oft mistaken for noise in the system—circulates as little vesicles that like white blood cells, neutralize seeds of entropy. These bits of extra are perhaps voids in and of themselves—materializing only in mutually destructive encounters with entropy particles.[28] Vesicles of aporia.

Serres contends that "states change phase, and systems change state, by transition of phases or of states."[29] But Serres does not posit an idealized steady state of equilibrium; equilibrium is "ideal, abstract, and never reached" (72). In reality, each entity "falls, it does not fall; it rights itself, it falls. It wears away; it is abraded; it is split by that flow. An aggregation, it loses parts like a vase covered with cracks" (72). This is not the consequence of degradation, or entropy, but is the originary state of things. All things and processes are, and always have been in transformation: "As soon as the world came into being, transformation began. . . . What we take as an equilibrium is only a slowing down of metabolic processes" (72). It is materiality that is the medium of transformation: "My body is an exchanger of time. It is filled with signals, noises, messages, and parasites. And it is not at all exceptional in this vast world. It is true of animals and plants, of crystals, of cells and atoms, of groups and constructed objects" (72).

Deleuze and Guattari posit a machinic model, in which the human organism is a collective assemblage of organic and nonorganic parts. The nonorganic parts—such as patterns of coherent electromagnetic energy and information stored in topological structures, or oscillations—once acknowledged as integral aspects of life, afford a new conceptualization of what it means to be a living being: "Dismantling the organism [means] opening the body to connections that presupposes an entire assemblage, circuits, conjunctions, levels and thresholds, passages and distributions of intensity, and territories and deterritorializations."[30] This dismantling of the organism is what Deleuze and Guattari mean by the becoming of bodies without organs. What is dismantled are the strata, the hierarchic domains of atom, cell, organ, system. To effect this requires a "production of intensities beginning at a degree zero."[31] Along these lines, Ho draws a distinction between equilibrium and nonequilibrium phase transitions, both of which "involve a reduction in the number of possible microstates in the system ultimately to a single one." However, in equilibrium systems, "the type of order achieved is essentially static—being that of a perfect crystal. In the nonequilibrium system . . . the transition is always to a regime of *dynamic* order where the whole system is in coherent motion."[32] According to Pearson, this dynamic order implies "the 'powerful nonorganic life' that escapes the strata and is implicated in transversal modes of communication, which are modes that cut across the evolution of distinct phyletic lineages."[33]

Thus Serres has argued: "I thought that . . . the interference was on the fringe, the translator was between the instances, . . . But there are no instances. Or more correctly, instances, systems, banks, and so forth are analyzable in turn as exchangers, paths, translations, and so forth. The only instances or systems are black boxes. . . . When we can finally open the box, we see that it works like a space of transformation."[34] The nature of the world has always been turbulent, in declension, out-of-equilibrium, composed of linked beings who defer to and differ from each other, and, therefore, there is stuttering. But what of this turbulence? What is its relationship to change, to evolution even?

Deleuze and Guattari contrast a "molar population, such as a species" with "a different kind of population, a molecular one, which is the subject of the effects of, and changes in, coding."[35] The individual person can be treated as if a species based on the molecular population of which it is composed. In making this distinction, Deleuze and Guattari are concerned with the mechanisms of evolution, and they propose that " 'change' . . . cannot be conceived as the passage from one pre-established form to another but rather in terms of a process of decoding."[36] This is a radical position. Indeed, Norman MacLean argues the opposite; he proposes that change can only be the passage from one preestablished form to another. He distinguishes between two different processes of change characterized by where the cells are in their life cycle. Cells develop scientific structures dependant on their genetically predetermined functions; this is referred to as a cell's "fate." Once a cell begins to respond to the chemical instructions to actualize its genetic program it is both rare and difficult to modify the developing structure.[37] Only in rare cases is there a change of commitment in determined cells, known as "transdetermination." MacLean considers these changes to be proof of the regulatory machinery that exists in the system (but outside the individual cell), as the cells don't switch in unpredictable fashion (that is, randomly) but only to a different preprogrammed structure that is somehow placed *in situ*.[38] Transdetermined cells are not the same as cells that have already differentiated, that is, cells that have already begun to express their function.[39] Transdifferentiated cells can also change both their shape and their function in response to a crisis; however, they do not do so by gradually changing directly into something else, without dissolving, so to speak, into an amorphous or undifferentiated form."[40]

MacLean depicts cells as given and then sets out to describe the modification that befalls them, whereas actor-network theory posits a "plane of pure action out of which networks subsequently emerge." Drawing on action-network theory, Steven Brown and Rose Capdevila claim that "first comes chance, disorder, hazard. Then come necessity, order, organization." To the question of how networks emerge, they answer, "when the accident occurs again repeatedly, and these repetitions are grasped as a series . . . [a] single accident is simple fate, a series of accidents starts to look like a programme."[41] But it is hard not to wonder how long the hiatus between accidents is that allows for the perception of a series.[42]

According to Pearson,[43] Deleuze and Guattari's more radical position depends on their concept of the "plane of consistency" that refers to "a different mode of 'evolution,' one which has the character of a 'becoming.' Such a 'becoming' involves neither . . . forms nor . . . subjects, but rather modes of individuation that *precede the subject or the organism.*"[44] Deleuze and Guattari write that "it is in the domain of *symbiosis* that bring into play beings of totally different scales and kingdoms."[45] They call "this form of evolution between heterogeneous terms . . . 'involution,'" the "becoming-animal" who resides (and evolves) on this plane "is defined not by characteristics (specific, generic, etc.) but by populations that vary . . . ; movement occurs . . . by transversal communications between heterogeneous populations" (238).

Here, Deleuze and Guattari offer a way to rethink the organism that fits Margulis's argument that an organism *is* a community of heterogeneous life-forms coexisting symbiotically, and, as I would propose, each of these life-forms is an ontic state that exists at its own rate of being. It is the turbulence of so many different rates of being coinhabiting one body that is the original "chance, disorder, hazard." From this evolves "necessity, order, organization." Not the homeostatic equilibrium of the well-run machine, but the dynamic coherence of Deleuze and Guattari's "Abstract Machine."

SLOW OSCILLATIONS AND COORDINATED MOVEMENTS
ON THE PLANE OF CONSISTENCY

Deleuze and Guattari write of the "plane of consistency" as a "univocality," or single plane (254). This is a different timescape/landscape from the x- and y-axied Euclidian topology of Cartesian space. This plane is akin to the concept of infinity, which can be defined as the place where a part is equal to a whole. On the plane of consistency, "Nature is like an immense Abstract Machine" (254). But for Deleuze and Guattari a machine is not a mechanical device but an ontic category in which heterogeneous linkages take place across phyletic lines and time zones. The plane of consistency is a "plane of immanence" where linkages allow "various assemblages" (254). The significance of this plane is that on it, "things are distinguished from one another only by speed and slowness" (254). The plane "has nothing to do with a form or a figure" (254), it is a location of intention and desire rather than of form or function. Likewise, in an economy of ontic rate, or rates of being, what matters is the different speeds of the linked parts, rather than their form or function.

Deleuze and Guattari go on to contrast the theories of Cuvier and Saint-Hilaire (255). Whereas Cuvier grounded his taxonomy on organs and functions, Saint-Hilaire went to "particles" and "pure materials" that assumed "a given function depending on their degree of speed or slowness" (255). In Saint-

Hilaire's work, "speed and slowness, movement and rest, tardiness and rapidity subordinate not only the forms of structure but also the types of development" (255). Deleuze and Guattari posit "[a] fixed plane of life upon which everything stirs, slows down or accelerates," on which "it is no longer a question of organs and functions . . . but of . . . [rate of] speed" (255). And they warn of "rifts between assemblages," where "elements . . . do not arrive on time" (255). However, not arriving on time is only one way that elements can be out of synchrony.

The simplest daily activities—smelling, walking, playing a piano—require a coordination of elements taken for granted. Deleuze and Guattari instead would speak of smelling as a "smelling-machine" consisting of a nose-breath-flower-olfactory bulb assemblage. Although using different language, Ho describes the body much as if it were an abstract machine on a plane of consistency. In her study of the body as a whole system susceptible to the rules of quantum mechanics, she writes of the apparent paradox that while "substantial parts of the brain are . . . involved in integrating inputs from all over the body . . . over long time periods," nevertheless much of the "coherent coordination of parts of the body . . . seems instantaneous."[46] Examples of this include the local coordination of smelling, where "slow oscillations in the olfactory bulb in the brain are in phase with the movement of the lungs," or (quadrupedal) walking, where "the coordinated movement of the four limbs in locomotion is accompanied by patterns of activity in the motor centres of the brain which are in phase with those of the limbs" (268).[47] The significance Ho draws from this is the instantaneous timing of the coordination. In writing of a skilled pianist, she says, "There simply is not time enough, from one musical phrase to the next, for inputs to be sent to the brain, there to be integrated, and coordinated outputs to be sent back to the hands" (47). Drawing on contemporary physics, Ho suggests that instantaneous (nonlocal) coordination of body functions is mediated . . . implicit in this suggestion is the idea that living systems have a special kind of coherence or wholeness, which is characteristic of macroscopic quantum systems. Here, coherence is not the rigid (classic) order of solid structures, but it is the fluid order of eddies—the oscillation through each possibility of a probability phase space.

HAECCEITIES AND EVENTS

To think of a body in terms of such a coherence, that is, in terms of the complex coordination of rates of being, it is necessary to think of agency in terms of haecceities and events that are subjectless individuations. These constitute collective assemblages and evolve through speeds and powers/affects. "Haecceity is . . . the domain . . . not of a subject but rather the agent of an infinitive. . . . in which the individual opens itself up to the multiplicities pervading and invading it."[48] Such agents point to a plane of nature that is both inside the body and linked to a world larger than one person—but a world that is subindividual and composed of both organic and nonorganic components.[49] These components constitute ontic states that are actual and virtual (manifest and perceivable while simultaneously latent in the circuit) and always in motion. The haecceities concern "longitudinal relations of movement and rest between molecules/particle and latitudinal capacities of affect and affectedness" (182). This is a phase space within which the haecceity is a point particle—virtual or actual according to its rate of ontology.[50]

According to Serres, a body is located in a phase space of three dimensions, with axes of an old trivium—"weight, fluidity, and heat"—within which atoms and void, as "residual bodies that are themselves limit states," are "the condition for the existence of other things . . . . Their matter is particular, their nature is relational."[51] We are back in the "conjunctive web of . . . topology,"[52] the actor network where the *thing* is indistinguishable from the *circuit* it travels. And it should be noted that the agency of haecceities presupposes a different understanding of things such as cells, circuits, and information, such that a problem arises around the descriptive and explanatory language left over from a previous worldview. For example, when Pollack and Ho write of the coherence of the cell and the organism, respectively, they require that we conceive of these entities in a way wholly different from their classical nontropic and reductionist identities. However, the language with which we now seek to describe them has not yet changed, instead hovering in some middle state of patched-together neologisms and idiosyncratically used terms such as *assemblage, actor network, différancial,* and the like.

Paul Feyerabend wrote, "Achilles . . . 'has no language to express his [thoughts]. He does it by misusing the language he disposes of.' He acts in a most 'irrational' way."[53] In fact, the inability to use the language of one worldview to discuss the elements of another is one of the ways by which to recognize that the two worldviews are incommensurable. Within a framework certain concepts cannot even be conceived or articulated. It is not a matter of their being controversial (or oppositional, e.g., "the devil is 'good'"), but of their being nonsensical (e.g., "the devil is causing my headache"). For these statements to make sense, one requires an entirely different framework (i.e., that illness is caused by the devil is incommensurable with the germ theory of illness).[54]

Indeed, Feyerabend claimed that "nor is it possible to *translate* [the] language [of worldview] A into [the] language [of worldview] B."[55] But I am interested in the way a particular language itself has traveled like a ferret through a circuit of sociology, philosophy, cybernetics and information theory, physics and biology. When Feyerabend says that "the discovery that certain entities do exist may prompt the scientist . . . to introduce new *concepts*" (270), I hold just the reverse. I would propose that neologisms precede a shift in conceptualization, and that words which imperfectly fit their borrowed context (e.g., the term *energy flows* used in all the subjects areas of the circuit enumerated above) accumulate and shed nuances as they shift disciplines, just as bacteria effect transversal symbiosis via viral vectors. Keep in mind John Law's observation that "to translate is to also betray."[56] In the realms of the cell, the virus, and the body without organs (*sic*), realms that exist in both the quantum and the macroscale reality, a language is needed to express complementarity (like Neil Bohr's) based on a degree of indeterminacy (like Heisenberg's).

THE MECHANISMS OF COHERENCE

Ho is committed to finding a language for explaining the mechanism of the complex coherence of different rates of being that would be legitimate in both classical and quantum frameworks. Citing research on synchronous firing patterns in widely separated areas of the brain, Ho has looked for mechanisms to account for such long-range coherence.[57] She asks about the oscillatory response in spatially separated regions which establish cell assemblies that have the phase and frequency of coherent oscillations. The key seemed to be in biotic sensitivity to electromagnetic fields, even those that are extremely weak. John McFaddan has addressed this same issue.[58] Like Ho, McFaddan is concerned with explanations that account for both wave (i.e., continuous and global) and particle (i.e., discrete and vectorial) phenomena. While the brain generates its own (endogenous) electromagnetic field, the question is how this field effects and is effected by the firing of individual neurons situated far from each other. The answer seems to lie in "phase-locks."[59] This is so because "the electrical field at any point in the brain will be a superposition of the induced fields from all of the neurons in the vicinity (superimposed on the fields generated by ion movement) and will depend on their firing frequency, geometry and the dielectric properties of tissue."[60] Thus, within the phase-locked coherent network, as in an actor network, everything happens both individually and severally, both instantaneously and eternally. The time it takes is one unit of time, thus there is no effort needed to synchronize: "Within that duration, which we can regard as the coherence time in that level of the nested hierarchy of time structure, processes coherent with it will generate no time at all."[61] Once one leaves clock time for the time of ontic coherence, one moves into a holistic measurement that resists subdivision into discrete segments. This would be the time scale appropriate to a Deleuzean assemblage of the seen and grasped object, one unit of eye-brain-hand-brain-object time describing the unit of time in which one sees and grasps an object and thus knows it. This moment of being can *not* be subdivided into the time it takes to know as separate from the time it takes to see and the time it takes to grasp.

Ho correlates this coherence with Henri Bergson's concept of duration, "biological rhythms . . . manifest a hierarchy of coherence times that define the time frames of different processes. This fits with Bergson's concept of pure duration, which, in one sense, we may identify as the time taken for the completion of a process."[62] Bergson argued that in our "inner lives," as well as "the universe," we dealt with "the continuous creation of unforeseeable novelty."[63] Pearson has argued that a "key aspect of time for Bergson is that it introduces *indetermination* into the very essence of life (this indetermination does become materially embodied: a nervous system, for example, can be regarded as a 'veritable reservoir of indetermination' in that its neurons 'open up multiple paths for responding to manifold questions' posed by an environment."[64] Here "time and space are no longer treated simply as universal *a priori* forms of sensible intuition, but rather are understood as components in the production of variation and difference."[65]

THE NATURE OF THE PASSAGE

Law has written: "[Actor-network] is *intentionally oxymoronic*, a tension which lies between the centered 'actor' on the one hand and the decentered 'network' on the other."[66] The method itself is a combination of "*relational materiality* . . . and *performativity*" (4), thus it describes "the semiotic insight . . . of the relationality of entities, the notion that they are produced in relations," with the understanding that "entities achieve their form" through being "performed" (4). Here Law returns to the same question asked by Serres: "How it is that durability is achieved. . . . that things get performed (and perform themselves) into relations that are relatively stable and stay in place" (4). How does the stable vortex in the rushing stream, homeorrhesis, arise? How does the molecular transport vessel recognize the correct docking site? How does the enzyme that "wishes" to secrete itself do so?[67]

So we face the question of the passage of the local to the global: Does it consist of discrete objects flowing through discrete channels that form a network?[68] Or is it composed of fields (chemical, electrical, magnetic, ontic) that are always real but that only sometimes actualize into discernable, measurable, and entropic modes of materiality. Rather than a boat flowing through a tunnel on a river (boat = molecule, tunnel = body passage, river = liquid), imagine a grape turning into and back from a raisin being moved by peristalsis through a dessert made of layers of Jell-O, custard, sorbet, and syrup. Serres gives the answer: "Thus everything flows throughout everything. There is always a network for a flow. The vault of grottoes oozes and our entire body sweats." But, "what is true in general has particular limitations. What goes through gold cannot pass through glass." Serres's conclusion is that "everything flows through every thing, but not in any manner whatever. There are conditions for the passage from the local to the global." The mechanism of passage is *specificity*.[69]

Pollock also addresses this issue of specificity, pointing to how "the quasi-permeable membrane of the gelatinous cell must be induced to . . . open a channel . . . to let the molecule out. And not just any door will do, mind you."[70] Specificity applies: "The molecule-to-secrete is neatly tucked into the matrix of a polymer gel . . . this vesicle . . . travels to the edge of the cell . . . . The contents; under 'pressure' due to the packing in of polymer gels in their most contracted state, explodes, releasing the secretion outside the cell."[71] The beauty of the system lies in how the molecule-to-secrete packages itself: "With rare exception, the agents responsible for keeping the matrix condensed—calcium, histamine, adrenaline, mucin, seratonin, etc.—are the agents to be secreted. Cut loose from cross-linkage, these agents are freed to carry themselves to their respective targets. Cross-linkers become agents of communication."[72] The agent-to-be-secreted is the very agent that triggers the mechanism. Self-reflexive specificity. Therefore the mechanism of the passage provides a passage from the virtual to the actual.

WHERE SINGULARITIES ARE FREE TO BE
DISTRIBUTED IN PURE INTENSITY

The transition from the virtual to the actual can be conceptualized in relationship to what Deleuze describes as "the Other-structure that ensures individuation within the perceptual world." The always present other (the actor to the network, or vice versa) gives "expression to those possible worlds in which that which is for us in the background is pre-perceived or sub-perceived as a possible form."[73] But what of the reverse, the transition from the global to the local, or from the actual to the virtual? Is it possible to rediscover the "pre-individual singularities as they are in the Idea"? To look for this, one would have to look backward in time—to a when/where before differentiation. Deleuze wrote that "departing from the subjects which give effect to the Other-structure, we return as far as this structure in itself, . . . then continue further, . . . far from the objects and subjects that it conditions, where singularities are free to be deployed or distributed with pure Ideas, and individuation factors to be distributed in pure intensity" (282). We continue into the kinematics of the egg.

Deleuze and Guattari sought the "full egg before the extension of the organism and the organization of the organs" that they characterized as the body without organs (BWO). Before the "formation of the strata," or layers of hierarchical organization, the "intense egg" is "defined by dynamic tendencies involving energy transformation and kinematic movements." In the body without organs, the organs "function . . . only as pure intensities" (153). Pearson clarified that for Deleuze and Guattari, "intensity . . . is not made up of addable and subtractable magnitudes . . . . Rather an intensity is a difference."[74]

In searching for ontic modes that "precede the subject or the organism,"[75] Deleuze found an answer in the fold: "Living creatures . . . need only *fold back* on this depth as a new dimension, or *fall back* on these forces of finitude. . . . The fold is what constitutes a 'thickness' as well as a 'hollow.' "[76] Deleuze wrote: "It is as if the relations of the outside folded back to create a doubling, allow a *relation to oneself* to emerge, and constitute an inside which is hollowed out and develops its own unique dimension."[77] He argues further: "It is never the other who is a double in the doubling process, it is a self that lives me as the double of the other: I do not encounter myself on the outside, I find the other in me."[78] This is close to the definition of symbiogenesis.

What Deleuze conceptualizes as the relation between the outside and the inside resembles the relationship between the actor and the network, and between the coherent field and the flow of the circuit. Deleuze is especially concerned about the relation of inside and outside, self and other in terms of the evolution of species, "the difference between humans and chimpanzees consists not in their genetic difference . . . but in the spatial organization and foldings of their cells."[79] Deleuze thus argues against the reductionism of genetic determinism and reinstates "the trace of genetic indetermination."[80] Indeterminate means, in this case, the chaotically random distribution of outcomes, subject to catastrophic (in René Thom's sense) slippages across planes (of phase space). The environment where the gene blinks into actuality determines everything, but it cannot itself be determined.

Not only can the outcome not be predicted but the state of the network cannot either, at any given moment, be concluded from its antecedent moment because the circuit encompasses (or, more accurately, is encompassed within) both the virtual and the actual. Or, as Stuart Kauffman has put it, "many of the highly ordered features of ontogeny are not to be regarded as the achievements of selection, but rather as the self-organized behaviours of complex genetic regulatory systems. . . . the properties of self-organization are . . . deeply immanent in these complex networks."[81]

TO FILL A SPACE IS VERY DIFFERENT FROM DISTRIBUTING IT

Here, indetermination refers to mathematical phase space, the space of quantum superposition, entanglement, indetermination. *Nunc hinc, nunc illinc—* now here, now there. Flickering. Statistical. Along these lines, Deleuze distinguishes types of distribution; there is "a type of distribution which implies a dividing up of that which is distributed." This is a suitable model of distribution for objects and subjects. Objects and subjects have attributes and form categories, but quasi objects/quasi subjects have tendencies and affects. For them, "there is a completely other distribution which must be called nomadic . . . no longer a division of that which is distributed but rather a division among those who distribute themselves in an open space a space which is unlimited, or at least without precise limits. To fill a space, to be distributed within it, is very different from distributing the space."[82]

What are the differences between a time that is distributed and a time within which matter is distributed? A différancial time, a time of difference and deferral. Surely different ontic modes must exist in a time that has a limit, and in unlimited time. In the first, discrete entities exist that can be added and subtracted. One pebble and two pebbles are three pebbles, each pebble recognizable and discrete, specific. The one can be subtracted from the pile of three, leaving the two again. Counting is possible. But, in the second, there is not counting, only measurement. When one ounce of water is added to two, there is no longer one ounce, or two ounces, only three. Likewise, one ounce of water can be taken from the three, but it will never be the molecules of the original ounce added. The trick is to think of the pebbles and water as different types of time, as Bergson did. It is difficult to even conceptualize such timescapes, whereas in space we can think of cows becoming equidistributed in a meadow,[83] in clear distinction from how plots of land are deeded to farmers.

Although not about time, Deleuze's description of the difference between distributed space and distribution in space is instructive. Deleuze writes about the space of games. Games are complex linkages of subjects, objects, and rules of interaction. Games are mechanisms of becoming. Evolution is a game, metabolism is a game, the moving ferret is a game. Deleuze suggests that the games people play create that space within which things are distributed. Such spaces can be filled by a sequence of events following a pattern of rule. Chance, at best, is excluded, at worst, it will create a glitch, a small irregular patch of unpredictability that will be quickly surrounded and encased by rule-determined entities.[84] Or, as Deleuze put it, this is where we subtract the consequence (of the throw of the die) from chance. The other type of space, the space that distributes itself, distributes itself though chance. Here, representation is not possible because there are no preexisting rules,

> the game includes its own rules. . . . Nothing is exempt from the game: consequences are not subtracted from chance. . . . The different throws can . . . no longer be said to be numerically distinct: . . . [But] are distinguished . . . *formally*, the different rules being the forms of a single ontologically unique throw, the same across all occasions. The different outcomes are no longer separated according to the distribution . . . but distribute themselves in the open space of the unique and non-shared throw; nomadic rather than sedentary distribution.[85]

Are the symbiogenetic origins of life, the phase-state shifting of cells, and the coherent dynamic of bioelectromagnetic fields constructed from/of pre-existing categories in which the results are distributed across a probability matrix? Or are they not numerically distinct, but rather formal, where the different outcomes migrate nomadically, rhizomatically? It is the second possibility that I have been exploring, a possibility that precludes the privileging of equilibrium, and with it, thermodynamics, in favor of far-from-equilibrium dynamism and homeorrhesis. No longer a vector (an arrow of time) moving forward, but a complex circuit of quasi objects now here, now there.[86] This is not to deny the role and the necessity of games of preexisting rules, operating in bounded space (or time, or time-space) where ontic beings (germs, enzymes, systems) evolve from one preexisting form to the next. But as we now know from the genome, not every gene specifies a protein. Splicing and shuffling occur; the chaperones may fold and package as many combinations as occur in the roll of the die, "first comes chance, disorder, hazard. Then comes necessity, order, organization."

The thing (whatever it is, (quasi) subject/(quasi) object, *furet*, cell, scrap of code, regulator gene) comes into being—solidifies, is made real, that is, present (presents itself as a gift)—at a moment of time, and then becomes invisible. Moving at the speed of light, or stretched out in tenuous hyperspace. Or, circulating in forbidden zones (not every passage is permissible). The message contains noise, the contracted state contains the seeds of its expansion within it, the indigestible symbiont is swallowed by its host, the gift is also the injury. Chaos is the state lacking contact, a cloud where no two particles collide, or a stream where no two drops commingle; stasis is the state lacking movement—neither is habitable to life. In between something else occurs: "Fluxion is a lamina of flux, it is a lamina of the laminar. Fluctuation is a tiny jot of chaos, indeed a tiny jolt. We do not, as a rule, know how to get from one to the other, from the local to the global and back again, from the chaos to the little jolt [*cahot*] and vice-versa."[87]

A new model of the organism is emerging, one that includes chaos and *cahot*, the jot and the jolt, electromagnetic fields and wave cavities that permit resonance, quantum entanglement and dynamic topology, memory and desire. Matti Pitkanen, working to define a topological geodynamics, writes,

> Topological field quanta assign to a given material system [a] kind of field body [which] is absolutely essential for understanding the physics of living matter. . . . Any system, be it electron, DNA molecule, human, earth, galaxy possesses this kind of field body. This field body serves as a kind of manual for the material system . . . . Topological self-reference is the term that seems good to express this. For instance, a new view about DNA as expressing itself also in terms of fields rather than only chemically emerges. Field bodies make possible also molecular recognition mechanisms explaining both the assembly of tobacco mosaic virus as well as homeopathy.[88]

Just as quantum electrodynamics needed to be reformulated as field theories, biology now desperately needs a reformulation to account for being *and* becoming, memory *and* chaos, the individual *and* the species. The tobacco mosaic virus exists in bits and pieces—how do they communicate? Pitkanen writes, "I believe that communication is based on 'electromagnetic bridges,' magnetic flux tubes, massless extremals (topological counterparts of light rays in very un-literal sense), or pairs of these forming magnetic mirrors. The communication involves classical signaling and quantum communication involving quantum entanglement. The components of tobacco virus have common mental image: a dream of becoming a full tobacco virus!"[89]

COOPERATION: A QUASI CONCLUSION

Ho has summarized the problem of finding a mechanism for dynamic coherence at metabolic temperatures. She reminds us that condensed matter physics is that study of "the collective behaviour . . . when molecular disorder—entropy—disappears and the systems no longer behave statistically but in accordance with dynamical laws."[90] Although it is typically true only of cold systems, biotic entities that are "nonequilibrium systems subject to energy flow can also undergo transitions to coherent, macroscopic activity" (89). Using a quantum model of the body, one where "exited molecules vibrate at various characteristic frequencies," Ho has drawn on Herbert Frölich's research that revealed "collective modes of both electromechanical oscillations (phonons, or sound waves) and electromagnetic radiations (photons)" (91). These "collective modes," called by Frölich "coherent excitations," could be synergistically linked. "Coherent excitations make the system sensitive to specific, weak signals . . . . Whole populations of cells may be poised in critical states so that a small, specific signal would set off a whole train of macroscopic, coherent reactions" (93), and, as in any other solid-state (condensed-matter) system, move through the system as a standing wave (or, soliton): "Frequencies are coupled together so that random energy fed into any specific frequency can be communicated to other[s]" (91).

Pollack documented the same sort of cooperative transition between condensed and expanded polymer states in which, "once a critical point is reached (in triggering conditions) the transition is inevitable." He suggested that its "inevitability presupposes some kind of cooperativity—a change that increases the propensity of additional change in the same direction," and described the mechanism involved, which "arises out of competition between two or more forces," in this case the equal tendency of polymer to bond with itself, or with water.[91] The cooperativity of fields is what enables them to be so fast: they create space. The link-by-link mechanism of neuronal and chemical networks is slower: it fills space.

I suggest that the economy of différancial rates within living entities is a consequence of the two complementary systems within them. The first is a step-by-step, rule-following, unidirectional (vectorial) circuit subject to entropy that could be adequately described by nineteenth-century thermodynamic metaphors. Contemporaneously and cospatially, there exists a field of flows (specifically electromagnetic, but as easily understood as intentions and desires) that predisposes and allows for rapid and global transition in the form of phase shifting. This field is best understood in terms of quantum field theory, with its vocabulary of nonlocality, entanglement, holography, and virtuality. These two modes of being (ontic modes) exist in a relationship where self and other, same and different, are superimposed.

These ontic modes differ in being continuous (fields) and discrete (molecules, cells, organs) and in that they call into being, and then exist in, different sorts of spaces. A metaphysics of biology in the twenty-first century will have to create a discourse that accounts for this dynamism. The vocabularies and concepts of twentieth-century actor-network theory and the economy of the gift (old as dirt) will prove useful. In addition, it is essential to read those biologists and biochemists who have been working for the past half century to redefine their field in light of the new paradigms of physics. It is my sincere hope that this brief overview of some of these issues will encourage this discourse.

NOTES

1. This is a theory of evolution based on the mechanism of symbiotic complementarity, holding that different life-forms permanently fuse into novel beings.

2. Luciana Parisi and Tiziana Terranova, "Heat-Death: Emergence and Control in Genetic Engineering and Artificial Life," *CTheory*, 5, *www.ctheory.com/article/a84.html.*

3. The original reference is to Lynn Margulis and Dorion Sagan, *What Is Sex?* (New York: Simon and Shuster, 1997), 32.

4. The original reference is to Gilles Deleuze and Félix Guattari, *A Thousand Plateaus: Capitalism and Schizophrenia*, trans. Brian Massumi (Minneapolis: University of Minnesota Press, 1987), 260.

5. Keith Ansell Pearson, *Viroid Life: Perspectives on Nietzsche and the Transhuman Condition* (New York: Routledge, 1997), 130

6. Gilles Deleuze, *Difference and Repetition*, trans. Paul Patton (New York: Columbia University Press, 1994), 217.

7. "Meticulous space-time organization in which energy is stored in a range of time scales and spatial extents." Mae-Wan Ho, *The Rainbow and the Worm: The Physics of Organisms* (Singapore: World Scientific, 1993), 70.

8. Ibid.

9. To the degree of accuracy that one knows *either* the location *or* the momentum of a particle the knowledge of the other aspect remains indeterminate. The significance of this is that it is not a measurement problem; indeterminacy is ontological rather than epistemological. The lack of determination lies in the particle's state of being, not in the scientist's measuring device.

10. Ho, *The Rainbow and the Worm*, 70.

11. See discussion of autopoietic structure and organization and the memorable example of a toilet in Humberto R. Maturana and Francisco G. Varela, *The Tree of Knowledge: The Biological Roots of Human Understanding* (Boston: Shambala, 1968), 47. They would consider space-time an organization rather than a structure. Terminology aside, they refer to "a type of phenomenon in which the possibility of distinguishing one thing from a whole depends on the integrity of the processes that make it possible" (46).

12. C. W. F. McClare, "Chemical Machines, Maxwell's Demon, and Living Organisms," *Journal of Theoretical Biology* 30 (1971): 1–34, qtd. in Ho, *The Rainbow and the Worm*, 70.

13. For example, energy storage as bond vibrations or as strain energy in protein molecules occurs within a spatial extent of 10^{-9} to 10^{-8} meters and a characteristic timescale of 10^{-9} to 10^{-8} seconds, whereas in terms of a whole organism such as a human being, the overall energy storage domain is in meter-decades. Ho, *The Rainbow and the Worm*, 70.

14. Ibid.

15. To "exchange" means to circulate, to swap, to trade, to give in order to receive. Constantin Boundas, "Exchange, Gift, Theft" *Angelaki* 6.2 (2001): 101. "Something is a gift when [it] cannot be 'paid back' by means of reciprocation . . . [where there exists an] inability to reach a 'zero sum'" (ibid., 102). It is an open system. It should thus be regulated by a thermodynamic of open systems that provides a complex theory for this state of imbalance. The word *homeorrhesis* is formed from the Greek words *homos*, meaning "same," and *rhysis*, meaning "flow." Serres replaces the normal term describing equilibrium of a self-regulating system, *homeostasis*, by *homeorrhesis* in order to express the idea of continual movement and exchange as opposed to the less dynamic idea of stasis. Michel Serres, *The Parasite*, trans. Lawrence Schehr (Baltimore, MD: Johns Hopkins University Press, 1982), 74.

16. Thanks to the efforts of Jean-Luc Marion, we have grown accustomed to the idea of working through the aporias of the gift by returning to the rich resources of a radical phenomenological reduction: after bracketing *donner*, *donnée*, and even the object of donation, one is left with the pure act of donation as the only phenomenal ideality for the investigation of the *eidos* of the gift—*there is giving*." Boundas, "Exchange, Gift, Theft," 109.

17. The *furet* is the animal, the ferret, as well as the marker in a game similar to hunt-the-slipper or button, button, who's got the button? Serres, *The Parasite*, 225.

18. See Donna J. Haraway, *Modest_Witness@second_Millennium. FemaleMan_ Meets_OncoMouse_* (New York: Routledge, 1997), on the cell as commodity.

19. Gerald H. Pollack, *Cells, Gels, and the Engines of Life: A New, Unifying Approach to Cell Function* (Seattle: Ebner and Sons, 2001), xi.

20. "The . . . hydrophilic surface . . . extends itself to maximize the number of water contacts, thereby minimizing the system's energy." Ibid., 117.

21. "The polymer is folded, with surface charges . . . contacting one another instead of water." Ibid.

22. That is, catastrophic, in the sense of René Thom's mathematical theory of catastrophic change. René Thom, *Structural Stability and Morphogenesis* (Reading, Mass.: W. A. Benjamin, 1975).

23. "Which is why it is interesting to work with the metaphor of the fractal. . . . A

fractal is a line which occupies more than one dimension but less than two. . . . Which is difficult to think because it defies the simplicities of the single—but also the corresponding simplicities of pluralism of laissez faire, of a single universe inhabited by separate objects. . . . It is difficult because what we study cannot be arrayed in a topologically homogenous manner either as a single object or as a plurality with a single space." Jacques T. Godbout, with Alain Caillé, *The World of the Gift*, trans. Donald Winkler (Montreal: McGill-Queen's University Press, 1998), 214, in John Law, "After ANT," in *Actor Network Theory and After*, ed. Law and John Hassard (Malden, MA: Blackwell, 1999) 12.

24. The transition between the cell's compressed and expanded states—triggered by the electromagnetic properties of structured water—allows the cell to store chemicals until they reach a critical amount, and to release the entire amount at once. Pollock's model thus describes one physical mechanism necessary for Ho's theory of stored energy. I am suggesting that this is similar to the way the gift stores value, which adheres to the gift until it is bestowed, at which moment it is then disbursed to adhere to the giver and the given-to.

25. See N. Katherine Hayles, *How We Became Posthuman: Virtual Bodies in Cybernetics, Literature, and Informatics* (Chicago: University of Chicago Press, 1999); and Tiziana Terranova, "Cybernetics' Surplus Value: Embodiment and Perception in Informational Capitalism," unpublished manuscript, 2001.

26. A nightmarish corollary includes an endless series of indistinguishable, half-drunk mugs of coffee. We have all drunk yesterday's coffee, but what happens when we drink tomorrow's?

27. "All we are saying is that the identity of effects, the continuity of genera, the totality of all BWOS [bodies without organs], can be obtained on the plane of consistency only by means of an abstract machine capable of covering and even creating it, by assemblages capable of plugging into desire, of effectively taking charge of desires, of assuring their continuous connections and transversal tie-ins. Otherwise, the BWOS of the plane will remain separated by genus, marginalized, reduced to means of bordering, while on the other plane the emptied or cancerous doubles [or, in this case the bodies emptied by heat-death and made lukewarm by entropy] will triumph." Gilles Deleuze and Félix Guattari, "How Do You Make Yourself a Body without Organs?" in Deleuze and Guattari, *A Thousand Plateaus*, 158.

28. Like matter and antimatter.

29. Serres, *The Parasite*, 72.

30. Deleuze and Guattari, *A Thousand Plateaus*, 160.

31. Ibid., 507.

32. Ho, *The Rainbow and the Worm*, 89.

33. *Transversals* is a term that can be found in Lazare Carnot and Rene Thom, where transversality concerns the ways in which the smooth curves of analysis intersect or cut each other. See Keith Ansell Pearson, *Germinal Life: The Difference and Repetition of Deleuze* (New York: Routledge 1999), 235.

34. Serres, *The Parasite*, 73.

35. Pearson, *Germinal Life*, 159.

36. Ibid. If forms of life are irreducible, then how can we explain novel becomings such as creative involutions and communications that take place across phyletic lin-

eages? The answer for Deleuze and Guattari lies in the insight that it is through populations that one is formed and assumes forms. The suggestion is that one can only
understand a molar population, such as a species, in terms of a different kind of
population, a molecular one, which is the subject of the effects of, and changes in,
coding. This molecularization of a population is obviously contingent since it is dependant on the ability of a code to propagate in a given milieu or create for itself a new
milieu in which any modification is caught up in a process of population movement.
See Deleuze and Guattari, *A Thousand Plateaus*, 52. Change, therefore, cannot be conceived as the passage from one preestablished form to another, but rather in terms of a
process of decoding. To support this view, Deleuze and Guattari appeal to the modern
theory of mutations and its claim that a code enjoys a margin of decoding that provides
supplements which are capable of free variation. Moreover, and as already noted,
innovation in evolution takes place not simply through a translation between codes but
equally in terms of the phenomenon of what Deleuze and Guattari call, drawing heavily
on the work of François Jacob (*The Logic of Living Systems: A History of Heredity*, trans.
Betty E. Spillmann [London: Allen Lane, 1974]), the "surplus value of code" or "side-
communication." Pearson, *Germinal Life*, 159.

37. The determination of the function of a cell is itself a complex interaction of
the location of the cell, how it expresses its genetic instructions, and how and *when*
it's affected by chemical communications controlled by regulator genes, that is, homeo-
boxes.

38. MacLean uses an example of a fly that grows a leg where an antenna should go. In
this case and others like it, the cells fated to become a leg accidentally drifted to the site
of the future antennae in the embryonic fly due to genetic malfunction—or were
inserted there by scientists. Once in the "wrong" site, they nevertheless grew a completely normal leg. There were no random or chaotic effects such as a quasi-antenna-
quasi-leg. MacLean holds this to be an indication of a mechanism that regulates the
development of the functional structure regardless of errors in placement. Norman
MacLean, *Genes and Gene Regulation* (London: Edward Arnold, 1989).

39. Whereas determined cells are virtual in their functioning, differentiated cells are
actual. In other words, a cell may be determined to become an eyelash follicle but has
not yet begun to express eyelashes, whereas cells that grow lashes are differentiated.

40. To illustrate transdifferentiation, MacLean uses an example of an eye whose lens
has been surgically removed. Epithelial cells at the edge of the iris attempt to become
lens cells, shifting both their shape and coloring, and eventually even synthesizing the
protein, crystalline, which is only produced by lens cells. They attempt to transdifferen-
tiate directly from iris cells to lens cells without any intermediate, undetermined stage.
MacLean, *Genes and Gene Regulation*.

41. S. Brown and R. Capdevila, "Perpetuum Mobile." In *Actor Network Theory and
After*, ed. John Law and John Hassard (Malden, Mass.: Blackwell, 1999)

42. What is the interval—every tenth of a second, every second, every ten seconds,
every ten years, every ten centuries?

43. Pearson, *Germinal Life*, 159.

44. Ibid.; emphasis added.

45. Deleuze and Guattari, *A Thousand Plateaus*, 238.

46. From the perspective of the whole organism, one might think that the brain's primary function is the mediation of coherent coupling of all the subsystems of the body, so the more highly differentiated the organism, the bigger the brain required. Substantial parts of the brain are indeed involved in integrating inputs from all over the body, and over long time periods. But not all the processing that goes on in the brain is involved in the coherent coordination of parts of the body, for this coordination seems instantaneous by all accounts. See Mae-Wan Ho, "Quantum Coherence and Conscious Experience," *Kybernetes* 26 (1997): 268.

47. Ho is here drawing on the work of Freeman and Barrie regarding the olfactory bulb, and on the work of Kelso regarding locomotion. See W. J. Freeman and J. M. Barrie, "Chaotic Oscillation, and the Genesis of Meaning in Cerebral Cortex," in *Temporal Coding in the Brain*, ed. G. Bizsaki (Berlin: Springer-Verlag, 1994); and J. A. S. Kelso, "Behavioral and Neural Pattern Generation: The Concept of Neurobehavioral Dynamical Systems," in *Cardiorespiratory and Motor Coordination* (Berlin: Springer-Verlag).

48. The original reference is to Gilles Deleuze and Félix Guattari, "One or Several Wolves?" in Deleuze and Guattari, *A Thousand Plateaus*, 37.

49. Subindividuals are, for example, the microorganisms living in one's blood. Information or energy would be examples of nonorganic components.

50. Nick Herbert, *Elemental Mind* (New York: Penguin, 1994), 182.

51. Michel Serres, *The Birth of Physics*, trans. by Jack Hawkes (Manchester: Clinamen, 2000), 122.

52. "Space is rich in complexities, it is divided, it bifurcates, it is filled with knots and confluences, it is the conjunctive web of the topology and of the *ars combinatorial*, it is the tattered strips of the *ars coniectandi*, of the event, of circumstance." Ibid., 51.

53. Paul Feyerabend, *Against Method: Outline of an Anarchistic Theory of Knowledge* (New York: Verso, 1975), 267.

54. "We have a point of view (theory, framework, cosmos, mode of representation) whose elements (concepts, 'facts', pictures) are built up in accordance with certain principles of construction. The principles involve something like a 'closure': there are things that cannot be said, or 'discovered', without violating the principles (which does *not* mean contradicting them). Say the things, make the discovery, and the principles are suspended. Now take those constructive principles that underlie every element of the cosmos (of the theory), every fact (every concept). Let us call such principles *universal principles* of the theory in question. Suspending universal principles means suspending all facts and all concepts. Finally, let us call a discovery, or a statement, or an attitude *incommensurable* with the cosmos (the theory, the framework) if it suspends some of its universal principles." Ibid., 269.

55. Ibid., 270.

56. "ANT set off with a notion of translation. . . . For translation is the process or the work of making two things that are not the same, equivalent. But this term translation tells us nothing at all about how it is that links are made. And, in particular, it assumes nothing at all about the similarity of different links. Back at the beginning of ANT the character of semiotic relations was thus left open. The nature of similarity and difference was left undefined, topologically—or in any other respect. Which means, no doubt, that it might come in many forms. Or, to put it differently, there was no assumption that an assemblage of relations would occupy a homogeneous, conformable and singularly tellable space." Law, "After ANT," 8.

57. The research Ho is referring to is cited in W. J. Freeman, *Societies of Brains: A Study in the Neuroscience of Love and Hate* (Hillsdale, N.J.: Lawrence Eribaum Associates, 1995); and C. M. Grey, P. Konig, A. K. Engel, and W. Singer, "Oscillatory Responses in Catvisual Cortex Exhibit Inter-Columner Synchronization Which Reflects Global Stimulus Properties," *Nature* 338, 334–37.

58. Johnjoe McFaddan, "Synchronous Firing and Its Influence on the Brain's Electromagnetic Field: Evidence for an Electromagnetic Field Theory of Consciousness," *Journal of Consciousness Studies* 9 (2002): 23–50.

59. "Synchronous firing of neurones 'phase-locks' em [electromagnetic] field effects and thereby increases the level of electrical coupling between the brain's em field and neurons." Ibid., 26.

60. Ibid., 29. "A dielectric material is a substance that is a poor conductor of electricity but an efficient supporter of electrostatic fields. If the flow of current between opposite electric charge poles is kept to a minimum while the electrostatic lines of flux are not impeded or interrupted, an electrostatic field can store energy. . . . In practice, most dielectric materials are solid. Some liquids and gases can serve as good dielectric materials. . . . An important property of a dielectric is its ability to support an electrostatic field while dissipating minimal energy in the form of heat." whatis.techtarget .com/definition/0,,sid9_gci211945,00.html.

61. Ho, *The Rainbow and the Worm*, 179.

62. Ibid.

63. Henri Bergson, *The Creative Mind* (New York: Citadel, 1992), 105.

64. Henri Bergson, *Creative Evolution*, trans. Arthur Mitchell (Lanham, MD: University Press of America, 1983), 125, qtd. in Keith Ansell Pearson, *Philosophy and the Adventure of the Virtual: Bergson and the Time of Life* (New York: Routledge, 2002), 77.

65. Pearson, *Viroid Life*, 129.

66. Law, "After ANT," 5.

67. One must be careful with anthropomorphic metaphors. What are the desires of an enzyme? Think more in terms of Elizabeth Grosz's contention that there are flows of desire and power and that we (humans, or matter in general) are merely the substance(s)/media through which they flow. In French this verb, *secrete*, would no doubt be a reflexive one: to self-secrete.

68. Channels that Haraway cautioned "get mistaken for nontropic things-in-themselves" rather than "material-semiotic bodies." Haraway, *Modest_Witness*, 142.

69. "The theory of flows . . . accounts, through shapes and movements, mechanism and transmissions, better, through forms and rhythms, for what we can call *specificity*. Serres, *The Birth of Physics*, 96.

70. Pollack, *Cells, Gels, and the Engines of Life*, 135.

71. Ibid., 136.

72. Ibid., 140.

73. "Notions necessary for the description of this world—such as those of form-ground, profile-unity of the object, depth-length, horizon-focus—would remain empty and inapplicable if the Other were not there to give expression to those possible worlds in which that which is for us in the background is pre-perceived or sub-perceived as a possible form; that which is in depth as a possible length, etc." Deleuze, *Difference and Repetition*, 282.

74. Pearson, *Germinal Life*, 156.

75. Ibid., 159.

76. Gilles Deleuze, *Foucault*, trans. Sean Hand (Minneapolis: University of Minnesota Press, 1998), 128.

77. Ibid., 100.

78. Ibid., 98.

79. Pearson, *Viroid Life*, 128.

80. Ibid.

81. S. A. Kauffman, *The Origins of Order: Self-Organization and Selections in Evolution* (New York: Oxford University Press, 1993), xvii, qtd. in Pearson, *Viroid Life*, 129.

82. Deleuze, *Difference and Repetition*, 36.

83. As goes the children's game: "Cows are in the meadow / huddled all together / first comes lightning / then comes thunder / down comes the rain / and the cows jump up." The lightning / the cows: *nunc hinc, nunc illinc.*

84. "Human games presuppose pre-existing categorical rules. . . . their games never affirm the whole of chance: on the contrary they fragment it and, for each case, subtract or remove the consequences of the throw from chance . . . this is why human games proceed by sedentary distributions . . . supposed to effect a distribution . . . the results of these throws are distributed according to their consequences . . . . This is sedentary distribution, in which the fixed sharing out of a distributed occurs in accordance with a proportion fixed by rules." Deleuze, *Difference and Repetition*, 282.

85. Ibid., 283.

86. "Entropic drift takes place in the forgetting of its initial condition. Or: the irreversible is without memory. . . . The universal does not require any memory. . . . And background noise is also the absence of code. There is no code for equilibrium, of the fall towards equilibrium. Equilibrium according to [Jean] Fourier, to [Ludwig] Boltzmann, is the forgetting of initial conditions." Serres, *The Birth of Physics*, 148.

87. Michel Serres, *Genesis*, trans. Geneviève James and James Nielson (Ann Arbor: University of Michigan Press, 1995), 99.

88. Matti Pitkanen, personal communication, April 18, 2002.

89. Ibid.

90. Ho, *The Rainbow and the Worm*, 87.

91. Pollack, *Cells, Gels, and the Engines of Life*, 118.

MYOCELLULAR TRANSDUCTION:

WHEN MY CELLS TRAINED MY BODY-MIND

DEBORAH GAMBS

WE CONTAIN ANTICIPATION

I quickly run up the two flights of stairs. My hand dusts across the gray steel railing. I come out of the stairwell and into the alcove of the soda machine. It is set back from the hallway around the corner from the rest of the fitness room. Still on linoleum tile, I have not yet reached the tight gray carpeting. I smooth the corners of a dollar bill and slide it below the red flashing arrows of the machine's opening, hoping there will be strawberry melon, 10 percent juice. Pink lemondade, 10 percent juice, is too acidic and produces a slimy film of mucous in my mouth as I run. My fingers press out the folds, and the dollar slot whirs and grabs my bill. My heart is picking up speed. Is it the endorphins coming before the run? The satisfactory pull and strain of my muscles, the desire for calories burned, the slick sheen of sweat that will drip from the underside of my forearms? Whatever, it is thumping now in my chest, and breath is shallow. The voice in my head comes, me talking to me, reminding me to breathe in, exhale, slow down, relax Deborah.

I drop the quarter in. It is solid, and it clangs against the metal box inside. This is the last bit before I turn the corner off the linoleum onto the carpet. Is it the machines that whir? The bodies flashing light glancing off sweat?

No. It is the approaching glass walls of your office. It is the bust of you above the desk, an arm stretched to the mouse, a wink over the monitor, the wave and pull of your hand, motioning me in to sit across from you at the corner of your wooden desk. It is me recognizing each of these parts, you in parts. It is anxiety holding me distant so that they come in slo-mo. I am careful in each step I take. It is you making me nervous. It is me crushing on you. It is my hormones run rampant. My lack of serotonin. It is my metabolism careening at breakneck speed now. I try to hold my cells tight. I will sit in the molded plastic chair, heart slowing, gradual smile, nod, waiting. For you to speak, smile, see me.

The bottle thumps down into the plastic slot. I reach my hand in for the drink, twist it sideways to pull it out, fingers slipping on its condensation. I step and turn around the corner. Anticipation has set in.

.....

I am compelled to record moments. To write through the changes. Bodily. Physical. Psychic. Political. The transformation that began to occur, which continues.

My mother did not recognize me when they met me at the airport at Christmas time. "You look so good! You look so good!" So many responses available to a statement like that.

I had dreamt of my extra flesh, waited to find my muscles and bones, the experiment I began to think of way back in 1999. Had I read of bodies without organs? Had I considered the theoretical possibility of the productivity of the anorexic? Production rather than lack. And do I produce as I shrink? As I work to lose my surplus value?

The trauma of physiological change is odd. Fractured, bizarre, confounding. What is the agent here? Not who, what.

Making a record, recording the moments, is a chance to think back, set down what occurs, describe a process. A very empirical kind of writing in this sense. I am compelled to say, I experienced these moments.
My autoethnographic will to power/knowledge.

SPEED

> speed - slow
> swishswish
> smooth
> sailing
> legsglide
> shouldersswing
> slightly forward tilting side to side
>> head straight upon the spine

7 to Times Square
Manhattan all times
express envy
gumstained cement
flyingfast
  center lane of tracks
  in the first car
  hand pressed fast
against the window
of the door between cars
as if to say
  stop, we're coming through.

we wait for the local
wish our train
  would go so fast

SLOW

  Sadness, its beautiful calm
gently pervasive
spreads through to red finger tips.
Sit carefully
  proper lady one
  leg crossed over
the other and
sandaled foot dangling
    artfully.

Papers carefully
  stacked
  atop the tiny oaken table itself
perched, on four tapered legs.

Tilt of the red and white
  straw leans at a
sympathetic angle, barely
dipped into the last drinks, of pale
  pear orange
tea small dots of ice waiting
for permission, to melt completely.

Allow the sadness   to
sift,   and filter through skin's
pores at a rate so slow
the draining   will last
    one hundred eighty   days.
        Slowseepage.

Salty water appears   on
    your forearms.
Speedwalk the treadmill at
    its highest
    incline

First a sheen   and
after about half a mile,   the droplets
    collect and merge.
miniature puddles.
the hairs of your arm will stand
    straight up,   become whitest blonde
against the flush   of pinkening skin.

During the next 2 miles
    large drops of water
fall from elbow tips   lie
    in the ridges   of the gray plastic
sides   at the base of the machine.

Afterwards, wipe your neck
    and hair line   mop
the moisture   from   the backs of hands, and
arms spray light green cleaner on a paper towel
Return to the machine
    Wipe the arms clean
    from the rubber hand holds
remove the marks   of your gripping palms.

OPPOSITIONS

Mindbody bodymind. Let me build an opposition. It won't be too difficult in this case. You'll see. Man Woman. Black White. Building body Developing mind. Easy oppositions if you want to oppose, you'd think.

Elizabeth Grosz explains that the problem with oppositions are the hierarchies that result. There are histories of oppositions to be undone.

This is an auto and ethnographic account. Myself and my trainer as not subjects, but bodies assembled in order to do something. Our bodies positioned and moving among global configurations of money (once mine, now his), information (once his, now mine), technology, power (ours). Ours. Our organismic bodies gendered, raced. Bodies of sexuality, nation. Our bodies becoming.
Those oppositions deconstructed, and more.

Teletechnology in the age of the unconscious: communication and information technology have the power to undo the distinctions between nature and culture, organic and nonorganic, machine and human. Mind is embedded in matter. Easy oppositions if you want to oppose, you'd think. Except that he's my personal trainer. I work with him to push myself. I pay him to help me with my body. I also pay my psychotherapist, and this helps me with my body. But it's the trainer who tells me it's all a state of mind. I argue with him over this, materialist that I am.

But apparently, changing your body requires your mind, changes your mind, and what can a human body do?

I love liking my trainer, the waves of affects that sweep through me.
Even the tight headiness of writing this is a turn-on.

When we work together, your voice is in my head. I mean you are speaking out loud to me but it is as if it comes from inside me and I hear the words and respond but sometimes I have no idea what you've said and my body just moves and I lift and lower. You say I should count to four as I lower the weights and you will keep track of the reps. The scored metal of the bar twists against my palm and after the sixth repetition my left triceps and pectorals begin to shake. I know my face scrunches up in fear and you remark upon it, tell me I am stronger than I realize, that I have a lot of upper body mass. Not to be afraid. I am not sure if I'm afraid. You think I am, my face expresses the affect fear but it does before I am even aware of what I feel I am not sure I feel afraid perhaps I do. Or am I constantly afraid?

AFFECTION

Two notions of affect, two spaces between conventional understandings of emotion and power. To understand the affects as Sylvan Tomkins describes them—fear, anger, shame, joy, satisfaction—as simply feelings would be to experience them in a kind of stasis. As Brian Massumi puts it, there is a kind of productivity in the affects, movement toward or away from something. A third state, prior to the distinction between activity and passivity.

Tomkins is seemingly playful in his discussion of the role of the affects in what a body wants, what a psyche wants and the capacities and limits for a social relationship between people in this regard.
It has nothing to do with a self.

> If you like to be looked at and I like to look at you, we may achieve an enjoyable interpersonal relationship. If you like to talk and I like to listen to you talk, this can be mutually rewarding. If you like to feel enclosed within a claustrum and I like to put my arms around you, we can both enjoy a particular kind of embrace.

If you would like to train my movement, and I would like my movements to be trained, we may both be pleased with ourselves.

.....

I strain backward against the Thera-Band, the giant rubber band that provides resistance. As I lean back and push myself across the track, my eyes fix at the center of your chest holds me there the center of you centers me where each of your pectoral muscles meet the top of your abdomen and the fold of your long-sleeved slick warm-up shirt creases right there and I always each time have the fast thought that I should focus somewhere else where I could focus instead of noticing your pectorals.

This was supposed to be about me and movement, my body's sensations. But these are not the sensations I meant. Your movements. My sensations.
Did I mention I love the way you move? Do you know how carefully the fabric of your nylon pants swishes between your thighs? Are you aware that your arms slide and flow at the socket of your shoulder?

> And now my mind moves
> view at a distance
> tassled corn tops about

the 4th of July
and sway in sync despite
the lack of breeze.

I strain back against the Thera-Band, unaware
the base of my red cut up Diesel T-shirt is soaked
and nearly
dripping.

He rewrites parables for the virtual, of sensation, movement, and affect. In this
we can see the actual relations of the molecular and the molar. The minutiae of
bodies, movements, affects, and sensations are not so far from culture. How
can one record, how can one show the emergence? The tiny cellular breakdown
of muscle fibers, rebuilding, reshaping this molar organism.

Focusing on the preindividual offers us the chance to recognize difference at
the cellular level. Not only is one whole bodily organism different from another but difference exists within the organism. An ontology of becoming is
evidenced here—if a thing "is" when it isn't doing, then a body in motion never
"is," and a body is always in motion. Even the earth's matter is in constant
motion, if at a speed we cannot perceive. This understanding at a microscopic
or preindividual level has implications for sociality, for culture. It is also on-
togenetic, it is becoming always.

This body finds pleasure in his movement
wish to walk with my head so high
my shoulders back
hips carefully encasing the head
of my femur, wish my body to move
    like my trainer's.

It is suggested that we can explore the relation of concrete and abstract by
looking at movement. "In motion, a body is an immediate, unfolding relation
to its own non-present potential to vary." The body as a site of movement,
sensation, and thus transformation challenges notions of positionality, stasis,
identity. Like an arrow moving across space in time. That arrow is always in
passage across points, it is never "in" any of the points, and these points are
only retrospective constructs of stasis.

DESIRE AND FEAR

I am afraid to be

of being

thin.

I am afraid of speed, quickness, lightness of being.
I am afraid
I will be blown away in the wind, be insignificant, empty,
    invisible.

I'm afraid
of speed
of running fast
of my body going off without me
if I move so fast where will I go?

My desire is producing my body
My desire is producing my body.
What desire? For whom?
Father.
What/whose body am I moving toward?
Toward becoming
Becoming woman for sure?

Not mother
Becoming woman away from my mother
Yet toward still

I saw that photo
mother and two friends
Circa 1965 according to the hair
Saw in her face mine.

The face that is becoming
Surface of a plane. Plane of consistencies
Desire has certainly reterritorialized my body

MOVEMENT

Pedaling rolling moving
across rattling blacktop
inner ears vibrating
knee high green soybean
plants on the left side of the road
taller than me corn
yet still tassle-less on the other side to my right
shoulders and back tingling
neck stiff from cycling on this old
racing ten-speed donated by my uncle
which my mother is afraid to ride on—
afraid to tip over on.

Affect :: Fear

Nervous about taking the
narrow tires on gravel
but I am tempted—
riding across the levee
the flat hot wind which
sweeps away the humidity
disappears as I reach
the top of the levee
which protects the town from
the flooding Nishnabotna.

Affect :: Satisfaction

Riding above the fields
made it to the top
of the levee
not afraid of the gravel
always try what you fear
it's all mental he says
satisfaction at conquering fear
satisfaction at finding fear unfounded
satisfaction at moving despite fear, with fear, through fear
because of fear?

Fear pulls me forward
fear is what interests me
entices me, it's how I know I'm interested.

Sensation :: Heat

She's right, the Midwest
Iowa summer is something
something on its own, apart.
There is a humidity yet
the sun bakes you dry
a moistness that the
wind clears away,
a wind
which blows my hair apart
yet the tree tops stand silent and still.

On the levee.
The sloped hills downward
thickly covered with
purple thistle plants
their round heads bobbing
next to the arching weeds.

Later, I sit and
a woman in a maroon 4x4 pickup,
window rolled down
cheeks tired and flushed
shuffles into the store
her keys slowly jangling
acknowledging her tiredness
hair flaming orange red
pulled back into a ponytail.
I knew her once in junior high.

It is a strange heat
the air is oddly still
yet my papers flap in the wind and the hairs
on my arm tickle in the breeze.
I look down the road
and no heat rises, no

mirage shimmers on the
blacktop,
yet somehow I must
squint to see through
the heat and everything
is farther, much farther
distant.

Movement :: Action

On the bike again,
I look down at my calves
just to see the muscles
at the side
clenched
in
action
feel my feet gripped in my sandals wrapped
around
the pedals
and my quads tensing as
I push the wheels
round and round

too far into my head
for enjoyment no
smile of enjoyment
no smile of satisfaction
no smile

POLITICS

These experiences, though mine, are not mine only. Experience is always
personal and also always layered over all others' singular experiences. We must
jump scale: preindividuals, parts, individuals, collectives; machines, rays, molecules; histories, archives, DNAs, futures, telefuture. Consider the political.
Consider the colonized cell. Consider the cell corporatized. Consider what a
cell can do.

I run indoors
legs pulled forward
feet thumping the moving band
   Concrete makes my shins ache

I like the turning whir
climate control
eyes drawn to the silent CNN
   Strings of words pass across my eyes

Music slams into my head
Walkman wired to my ears
what I call girlydance music, bippy-bop
   A surprise that it is this femme-chick girl stuff that gets me going

I ask my trainer
if when I run my first marathon
I can remain connected to him by cellular phone
   My dream is to run with my headphones.

Dan Browne lives in Portland in a house in which the oxygen in the air is as if they are at an altitude of twelve thousand feet. He trains, he pushes his body. His body trains, his body pushes him. He runs a race down at sea level. Salazar, his trainer, is open to the new, open to the future. "Live high, train low." He will try anything to have a "nonforeigner" win a long-distance race.

He would like to use technology to "counter the increasing domination of African runners, many of whom were born and train at altitude." The humiliating truth is that "the rest of the world has gotten faster, and Americans have gotten slower."

And so Dan Browne stands atop the Nemes, a machine that vibrates the muscle fibers in his legs, to train his body. He is a running machine. Nike would love to help him succeed, and so they pay for the house, the house with thinner air and the Nemes machine vibrating Browne's muscle cells into high performance.

Miles and months away the newscaster announces that the Kenyans have won the New York City marathon. Better still—they have dominated the race. Four

Kenyans in the top ten, both men's and women's. This is an Olympic-worthy human interest moment.

The voice-over importantly intones manufactured suspense, "The natural resources of Kenya: gold, hydropower, rubies . . . and marathon runners." The irony is both intended and lost.

Lorna Kiplagat founds the Safari High Altitude Training Camp near Iten, Kenya. Runners from Uganda, Nigeria, Scotland, and Holland travel there to run at high altitudes. Their low-tech GeoCities Web site offers anyone the opportunity to train where the Kenyans have. To train in the dusty traces of the Kenyan earth. I am told hypothesized stories of the training African runners endure. Told it is their environment and will that are key. If you walked six miles for water each way carrying the container on your shoulders, ran in heat like that. If this was your best shot. Your best dream. What is the political economy of the marathon runner?

And I began to run in slow motion.

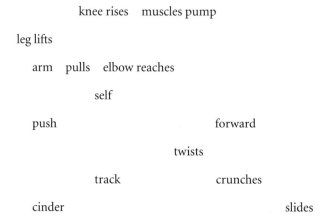

knee rises   muscles pump

leg lifts

arm   pulls   elbow reaches

self

push   forward

twists

track   crunches

cinder   slides

I had seen it on television. Close up slow-motion shots of athletes at the end of the race. An image transmitted from my quadriceps through to my brain. Made a picture in the brain. Slow motion. Teletechnologies in the brain.

DAVID STAPLES

Rather than the refusal to work of the Jamaican slaves in 1834, which is cited by Marx as the only example of zero-work, quickly recuperated by imperialist maneuvers, it is the long history of women's work which is a sustained example of zero-work: work not only outside of wage-work, but *in one way or another*, "outside" of the definitive modes of production. The displacement required here is a transvaluation, an uncatastrophic *im*plosion of the search for validation via the circuit of productivity. Rather than a miniaturized and thus controlled metaphor for civil society and the state, the power of the *oikos*, domestic economy, can be used as the model of the foreign body unwittingly nurtured by the *polis*.
—Gayatri Chakravorty Spivak, *In Other Worlds*

The State guarantees equality and equity between men and women in the exercise of their right to work. The State recognises work at home as an economic activity that creates added value and produces social welfare and wealth. Housewives are entitled to Social Security in accordance with the law.
—Constitution of Venezuela, Article 88

The specter of women's work haunts capitalism. From women and children being set to work in the nineteenth century by what Karl Marx called the "invisible threads" of capitalism to today's globalized homeworkers, domestic workers, and caregivers, the hidden, invisible, and cyclically forgotten labor of women—derogated by Marx as a natural and thereby "freely appropriated" force of social production—marks a recurring, ghostly passage through materialist formulations of subjectivity, history, and culture.[1] The historic appearance of women's work in late-twentieth-century decrees of the International Labor Organization or the Venezuelan constitution of 1999—insistently reminds feminists and critical political economists (undoubtedly in different registers) that cultural, political, and social struggles over reproduction, gender, and sexual equality are fully implicated in what is thought today as both neoliberal economic crisis *and* counter-hegemonic politics. The ghostly reappearances of sexually as well as racially divided labor constitute the ontological inside of long and complex histories of human struggles over the accumulation and circulation of time, starting with nineteenth-century capitalist efforts to socialize labor time.

The modulation of what Marx called "living labor," typically through its refusal by organized workers, constitutes the historical ground on which ethico-political struggle over wages and over time—and the consequent composition of political classes (and, as we know from labor studies, gender and races)—is still theorized and enacted.[2] Yet lurking in the workingman's historic demand for higher wages and a shorter working day is the ghostly figure of workingwoman. Class has long been a ghostly appearance of what we have come to think of as gender—and with gender always race.[3]

How are contemporary Marxist theorists attending to this aporia, or ghost effect? The so-called autonomia school of Marxism, particularly the work of Antonio Negri and his collaborators, took its cues from the organized mass refusal of capitalist work and restructuring in Italy in the 1960s and 1970s. In short, Negri and others argued that a qualitative leap in global working-class struggle led to something more than the traditional refusal by workers to give alienated labor time in conditions of exploitation.[4] Unlike prior class struggles for shorter hours and higher wages, struggles in the 1960s and 1970s, near in time to what we now understand as the close of the Fordist period, were at best isomorphic with previous ones. In the more recent period, autonomist Marxists ascribe the antagonistic relationship with capital that constituted the working class to a more extended and immaterial laboring body than the stereotypical assembly-line worker of the previous era. Rather than the length of the working day or size of the pay packet, it was the communicative and cooperative capacities, the social organization—in short, the highly developed social and affective capacities of workers that were being struggled over, according to the autonomist view. By the 1960s, class struggle in Europe and the United States had expanded well beyond the factory floor and beyond traditional working-class demands. The era of the "social factory" saw capital increasingly exploiting labor outside the factory walls, in the substrata of everyday life, that is, in the hyperfashioning of consumer bodies, needs, and tastes; in the commodification of knowledge and information; in the creation of a service economy; in the rise of lifelong education; and so on. The social-factory thesis signified that labor increasingly responded in kind by exposing and rejecting the society of the spectacle and gaining through direct action and political organization reductions in the costs of living and a valorization of other aspects of life, that is, what was termed a social or political wage.[5]

My purpose here is not to dispute this analysis, but rather to argue that what historically and theoretically modeled the shifts in industrial and post-industrial class power and organization in the latter half of the twentieth century is lodged—or held hostage—inside the analysis itself. The succession of the era of the mass worker by that of the socialized worker was premised on the shift to "a working day so extended as not only to comprise within itself *the relation between production time and reproduction time, as a single whole,* but also and above all to extend the consideration of time over the entire life-space of the labour market."[6] Embedded in this singular transition, I am arguing, is the body whose labor had been socialized long before any other—that of the female worker.

In what follows, I attempt to explore the technological and biopolitical transformations of reproductive labor in the twentieth century, changes that have engendered new techniques of reproduction, a novel control of bodies and labor power, as well as sites of resistance and refusal. In doing so, I offer, via a critical reading of autonomist Marxism, a theoretical supplement to the Marxist-feminist theoretical revelation of the productivity for capital of un-paid reproductive labor (traditionally conceived woman's work)—indeed, a theory of reproductive labor value that both embraces and critically interrogates the implications of neo-Marxist conceptions of value for understanding social movement and political change today. The elaboration of a more generalized economy is needed in order to account for what Gayatri Chakravorty Spivak has termed "the expanded textuality of value" in late twentieth-century capitalism, as well as for the decodified flows of sexual and racialized affect-value production, which are informing early twenty-first-century capitalism.[7] I examine the expanded textuality of affect-value production in terms of the diverse milieus of capitalism, going beyond the restricted economy of more orthodox Marxist and neoclassical political economic approaches finally to discuss the so-called gift economy in the context of socially reproductive labor.

Leopoldina Fortunati's trenchant analysis of housework, prostitution, and re-production challenges the obscuring of the sexual division of labor in the political economy built up around the socialized stereotypical European and North American household. Beginning with Marx's dualistic analysis that work must appear as waged work in capitalism and that value in capitalism is measured by alienated labor time (or the capacity of what in the *Grundrisse* Marx called living labor), Fortunati argues that the dialectic which, for Marx, pervades capital—the ghost effect of paid/unpaid or necessary/surplus labor in capital—must be held equally to apply to non-wage work such as housework and the physical and affective reproduction of living labor. The reproductive labor of housework, childcare, and sexual reproduction, seen as nonwork (because unwaged and engendered), enables capital to interpret productive labor as work (in the material-ideological sense) and to exploit it as sur-plus value-producing labor. Taking this logic to its end, Fortunati insists that housework *must* appear under capitalism as a "natural force of social labor" *in order for* waged work to appear as value production. Finally, consonant with other Marxist feminists of recent decades, Fortunati recasts the debate over whether women's household labor should appear as simply any other form of productive social labor: "The real difference between production and repro-duction is not that of value/non-value, but that while production both *is* and *appears as* the creation of value, reproduction *is* the creation of value but *appears otherwise.*"[8]

Such an understanding radically extends Negri's reading of Marx that "cap-ital is not just specific exploitation within production, but it *also acquires for itself, gratuitously, social dimensions which are only produced by the living force of labor*"; and that what is added "gratuitously" is accomplished by a different composition of living labor that "preserves the value of capital as well as . . . comes to be enriched in the cooperation of large masses, the labor which follows the scientific potential of society *as well as that which results from the simple increase of the population.*"[9] The gratuitousness of the "simple increase of the population" is, I am arguing, one of the ghostly effects of reproduc-tive labor—which in the context of capitalism is also, we will see, both a gift of time and a nurturing of the political.[10] I return to these points in the final section.

While classical political economy understood the extraction of value from surplus labor to produce a measurable profit—which, when reintroduced into productive circulation, became capital—Negri and Michael Hardt have argued that in the late twentieth century, money (capital's forceful claim on future labor) has broken free of production. Neither exchange value (the wage) nor surplus value (capitalist profit) any longer function as measures of value. Production time, understood by Marx as the relative and absolute ground of surplus-value extraction, no longer adequately measures either the quantity or quality of value production, which proceeds on an expansive social (i.e., subjectivized, but also pre-individual) and indeed, global, scale. Labor power, in Negri and Hardt's view, is mobile and cannot be commanded as it could in the Fordist era. Money, once the expression of a narrowly conceived "regime of exchange between capital and more or less subjectivized labor-power," now launches an entirely new regime of exchange. Money as the "claim on future labor" assumes a more expansive role, and the labor theory of value has been "transfigured into monetary theory—constructed on the horizon of globalization, organized by imperial command."[11]

While Negri argues that labor no longer operates as the limit or measure of value or productivity, but rather as the "living antagonism" within capitalism, he also argues that labor power "is presented as the social fabric, as population and culture, traditions and innovation, and so forth—in short, its productive force is exploited within the processes of social reproduction."[12] What grounds labor and simultaneously pulls it back from what Negri describes as the "non-place" of value with respect to labor, are forces as much premodern as postmodern: population, culture, traditions, and so on. Thus labor power in Negri's take on postmodern political economy refers to the biopolitical expansiveness and mobility of the production, appropriation, and distribution of what Hardt and Negri in *Empire* term "immaterial labor" (a term which, we will see, is not the same as *reproductive labor*).[13] In the literature of economic globalization, on the other hand, we are presented with the old story of capital's reply to zero-work: with the slightest hint of social or political turbulence, capital's subcontractors pack up and leave waged women workers (long ago socialized, or "housewifized," in Maria Mies's singular expression) in a flash, in search of cheaper, more flexible, more cooperative labor power.[14] What results from these two distinct but overlapping perspectives is a spectacular doubling of the specter of women's work, which has led many researchers of today's home-based labor/homeworking phenomenon to speculate that for labor power exploited in the cycles of global (re)production, there is literally "no-place" like home.[15]

Capitalist globalization, as David Harvey, Sassia Sasken, and others showed over a decade ago, has reached a nonlinear point of more or less instantaneous local and global mobility. Its extensiveness has taken the form of an intensification of the social and communal forms of development that modulate and enmesh productive and reproductive forces: for example, massive increases in the educational, information, and service sectors (including commodified women's work such as childcare) in industrializing and postindustrial economies; the communication-, knowledge-, and affect-orientation of a greater number of labor sectors in these economies today; and the proliferation of so-called informal, precarious, home-based, and other kinds of labor. When Hardt and Negri term this new composition of labor, wholly subsumed in capitalist production, immaterial labor, one may take pause. With the notion of immaterial labor, Hardt and Negri ask us to recall in particular Marx's distinction between the *formal* subsumption of labor (when capital encounters labor in alien forms, with their own distinct rules, traditions, and cultures), and the *real* subsumption of labor (when capital has internalized labor in its own specifically capitalist sociality and mode of production). The real subsumption of labor does not signify a loss in antagonism. If capital no longer encounters labor outside itself—as alien to capital—it does not mean that labor is no longer antagonistic to capital. On the contrary, "the social capacity of reproduction, the productive surplus of cooperation, the 'small-scale circulation,' the new needs and desires produced by the struggles"—such aspects of the real subsumption of labor have led to a situation in which, at least in the high-tech creditor economies (although many, including Hardt and Negri, argue that this is more or less universal today), virtually all productive and reproductive work is either directly or indirectly waged work, meaning that there is no labor time standing outside capital as the external reference or measure for labor time expended within capitalism.[16] Consequently, the objective relationship of the antagonism between necessary and surplus labor (at the heart of Marx's *Grundrisse*) has progressively expanded and intensified—and labor is now *subjectively* antagonistic to capital. We are in a time, as Negri famously put it, of "Marx beyond Marx," where the struggle over the time and subjectivity of labor has assumed a wholly different texture.[17]

What has transformed the antagonism is both the loss of labor time as the measure of value, and the displacement of value production onto affect. That is to say, in purely spatial terms, the antagonism focused on the factory floor in Fordism has extended to all sites of capitalist sociality: the home, the office, transportation, the Internet, health care, education, child care, popular culture, body culture, morality, political organization, and so on. Such a shift does not imply traditional concepts of class, to be sure. There may indeed be new (and old) sectors of stereotypically affective laborers—therapists and caregivers are two that come quickly to mind—but that is not what Hardt and Negri mean by affective labor. On the one hand, affective labor is meant to highlight the permeability of the line between paid and unpaid labor (and in this respect implies a rethinking of the phase shifts between commodification and decommodification).[18] On the other hand, given the tremendous mobility and shifting both within globalization as well as on the microlevel of everyday life, value is now being produced more or less everywhere and all of the time: from the patenting of genetically modified food, to the shaping of appetites, to the marketing of fast-food franchises—to give just a few examples of the production, circulation, and distribution of value today.

Nevertheless, it is important to recall that in the Fordist era of the mass worker there was never any abstract or statistical measure of value for specifically reproductive labor other than the workingman's socially necessary labor. And this, too, was always limited to a sexually, racially, and colonially divided society. So were the classes being reproduced differently? Or was the scission of value from measure already affective inside the developing states of capitalist sociality—especially as it related to the microlevel of power, on the one hand, and colonialism, on the other? There is ample documentation, as we know, of the changing social norms and governmental forms—what Michel Foucault termed the "biopolitics"—of nineteenth-century European social policy, including housing, sanitation, education, philanthropy, child care, and marriage, to name just a few. As Foucault, Jacques Donzelot, feminist historians, and others demonstrated so clearly, the *dispositifs* of these fields were always bound to the abstract value measures of labor, even as they were directly mobilized by and for governmental apparatuses such as security and public health. By the turn of the twentieth century, if not earlier, a robust science of home economics had been created around the household whose explicit purpose was to increase the productivity of domestic labor. Throughout, there was the violent capitalist accumulation revealed in the stark form of imperialism and colonial genocide.[19]

To suggest today, as Hardt and Negri do, that affective labor is *now* hegemonic within the field of class struggle may be correct, but also misleading in a way. As in the ritual economy—where woman's gift of time must be forgotten, and therefore the supposed prestige, sacrifice, and obligation that were to accompany her gift also became effaced—so apparently in the theory of value-affect.[20] It bears repeating that women's work has long invested supposedly universal (not to mention global) wage and value production not only with energy but with affect and subjectivity too.[21] And although Hardt and Negri gesture to the problem, there remains the troubling prospect that the well-educated artisans and radical biopoliticians of the information economy will not only forget, in the political/policy realm, but continue to exploit, in the affective realm, the gratuitousness of the very complex "simple increase" in (global-local) population and change in social fabric and culture.

And thus I return to the opening citation on women's work as the sustained historical example of zero-work, work outside waged labor, or value production beyond value, which capital has continuously sought to colonize, discipline, and subsume in the sense of the old (but certainly not passé) imperialist and patriarchal orders, and which today it seeks increasingly to control in the turbulent expansiveness of global production and value extraction (e.g., ongoing and wrenching policies of structural adjustment). Today again, in ways that Marx only gesturally anticipated, there is an opening to contested claims on affect (in the form of attention, training, education, care, and children), on the one hand, as well as to capitalist claims (via material debt and consumption) on future reproductive-productive labor (that is, to a turbulent recoding of specifically female workers), on the other hand—in both old and new class categories and terms.[22]

These arguments could be important for understanding not only the divides at the heart of contemporary global class politics. They could also be important for understanding the displacements and modulations of the female worker's body in the full assertion of affect and the extended crisis of global capitalism. For once broken out of the circuit of value, either through social organization or violent displacement into the structure of debt, reproductive labor is returned in another ghostly form, marked both by shocks to the system and highly focused sexual and racial politics. Agency from the bottom up emerges not as the disciplined, organized body of counter-hegemonic struggle, but as indeterminate forces of life both actively circulating their gifts and struggling against neoliberal capitalism's piratical treasuring of them.

With these prefatory remarks in mind, I turn to examine how, in the twentieth century, the long line of affective labor came to further change the relationship between production-time and life-time such that, in the words of Hardt and Negri, life

> is now completely inverted with respect to how the discipline of political economy understands it. Life is no longer produced in the cycles of reproduction that are subordinated to the working day; on the contrary, life is what infuses and dominates all production. In fact, the value of labor and production is determined deep in the viscera of life. Industry produces no surplus except what is generated by social activity—and this is why, buried in the great whale of life, value is beyond measure.[23]

This reversal displacement of the relationship of production and life, however, requires a momentary return to the specter of Marx and the nineteenth-century question of the technological forces of production and reproduction, beginning with capital's relationship to thermodynamics.

MARX AND THERMODYNAMICS

In the *Grundrisse*, Marx wrote: "Human anatomy contains a key to the anatomy of the ape. The intimations of higher development among the subordinate animal species, however, can be understood only after the higher development is already known. The bourgeois economy thus supplies the key to the ancient, etc."[24] Economistic readings of Marx always saw in this and similar pronouncements a useful determinism. Marx's complicity with deterministic science is a somewhat different problem, however, for at the same time that Marx was turning Hegel right-side up politically and philosophically, a generation of proto-technoscientists was transforming thought about physical forces of the cosmos (as well as about what some today might call cosmopolitics). Marx and the class subjects of his own time were affected not only by the emergence of colonial anthropology and race theory, two of the better-known confluences of critical political economy. They were affected, arguably at a deeper level, by the groundbreaking studies and experiments on the conversion of force, energy, and heat in the new engines of industry—what came to be known as thermodynamics.

The technoscientific understanding of thermodynamics contributed to shifting not only the scientific and popular understanding of the universal forces of nature but also the paradigmatic appreciation of human labor—labor no longer theorized as a singular exchange with nature, but as a universal force (*Arbeitskraft*) equivalent to all other natural forces. That is to say, the new machine sciences of the mid-nineteenth century were beginning—at about the same time as political economists—to conceive of human labor like other physical forces in the universe, as one essential, timeless, energetic force (*Kraft*) that could neither be created nor destroyed.

We can trace the thought of universal work energy, which so captivated both new industrialists and political economists (including critical ones such as Marx), at least in part to Hermann von Helmholtz's 1847 elaboration of the law of conservation of energy, better known as the first law of thermodynamics.[25] Well before Marx began theorizing the production of value under capitalism, the study of thermodynamics had already begun shifting the natural sciences paradigm. The widespread presence of machine technology had the circular (or what we would call today, the cybernetic) effect of informing scientists about the dynamics of energy flows, including the dissipation of energy. A landmark development of machine-informed technoscience was encapsulated in what became known as the second law of thermodynamics, articulated by Rudolf Clausius at about the same time as Helmholtz's conservation of energy theory. This second law viewed the conversion of force, specifically the transfer of heat energy from a warmer source to a cooler source in a closed dynamic system, as a process accompanied by the gradual decrease in the amount of total energy available for work. This dissipative effect of heat energy was termed entropy.

The parallel developments in political economy and physical science in the early to mid-nineteenth century were arguably not pure coincidence. The simultaneous political expansion of *liberté* and *égalité* had the practical effect in bourgeois political economy of conceptualizing previously alien forms of labor as abstractly free and equal (as much in theory as in practice). With labor power established scientifically as a general equivalent of energy, the free laboring subject could also be thought, mutatis mutandis, to be able to produce more or less universally, that is, to produce out of proportion to its previously understood nature. Most important to Marx's critique of political economy, as well as to mid-nineteenth-century artisanal class politics, the subject of bourgeois political economy and the capitalist-controlled labor process could be regulated systematically and put to work *like a machine*. As Marx was quick to recognize, in the theoretical shift from labor to labor power (a recognition corresponding to what Marx would term the real subsumption of labor in the emerging metropolitan centers of capital), the free laboring subject of bourgeois political economy could be thought of as equivalent to all other kinds of productive energy, including machines. Conceptually, production centered on this subject was no longer a process of metabolic exchange with nature, but rather a pure expenditure and consumption of energy (Marx would refer to this expansive production as a "social metabolism" in *Capital*). Whereas mercantilist wages of the previous epoch were kept artificially low in order to enforce work discipline (i.e., to keep shiftless workers coming back for more), capitalist wages would manage a profitable circulatory flow between the time required for reproducing labor capacity and the time available for surplus production. In the translation between the natural and social sciences of the day, the problem of entropy became the part-political, part-technological problem of how to keep slowly dying labor going, that is, how to extract as much as possible from labor before it could no longer produce, or needed to be replenished. At the risk of much overgeneralization, one might argue that for

Marx, the second law of thermodynamics—the law of entropy—would become, by turns, the radical scientific basis for the long-term tendency of the rate of profit to decline in capitalist production, and an evolutionary step on the road to the "heat death" of capitalism.

The attraction of the emerging machine-based economy was powerful for scientists and laboratory researchers in the middle decades of the century and, later, became the raison d'être for the growing contingent of industry-based scientific theorists and experts who would be responsible for, among other things, Taylorization, time-motion studies, and other synthesized forms of systematic industrial organization. Between thermodynamics and political economy, a radical correspondence developed, as Anson Rabinbach has noted: "Taylorism, bolshevism, and fascism . . . conceived of the body both as a productive force and as a political instrument whose energies could be subjected to scientifically designed systems of organization. . . . The laboring body was thus interpreted as the site of conversion, or exchange, between nature and society—the medium through which the forces of nature are transformed into the forces that propel society."[26] What would become crucial for anticapitalists to determine was whether and how the forces of nature, once converted into labor, might be in contradiction with the social relations they propelled. If capitalism were conceived as a (thermo)dynamic system, did this not necessitate a view of the ultimate collapse of capitalism (brought on as a result of the entropic decline of all thermodynamic systems)? As Marx wrote: "The growing incompatibility between the productive development of society and its hitherto existing relations of production expresses itself in bitter contradictions, crises, spasms. . . . These contradictions lead to explosions, cataclysms, crises in which by momentaneous suspension of labour and annihilation of a great portion of capital the latter is violently reduced."[27] Varying understandings of this tendency of capital to dissipate or implode as a result of the increasing share of systemic entropy propelled Marxian political economy far into the future. For a more nuanced understanding of the entropic tendencies within capitalism, I turn now to a Marxist-feminist analysis of one of these capitalist crises—the 1973 energy crisis.

THE WORK/ENERGY CRISIS AND ENTROPIC LABOR

Beginning in the mid-1960s, a gradual decline in the overall rate of profit in the United States culminated in a period of political economic crisis brought on, as many then argued, by the success of OPEC (Organization of Petroleum Exporting Countries) in tightening the world supply of oil and inducing a drastic increase in energy prices worldwide. Generally, OPEC was seen as the culprit in energy inflation and economic recession. Yet some Marxist political economists have suggested a different history of the energy crisis, part of it drawn from the pages of nineteenth-century thermodynamics, namely, that the energy crisis of 1973 and onward was, properly speaking, a labor crisis. As George Caffentzis and other members of the Midnight Notes Collective argued over the years following the crisis, the calculable relationship of work (here understood as expanded productive/reproductive labor) to energy (understood as financial capital that supplants competitive capital) was "from capital's point of view . . . a more generalized form of the exploitation (profit) rate."[28] Out of capital's struggle against rising social costs and declining profits, the so-called energy crisis, or work/energy crisis, was born.

Why a *work*/energy crisis? By 1970, the Keynesian-Fordist regulation of the U.S. economy had all but broken down. After 1945, one could already begin to see an unhinging from value productivity of a mass-socialized labor force traditionally centered in the home, factory, and school and typified by the socialization of a capitalist work/family ethic, on the one hand, and a broadly trade unionist class discipline, on the other. The orderly transformation of labor power into work conceived under Keynesian-Fordist regulation depended on the continually expanded social reproduction of labor. Emphasizing the importance of the sexual/reproductive nexus, Caffentzis explained how the figure of the housewife assumed an increasing importance in Keynesian-Fordist calculations of social reproduction—not merely as consumer but also as a producer of labor itself. The latter, according to Caffentzis, required capitalizing the home itself.

With such an analysis, carefully noting the crossing political-economic lines of socialized production and reproduction, it is possible to see what would become a serious challenge to capital in the postwar period, requiring it both to overcome its limits in neoliberalism and the challenge to its reproduction in broadly sexual, racial, and ideologico-affective terms. It is also possible in this conjuncture to see how the invasion of entropic energy, energy not available to work, began to pressure capitalist class strategy and put the latter, as Marx had suggested it would, into crisis mode. This time, however, it would be the reproductive forces of labor, and the domain of social reproduction more generally, that would force the crisis. As Caffentzis put it:

> In the period from the late 1960s to the mid-1970s the mesh began to tear. Divorce, for example, accelerated with the wage, which revealed a new tension between the poles of the Keynesian synthesis. . . . They were "boom"

years, but not for capital. Not only did the struggle in the factories, homes and streets force capital to pay more for factory work; increasingly, capital had to pay, through the state, *directly* for reproduction work that had previously come financed via the male, factory wage. Women and young people would no more "naturally" do what they used to do under the direction of husband and daddy. Thus, though there was an enormous increase of energy generated by the working class during that period, it proved especially resistant to the transformation into work. There was a precipitous drop in the work/energy ratio; this was translated into a "profits crisis" and a subversion of the axioms of Keynesianism.[29]

Pushing the limits of the Fordist factory-home/production-consumption cycle, the working class in the United States, parts of Europe, and Latin America increasingly forced capital, largely though not exclusively through struggles directed at the state, to guarantee more and more of its subsistence, to the point of forcing abstractly a rupture in capital's configuration of profit as productivity. The multinational capitalist response to this resistance to the transformation of energy into work was to change the ratio of energy prices to other prices, including wages, and thereby redirect the composition of labor and the work/profits crisis. That is, to "centralize the accumulation process" while "decentralizing the exploitation process."[30] There was a correspondence, then, between deindustrialization in the United States and Europe—signaled by the rise of the information, energy, and service sectors—and the increase of women in development and women worker–centered offshore assembly and export processing strategies in the becoming global South. And each of these ultimately corresponded to the rise in energy prices.

In the slow but growing transfer of work from one sector and geographic region to another, a new idea arose for the cadres of multinational capitalism—prompted in part by the dispersed social and sexual struggles of the 1960s, as well as by the decline of profits in the early 1970s: everyone (who was on the power grid at least), working everywhere (again, within the limits of the world market), would have to pay for (the higher price of) energy, that is to say, for the apparent loss of value in the leading sectors and regions of the international economy.[31]

The success of the U.S. and European working classes in forcing more surplus profit for themselves through struggles for the social or political wage (pensions, health care, housing, welfare, child care, education, mass transit, etc.) forced capital to increase basic commodity prices (energy in particular) and simultaneously intensify absolute surplus-value extraction in newly industrializing zones of the globe (by extending working hours in industrial production, as often today through home-based production and outsourcing as in Marx's day). In other words, there was a shift of value production from so-called high organic composition industries such as oil (where labor costs are comparatively low) to the low organic, labor-intensive sectors such as clothing manufacture, tourism, for-profit education, health, and other care sectors in increasingly valuable world regions and zones.[32] The rise in oil prices, thus, did not signify increased profits in the oil industry. Higher oil prices were instead a direct response to the profit crisis (i.e., the crisis in value extraction) in the imbalanced, post-Fordist economies of the global North. Value, in other words, was being shifted around, both between sectors with lower and higher concentrations of labor and between places in the international division of labor with lower and higher waged workforces, both at the top and at the bottom.

With value unhinging itself from productivity in regions with higher densities of high organic composition industries (North America, Western Europe, the oil fields of the Middle East), the struggle over profits would be thrown back partly to labor time as measure of value in the developing world, as well as (if not more) to the structural adjustment of the latter economies by the World Bank, International Monetary Fund (IMF), and other multinational capitalist hustlers in search of profit via privatization, international debt, and the creation of easily expendable, low-wage, female-centered industrial and domestic labor forces. In the decades following the oil shock, energy prices would eventually settle down; however, real average wages would not go up for another twenty-five years in the United States, and then only slightly. In this view, capital's oil price shock to the system was indeed its powerful rejoinder to the social struggles of the 1960s. In the twenty or so years after 1973, as Juliet Schor, Pietro Basso, and others have documented for the United States and Europe, wageworkers (in particular waged women workers) would work more wage hours than they ever did in the Fordist era—and earn less over time for it.[33] Productivity—the linchpin of the U.S. postwar economic equilibrium—would increasingly be imported as a result of longer and longer global commodity chains.

What the Midnight Notes analysis makes particularly clear is that for the energy price rise to succeed, surplus value had to be shifted from the high-organic to the low-organic sectors. This transformation required the "creation of a new figure of exploitation": the twenty-four-hour, social factory woman. And while the political arrival of this figure was at first reduced to women's challenges to patriarchy ("the fights, the visits to the therapist, the affairs, the divorce, the welfare line, the service sector job"), there also were implications for capital's claims on future labor.[34]

Women's revolt against patriarchal oppression at home and in society, and the consequent demands for free and equal participation in the wage-labor market, presented a shock to capital on one level (with the rupturing of the male wage as a regulatory gauge of the thermodynamic economy), but an opening on another, with an extension of exploitation, supplemented by patriarchal controls, in the increasingly privatized and precarious workplace. In Caffentzis's analysis, the work/energy crisis is centered as much on reproduction as production. Both in terms of housework's commodification ("only when women struggle against this unwaged work does it become a commodity") and in terms of the entropic energy of domestic labor ("the woman refuses her place in unwaged housework, at a time of energy shortage"),[35] there remains for capital the problem of self-reproduction, of the labor power necessary to make other labor power available for work. If, as Marx claimed (and multinational capitalists appeared to be confirming in practice), value could only be produced through the exploitation of human labor power (with its capacity of refusal) and, more important, if the capitalist system depended on this source of value for its ongoing reproduction, then who or what (by way of force, including conceptual metaphor) would produce this originating labor power?

Capital's reproduction, because it is not ever autoreproductive (at least according to thermodynamic Marxism), needs to appropriate freely the forces of nature that precede the transformation of labor power into profit in order to perpetuate. Like some Marxist feminists, more ecologically minded Marxists have sought in recent decades to note a contradiction in Marx's thought on the contribution of the "free gift of Nature" to value production. However, to paraphrase Paul Burkett on this point, rather than a contradiction in Marx's thought, there is a contradiction in capitalism rooted in its appropriation of natural resources and processes (including what Marx considered naturalized forces such as domestic labor) to speed the rate of reproduction and lower the costs of exploitation.[36] Thus, ideologically, capitalism needs to make a claim on *future* natural resources and reproductive labor (more and more via biotechnology, waged home-based work, as well as the commodification of affective labor), especially when that labor in particular produces resistance, loss, decay, waste, and dissipation within the patriarchal order. Thermodynamic capitalism, in the European and American social factory of the 1960s and 1970s, therefore needed to somehow transform or eliminate those entropic labor forces whose energy could not be put to work—the recalcitrant shift workers, the unhappy housewives, the social deviants, the rebellious colonials, and so on. I say "transform" because not all entropic energy is unproductive (and can be shifted around between more and less entropic sectors of labor); "eliminate" because some sectors (i.e., armed or revolutionary social movements of workers, peasants, the oppressed) are so destabilizing that they represent a threat to the vitality of the system. Capital's productive effort, as Caffentzis saw it, was to shift the low entropic sectors and wastes around in order to get *some* work out of them (housework, child care, prostitution, prison industry, toxic cleanup) and to eliminate the highest entropic sectors and wastes (oppressed nationality militants in the First World and anti-imperialists within the Third World) to the extent that this was possible.

However, waste/heat death—and woman, in this conceptual place of destructive excess and loss—is again made useful by capital, albeit differently from before. Keeping with Marx, it is important to reiterate that capital does not flourish automatically. Entropic labor is launched into exchange, differently and more precariously than before, requiring ever more contingent developments on the part of specifically capitalist sociality. The mechanisms of the movement and control of labor power subjectively unavailable for work in capital-productive exchange, become, in this period, as important as exchange itself. In this frame, the "woman worker," less ghostly than before, nevertheless appears now in a metaphorical (and technoscientific) place of excess. Capital cannot appropriate her labor so freely—but it still manages to make abundant use of its excess. How?

FROM THERMODYNAMICS TO TECHNOSCIENTIFIC CONTROL

Thirty years in the wake of the work/energy crisis, the expansion and intensification of thermodynamic capitalism has prompted revisions of the labor-entropy thesis. At the beginning of the twenty-first century, a reformulation of thermodynamic capitalism via developments in cybernetics and biotechnology has marked capitalist sociality as a radically modulated configuration of labor and human bodies. In "Heat Death," Luciana Parisi and Luciana Terranova theorize the evolutionary movement within capitalism from one crisis to another as the progressive transformation of entropic labor into productive-reproductive forces of capital. Following in the tracks of Gilles Deleuze's interpretation of Marx, they draw a positive, nondialectical connection between the threat of the invasion of entropy and the expansive, social reproduction of capital.[37]

Where Caffentzis theorized a thoroughly antagonistic movement between multinational capitalists and the feminist-fueled forces of reproductive social labor, Parisi and Terranova theorize the emergence of turbulent flows of female labor whose diverse and infinite capacities for social reproduction have become the starting points for technoscientific development and the broad transformation of the disciplinary society of the Fordist-Keynesian era into a "society of control." In these terms, entropic death no longer marks the point of exhaustion that must be rechanneled into reproductive lineage. "Death is now stretched. . . . The female body therefore appears as no longer enclosed into the organism and limited exclusively to reproductive sex (meiotic sex). It is no longer exclusively defined by exchange, but by *circulation*."[38] Drawing on late-twentieth-century developments of technoscience, cybernetics, and social theory, Parisi and Terranova find that far from seeking the preservation of the female laboring body for the sake of homeostatic equilibrium, capitalism and its allied technosciences of social bioengineering and control have sought, and must contend with, the radical dispersal and displacement of the female laboring body. Paraphrasing the seventeenth-century philosopher Baruch Spinoza, they argue that the capacities of this body are never finally known. They are in a continuous state of flux and flows. The grounding metaphors of machine, organism, and subject for the human body, so important in the thermodynamic conception of capitalism, are literally washed away by the complex flows of preindividual force and artificial life-time emerging in the political economic era of structural adjustment.

Indeed, Parisi and Terranova refer throughout "Heat Death" to genetic engineering, artificial life, and the technoscientific movement toward unpredictability and risk as particular hallmarks of global financialization. Capital's corresponding need for global management and control reorders and revises fiscal discipline (e.g., structural adjustment and privatization). Fiscal discipline is accompanied, or accomplished, by myriad movements away from the disciplinary modes theorized by Michel Foucault, among others. The outcome of the capitalist financialization and privatization of natural resources, transportation, and health sectors in the global South has been tremendous economic disorder and chaos—not the opposite, as neoliberal apologists claim. In this respect, entropy is being partially reabsorbed by turbulence. Viewing this movement in a somewhat different context, the *strategic* effort for capital may be less to manage through deferment and pollution credits the crisis of global warming than to mine for energy in the ocean depths of life itself (although it should be acknowledged that both strategies are presently being pursued).

The political-economic shifts from discipline to control, from entropy to turbulent flows, are informed by the twentieth-century passage of capitalism and political economy through, among other major influences, cybernetics. Most important for theorizing the social are the successive waves of cybernetic theory that have transformed the understanding of entropy from the thermo-dynamic principle of heat death into a positive identification with informa-tion.[39] Noise, uncertainty, death, resistance—all have become productive in ways that the closed-system theorists of thermodynamics could not account for. By the 1990s, the cultural and political struggles of the 1960s and 1970s had been more or less fully recuperated in the United States and Europe. Capital found ways to devalue resistance—and in some instances equate resistance with value itself. Capital's global scale, now a more or less open system from the standpoint of physics, positions it to process resistance (increasingly through rapid computation and the mobilization of financial flows) as *information*, rather than as an entropic threat to the system. In political-economic terms, the postthermodynamic shift, with entropy recoded through the principles of cybernetics and information theory, poses, "rather than an ultimate collapse of the universe[,] . . . an indefinite and discontinuous process of production, where nothing gets lost or wasted, but everything becomes useful."[40] The differences between this conceptualization and zero-work (or the organized refusal to work) appear considerable, and yet not entirely incommensurable.

The implications of such a shift are important for labor and gender studies, as much as for labor organizing and feminist social movement. In thermo-dyamic capitalism, the apparatuses of society required a body that could be disciplined in order to manage the inevitable entropy of its value-producing labor. At times, Marx theorized a thermodynamic capitalism moving steadily toward its own collapse, with the revolutionary energies of entropic labor bursting out into political crisis and social paroxysm, a disorder that capital-ism would ultimately be unable to contain or put to use.[41] By the latter part of the twentieth century, Marxist feminists theorized the possibility that capi-talism and its technoscientific forces would seek to overcome the limits posed by entropic labor not merely through the expansion of the world market, that is, by shifting value production from high to low entropic sectors, but also through the reorganization of reproductive labor in such a way that it would ward off the entropic excesses posed by the successful demands for national liberation, sexual liberation, and the social wage. But the rethinking of en-tropic labor proposed by Parisi and Terranova supplements this analysis with a theory of a fluid human body and extended social organism. In so doing, it exposes the microlevels of social organization to see the intensification of capital's efforts to recode labor and revise its own strategy for social control.

For Marxists and Marxist feminists, the laboring body—the racialized female body, in particular—has been the placeholder for both value and subjectivity in capitalist sociality. In the social thermodynamics of the work/energy crisis, the identification of woman with reproductive labor offered a way to see the emergence of a new figure of anticapitalist entropic labor. In the post-thermodynamic state between order and disorder, however, one sees not so much a subjective identification as a kind of kinship, a biodiversity of sexual and familial relations, between turbulence (as the emergence of a paradigm of flows and controls of vastly differentiated labor energies and forces that seeks only its own infinite social reproduction) and the global (female) worker, for example. Thus while Marxist feminists have argued that capital's strategy is premised on the claim on future reproductive labor, some theorists are pointing to the prospect of capital's no longer registering (that is, not registering in the same way or places) whether labor does or does not recognize capital's claim on its self or its futurity, much as petty commodity producers (*capitalists* is not the right term historically or politically) did not recognize the claims on their future by a feudal aristocracy in the early modern period.

Given such a thought, strategies of capitalist state control, as well as approaches to organizing reproductive labor/energy, do appear turbulent. Where entropy spelled universal heat death, turbulence spells the indefinite production of increasingly simulated life. Thus, on the shaky ground of the division of reproductive labor/energy, wage labor no longer describes every form of value production—even as most labor, particularly in the service-based capitalist economies, becomes either directly or indirectly waged. The flows of female labor in the bodily mode (e.g., productivity increases imported into the United States from China) and reproductive energy (e.g., experimentations with bio-materialization and artificial life) emerge as new sources of valorization, as well as as new sites of control for global-nationalist class governmentality. Confronted with these (precapitalist and emerging) needs for primitive accumulation and free appropriation of forces of nature (including the ghostly "woman worker" and life itself in today's biotech laboratories), how are we to theorize the circumvention, if that is the right word, of the shifting needs of the capitalist class for the theft of nature and the treasuring of nature's "free" gifts?

Missing in this question are the interactions undoubtedly occurring between the old entropic and the new turbulent flows of labor, as well as, in a different way, between the remnants and new configurations of thermodynamic capitalism and the emerging forms of cybernetic capitalism—that is, the ongoing international division of labor and energy. Surplus value in the old thermodynamic sense is still being extracted, particularly at the ends and along the edges of the long global commodity chains that home-based labor studies, for one, document.[42] But the difference between home-based work at the bottom and home-based work at the top remains important as capitalism demands disciplined female labor forces in the short run and controlled reproductive labor/energy in the long run. Home-based work, sexual reproduction, education, and child rearing—all with affinities to female labor and reproductive flows—are not the same everywhere one finds them. Thus I am arguing that to think of ways in which affective labor in the woman-worker mode is potentially nurturing the (bio)political is a good deconstructive move if it is supplemented with a Marxist- and feminist-informed ethics of post-thermodynamic class power. In this context, one could cite diverse movements such as the women-led protection of oil and water commons in Africa and Latin America, the formation of home-based and street-based women worker unions and cooperatives in Asia, the contestation over state-subsidized care industries in the United States and Europe, and indeed, the fight for inclusion of housewives in the new constitution of Venezuela. Yet how these are rendered visible and invisible—how, in short, they remain ghostly or not—is a deconstructive question that remains lodged, as Marx indicated, as much in an ethical approach to political economy as in today's new (bio)machinery.

WHEN ISN'T ENERGY WORK? THE EXCESSIVE GIFT OF TIME

In the *Accursed Share*, the surrealist philosopher Georges Bataille's two-volume work on economics, eroticism and sovereignty, Bataille proposed a novel categorization within political economy. In what he termed the "restrictive economy," the form taken by capitalist political economy, for example, the primary interests constitute the limited ends of production and consumption: exchange, utility, scarcity, and above all, profit. To this Bataille opposed the "general economy," where the interest or stake is what he termed "pure expenditure," that is, the unreserved use and dissipation of wealth and energy. The radical implications of this difference for critical political economy become more apparent as one understands how closely related Bataille's thought was to seminal developments in social theory. Indeed, Bataille's notion of the general economy directly applies the second law of thermodynamics to political economy—and explodes it. "On the surface of the globe," he wrote, "for *living matter in general*, energy is always in excess . . . the question is always posed in terms of extravagance. The choice is limited to how the wealth is to be squandered."[43] Emphasis on such a choice may put an orthodox Marxism, or even Marxist feminism, in a difficult starting position for analyzing class power. Bataille was certainly sympathetic to Marxism in the *Accursed Share*, which is important for understanding what follows.[44] And while the complexities of Bataille's argument should not be reduced merely to a deconstructive gesture, here, interested in signaling a resource for future thought, I am forced to condense his argument considerably.[45]

In the restrictive economy, one is operating on the plane of traditional political economic approaches to capitalism, where surplus production, investment, and consumption are well understood (by capitalists and Marxists alike). With the notion of the general economy, we are led to consider what this frame is leaving out—much as Marx had done in the nineteenth century. Unlike Marx, however, for Bataille the site of exposure of capitalist political economy is not ultimately (or even to start with) the commodity fetishism that conceals the theft of labor power and time. Rather, Bataille begins with the obverse sites of theft—that is, he begins with sites that inscribe the "social metabolism" (see Marx) of contemporary capitalism: gift, sacrifice, potlatch, war, alms, philanthropy, debt, and the like.

For Bataille energy is always in excess, and the ultimate question or problem is how the excess is to be dissipated. The capitalist, or restricted, economy is primarily concerned with the increase or decrease of labor and capital, that is, with the reified inputs and outputs that add up to profit and loss, equilibria and disequilibria. What Bataille proposed by way of the general economy is that the economy is complicated by its excess energy, by entropy, and that the dissipation of the excess is never simply a question of achieving equilibrium (war being the classic case of pure, disequilibrating expenditure), but rather an ethical and political question of sovereignty. Bataille cannily theorized that the excesses of the economy must be dissipated "without reserve," that is, with unlimited and ambivalent ends: "If a part of wealth (subject to a rough estimate) is doomed to destruction or at least to unproductive use without any possible profit, it is logical, even *inescapable*, to surrender commodities without return."[46] This understanding of the genesis of the gift, while moving in intriguing ways within the sociological tradition, is also infused with an intuition of the ontological limits posed by thermodynamics. Such a perspective puts us, on balance, a step closer to the cybernetic recoding of entropy accomplished in the years just following the writing of the *Accursed Share*: pure dissipation or loss of energy requires in turn a loss of signification—an unreturnable gift—and a formative ambivalence in the economy itself.[47]

In the general economy, the gift-without-return, the violent destruction of wealth, and philanthropy all launch exchange in one way or another. In this respect, the forms of the general economy precede the subject of labor or capital. Pure expenditure shifts the ground of the narrowly conceived political economy. What happens, for instance, when class analysis begins not from asking how labor is opposed to capital, but from how the dissipation of the excesses of wealth, energy, and work in a given economy are being used to manage, divert, or mitigate class, race, and gender antagonisms? How is pure expenditure being used to militate against the political resistance to neoliberalism (as is the case with much military and police expenditure today)? How is the pure expenditure of wealth—for example, liberal philanthropy—being used to underwrite class hegemony?

To put it another way, if the ambivalent future of the nonproductive expenditure retains altogether different information (including turbulence) about labor, even as it continually launches exchange, including the most powerful forms of capitalist exchange, might critical political economy at the start of the twenty-first century likewise be shifted by the practical politics presented by the ambivalence of the (entropic) gift or pure expenditure of wealth?

The gift, in a general economic sense, has always underwritten power, sovereignty, or mana, much as it underwrites hybrid and neoliberal capitalisms today.[48] Recalling Negri's reading of *Grundrisse*, capital's claims on future labor are "constituted *gratuitously*, by the totality of social labor"—including social reproductive labor.[49] I am arguing that it would be an underestimation to read this abstractly or metaphorically—even as most Marxists, in all correctness, continue to emphasize capitalism's theft rather than labor's gift. George Gilder, the high priest of supply-side economics and the Reagan counter-revolution, in his (at the time influential) *Wealth and Poverty*, interpreted "giving without return" as, on the one hand, capitalist investment, and on the other, the "x-factor" of productivity—"the metaphysics of freedom and creativity." The danger to contemporary capitalism, he wrote at the start of the era of structural adjustment in the United States, "lies not chiefly in a deterioration of physical capital, but in a persistent subversion of the psychological means of production—the morale and inspiration of economic man—undermining the very conscience of capitalism: the awareness that one must give in order to get, supply in order to demand."[50]

I write this in partial awareness of Gilder's more recent status as a guru for the new economy of broadband and information technology. But in 1981, he juxtaposed socialism, where planned expenditure begets egalitarianism ("from each according to ability"), to unfettered capitalism, where giving begets capital. On the other hand (and unsurprisingly), for Gilder and other notables among today's capitalist metaphysicians, "egalitarianism in the economy tends to promote greed over giving." Precisely the heart of liberalist ethics! Here, the second half of the *Communist Manifesto* mantra, "to each according to need," is subverted for the sake of the x-factor of the gift economy—and a complementary ethics of free appropriation of unpaid labor—preliminary to the extraction of surplus value. Capital's claim on future labor, this reading makes abundantly clear, is all about the treasuring of the turbulent gift.[51]

Bataille references the observations on gift and ritual economies of his contemporaries Marcel Mauss and Claude Lévi-Strauss, whose writings gave rise to well-known schools of sociological thought. To briefly recap these, Mauss interpreted the gift (in the narrow sense) as an elemental form of a total social system of exchange. The phenomenology of the gift could be seen in the way its spirit always brought it back to the giver. Lévi-Strauss took this several steps further: the gift produced an obligatory countergift as a function of the unconscious collective-symbolic exchange of everything from language to marriage partners to, most famously, women.

So what are the protocols of an analysis of the general economy, of giving in particular, for class analysis? The expansion of the textuality of value, which Gayatri Chakravorty Spivak suggests deconstructive Marxist feminists be attentive to, not only must account for the interruption of the gift economy through the genealogical remembering of the valorization of reproductive (including domestic) labor. It also must take into account the subjection (including the desubjectification) of the race- and sex-divided global-local, home-based woman worker (among others). In other words, it would be necessary that workers, when demanding equality of treatment with other legally constituted laboring subjects, also remember the biopolitical valence, the ambivalence, of housework (including, for example, the care of their own children). As low-wage homeworkers, domestic laborers, and similarly situated workers are made more visible through organizing and exposure of all kinds, one can begin to see the intricate governmental relations of social and sexual reproduction on a global scale.[52] And who or what will organize (or counterorganize) those expanded forces of reproduction? The gift economy text itself does not respond to these questions, for the most part. And if these questions are passed over in silence, what, once again, is being given over gratuitously?

In partial response to some of these problems, I turn to Jacques Derrida's reflection on the gift, confining myself for the most part to Derrida's gloss on Mauss in *Given Time*. In what is perhaps a familiar theoretical move for his readers, Derrida holds up the gift—takes it hostage as it were—as the figure (or experience) of the impossible. The experience of the impossible is a theoretical and ethical aporia: an erasure of Being through which one nevertheless passes.[53] In the Derridean aporia, that is, in the experience of the impossible, the loss of metaphysical grounding occurs in complementary relation with the undecidable. The importance of this in terms of the economy of the gift, for Derrida, is that it carries the added weight of an ethical relationship rooted in a kind of justice where, as Elizabeth Grosz points out, one must first do violence in order to do justice.

Derrida's reflections on Mauss's analysis shift the gift not so subtly from the restrictive economic space of a certain kind of productive agency to the general economy. "On the one hand," Derrida writes, "Mauss reminds us that there is no gift without bond, without bind, without obligation or ligature; but on the other hand, there is no gift that does not have to untie itself from obligation, from debt, contract, exchange, and thus from the bind."[54] Derrida's fascination with the disappearance, the inexorable loss or escape, of the thing itself causes him to question repeatedly the exacting nature of the (pre)social relation that, in the case of the gift, resides in the loss of any property of the gift as a thing itself. The condition of the gift, for Derrida, as for Mauss in a less emphatic way, is the condition of forgetting that the gift is a gift. "Forget it," says the giver to the recipient, who must already have forgotten the giving for the gift to *be* at all.[55]

Derrida transports us in this characteristic manner to Martin Heidegger, specifically to the paradigmatic thought of "es gibt." "Es gibt," which one might translate as "giving without giving," or "giving without reserve" (in Bataille's general economic sense), is a thought analogous to what, in other essays, Derrida terms the presencing effects of *ousia* [being, property].[56] The gift itself escapes and flows—as the condition of forgetting of "es gibt": "The gift must not even appear or signify, consciously or unconsciously, *as* gift for the donors, whether individual or collective subjects. From the moment the gift would appear as gift . . . it would be engaged in a symbolic, sacrificial, or economic structure that would annul the gift in the ritual circle of the debt."[57]

To give a gift already requires, in itself, a duty (a debt, an ought, structured as *is*), *not* to return the gift (including, as well, not to give or return excessively). For Lévi-Strauss, the solution to this dilemma, the formation of the debt-bond structure, was to reconstitute the gift according to the laws of the unconscious, as being in the symbolic social order of the gift relation (which itself was Mauss's gift to sociology, and possibly his own debt to Émile Durkheim). Derrida's solution, by way of Heidegger, is to "pre-pone" the gift before the exchange of symbols and signs—linguistic, unconscious, or other—that is, to trace the originary structure of the gift, as well as the force or forces that ground it in Being itself. Such an analysis presupposes, like much other post-structuralist thought of the present era, at least a partial movement prior to the constitution, or even the possibility, of a subject of giving or exchange. "One would be tempted to say," Derrida writes, "that a subject as such never gives or receives a gift. It is constituted, on the contrary, in view of dominating, through calculation and exchange, the mastery of this hubris or of this impossibility that is announced in the promise of the gift."[58] The subject of the gift does not exist as such, but rather exists as an effect, a momentary arrest of the gift, serving to underscore the importance of the gift and giving for a more general movement of subjectivation, that is to say, the originary importance of the circulation of the gift in thought about the subject.

With Mauss, who saw in the originary importance of the gift a total social phenomenon, the gift had neither the structural unconscious effect theorized by Lévi-Strauss nor the movement of presubjective displacement given it by Derrida.[59] Mauss's gift was, as Derrida notes, as much a *name* for the object of gift exchange as the splitting of itself from exchange, that is, the gift's differentiation from calculated, rational economic exchange and its consequent phenomenological stature as an object of countereconomistic social fact—and thus, as I am suggesting, another source of controlled, biopolitical value.

The continuous, and typically violent, displacement of the gift that Derrida pursues has been interpreted by some as antagonistic with the tradition of Maussian gift scholarship.[60] Rather than antagonism, I would surmise, Derrida proposes a momentary departure from tradition in order precisely to acknowledge the possibility of violence in the tradition itself: not to destroy or annul, but to maintain the gift, still repressed, as the social mediating experience of the impossible—of both zero-work and nonwork, if you will: "Even if the gift were never anything but a simulacrum, one must still *render an account* of the possibility of this simulacrum and of the desire that impels towards this simulacrum."[61] The obligation to give, even, or especially, in the account of giving, is the *unheimliche* [uncanny] experience of the impossible, of ambivalence, and indeed, of turbulence.

I make this final point with the following argument in mind: that capital is accumulating in the domain of affect, socializing capacities for living. As we have seen, although it is not new, this socialization is more virtual and massive than ever. Continuing with *Given Time*, what one gets specifically is an account of charitable giving that poses the ethical question of giving in terms of the secret of time. In an abridged version of the argument he makes in *Specters of Marx*, Derrida speculates in *Given Time* that the obligation to pay the debt to capital is presented as the obligation "to give time." But how is this possible? Time, Derrida considers, is the only thing that cannot be given, precisely because it cannot be possessed—it cannot *be*. Time thus fulfills the deconstructive criteria of giving—that is, the "es gibt" that does not demand repayment or create a debt: "If there is something that can in no case be given, it is time, since it is nothing and since in any case it does not properly belong to anyone; if certain persons or certain social classes have more time than others—and this is finally the most serious stake of political economy—it is certainly not *time itself* that they possess."[62]

In Derrida's hands, the gift gives time, or according to Elizabeth Grosz, "the gift gives a possible future, a temporality in excess of the present and never contained within its horizon, the temporality of endless iteration."[63] In the Marxist feminist text, as we have seen, it is tempting to get caught up in the thought structure of a duty to repay debt in acknowledgment of a claim on future reproductive labor. But this is not giving as such. Reflecting on woman's sexual labor in global-local debt bondage, Gayatri Spivak has remarked that, supplemented with male exploitation, "internalized gendering perceived as ethical choice is the hardest roadblock for women the world over."[64] This inspires a more extended analysis of time in the circulation of the gift as biopolitical affect than I can hope to accomplish here; however, a few short reflections are possible.

In discussing the relationship of the gift to calculability and rationality, Derrida writes that the gift, "if there is any, does not even belong to practical reason. . . . It *should* surpass *duty* itself: duty beyond duty."[65] I choose Derrida's deconstruction of the gift because it bears a more or less equivalent (though by no means similar) load as Bataille's principle of expenditure without return. Each offers a slightly different framing of the gift as the necessary iteration of a different kind of economy altogether: forgotten, invisible, hidden, secret, ghostly, infinite, double, obverse. The time that is given, the ghostly, incalculable time of reproductive labor, for instance, must be expended and cannot be returned. It is informative, in the cybernetic sense of entropy. It is always available, and when it is not—for example, when it is refused—it flows into other reaches of the general economy, including commodification, but also social and political networks, and as we are reminded by Negri and Hardt, into life itself.

In commodities and networks, reproductive labor is not exactly what it was before in the system. In this sense, the giving of reproductive labor time cannot be organized for capitalism to function just so. And yet we know it will have been. This double bind or aporia brings us back to the issues of valorization and control in the affect economy that autonomist Marxists and Marxist feminists are exploring (somewhat differently) today. What I am arguing, by way of Derrida and Bataille, is that any response to the question of how reproductive labor must appear in the affect economy must also appear to be deontological, to be answered in terms of duty beyond duty. This might mean considering in ethico-political terms the sheer quantity of women's work—especially what does not currently count—as a temporary means of banishing its ghost. The ethical duty or responsibility implicit in child care cannot be measured, or estimated, or valorized as such—although the time of child care can. We can see the latter in the 1999 rewriting of the constitution of Venezuela, in the prolific rise of time-use studies of housework and other forms of traditional women's work in South and Southeast Asia, and in commodified child-care provision around the world. Such "a transvaluation, an uncatastrophic implosion of the search for value via the circuit of productivity," to return to the citation by Spivak with which I started, should give contemporary biopoliticians openings to new kinds of political struggle and social theory.

Even more, the gifts of what I am calling reproductive life-time will undoubtedly keep giving, and attention to the turbulence and modulation of these gifts—in technoscience, in biopolitics and affective labor—remains paramount. Some, including possibly some socialist feminists, may see in all of this a revised nineteenth-century romanticism of domestic labor or essentialized femininity. Yet class struggle has always been overdetermined as population struggle, as whole ways of life, structures of feeling, and nowadays, as affect economy. Cultural studies have succeeded (rarely unproblematically) in transmapping and transfiguring Marxism in and throughout the overlaid critical-theoretical matrices of race, nation, sex, mobility, generation, gender, migration, and location—as well as in challenging the residual economism of restrictive Marxist political economies, precisely because of an (often fleeting) appreciation of this ghostly duty to give prior to and beyond the claim on future labor—that is to say, prior to and beyond the end of capitalism. Being responsible to the worker who labors to produce and reproduce the population gratuitously is not a romanticism, but a necessarily ambivalent class-cultural biopolitics that infuses the micro- and global-local politics of life itself in the twenty-first century.

NOTES

1. Karl Marx, *Capital: A Critique of Political Economy*, Vol. 1. New York: Vintage, 1977; Marx, *Grundrisse.* Trans. Martin Nicolaus. New York: Vintage, 1973.

2. Marx, *Grundrisse*, 263, 272.

3. See Harriet Fraad, Stephen Resnick, Richard Wolff, eds., *Bringing It All Back Home: Class, Gender, and Power in the Modern Household* (London: Pluto, 1994), for a sustained effort to analyze the displacement of gender into class.

4. See Nick Dyer-Witheford, *Cyber-Marx: Cycles and Circuits of Struggle in High*

Technology Capitalism (Urbana: University of Illinois Press, 2000), for an appreciative analysis of autonomist Marxist writings.

5. See Mario Tronti, *Operao e Capitale* (Turin: Einaudi, 1966). See also Red Notes, *Working Class Autonomy and the Crisis* (London: Red Notes and CSE, 1979).

6. Antonio Negri, *Revolution Retrieved: Selected Writings on Marx, Keynes, Capitalist Crisis, and New Social Subjects, 1967–83* (London: Red Notes, 1988), 219.

7. See Gayatri Chakravorty Spivak, "Scattered Speculations on Value," in *In Other Worlds: Essays in Cultural Politics* (New York: Methuen, 1987); 161–63; Antonio Negri, "Value and Affect," *Boundary 2* 26 (1999): 2.

8. Leopoldina Fortunati, *The Arcane of Reproduction: Housework, Prostitution, Labor, and Capital*, trans. Hilary Creek, ed. Jim Fleming (Brooklyn, NY: Autonomedia, 1995), 8. See also Marx, *Grundrisse*, 400. I agree with Fortunati when she refers to the productive disappearance of reproductive labor as the "line of value" (161). This must be supplemented with further recognition of the international division of (reproductive) labor value. Reproductive labor is not the same everywhere. Gayatri Spivak, who sees the "line of value" as a "multinational," or even, with much redaction, a "multicultural" enclosure, has discussed this point in various ways over many years. For a recent instance, see the chapter entitled "Culture" in Gayatri Chakravorty Spivak, *A Critique of Postcolonial Reason* (Cambridge, MA: Harvard University Press, 1999), 312–421.

9. Antonio Negri, *Marx beyond Marx: Lessons on the "Grundrisse,"* trans. Harry Cleaver, ed. Jim Fleming (Brooklyn, NY: Autonomedia, 1991), 86–87; emphasis added. See also Fortunati, *The Arcane of Reproduction*, 143–56.

10. Biotechnology and its key offshoot, biomaterialization, represent possibly the most powerful of the recent phase shifts in the biopolitical economy. Thanks to Patricia Clough for drawing my attention to this and recent works on the subject, especially Eugene Thacker, *The Global Genome: Biotechnology, Politics, and Culture* (Cambridge, MA: MIT Press, 2005).

11. Negri, "Value and Affect," 82; *Marx Beyond Marx*, 87.

12. Negri, "Value and Affect," 83.

13. Michael Hardt and Antonio Negri, *Empire* (Cambridge, MA: Harvard University Press, 2000), 292–93.

14. Maria Mies, *Patriarchy and Accumulation on a World Scale: Women in the International Division of Labour* (London: Zed Books, 1998), esp. 100–110.

15. For the thousands of small-scale capitalists roaming the globe in the service of large-scale capitalists, as well as their own profit, labor is literally everywhere, or when refused as such, "anyplace but here." For diverse instances of this, see Radhika Balakrishnan, ed., *The Hidden Global Assembly Line: Gender Dynamics of Subcontracted Work in a Global Economy* (Bloomfield, CT: Kumarian, 2002); David Staples, *No Place Like Home: Organizing Home-Based Labor in the Era of Structural Adjustment* (New York: Routledge, 2006).

16. There certainly will be disagreement over the politics resulting from this perspective, which might be more evident when presented with the utterly contrary view elaborated by Jeffrey Sachs that the billion or more inhabitants of the planet subsisting on less than one dollar a day must become waged in order for them and capitalism to survive. Such a view begs the question of how people actually are surviving on less than

a dollar a day—and what politics this mass survival may portend. See George Caffentzis, "Dr. Jeffrey Sachs' *The End of Poverty*: A Political Review," July 18, 2005, info.inter activist.net/article.pl?sid=05/07/19/0242219&mode=nested&tid=2.

17. See Negri, *Marx beyond Marx*, 69–70; Negri, "Value and Affect," 82. In an essay entitled "The Constitution of Time," Negri put it somewhat more bluntly: "Does this mean that Marx's theory of value and time should be put out to pasture? The answer is probably yes for a sizeable part of it. . . . For now we know that time cannot be presented as measure, but must rather be presented as the global phenomenological fabric, as base, substance and flow of production in its entirety." Antonio Negri, *Time for Revolution* (New York: Continuum, 2003), 29.

18. See Ursula Huws, *The Making of a Cybertariat: Virtual Work in a Real World* (New York: Monthly Review Press, 2003), especially chapter ten, for a discussion of these phases.

19. There is an abundant literature one could cite on the formations of biopower and biopolitics. See, among others, Jacques Donzelot, *The Policing of Families*, trans. Robert Hurley (Baltimore, MD: Johns Hopkins University Press, 1997); Barbara Ehrenreich and Deirdre English, *For Her Own Good: One Hundred and Fifty Years of the Experts' Advice to Women* (Garden City, NJ: Anchor, 1978); Michel Foucault, "Governmentality," *I and C* 6 (1979): 5–21; Dolores Hayden, *Redesigning the American Dream: The Future of Housing, Work, and Family Life* (New York: Norton, 1984); and Achille Mbembe, "Necropolitics," trans. Libby Meintjes, *Public Culture* 15.1 (2003): 11–40.

20. See Annette B. Weiner, *Inalienable Possessions: The Paradox of Keeping-While-Giving* (Berkeley: University of California Press, 1992); Negri, "Value and Affect," 79–80.

21. Gayatri Chakravorty Spivak, "Ghostwriting," *Diacritics* 25.2 (1995): 67.

22. There is a growing body of literature that documents these claims. See, for example, Barbara Ehrenreich and Arlie Russell Hochschild, eds. *Global Woman: Nannies, Maids, and Sex Workers in the New Economy* (New York: Metropolitan Books, 2003).

23. Hardt and Negri, *Empire*, 365.

24. Marx, *Grundrisse*, 105.

25. This law states, in short: energy can neither be created nor destroyed, only transferred; therefore the total amount of available energy in the universe is constant.

26. Anson Rabinbach, *The Human Motor: Energy, Fatigue, and the Origins of Modernity* (New York: Basic Books, 1990), 3.

27. Marx, *Grundrisse*, 749–50.

28. George Caffentzis, "The Work/Energy Crisis and the Apocalypse," in *Midnight Oil: Work, Energy, War, 1973-1992*, ed. Midnight Notes Collective (Brooklyn, NY: Autonomedia, 1992), 228.

29. Ibid., 232.

30. Without, however, leaving the terrain of the labor theory of value. Here we have to resort with Caffentzis to the other face of capitalist subjectivization—planetary domination, not to be confused with intraclass capitalist competition: "[Capital] no more rewards capitalists to the extent that they exploit than it rewards workers to the extent that they are exploited. There is no justice for anyone but itself." Ibid., 236.

31. The global energy price fix continues today in more and less heralded ways, for example, in the extreme natural and built environmental conditions of the 30 to 40 percent of the world's population who are off the power grid. See David Lipschultz, "Solar Power Is Reaching Where Wires Can't," *New York Times*, September 9, 2001.

32. The organic composition of a given industry refers to the ratio of fixed versus variable capital, or the value of the automation versus the value of the labor power employed. Caffentzis elsewhere discusses the 1980s era of debt-equity swaps and structural adjustment programs in Africa; one would also have to reference low-tech export-processing strategies in Latin America and Asia, and ultimately, international "house-wifization," Maria Mies's term for the material-ideological process of the exploitation of women's productive-reproductive labors. See George Caffentzis, "On Africa and Self-Reproducing Automata," in *New Enclosures*, ed. Midnight Notes Collective (Jamaica Plain, Mass.: Midnight Notes, 1990), 35–41; Maria Mies, *Patriarchy and Accumulation*, 114–27.

33. See Juliet Schor, *Overworked American: The Unexpected Decline of Leisure* (New York: Basic Books, 1993); Pietro Basso, *Modern times, Ancient Hours: Working Lives in the Twenty-first Century*, trans. and ed. Giacomo Donis (New York: Verso, 2003). One should recall that during the same period, industrial wages in Japan experienced a long rise. On the other side of the intensifying international division of labor during this period, a home-based child-care worker in the United States would come to make five to eight times more per day than a maquiladora worker in Central America, or just across the border in Mexico. Low organic composition industries such as child care and electronics assembly are analogous in some ways, but not necessarily comparable, given factors such as primitive accumulation, hemispheric indebtedness, and regionalism. For a greater sense of this, see Spivak, "Ghostwriting."

34. Caffentzis, "The Work/Energy Crisis and the Apocalypse," 249.

35. Ibid., 251.

36. Paul Burkett, "Nature's 'Free Gifts' and the Ecological Significance of Value," *Capital and Class* 68 (1999): 89–110.

37. Luciana Parisi and Tiziana Terranova, "Heat-Death: Emergence and Control in Genetic Engineering and Artificial Life," *CTheory*, 5, *www.ctheory.com/article/a84.html*.

38. Ibid., 1, emphasis added.

39. Patricia Clough clarifies this point in the introduction to this book.

40. Ibid., 10.

41. This is a local interpretation of Marx, to be sure. More open Marxisms would not posit or infer the revolutionary versus evolutionary perspective that I do here. The problem, for me, remains one of the differing speeds and scales of capitalism, as well as the capacities of Marx readers to note these differences.

42. For a representative sampling, see Eileen Boris and Elisabeth Prügl, eds., *Home-workers in Global Perspective: Invisible No More* (New York: Routledge, 1996).

43. Georges Bataille, *The Accursed Share*, vol. 1, trans. Robert Hurley (New York: Zone, 1991), 23; emphasis in original.

44. For insightful elaborations of this point, see John Hutnyk, *Bad Marxism: Capitalism and Cultural Studies* (London: Pluto, 2004), 155–82.

45. See Michele Richman's overall review of the relationship of Bataille's work on the gift to critical theory and deconstruction, *Reading Georges Bataille: Beyond the Gift* (Baltimore, MD: Johns Hopkins University Press, 1982). See also Jacques Derrida,

"From Restricted to General Economy: A Hegelianism without Reserve," in *Writing and Difference* (Chicago: University of Chicago Press, 1980), 251–77.

46. Bataille, *The Accursed Share*, 25.

47. With Gilles Deleuze, Patricia Clough sees in the technoscientific crossing from meaning to information one of the paradigmatic shifts from disciplinary to control society. Patricia Clough, "Future Matters: Technoscience, Global Politics, and Cultural Criticism," *Social Text* 80 (2004): 1–24. Following Derrida, Arkady Plotnitsky reads entropy as the loss of critical meaning. See Plotnitsky, *Reconfigurations: Critical Theory and General Economy* (Gainesville: University Press of Florida, 1993).

48. Mayfair Mei-hui Yang's study of Wenzhou province in China's fast-mutating general economy advances such an analysis. See "Putting Capitalism in Its Place," *Current Anthropology* 41.4 (2000): 477–510.

49. Antonio Negri. *Marx beyond Marx: Lessons on the "Grundrisse,"* trans. Harry Cleaver, ed. Jim Fleming. (Brooklyn, NY: Autonomedia, 1991), 87.

50. George Gilder, *Wealth and Poverty* (New York: Basic Books, 1981), 28.

51. Ibid., 30. For a critical reading of the gift economy in today's information technology societies, see Tiziana Terranova, *Network Culture: Politics for the Information Age* (London: Pluto, 2004).

52. Among those laboring in this vast and relatively unexplored corner of the global domestic economy, see Rhacel Salazar Parreñas, *Servants of Globalization: Women, Migration, and Domestic Work* (Stanford, CA: Stanford University Press, 2001), as well as Ehrenreich and Hochschild, *Global Woman.*

53. This has been understood by some as the experience of the double bind, or, in an early phrasing by one of Derrida's most critical and sympathetic readers in the United States, Gayatri Spivak, the experience of operating in the "structure that one cannot not wish to inhabit." See Gayatri Spivak, *Outside in the Teaching Machine* (New York: Routledge, 1993), esp. 5–6, 60.

54. Jacques Derrida, *Given Time*, trans. Peggy Kamuf (Chicago: University of Chicago Press, 1992), 23.

55. For Derrida, the force of forgetting as the condition of the gift lies not in the unconscious, however. In the unconscious, the gift would only be displaced in one way or another by repression, and hence un-forgotten. The gift would not be, would not exist, as such.

56. That is, the making present of giving without giving, of how what Being gives is present (in Heidegger's language: "What 'Being' means, which—It gives (*das—es gibt*); what 'time' means, which—It gives (*das—es gibt*)," quoted by Derrida, *Given Time*, 21.

57. Ibid., 23.

58. Ibid., 24.

59. Ibid., 31, 37–39. Although, as Derrida notes, it turns out that Mauss, too, was equally carried away by the violent destruction of wealth, the protodeconstruction of the gift as such, in the American potlatch observed by the French sociologist Georges Davy.

60. See David Graeber, *Toward an Anthropological Theory of Value: The False Coin of Our Own Dreams* (New York: Palgrave, 2001). Derrida's statement that "there is no longer any 'logic of the gift,'" may indeed be a reference to the work of Marxist anthropologist Maurice Godelier, who in turn takes a jab at Derrida in his *Enigma of the Gift*. I leave to others to judge the merits of such claims and counterclaims. See Derrida, *Given Time*, 24; Maurice Godelier, *The Enigma of the Gift*, 2d ed. (Chicago: University of Chicago Press, 1999).

61. Derrida, *Given Time*, 31.

62. Ibid., 28.

63. Elizabeth Grosz, "The *Time* of Violence: Deconstruction and Value," *College Literature* 26.1 (1999): 15.

64. Spivak, translator's preface, xxviii.

65. Derrida, *Given Time*, 156; emphasis in original.

VOICES FROM THE *TEUM*: SYNESTHETIC TRAUMA
AND THE GHOSTS OF THE KOREAN DIASPORA

GRACE M. CHO

To bear the imperative to survive . . . as the one who must tell
what it means to not see.
—Cathy Caruth, *Unclaimed Experience*

*Forgive me for not knowing about our history, but you wouldn't tell me
the truth about your life. Only once did I ask you why you were born in
the country that was not the one you called home. But you did not
answer me with words. You were quiet and stared straight ahead as if
there were something else in the room, something I could not yet see.
You never talked about the circumstances of your birth, or of mine, or
about any of the events that took place before I could witness them. And
I took for granted that the things you did say were true and that the
truth was available to you. Maybe you were too young to remember
what had happened before you began your life in Korea, and too broken
to remember what had happened after. Maybe you did not know to
question your relationship to the woman you called mother or the
woman you called sister. But you see, I began recording these events
that you do not talk about long before either of us knew what would
happen at 9:45. And then the steady repetition of the date activated my
memory. And I listened carefully to your speaking, and the gaps in
between, and the patterns of noise and silence. Always at the same time
every day, your voice sounding with the clock told me that something
happened at that time, or that something was about to happen. It is
only now that I have the capacity to read the information I've had
stored all these years. I am beginning to see these images of you sailing
on the water, not knowing that you were moving toward a future that
would silence you. Slowly I am beginning to see what you could not.*

I began searching for a history . . .

August 24, 1945, 5:20 PM: A Japanese naval vessel carrying ten thousand Korean passengers sails through calm waters off the coast of Japan. There is an explosion from the front half of the ship, which becomes engulfed in flames. Pieces of ship and bodies of passengers are propelled into the ocean by the force of the explosion. A few bodies cling to the deck but eventually fall away into the water as the vessel splits in two, each half descending into the ocean. The passengers locked below panic as the lower decks of the ship fill with water. Two lovers search for each other even as their bodies are carried against their will by currents stronger than their desperation. Only after the split ship is fully submerged is there calm once more, the water flecked with dead bodies and debris. It is silent at first, but then there are rumblings of life. A child's sobbing becomes audible. He is perched atop a floating fragment of the ship, and nearby a hand emerges from the water and reaches upward. It is the hand of the man who searched years for his lover, from whom he was separated after having been conscripted into the labor camps. He finally finds her aboard this ship—until they are separated once again by the disaster. The man and the little boy are the sole survivors of this event as it is rendered in the movie, sometimes called "the Korean Titanic."[1]

The North Korean film *Soul's Protest* melodramatically reenacts the story of the first shipload of Korean slaves that set sail for Korea from Japan on August 22, 1945. The film dramatizes the actual incident of August 24, 1945, when the *Ukishima Maru*, a Japanese naval vessel full of thousands of newly liberated Korean slaves, exploded off the coast of Maizuru, Japan, just nine days after the end of World War II. Weaving together memories of working in Japanese labor camps with the mundane occurrences of life on the *Ukishima Maru* as it sails toward Pusan harbor, the film not only narrates the atrocities of Japanese slavery made even more tragic by the deaths of thousands of Koreans on board the ship. It also expresses the Koreans' frustrated longing for freedom and a homeland. The film's depiction of a vessel split in two, rendering its passengers dead or separated from their loved ones, symbolizes the Koreans' return to a country already divided and occupied by external forces and soon to be decimated by war. The return home, however, is made impossible in the most literal sense.

It was the fate of those on board the Ukishima Maru *to never arrive in Korea.*

It must have been fate also that decided that you would not be on that first ship. The Japanese officials would wait to put you and your mother on the second ship, or maybe it was the third.[2] But in any case, not the first. You would not die that day in 1945.

.....

Much of *Soul's Protest* takes place over two days in August 1945 as the ship circles the waters between Korea and Japan, while the Koreans on board grow restless anticipating the freedom that awaits them in Korea. The ship circles the waters never reaching its purported destination, never returning the Koreans to their homeland. Instead, the plot of the film reveals the Japanese ship crew's plans to blow up the vessel with the Koreans on board.[3] One Korean character does witness this scheme, but because his tongue had been cut out during his days as a slave, he fails to speak at the very moment when speaking becomes most urgent. He must inform the others without the use of his tongue, through wild bodily gestures, grunts, and panicked eyes that warn of danger. Through his movements and sounds, the passengers decipher that the ship is about to explode, but it is too late to prevent the tragedy. The ship full of Koreans goes nowhere and eventually does explode. There are survivors of this disaster, however, like the little boy in the film who is too young to understand anything that has happened, who perhaps does not see anything, yet returns to the site of the sinking ship years later to tell the story.

Besides being a heavy-handed tale about the cruelty of Japanese colonizers, *Soul's Protest* can also be read as a story of being left homeless by a history one can never know with certainty, yet a history that longs to be spoken nonetheless. Although the film expresses a North Korean nostalgia for a homeland prior to its division whose unity could be measured against the Japanese suppression of national identity, the final images of a return never completed suggest that Koreans remain in a state of permanent dislocation. Despite the political and geographic divisions between the two Koreas, the making of the film, in concert with the lawsuits brought against the Japanese government by a group of South Korean survivors of the incident, shows the ways in which both halves are similarly unsettled by an obscured and uncertain history. Both *Soul's Protest* and the actual events on which the film is based raise questions about seeing, speaking, and surviving for the displaced subject.

.....

I began searching for a history. My own history. Because I had known all along that the stories I had heard were not true, and parts had been left out. I remember having this feeling growing up that I was haunted by something, that I was living within a family full of ghosts . . . There was this place that they knew about. I had never been there yet I had a memory for it. I could remember a time of great sadness before I was born. We had been moved. Uprooted . . . She tells the story of what she does not remember . . .[4]

.....

The *Ukishima Maru* tragedy had almost been forgotten in Korea, and was practically unknown in other parts of the world, but a series of events would unfold to bring the 1945 sinking of the fated vessel back to memory.

June 21, 2001: *Soul's Protest*, entitled *Sa-ra innun yong-hongdul* (literally, "living souls") in Korean, makes its international debut at a film festival in Moscow.

June 27, 2001: *Soul's Protest* opens at the Hong Kong Film Festival and is purchased by a Hong Kong film import company for distribution.

August 23, 2001: A Japanese judge makes a ruling in a lawsuit against the Japanese government for failing to provide safe transport for Korean forced laborers on board the *Ukishima Maru*. "The [Japanese] government contended that there was no employment relationship between the government and the Koreans that required the state to ensure their safety."[5] The court rules in favor of some of the plaintiffs and orders that the government pay a total of $375,000 to fifteen Korean survivors of the disaster. The other sixty-five plaintiffs are dismissed because they cannot prove that they were on the ship.

August 24, 2001: It is the fifty-sixth anniversary of the *Ukishima Maru* incident. South Korean protesters hold a memorial service for the victims and "urge Japan to take full responsibility" for the other sixty-five plaintiffs not awarded payment, to reopen an investigation into the cause of the explosion, and to give an official apology to the survivors and the victims' families.[6] Meanwhile, *Soul's Protest*, along with a Japanese film also commemorating the incident, is screened for the first time in Seoul.

August 24 and 25, 2001: Korean and Japanese newspapers report on the renewed controversy, casting doubt on official reports of what happened on

August 24, 1945. According to government records, "there were 4000 people on board . . . Korean sources speak of 7000, 7500 or even 10,000 passengers . . . The dead numbered 524 Koreans and 25 Japanese."[7] Korean groups claim that five thousand Koreans died, yet these victims do not exist in the official Japanese record. According to Japanese numbers, close to thirty-five hundred passengers should have survived, but only eighty Koreans have come forward as survivors in the lawsuit against the Japanese government. Sixty-five of their cases were dismissed "because their presence aboard the ship could not be confirmed."[8] Their survival, their existence, did not appear in official documents.

More controversial still are the discrepancies in the explanations of what caused the explosion: "The Japanese government claims that the ship hit a mine planted in Maizaru Harbor by U.S. forces. However, survivors remembered seeing Japanese sailors fleeing the ship in boats before it sank, which raised their suspicions that the Japanese blew up the ship themselves to get rid of Koreans who were witnesses to the heinous deeds the Japanese committed during the war."[9] Another report confirms that "data and collected information on the incident indicate that the explosion was a plot concocted by the Japanese military leadership in an attempt to destroy its dark records on and atrocities against those Korean victims and survivors."[10] Kim Chun Song, the director of *Soul's Protest*, claims that the film is historically accurate and that "a number of North Korean historians and researchers cooperated with the scenario writer in his effort to further probe into the historical fact and collect all the relevant information available before this half-documentary film was completed."[11] The *Korea Herald* reports that "the group [of plaintiffs] considers cooperation with North Koreans in its efforts to find out the truth behind the incident and possibly in its further legal actions."[12]

.....

I began searching for a history. My own history. Because I had known all along that the stories I had heard were not true, and parts had been left out . . . I felt lost, ungrounded. Like I was a ghost watching others live their lives without one of my own . . .[13]

.....

In mapping out the events of the *Ukishima Maru*'s return, what becomes apparent is a kind of haunting, as if the "living souls" in the title of the film might refer to the thousands of people on board the ship whom official records can claim as neither dead nor alive, or to those who testify to having survived the ship's sinking but were rendered nonexistent by their absence from government documents. The living souls haunt a history that is perforated by attempts to erase it and then left to die out along with its witnesses. As the story goes in the Korean imagination, the Japanese wanted to ensure that there were no eyewitnesses to their atrocities, no trace of evidence. Even the ship itself was left on the ocean floor for nine years after the incident, as if the memory of the event could also be submerged. Accident or not, the first shipload of witnesses to the cruelties of Japanese slavery were eliminated, except for those eyewitnesses who describe scenes of Japanese soldiers fleeing the *Ukishima Maru* in rowboats prior to the explosion but who nevertheless have been banished from official memory.[14] The fact of the *Ukishima Maru*'s sinking remains unsettled, however. There are gaps in what gets legitimated as history.

These holes in history come to be lived as "transgenerational haunting," what Nicolas Abraham and Maria Torok describe as the phenomenon of an unspeakable trauma being passed unconsciously from one generation to the next in which the transgenerational phantom inhabits "the depths of the unconscious, dwells as the living-dead of knowledge of *someone else's secret*."[15]

.....

She tells the story of what she does not remember. But remembers one thing: Why she forgot to remember . . .[16]

.....

When the object of analysis lies outside the field of vision, erased from the official record, as in the case of the *Ukishima Maru* and countless other incidents like it, one must employ "radical new methods of seeing" such as "focusing on personal memories and the dreamwork—on the unconscious aspects of looking."[17] While *Soul's Protest* focuses on the personal memories of the survivors, as well as on the unrecorded memories of the dead, the film not only resurrects these memories for viewers who lived during August 1945 but also creates new memories for those not eyewitnesses to the event. "The unconscious aspects of looking" belong not only to Korean colonized subjects but are distributed across the diaspora, across bodies and generations. As John Johnston points out, "what is perceived is not located at any single place and moment in time, and the act by which this perception occurs is not the result of a single or isolated agency but of several working in concert or parallel."[18] *Soul's Protest* offers an example of this distributed perception because equally important to the telling of its story are both the man who sees but cannot speak and the child narrator who does not see the event but returns to tell the story years later. It is as if the mechanism for remembering were not an individual one at the site of the tragedy, but an assemblage of eyes, tongues, and other parts distributed in time.

This assemblage extends beyond the boundaries of the semifictional story to include the eyes of those watching the *Ukishima Maru* fifty-six years after its sinking. Drawing from Gilles Deleuze's notion of decoded perception and deterritorialized organs, Johnston calls this type of seeing "machinic vision," one not merely the function of a passive sense organ, the eye, but an assemblage of eyes distributed and working in concert with heterogeneous terms in an environment: "Within the social space of these assemblages (which amount to a new form of collective psychic apparatus), the viewing or absorption of images constitutes a general form of machinic vision."[19]

If, as Johnston suggests, machinic assemblages are "a new form of collective psychic apparatus," then we might consider transgenerational haunting as an example of machinic vision, and of distributed perception more generally. In response to an inability of the subject to see the trauma that takes place before her or his very eyes, these eyes are then distributed across bodies and generations. The paradox of trauma is that the closest encounter with it often results in a "belatedness" of seeing or in not seeing at all, so that the imperative of witnessing is passed along to another as trauma's legacy.[20] These events are transmitted through images, words, affects, and performances, and are folded into the body along with traces of their contexts.[21]

.....

> There are things which have happened in the world while there were cameras watching, things that we have images for.
> There are other things which have happened while there were no cameras watching which we restage in front of cameras to have images of.
> There are things which have happened for which the only images that exist are in the minds of the observers present at the time . . .
> There are things which have happened for which there have been no observers, except for the spirits of the dead.[22]

.....

A diasporic machinic vision is perhaps the only means by which haunted histories can be seen, through a distribution of the senses that at once resides in the film images of the *Ukishima Maru* exploding, in the eyes of the viewers of the film, in the court transcripts of eyewitness testimonies, in what is absent from official records, in the silences of those who remember the incident but never speak about it, in the paintings of the artists who memorialize drowned women and sunken ships, in the grief of survivors, in the bodies of those who absorbed their grief, in the remains of the disaster itself. Diasporic machinic vision constitutes an assemblage of the body memory of transgenerational haunting and the haunted subjects' own cultural productions disseminated through technological apparatuses that make visible the trauma that their own eyes could not see in time.

.....

틈 (teum)

틈

teum

(aspirated *t* sound ti-gut, followed by short vowel *eu*, ending in *m* sound mi-um)

Teum, depending on the context can mean

1. "spare time" or "time to spare";
2. "a gap" or "crack";
3. "chance";
4. "an unguarded moment";

as in

문틈에서 바람이 들어와요.
Moon teum eh-suh param-i deuruh wayo.
The wind is coming through a chink in the door.

저는 틈이 없어요
Juh-neun teum-i upsuyo.
I have no leisure. (Or: I am pressed for time.)[23]

.....

April 14, 2002: *Soul's Protest* is screened in New York City at what the organizers believe is the first ever North Korean film festival in the United States, although no one can be certain since few public records regarding North Korean culture in the United States exist. The screening room is packed, with standing room only. The mostly Korean American audience watches horrific scenes of forced laborers being humiliated and beaten, body parts severed. The Korean body is subjected to direct control, to an exacting punishment that removes the disobedient tongue, dismembers the legs that try to run. At times, the viewers gasp in disbelief, but the film draws them in closer and closer until they, too, are living in 1945, as if the image is no mere representation, as if the moment is now. There is a clear political urgency in watching this movie. It is not a luxury. We are not watching out of leisure. *Juh-neun teum-i upsuhyo.*

After the screening there is a discussion about how much of the film is historically accurate and the extent to which Korean Americans and Koreans living in the United States can identify with this film. My identification comes most at the end, when I am watching the little boy who survived, floating among the dead. And I am left thinking about fate.

It was the fate of those on board the first ship to never arrive in Korea, to never return. It must have been fate also that decided that my mother would not be on that first ship. The Japanese officials would wait to put her and her mother on the second ship, or maybe it was the third. But in any case, not the first. My mother would not die that day. The little boy in the film, who was about the same age as my mother was in 1945, also did not die that day. The little boy who survives the sinking of the ship, he is my mother, because she, too, survived the sinking of the ship by virtue of being on the next one. But what does it mean to survive to the kind of life from which you want desperately to be relieved?

.....

> In 1946, the year I turned 24, a ship came to take us back home. I didn't want to return, but I had to get on board as all Koreans had been ordered by the government to return home. The ship was filled with comfort women. I had no family, no relatives and no home to go to. I thought it would be better to drown than to return to my country, but I didn't have the courage to throw myself overboard.[24]

> 1946 년, 그러니까 내가 스물 네 살 되는 해, 배가 와서 우리를 집으로 데꼬 갔어. 난 돌아가고 싶지 않았는디, 정부에서 조선사람은 모두 타고 집으로 돌아가라고 혀서 . . . 타봉께 전부 위안부 밖에 없었어. 돌아갈 집도 친척도 가족도 없었는디. . . 조국으로 돌아가느니 차라리 풍덩 바닷물에 빠져 죽는게 낫다 혔느니 . . . 그럴 용기가 차마 없었어.[25]

.....

Do you consider throwing your body into the ocean so that you can be spared the fate of living? My mother was too young in 1945 to be tempted by such ideas, or to know that she would wish for death later. She was four years old then, moving toward . . . .

The image of a sailing ship packed with slaves suggests, as Hortense Spillers has pointed out, a suspension in the "oceanic," in what Sigmund Freud described as "limitlessness . . . a bond with the universe," or, in other words, a feeling reminiscent of a pre-oedipal state in which the baby does not sense its separation from the mother and the breast and the milk.[26] This oneness of the infant with its surroundings, followed by the development of an individuated identity, is assumed as universal in a Freudian narrative of oedipalization. Spillers, however, looks at the paradoxical situation in which enslaved Africans were subjected to the oedipal fiction as a tool of normalization even in the absence of the conditions for making that normalization possible. Slavery separated children from their mothers, obscured bloodlines, always putting in question one's parentage, and therefore laid the ground for nonoedipal psychobiographies, perhaps ones that Western psychology would call fractured.

In the context of the slave vessel, the oceanic feeling associated with a oneness with the universe/mother is displaced by an oceanic of "undifferentiated identity removed from indigenous land and culture."[27] These captives were "culturally unmade" beings whose destinies were "exposed . . . to an unknown course."[28] The vessel's movement toward an unknown destination implies not only the vulnerability and the erasure, or unmaking, of the subject but also a moment of radical possibility. In *Soul's Protest*, the circling of the ship and its seemingly endless movement toward a never arrived-at destination suggests that time itself is suspended, unaccounted for—*an unguarded moment . . . .*

.....

I could remember a time of great sadness before I was born.
We had been moved. Uprooted . . . .[29]

.....

Unlike the slave vessel in Spillers's text, however, the *Ukishima Maru* was not transporting slaves to an unknown land, but rather returning many of them to a home that was once known but only existed phantasmatically for the returnees, a home that was always already fragmented and to which the return was impossible. This ship's course is charted in an unguarded moment that simultaneously forecloses the future imagined by those "going home," and opens up another future. This ship's trajectory is played out in the cracks, in *teum*, in the imperceptible spaces in between.

Spillers describes the captive Africans sailing across the Atlantic as not-yet American subjects. Yet most post–World War II Korean returnees submitted to an additional layer of subjectification. They became not-yet subjects once again in that they were both culturally unmade as Koreans and remade as Japanese colonial subjects who were later returned to an alienated homeland to which they were not yet assimilated. But what of those Koreans who were children at the time of the "return," the not-yet Korean subjects whose bodies only ever inhabited Japan, like the little boy in *Soul's Protest*, like my mother? What paths were traveled by the colonized children whose mothers' bodies were unavailable to them, whose origins were as uncertain as their destinations? To what did they return?

.....

Mother. You went to great lengths to make this history inaccessible to me, but some secrets have already exposed themselves, as if my eyes were there in 1941 when you were born into the labor camp. To labor in the same way as your mother, only for another country's army. My eyes were already there when your mother's body was forcibly moved from her home in Kyung-Sang province to Osaka where it was her duty to serve the Japanese Empire, where to speak Korean was to risk having one's tongue cut out. Your sister was fifteen in 1941, close in age to her other siblings. She was your eldest sibling, and you her most beloved. Grandmother was always so old to me. She seemed too old to be your mother. Sister was fifteen in 1941 when you were born in Osaka. My eyes were already there.

I have only pieces of a story, drops of sorrow that fall from your lips. Sister's sons are not her sons, but flesh of her husband's mistress. In 1945, she married this man who had two children (boys even) and took them as her own. Took cover in their desire to suck because she was unable to produce children, like many of the girls shipped back to Korea who had been "sanitized" with routine injections of an antibiotic called 606, an antibiotic later found to contain mercury. Her husband's baby boys saved her womanhood, because you are almost not a woman if you can't carry a child on the inside, if your body doesn't own that kind of knowledge. And you can't remember if her body once knew and was made to forget, if your family's honor was more powerful than the memory in her belly. One thing is certain, though. Those boys were not the only ones she loved like her own.

I had not yet been planted into your womb when it happened, but parts of me were already assembled and set into motion. My eyes were already there when you dropped out of school to look for work in the city, and I saw how she wanted to protect you, her baby sister, as if you were her own child. She wished she could have kept you safe from the maengsu *American soldiers and took the blame for your fall like any Korean mother would do. When one of them finally took you away, she followed you with her grief, and begged you to stay because she knew that this time you would not return.*

.....

She tells the story of what she does not remember . . .
a beautiful woman who lost her mind . . .[30]

.....

1941: Born in Japan, under what exact circumstances, I do not know. Born in Japan, of whose body I am uncertain. Of a woman conscripted for what purpose? Born to what father?

1945: Returned to Korea, shortly after liberation. "Returned," let us say, even though she had never been there before. The exact date of the return is undocumented. Maybe it was in September, shortly after liberation. "Liberation," let us say, even though she would find no freedom in her homeland either. "Homeland," let us say, even though she had never lived there. Returned to her homeland in 1945 shortly after liberation, maybe in September.

June 25, 1950: A few days before her birthday, not quite nine years old. Years later she would tell no stories to her children about what she did on that day, or on the next thousand days. She would tell no stories about stepping over severed limbs and discarded babies, or about eating the Americans' garbage full of napkins and toothpicks, or about watching bombs fall from the sky.[31]

1971: Married an American, a high-ranking officer twenty-five years her elder. Maybe the other women with whom she worked reassured her that older men knew how to take care of a woman. But I cannot be sure of this either.

1975: Moved to America with her children and never returned.

.....

I began searching for a history. My own history. Because I had known all along that the stories I had heard were not true, and parts had been left out. I remember having this feeling growing up that I was haunted by something, that I was living within a family full of ghosts . . . . There was this place that they knew about. I had never been there yet I had a memory for it. I could remember a time of great sadness before I was born. We had been moved. Uprooted . . . . She tells the story of what she does not remember. But remembers one thing: Why she forgot to remember . . . a beautiful woman who lost her mind . . . .[32]

.....

August 22, 1945: The *Ukishima Maru* sets sail for Pusan harbor, returning an estimated ten thousand Koreans to their homeland. It was the fate of those on board the first ship, to never arrive in Korea, to never return. It must have been fate also that decided that my then four-year-old mother would not be on that first ship. The Japanese officials would wait until September to send my mother and her mother back to Korea.

Before that, she must have been a subject of the Japanese Empire, though I do not know for sure. I have seen no records to prove that she was ever Japanese. The only evidence is her own admission of guilt—that her birthplace is Osaka, that her first tongue was Japanese, and not Korean. Documents later reconstructed her as a Korean national, daughter of a Korean mother and a Korean father. The document says so. But her beginnings as a not-yet Korean subject aboard a Japanese naval vessel would set her on an uncharted course, moving toward . . . moving toward . . .

September 1945: U.S. forces arrive in Korea just eighteen days after the liberation from Japan, installing an occupation government. In response to the Japanese colonial system of sexual slavery, the United States officially outlaws prostitution in Korea, but unofficially transfers the comfort stations from Japanese to U.S. control. By 1953, there would be an estimated 350,000 women working as prostitutes in Korea, 60 percent of whom would service the U.S. military. *My eyes were already there.*

I have never heard the word *wianbu* spoken in my family. Nor have I heard *yanggongju*. These are the unspeakable words never spoken in my family. Words wrapped in silence. Words that Abraham and Torok would call "phantomogenic," "secreted . . . words giving sustenance to the phantom . . . . These are often the very words that rule an entire family's history."[33] Words mapped in blood. But I had no memory of them. Perhaps the sounds of these words never entered consciousness and therefore could not be remembered, but traces of *wianbu* and *yanggongju* were folded in and stored in the "resonating vessel" of brain and skin.[34]

Wianbu, the word used to refer to the so-called comfort women who were forced sexual laborers for the Japanese military, was also used to describe the women who were sexual laborers for the U.S. military. That is, until another word replaced *wianbu* in order to connote a different kind of shame. *Yanggongju* would draw the line between the violated virgins and the willing whores.[35] *Yanggongju*, literally meaning "Western princess" and commonly translated as "Yankee whore" replaced *wianbu* as the popular name for women who are prostitutes for the U.S. military. *Yanggongju*, when translated as "GI bride," is extended to those women who date or marry American men. Although my *um-ma* fit this definition, I have never heard the word *yanggongju* spoken in my family.[36]

Who or what gets implicated in not speaking? In *Soul's Protest*, there is another character who literally cannot speak. Besides the tongueless man who warns that the ship is about to explode, there is a young woman who had been enslaved as a comfort woman, a *wianbu*. This young woman embodies the unspeakable word *wianbu*, but she cannot speak the horror of being *wianbu*. She ultimately cannot speak at all. Instead of speaking, she laughs while her body hangs limp, an emptied-out body that must be moved along by the force of others.[37] In one scene, another returnee asks why she does not speak. At the precise moment when the word *wianbu* is uttered to explain her unusual condition, a hush falls over the women in her company who cast their eyes downward at the sound of *wianbu*. When her own voice becomes incapacitated, who or what speaks for her? Who or what speaks to her?[38] *Soul's Protest*, as well as writings about comfort women, figures the *wianbu* as the tragic woman who loses her mind and her place in the symbolic order. Like the *wianbu*, the *yanggongju* is also placed on a trajectory toward madness.

The narrative pattern now familiar in writings about the life histories of Korean women who migrated to the United States through marriage begins in rural poverty and ends in psychosis.[39] This is a madness marked not only by one's own voice being silenced but also by the hearing of other voices, what Slavoj Žižek would describe as a psychosis induced by excess rather than lack: "[Jacques] Lacan pointed out that the consistency of our 'experience of reality' depends on the exclusion of what he calls the *objet petit a* from it: in order for us to have normal 'access to reality,' something must be excluded, 'primordially repressed.' In psychosis, this exclusion is undone . . . : the outcome of which, of course, is the disintegration of our 'sense of reality.' "[40] The hearing of voices constitutes an undoing of the exclusion of the Real from the symbolic enclosure that produces the subject of speech. In this case, flooded by the Real, silence resonates with the voices of a haunted history.

In an unconscious haunted by an unspeakable trauma, there is a constant tension between speaking and not speaking. According to Abraham and Torok, there are two alternatives for relieving the unconscious from being haunted—to remain silent and allow the ghosts to wither away after several generations, or to speak and set the ghosts free. When a secreted word remains secret, it will be passed down through several generations, but eventually the phantom effect will wear off as long as the words remain unspoken. But if the unconscious attempts to speak secreted words, the ghosts do not simply disappear. Speaking and releasing the phantom words into the social realm is what Abraham and Torok describe as "staging words," an act through which "shared or complementary phantoms find a way of being established as social practices."[41] A staging of words implies exposing the ghosts, not only to the world but to one another so that the ones that have something in common find each other, like *wianbu* and *yanggongju*.

These ghosts have an agency of their own in that silence shows itself to be inherently unstable as it becomes the background against which secreted words become audible, often to one who is a witness. Put another way, a ghost can express itself in the form of a voice that comes through the wound. It is an alien voice, disembodied, but one that has witnessed something that the hearer has not. It is a voice that has *seen*, and that demands to be listened to. "We can also read the address of the voice here . . . as the story of the way in which one's own trauma is tied up in the trauma of another, the way in which trauma may lead, therefore, to the encounter with another, through the very possibility and surprise of listening to another's wound."[42] Together the listener and the voice speaking from the wound constitute a kind of storytelling machine, an assemblage of seeing, speaking, and listening components.

. . . . .

There were voices that came out of the oak tree in front of the house, others that came out of images on television, newsprint, clocks . . .

They gave her directives: "Kill yourself tonight. Do it while your children are sleeping." But usually their orders were far more mundane: "Stop fermenting the dwenjang. *It has been long enough"; and "Get chocolate cake for* mangnei's *birthday." Sometimes they spoke in verbal language, to her, about her. In other moments, their communication took the form of nonverbal, nonhuman sounds . . .*

The pattering of acorns falling on the roof of her car signaled her involvement in government conspiracies. The kitchen timer ringing meant that Ronald Reagan set up surveillance equipment in her house. Eventually, many of the communicators stopped speaking from their original sources, so that she always questioned whether or not to believe what she was hearing. The voice of technology often spoke as the oak tree, sometimes disguised as a small dog. The messengers even took the form of her own voice from time to time, speaking to her, through her. Every twelve hours at 9:45, the clock would borrow her voice to an-nounce the time, but in the form of a date. September forty-five. *Maybe it was a voice from another time speaking through the clock voice speaking through her voice. But she could not hear the clock voice when it spoke, otherwise she might have noticed that this date was significant for her too. But maybe she was not even old enough to have remembered what happened in September 1945. She was four years old then, moving toward . . . moving toward . . .*

. . . . .

At the end of *Soul's Protest*, when the little boy is a grown man, he and the other survivor return to the site of the sinking ship to search for living souls, the ghosts of 1945 still living in the waters between Korea and Japan. The wounded child survivor in *Soul's Protest* can be read as the conduit for the voices of the dead and the silenced. It is his fate as a survivor to bear witness to unspeakable events. But what does it mean to survive when you are unable to tell of the trauma, indeed, unable to even know it? The little boy in the film who grows up to return to the place of trauma, he is not my mother. Because this return to the place of trauma, in order to tell a story, would be for my mother a fate that could never be fulfilled. Her seeing would come too late, but she is not the only one who could not see in time. Perhaps it was my fate to return to the place of trauma to tell what it means to not see. The story of the *Ukishima Maru* is not just a personal narrative of the survivor but also an embodiment of the voices that emerge from *teum*.

NOTES

Portions of this essay have been published as Grace M. Cho, "Murmurs in the Storytelling Machine," *Cultural Studies–Critical Methodologies* 4.4 (2004): 426–32, and Grace M. Cho and Hosu Kim, "Dreaming in Tongues," *Qualitative Inquiry* 11.3 (2005): 445–57.

1. In *Soul's Protest*, the semifictional film version of the *Ukishima Maru* incident, we see only two survivors. However, at least eighty people have come forward as survivors of the actual incident.

2. The *Ukishima Maru* was the first of a series of Japanese naval ships that would return the conscripted Koreans, many of whom were comfort women, to Korea.

3. While the historical accuracy of *Soul's Protest* is debatable, the story is based on the survivors' eyewitness accounts of the *Ukishima Maru* incident in which they testified that some of the Japanese crew members evacuated the ship shortly before the explosion.

4. Rea Tajiri, dir., *History and Memory* (Women Make Movies, 1991). The narrator in the film recounts her mother's experiences in a Japanese American internment camp during World War II. These are experiences that the mother never speaks of, and perhaps cannot even remember, yet the daughter inherits the memories through dreams, screen images, and affects of feeling haunted.

5. "Japan/Korea: Fifteen South Koreans Awarded 45 Million Yen over Ship Blast," *Japan Times*, August 24, 2001, www.archk.net/news/mainfile.php/ahrnews_200108/ 1818/?print=yes. www.japantimes.co.jp/cgi-bin/getarticle.pl5?nn20010824a1.htm.

6. Jang-jin Hwang, "South Koreans Urge Japan to Take Full Responsibility for 1945 Ship Blast," *Korea Herald*, August 25, 2001, www.koreaherald.co.kr/servlet/kherald .article.view?id=200108250034&tpl=print.

7. Richard Lloyd Parry, "Korea Rallys Round Kim Jong Il's 'Titanic' Tale of Slave Ship," Independent News, August 24, 2001, news.independent.co.uk/world/asia_ china/story.jsp?story=90376.

8. "Japan/Korea."

9. Hye-jean Chung, "Two Films Shed Light on 1945 Ship Tragedy," *Korea Times*, September 17, 2001, http://koreatimes.co.kr/kt_culture/200109/t2001091717180856110.htm.

10. "Korean 'Titanic' Amazes Moscow and Hong Kong Audience: To Be Exported to West," *People's Korea*, July 25, 2001, www1.korea-np.co.jp/pk/165th_issue/2001072515 .htm.

11. Ibid.

12. Hwang, "South Koreans Urge Japan."

13. Tajiri, *History and Memory*.

14. The work of the Japanese artist Tomiyama Taeko, as well as the paintings of former comfort women such as Kang Tok-kyong, bears witness to that which gets omitted from historical documents. Tomiyama's images of drowned women and sunken navy ships depict a world in which the story of the *Ukishima Maru* is not only likely to be accurate but also a commonplace occurrence.

15. Nicolas Abraham and Maria Torok, *The Shell and the Kernel: Renewals of Psychoanalysis* (Chicago: University of Chicago Press, 1994), 188.

16. Tajiri, *History and Memory*.

17. David L. Eng, *Racial Castration: Managing Masculinity in Asian America* (Durham, NC: Duke University Press, 2001), 37.

18. John Johnston, "Machinic Vision," *Critical Inquiry* 26.1 (1999): 44.

19. Ibid., 46.

20. Cathy Caruth, *Unclaimed Experience: Trauma, Narrative, and History* (Baltimore, MD: Johns Hopkins University Press, 1996), 92.

21. Brian Massumi, *Parables for the Virtual: Movement, Affect, Sensation* (Durham, NC: Duke University Press, 2002).

22. Tajiri, *History and Memory*.

23. See Sang Oak Lee, et al., *Korean through English* (Seoul: Hollym, 1993), 38.

24. This comes from an interview with Yi Yongsuk, a former comfort woman. For the full transcript, see "I Will No Longer Harbor Resentment," in Keith Howard, *True Stories of the Korean Comfort Women* (London: Cassell, 1995): 50–57.

25. Translated by Hosu Kim. The original interview transcript in Korean is unpublished, therefore this is a translation of a translation, from Korean to English to Korean. The translator of the version that appears here chose to translate the word *Koreans* as *Chosun saram*, or "people from Chosun," using the name of the peninsula prior to its division rather than the present-day name for South Korea, *Hanguk*.

26. Hortense J. Spillers, "Mama's Baby, Papa's Maybe: An American Grammar Book," *Diacritics* 17 (1987): 15. Sigmund Freud, *Civilization and Its Discontents*, trans. Peter Gay (New York: Norton, 1989).

27. Spillers, "Mama's Baby," 72.

28. Ibid.

29. Tajiri, *History and Memory*.

30. Ibid.

31. This vignette is based on Ramsay Liem's oral histories of Korean War survivors, as well as memories that have been passed down to me through transgenerational haunting. For a discussion of traumatic wartime memories, see Ramsay Liem, "History, Trauma, and Identity: The Legacy of the Korean War for Korean Americans," *Amerasia Journal* 29.3 (2004): 111–29.

32. Tajiri, *History and Memory*.

33. Abraham and Torok, *The Shell and the Kernel*, 188.

34. Brian Massumi, *Parables of the Virtual* (Durham, N.C.: Duke University Press, 2002), 29.

35. For a discussion of the way in which boundaries are drawn between the two types of military sexual labor, see Katharine H. S. Moon, "South Korean Movements against Militarized Sexual Labor," *Asian Survey* 39.2 (1999): 310–25.

36. *Um-ma* is a colloquial Korean word for "mother."

37. See Chungmoo Choi, "Introduction: The Comfort Women; Colonialism, War, and Sex," *Positions* 5.1 (1997): v–xiv, for a discussion of psychological effects of forced sexual labor on surviving comfort women.

38. Does the character's inability to speak point to a "contested historiography," as Kyung Hyun Kim has argued about other figures in "post-traumatic Korean cinema" who have lost both their language and their sanity? In his reading of *A Petal*, a film that depicts the 1980 Kwangju massacre, Kim posits the character of a mentally disturbed homeless teenage girl as the ghostly embodiment of Kwangju itself: "A specter that resides on street corners and in everyday life," whose inability to intelligibly speak of her own traumatic memories of the massacre parallels the obscure and fragmented narratives of the Kwangju massacre as a larger historical event. Kim points out that "if language, according to Lacan, is the crucial means for the child to free him or herself from the preoedipal crisis, then the girl's identity will forever be impaired without the return of language. However, she remains hysterical: narration is ruptured, and her ability to recount history and to translate scattered images into verbal discourse is denied." Kyung Hyun Kim, "Post-trauma and Historical Remembrance in Recent South

Korean Cinema: Reading Park Kwang-su's *A Single Spark* (1995) and Chang Son-u's *A Petal* (1996)," *Cinema Journal* 41.4 (2002): 109.

39. For an example of this narrative, see Alexandra Suh, "Military Prostitution in Asia and the United States," in *States of Confinement: Policing, Detention, and Prisons*, ed. Joy James (New York: St. Martin's, 2000), 144–57.

40. Slavoj Žižek, " 'I Hear You with My Eyes'; or, The Invisible Master," in *Gaze and Voice as Love Objects*, ed. Renata Salecl and Slavoj Žižek (Durham, NC: Duke University Press, 1996), 91.

41. Abraham and Torok, *The Shell and the Kernel*, 188.

42. Caruth, *Unclaimed Experience*, 8.

MELISSA DITMORE

*My second day in Calcutta, before visiting the Dur-
bar Mahila Samanwaya Committee (DMSC), I took
a walk through Sonagachi, the largest red light district in Calcutta. I arrived at about 4:30 in the after-
noon and was immediately surrounded by a group of non-English
speaking men, who were possibly shocked that any woman not working
in the red light district would venture there and who definitely wanted
to assist me in leaving the area. One man asked what was I looking for.
I said, in my probably incomprehensible Bengali, that I was looking for
the Durbar Mahila Samanwaya Committee. Eventually, after some
Bengali conversation that I could not understand, he said, "Social
services for women? There, and to the left." I never made it to the office
he recommended, because fifty feet further down the street, some of the
women on the road approached me. Our limited conversation mostly
relied on gestures and smiles, despite attempting Bengali and English.
People come from many places to work in Calcutta, and this is especially true of Sonagachi. The largest number come from nearby Bihar,
Orissa, and Bangladesh, but significant numbers also hail from further
away in India and Nepal as well, and so many speak other languages
better than they speak Bengali, just like myself. "What language is she
speaking?" came from the Nepali and Hindi speakers of the seven of us
standing in a circle. Perhaps I was being questioned to discover whether
I had been brought there against my will.*

.....

The world's oldest profession is also the world's oldest form of affective labor.
Looking at prostitution through the lens of affective labor not only shows that
sex work is an apt term for prostitution in that it allows recognition of prostitution as work, work that increasingly seems akin to much of the work done in

contemporary capitalism. Thinking of prostitution as sex work also allows for an application to prostitution of the empowerment approach to labor practices, suggesting a politics not reducible to "rescuing" the prostitute. In what follows, I want to explore the affective labor of sex workers and the influence of an empowerment approach to labor that has resulted in political organizing among sex workers linked to the Durbar Mahila Samanwaya Committee (DMSC) in India. Founded in 1992, DMSC is funded in part by the Department for International Development (DFID), a British agency concerned with international development, and, in part, the DMSC is also self-funded. While the committee was founded by a doctor, it is especially successful in involving sex workers in all aspects of the organization. The DMSC has sixty thousand sex worker members and is possibly the largest organization of sex workers in India and the world.[1]

SEX WORK AS AFFECTIVE LABOR

> Immaterial labor produces first and foremost a "social relationship" . . . . Only if it succeeds in this production [of a social relationship] does it have an economic value.
> —Maurizio Lazzarato, "Immaterial Labor."

Affective labor can be understood as work that aims to evoke specific behaviors or sentiments in others as well as oneself, rather than it being merely about the production of a consumable product. Arlie Hochschild's term "emotional labor" describes a form of affective labor, one certainly characteristic of sex work.[2] And indeed, the term *emotional labor* has been usefully applied to sex work by Wendy Chapkis.[3] However, these analyses of the work in service industries including the sex industry have not delved deeply into the components of labor that create value. Maurizio Lazzarato goes further in elaborating the value-producing aspects of affective labor;[4] he proposes that the interpersonal relationship created by affective labor is the crystallization of capital. For Lazzarato, affective labor produces value through a synthesis of different types of know-how and physical labor. Affective labor especially makes use of interpersonal skills often as part of entrepreneurialism, where the relationship with clients and potential clients is paramount. So there also is the marketing of skills not previously deemed labor, such as creating a relationship with the client. For Lazzarato, affective labor involves work that often proves hyperexploitable, precarious, and unstable precisely because it is hard to determine when affective labor begins or ends, therefore rendering its value immeasurable.[5]

While sex work constitutes value-bearing affective labor, the aspects that make it so have not been well examined, in part because they are seemingly nonsexual aspects of sex work, and in part because the value of the affective labor of sex work is beyond measure. For example, sex workers use intellectual skills to make and maintain personal connections. Some of this work is about constructing an image: sex workers present themselves in various ways, and many such images are as carefully constructed as those of other kinds of affect laborers. Some present a sophisticated veneer, others a hypersexual persona, and many work to appear like the "girl next door." This aesthetic labor very much resembles that done by models in crafting and projecting personalities. Physical appearance may lead to the initial contact between the sex worker and the client, but sex workers also cultivate those aspects of their work that lead to repeat customers, who provide sex workers with their most reliable source of income. The creation of bonds between a sex worker and the client can be based on shared interests (sometimes feigned) or conversational skills. There is energy expended to maintain the illusion of recreation to be enjoyed by both the client and the sex worker. This is akin to performers in the arts working to make their art look easy, to athletes who make their work in sports look like fun, and to others whose work consists of putting people at ease. Sex work frequently consists of a great deal of activity before sex commences. And the work involved in the sexual activity itself has many aspects, including stripping, engaging in sadomasochistic practices, acting out fantasies, or maintaining the illusion that the sex is a matter of romance or pleasure for the worker.

While entrepreneurialism constitutes an aspect of all sex work, the level of entrepreneurialism involved in sex work is often relative to the venue in which the work is done. There are independent sex workers who do their own advertising and do not share any portion of their money with management, but instead rent their own space and serve as their own management. Yet women who work in brothels are managed. Management provides the workplace and often does much of the work of finding clients. Brothel workers keep approximately half of the money taken in, while the other half goes to management for overhead and their own income. In sex work, the levels of entrepreneurialism are connected to levels of income, as well as levels of independence. While sex workers in brothels rely on others for obtaining work, and must manage a relationship with them, the independent worker depends more on personal relationships, a working in tandem with others who will refer clients.[6]

Of course, prostitution is not easily treated as affective labor, or as labor at all. This is because the law in many places defines prostitution and/or its attendant activities such as soliciting as illegal and therefore refuses to recognize it as work. As such, many sex workers around the world are denied the regulation of working conditions, and illegal practices that would be subject to correction in other industries are ignored. Sex workers, therefore, are usually denied legal recourse in the face of abusive work practices. Workers in the sex industry are unlikely even to seek legal recourse if they are themselves in jeopardy of prosecution. And even where prostitution is not against the law, it is not necessarily the case that the law will not be used against the prostitutes themselves. For example, in Calcutta, laws against the prostitution of minors (which is classed as a trafficking offense) are used as a pretext to raid legal brothels. In the context of such raids, legal prostitutes often have been exposed to illegal abuse by the authorities, including graft and theft.[7] This adds weight to prostitutes' fear of seeking police aid, since often when they do seek police attention in cases of violence or abuse, they usually are refused assistance.[8]

The existence of abuses within the sex industry should not, however, lead to equating all sex work with abuse; rather, it should highlight the need for the application of labor regulations to the sex industry. Only if sex work is recognized as labor can labor violations become criminalized. As a person cannot consent to abusive conditions, including violence, coercion, debt bondage, or confinement, abuses like these constitute crimes regardless of the industry in which they are committed. The presence of such abuses in other kinds of work has led to workers' organizing and to the introduction of occupational safety regulations.

Indeed, the International Labour Organization (ILO) report *The Sex Sector* recommends recognition of the sex industry as labor in light of the economic and social realities of those engaged in it.[9] It is fitting that the ILO recommends recognition of sex work as labor since ILO statutes governing minimum standards of working conditions could be applied to the sex industry and modified where necessary to accommodate conditions specific to sex work. Examples of such specifics include the right to decline a client. Regulations might also make possible addressing health concerns such as the use of condoms and the use of postexposure prophylaxes for HIV in the case of broken condoms.

In contrast to a labor approach to sex work, attempts at "rescuing" prostitutes typically assume that no one would choose to engage in prostitution under any circumstances. Rescue attempts of women in the sex industry have long formed part of, if not a cover for, a moral agenda that does not value the autonomy of women. Rescue perpetuates a morality that seeks to protect women and girls by restricting them, rather than enabling their self-determination.[10] Thinking of prostitution as sex work affords another approach to prostitution, which provides a rethinking around issues of crime, protection, and morality. Thinking of prostitution in terms of labor and labor violations opens up the possibility of sex workers' organizing on their own behalf, organizing for their empowerment.

In his discussion of empowerment and sex work, Ivan Wolffers makes a useful distinction between three types of empowerment in order to evaluate the benefits each offers. The first and most limited is "personal empowerment," empowerment at the individual level. This empowerment works through "making people aware of their skills, possibilities and choices and giving them control over ways to change things that cause them problems."[11] This is the tack taken by many sex work projects that focus on health, such as projects aimed at education about the use of condoms. However, knowledge alone is not sufficient to address problems, including health problems, and it has never proven sufficient in explaining human sexual behavior.

Second, there is community empowerment, involving "the strengthening of the sex work community as a whole to demand changes in their communities and to call for a supportive environment." But, as Wolffers points out, community empowerment does not necessarily include sex workers themselves in the decision making, nor does it do so in the direct control of projects. Rather, community empowerment often involves sex workers acting en masse, as in approaching the police when dealing with the harassment by a police officer. Thus Wolffers explores a third kind of empowerment, "social empowerment." As he puts it: "Social empowerment defined as empowering sex workers to fight for their rights and for acceptance of their profession by the larger society, is a more ambitious goal." Wolffers points to sex workers' organizing and the demand for recognition of sex work as labor as important steps in their social empowerment.

Wolffers's discussion of empowerment points to the numerous levels on which organizing has occurred among sex workers connected to the DMSC in Calcutta. The committee has used an empowerment approach at the individual, community, and social levels. While the DMSC is managed in part by social workers and medical personnel, it also includes sex workers at every level of the organization. Sex workers are paid for their work as peer educators and manage the credit union and condom-buying cooperative on their own. The current director is the son of a sex worker and a member of the community in the red light districts. Indeed, the DMSC is widely recognized for its groundbreaking work in organizing on behalf of sex workers' rights by including sex workers in all aspects of the process. The efforts of sex workers on behalf of themselves strongly contrast with the more usual attempts by the authorities to close red light districts, as well as with the well-intentioned but misguided effort to "rescue" women and girls from brothels.

DMSC SERVICES AND WORKING CONDITIONS IN
CALCUTTA'S RED LIGHT DISTRICTS

> *Women in Sonagachi were as curious about me as I was about them. Most of our rudimentary conversation, almost incomprehensible to me, seemed to focus on me. I became an object of curiosity, turning tables on my intentions of questioning them. Our bits of conversation focused on where I was from, my clothes, the color of my eyes, and whether I was Hindu. I could not accurately guess how old most of the prostitutes there were, but the overwhelming majority of sex workers I saw outside looked healthy and clean, qualities valuable to a prostitute's business. Eventually our numbers grew until I was surrounded by many of the women working in the district, one of whom held my right hand tightly in hers while we tried to communicate. These women were vibrant and friendly and smartly dressed, and as full of questions as I was. They had freedom of movement and seemingly could waste time that could be spent working, talking to me instead. At this time, I was unable to distinguish the different types of sex workers there. This was, in part, because attracting clients (no matter which venue) largely consists of standing by one's doorway, visible to potential clients. This makes it difficult to distinguish between those who work for themselves or alone, those who work in a brothel and those who work on the street.*

.....

The DMSC distinguishes three types of sex workers. Besides the independent contractors and brothel workers already mentioned, there are indentured prostitutes. These distinctions are recognized among most sex workers around the world and refer to the working conditions of prostitutes. Independent contractors enjoy the best conditions. They rent their rooms and work for themselves. Independent contractors negotiate with their clients themselves, usually without a third party. This means that they do not give any part of their earnings to anyone else. They are like call girls elsewhere or women who work in the windows in Belgium and the Netherlands. To make a parallel with other industries, and particularly with other affective labor, they are most like self-employed people, perhaps working as consultants or freelancers, who accept jobs with conditions acceptable to them in regard to wages, time commitments, and scheduling.

Brothel workers in Calcutta live with and work with a madam, or brothel manager, and keep approximately half their earnings. However, while brothel work in the United States is more discreet, relying perhaps on regular clientele or on advertising in local media, some brothel workers in India stand outside to meet clients. Negotiations may be made by the brothel management. This can restrict a sex worker's autonomy, but, on the other hand, it can remove the responsibility of the difficult task of getting clients. Brothel management can be good, neutral, or malevolent, the latter, for example, by denying the sex worker the right to decline clients or to use condoms.

The workers with the least autonomy in the sex industry are indentured workers. They may enter a contract in which they or their families borrow money or incur expenses that they will pay back against future work. For people without collateral, this may be the only option to obtain a loan. Some indentured workers receive a fair deal and are able to get out of debt in a fixed amount of time. However, some indentured workers are held in debt bondage, in which their debt spirals out of control and out of proportion to the expenses incurred. Debt bondage is illegal and defined as a contemporary form of slavery in international law.[12]

Conditions of debt bondage vary. Prostitutes in debt bondage may not be allowed to either turn down clients or difficult and/or unsafe requests. These are the prostitutes who are most supervised and who have the least time away from those who control them. These often are abusive cases that constitute proper examples of trafficking. In other cases, indentured workers may enjoy good conditions, seeking to work off their debt and then move on. These prostitutes often do not view their condition as criminal; they may also see the person to whom they are indebted as providing a valuable service, such as assisting in migration. The social empowerment that the DMSC offers targets all of these sex workers in various ways.

.....

> We visited the DMSC office in Bowbazar, which held both a small
> medical clinic and a branch of their credit union. The credit union was
> busier than any other financial institution I have ever seen. The build-
> ing had a concrete floor and painted walls, and all volunteers and staff
> wore smocks—white smocks in the clinic and blue smocks in the credit
> union. It was clear that these services were valued and utilized by an
> incredible number of people, mostly women, but also men at the clinic,

mostly the lovers and clients of the prostitutes in the district. The women all wore saris with the exception of one doctor in slacks. Some carried children. The sheer numbers of people coming and going demonstrated the enormous popularity of the credit union, while the small talk and interactions between people indicated that the office also served as a community hub.

.....

Each of twelve red light districts in Calcutta has a branch office of the DMSC. The DMSC offers many services to all types of sex workers, including health services, a credit union, literacy and English classes, and education programs for the children of sex workers. It would be difficult to downplay the importance of the credit union in empowering sex workers in Calcutta. Sex workers are not able to open traditional bank accounts in India, where "good moral standing" is a requirement for banking. For this reason, sex workers keep their savings in cash and jewelry. Such savings can be lost in a moment if one is robbed or "rescued." Without banks in the red light district and usually without the papers necessary to open an account, sex workers in the red light districts must save their money on their person, leaving them prey to attack and robbery. All this has been changed with the operation of the sex workers' credit union, which now has sixty thousand members. Laying the foundation of this credit union may be the single most effective project of the DMSC. It has eliminated the need to save money in the form of jewelry and cash and has therefore eliminated the risk of losing one's life savings in a single event.

.....

From the Bowbazar office of the DMSC, we went to a brothel, which was apparently a typical brothel there. On the way to the top-floor brothel, we walked to the rear of an entryway and across a muddy, puddled, dirt ground floor to an uncovered stairway that would be condemned anywhere in the developed world. Nonetheless, according to my sources, the sex workers in the areas I visited live in much better conditions than what would be deemed Indian slums. The area was crowded, but certainly not overcrowded. After all, the middle-class neighborhood where I stayed on the south side of Calcutta included many families who slept together in one room. We went up three flights to the madam's room, where she and the three brothel workers welcomed us. We discussed her business over tea. The brothel had one room, with two beds and a curtain to draw between them. This room was not large, possibly 150 square feet, about the size of a small studio apartment. The four women—three workers and the madam—all slept here as well. There was a small stove at the end of the room close to the doorway. This room was painted yellow, and the beds were neatly made up with plaid spreads. There were other rooms accessible from the landing at the doorway, but I was not shown them and do not know if they were also held by the madam in addition to the room in which we met. To my eye, the women looked much like the women I had seen elsewhere in Calcutta—no one wore a lot of makeup, and each wore her long dark hair pulled back. I am sure that I was unable to discern whatever it might be that would mark an Indian woman as a prostitute.

.....

In most brothels linked with the DMSC, it is more certain that the madam and the workers will share the client's fee. The sex workers are usually well fed and healthy. Condom use is encouraged by the DMSC, which also offers sex education and negotiation training. Some members have begun a condom-purchasing cooperative with a social marketing plan to sell condoms to others in the red light districts below prices charged elsewhere, while still making a profit. Since prices for almost everything in the red light districts are reported to be much higher than elsewhere, this marketing scheme ensures access to condoms.[13] It also allows sex workers who work in brothels to find a way to become independent. Sex workers often hope to save enough money to eventually rent their own rooms and work independently. These sex workers are among the very many members of the DMSC interested almost solely in improving working conditions, rather than devoting more time to activism. But there are others who engage in activism.

THE DMSC AND ORGANIZING

The DMSC's organizing work has three important characteristics contributing to its success. First, the DMSC is comprehensive and addresses far more than only one issue, be it health or trafficking or "rescue." This stands in contrast to many of the so-called rescue efforts, which are only able to focus on one issue, say antitrafficking efforts (like Western Europe's TAMPEP, Transnational AIDS/ STD Prevention among Migrant Prostitutes in Europe) or health issues (like NYC's FROSTD, Foundation for Research on Sexually Transmitted Diseases). Second, the DMSC involves sex workers, working at every level of decision making, planning, and outreach. Finally, with sixty thousand members, the size of the DMSC alone enables it to address a variety of issues. Most other efforts around sex workers' organizing usually have many less participants, giving them neither the personnel nor the long-standing relationships with other local organizations that enable the DMSC's exceptional strategy of organizing.

Perhaps the most important characteristic of DMSC's organizing is sex workers' involvement at every level of organizing, proving central to the organization's empowerment strategy. The DMSC started as an HIV-prevention program, but was expanded by its first director when it became obvious that knowledge about prevention did not suffice to promote safe sex. What seemed necessary were efforts addressing the self-respect, self-reliance, and responsibility of the red light districts' residents. Ultimately, all DMSC empowerment efforts came to focus on increasing the self-determination of the sex workers and negotiating among sex workers to function as a bloc to improve the conditions of their work.

It is important to notice that this is not merely a matter of addressing a sex worker's self-hatred. Rather, what is emphasized is the process of self-determination, in other words, a social empowerment. The DMSC strategy of empowerment, therefore, aims to expand women's agency and thus refocuses the aims of research, which often expects to find low self-esteem among sex workers. Of course, sex workers' self-esteem may be affected by the knowledge that some others imagine them to be tainted, untrustworthy, oversexed, dumb, duped, helpless, and so on.[14] Indeed, sex workers and others would be blind not to realize that their work will color some peoples' opinions in ways that other kinds of work would not. This almost certainly contributes to the phenomenon of telling researchers, journalists, and others what they seem to want to hear.

But for DMSC, empowerment is conceived as social, beyond the individual level, and this is what is necessary for organizing around sex workers' affective labor. As such, a lack of self-esteem, where it may exist for sex workers, is understood as a reasonable reaction to poor working conditions. A spokesperson for TAMPEP, an antitrafficking organization that works with prostitutes in Europe and that has influenced DMSC's approach to antitrafficking, proposes that

> by making the women more assertive and raising their self-esteem, the
> TAMPEP worker is able to convince them they can resist the pimp and to
> decide the future course of their lives. TAMPEP knows of many women who
> have set themselves free from pimps (often with the help of a TAMPEP

worker) and who have remained in prostitution. Their working conditions have drastically improved, they seem like completely different persons and they take better care of themselves. This suggests conclusion [*sic*] that AIDS prevention should start by improving the working conditions of the women concerned.[15]

ANTITRAFFICKING EFFORTS AND DMSC ORGANIZING

> *A former director of the DMSC, Dr. Jana, told me that when he asked if the women knew, when they first came to the red light districts, that they would be prostitutes, they all said no. Later it came out that they all did know, but social strictures prevented them from ever saying so. He asked them why they had lied to him, and they said they wanted to give the answer he wanted to hear and that this answer gave them less shame as "bad" women. He told me that everyone in a family knows when the daughter leaves home to go to a red light district. Even the daughter knows. But no one says so overtly. All conversation proceeds as if she will do something else. Honesty, he told me, is even less likely when there are substantial reasons beyond social acceptance to claim that one was duped into prostitution, as when securing a visa and evading deportation in the West. This indicates that the overwhelming number of workers in the districts was not duped.*

.....

Clearly, DMSC's organizing contrasts with those efforts presuming that all prostitutes are unwilling victims and that sex workers' rights advocates are enabling, even encouraging, trafficking in women and children.[16] This presumption is not new. Josephine Butler, who spearheaded efforts against so-called white slavery in Victorian England, was appalled by prostitutes who favored the regulation of prostitution (because it freed them from the risk of arrest) over the abolition of all prostitution.[17]

Trafficking in persons, of course, is a problem, especially involving children, adolescents, and adults put to work in industries as varied as sweatshops, agriculture, and begging.[18] Yet trafficking has been most often associated with prostitution. In India, prostitution is defined as trafficking when it involves a person under the age of eighteen and in all situations of deception or force. So in contrast to the legal status of prostitution by adults, it is illegal for minors to work in the sex trades, even though minors may legally work otherwise. Furthermore, law enforcement has used this prohibition to raid brothels in the red light districts even at the mere suspected presence in brothels of underage girls. During these raids, women are arrested even when there are no minors present. Other forms of police abuse have included violence, graft, and sexual harassment. When minors are illegally employed in other industries, these industries are not targeted in the same way.

The DMSC's organizing among sex workers, however, offers a unique approach to trafficking that aims to involve sex workers and reduce the violence and abuses of the authorities. In many of the districts, this represents a sea change from the control of the *goondah* (a kind of mafia) and the abuse of the police. The DMSC works against trafficking in two ways: It has created a committee on trafficking without any police membership. It also has developed a grassroots approach that involves trafficked persons, prostitutes, and nongovernmental organizations in simultaneously addressing the trafficking of minors and the alleviation of police abuse. This hands-on, grassroots approach has proven effective.

The DMSC has sought a nonjudicial, even nonprosecutorial, solution, in contrast to recent efforts by the United States and the United Nations that focus on law enforcement. This is desirable in India, where court cases may drag on literally for decades. Bureaucratic solutions, including trials, are thus unlikely to be pursued due to expenses and the extremely time-consuming aspects of such actions. Instead, the DMSC has turned to direct negotiations with the police and politicians. A twelve-person committee—made up of representatives from various organizations, politicians, and six prostitutes—conducts these negotiations. The committee works to facilitate relations between residents of the red light areas and law enforcement, and helps the DMSC use the law as a guideline in their antitrafficking work.

The committee was formed when the DMSC approached other nongovernmental organizations in order to form a bloc for negotiations with police in the red light districts. Initially, the nongovernmental organizations involved were health oriented, but now they contribute to the work of replacing the police with the vigilance of the sex workers themselves, except when police are needed · and called for. The kind of coalition the DMSC has initiated between politicians and sex workers works in India because the politicians accept negotiating with DMSC, which has a support base of a good number of nongovernmental organizations, as well as having a large number of participant sex workers. On the one hand, the politicians need the support of the members of the supporting NGOS; on the other hand, the large number of sex workers affected by certain issues enables, even encourages, them to organize both to tackle issues and to successfully gain the support of others. It would not be possible to focus attention on their issues if there were not so many sex workers affected and ready to organize. For example, if the numbers of people subjected to violence and extortion by the police did not run in the tens of thousands, the DMSC efforts to address these issues might not receive attention. And because there are so many sex workers interested in supporting a credit union and a condom-buying cooperative, these endeavors have also proven successful.

ANTITRAFFICKING INSIDE THE RED LIGHT DISTRICT

> *The former director of the DMSC stressed that assistance must be offered immediately when it is first suspected that trafficking is occurring. He felt it would be difficult, even impossible, to return to society after any time spent in the red light district. This is one reason to engage young women new to the district. Thus certain efforts in the red light districts often focus on new arrivals, with veteran residents interviewing them to discern their ages and the conditions under which they have come to undertake sex work.*

.....

The DMSC organizes sex workers to survey their own red light districts in order to prevent underage persons and coerced adults from entering the trade. The surveillance, followed by an interviewing of newcomers, is conducted by long-term residents of the district. Of course, sex workers are both transient and stable. While many sex workers come from various parts of India, as well as from neighboring countries, without intentions to settle permanently, they frequently stay for a number of years in one red light district. These sex workers become established members of the neighborhood community. Because they are very familiar with the area, they know who is from the district, who has been in the district before, and who is new.

Once a minor is found working in a brothel, she is taken to a residence outside the red light district. If an adult is found to be in the red light district under duress, she, too, is helped to leave. Leaving the red light district both for minors and legal adults means being accompanied away from the district and away from prostitution. These women are supported for a short time while deciding what to do next. This can mean returning to her family or starting in another line of work, and in some cases, in situations involving those who have attained the age of majority, staying in the red light district. Youths are accompanied back to their families if and when they choose to return. However, not all of them choose to return to their families because returning home is not always a solution. As of June 15, 2001, forty-three trafficked persons had been assisted by the DMSC, thirty-five of whom were minors. Numbers have increased since then, and over two hundred people have been helped to leave the red light districts in the past two years.[19] The majority of people who have found job training with the DMSC have turned to health care training (417 as of 2001), while others have entered nursing, the care of people living with HIV and AIDS, food production, manufacturing, and research. (This training is not limited to trafficked persons.)

Those who enter and/or stay in prostitution do so for a number of reasons. Unfortunately, some people who have left the red light districts feel indebted to their original helpers, having incurred expenses for food, lodging, and basic care, as well as transportation to one's village or to another location. These persons feel pressured to return to the red light districts to be able to work off the debt, given that there is little other work, especially for migrants. In this situation, there can be very few options. While the woman's decision as to what to do next is hers, money certainly makes for a pressing concern influencing her. For this reason, the programs offered to sex workers by the DMSC do not require that the women stop doing sex work.

Few vocational programs teach skills that would provide an income comparable to that made in prostitution, so many who benefit from the DMSC programs often supplement their "legitimate" incomes by doing sex work. This makes the DMSC different from most so-called rescue programs, which require sex workers to leave the industry, and if they do so with any vocational training, most likely for a vocation less lucrative than sex work. Instead, the DMSC supports sex workers and incorporates them at every level of organization. This fosters a level of cooperation impossible with those efforts antagonistic to sex work and sex workers, and it also makes it possible for sex workers to form blocs with other organizations in order to influence local authorities.

Despite the difficulties facing the organizing of sex work, the strategies and actions of the DMSC are quite successful. Based on the premise that "sex workers are part of the solution,"[20] the DMSC not only addresses the trafficking of minors and coerced adults but does so while providing sex workers with literacy training, peer education about safe sex, and schooling for their children. It also encourages the self-representation of sex workers at local, national, and international events.[21] It has contributed to creating the Millennium Mela gathering in February 2001, a successful meeting of sex workers from all over Asia.

Of course, the DMSC demands that sex workers engage in self-regulation and self-surveillance, which can be a form of self-restriction and self-censorship, encouraging greater and more pervasive control of sex workers by other sex workers. Nonetheless, self-surveillance seems an appropriate ethical choice, choosing self-regulation over the uninvited presence of police with their abusive practices and without access to negotiation. Furthermore, the self-surveillance by sex workers usually makes use of well-defined legal guidelines, rather than arbitrary punishment based on an individual's egregious abuse of power. It is, at least, a way to begin, a way that allows for the ongoing organizing of sex work.

The work of the DMSC shows the importance of inclusive organizing for sex workers and suggests that such organizing might also prove important for those engaged in other forms of affective labor. The DMSC's efforts are successful because they are focused on specific concerns, rather than constituting a blanket approach to sex work. Distinct from the organizing style more typical of unions, DMSC organizing is rather more a matter of assuring that sex workers can voluntarily adhere to a code of conduct. It also offers a welcome alternative to the many "rescue" programs for prostitutes in which outsiders press their moral agendas without any input from those affected. The DMSC's inclusion of sex workers in the implementation of programs and their encouragement of sex workers' efforts to create coalitions, go toward achieving better working conditions, rather than focusing on the morality of sex work. In this, the organizing aims for social empowerment, rather than the empowerment of an individual. In doing so, the overall conditions have improved for everyone in the red light districts.

The inclusion of sex workers at all levels of the organization and in determining the issues to be addressed makes for an ideal difficult to emulate, but the DMSC has shown the possibilities of such organizing. Like all affective labor, sex work draws on human capacities as its resource, so sex workers' organizing for social empowerment can serve as model for other affective laborers, especially those at the bottom levels of the affective labor hierarchy. There is some irony in the fact that the DMSC works with immaterial affect laborers in the world's oldest, but as yet unrecognized, profession to advance their cause at a far deeper, more meaningful and effective level than has been achieved by recognized workers in affect labor.

NOTES

1. The DMSC's clients come from a cross section of the population. Some may be aware of varying conditions in the sex industry, and some may be appalled at the level of engagement enjoyed by the "uppity" sex workers of the DMSC. Clients have often

assisted trafficked women to leave brothels on their own terms, rather than in coercive rescues.

2. Arlie Russell Hochschild, *The Managed Heart: Commercialization of Human Feeling* (Berkeley: University of California Press, 1983).

3. Wendy Chapkis, *Live Sex Acts: Women Performing Erotic Labor* (New York: Routledge, 1997).

4. Maurizio Lazzarato, "Immaterial Labor," in *Radical Thought in Italy: A Potential Politics*, ed. Paolo Virno and Michael Hardt (Minneapolis: University of Minnesota Press, 1996), 142.

5. Ibid., 137.

6. Other characters include people who direct potential clients to various venues, possibly cab drivers or touts. This is another lower-level entrepreneurial stage worthy of inquiry, but outside the scope of this project.

7. Minu Pal et al., "The Winds of Change Are Whispering at Your Door," in *Global Sex Workers: Rights, Resistance, and Redefinition*, ed. Kamala Kempadoo and Jo Doezema (New York: Routledge, 1998), 200–203.

8. Juhu Thukral and Melissa Ditmore, "Behind Closed Doors: An Analysis of Indoor Sex Work in New York City" (New York: Urban Justice Center, 2005). Juhu Thukral and Melissa Ditmore, "Revolving Door: An Analysis of Street-Based Prostitution in New York City" (New York: Urban Justice Center, 2003), www.sexworkersproject.org. Melissa Ditmore, "Report from the USA: Do Prohibitory Laws Promote Risk?" *Research for Sex Work* 4 (2001): www.nswp.org/r4sw.

9. Lin Lean Lim, ed. *The Sex Sector: The Economic and Social Bases of Prostitution in Southeast Asia* (Geneva: International Labour Organization, 1998).

10. For example, in 2003, women "rescued" from a Thai brothel by the International Justice Mission/Trafcord were detained and questioned against their will by Trafcord, a U.S.-funded antitrafficking nongovernmental organization (Shan Women's Action Network, "Report by the Shan Women's Action Network (SWAN) on Services Provided to Trafcord on May 3, 2003" [Chiang Mai, Thailand: Empower Chiang Mai, 2003]). Most detainees later escaped, and their choice of the word *escape* in their reports undermines and belies the ostensible rescue. See Empower Chiang Mai, "A Report by Empower Chiang Mai on the Human Rights Violations Women Are Subjected to When 'Rescued' by Anti-trafficking Groups Who Employ Methods Using Deception, Force, and Coercion" (Chiang Mai, Thailand: Empower Chiang Mai, 2003); and Empower Chiang Mai, "US Sponsored Entrapment," *Research for Sex Work* 8 (2005): *www.researchforsexwork .org*, 25–27. Such supposed rescues demonstrate that often the well-intentioned people who promote them have neglected to ask fundamental questions as to why someone would want to work in the sex industry, and what makes it advantageous for them

11. Ivan Wolffers, "Empowerment of Sex workers and HIV Prevention," *Research for Sex Work* 3 (2000): 2.

12. See the United Nations Supplementary Convention on the Abolition of Slavery, the Slave Trade, and Institutions and Practices Similar to Slavery (1956).

13. In the developing world, condoms can cost up to 40 percent of the price of sex, making them prohibitively expensive. Cheryl Overs and Paulo Longo, *Making Sex Work Safe* (London: Russell, 1997), 42.

14. I attended a session highlighting this situation at the Thirteenth International

Conference on AIDS in Durban, South Africa, in 2000. One presenter noted a lack of self-esteem in sex workers as an obstacle to safe sex. A representative of the Network of Sex Work Projects asked whether self-esteem was really the crux of the issue, or whether poor working conditions could lead to difficulties in practicing safer sex. She further questioned whether the researcher's own expectations, enforced by widely held stereotypes of sex workers, led to the conclusion that sex workers had low self-esteem.

15. Licia Brussa, ed. *Health, Migration, and Sex Work: The Experience of* TAMPEP (Amsterdam: TAMPEP International, 1999), 69.

16. Ellen Carol DuBois and Linda Gordon, "Seeking Ecstasy on the Battlefield: Danger and Pleasure in Nineteenth-Century Feminist Sexual Thought," in *Pleasure and Danger: Exploring Female Sexuality*, ed. Carole S. Vance (Boston: Routledge and Kegan Paul, 1984), 31–49. Gayle Rubin, "Thinking Sex," in Vance, *Pleasure and Danger*, 267–319.

17. Judith R. Walkowitz, *Prostitution and Victorian Society: Women, Class, and the State* (Cambridge: Cambridge University Press, 1980).

18. Amy O'Neil Richard, "CIA Report on Trafficking" (April 2000).

19. Statement by a DMSC representative at the Fifteenth International Conference on AIDS, Bangkok, July 15, 2004.

20. This is a Network of Sex Work Projects slogan.

21. Pal et al., "The Winds of Change."

MORE THAN A JOB: MEANING, AFFECT, AND
TRAINING HEALTH CARE WORKERS

ARIEL DUCEY

> Neither love nor hatred of work is inherent in man, or in-
> herent in any given line of work. For work has no intrinsic
> meaning.
> —C. Wright Mills, *White Collar: The American Middle Classes*

E-mail still seems to me like a mode of communication most valuable for conveying new and urgent matters, though apparently not everyone agrees. I recently received in my inbox a "summary brief" on trends in career development, in which it was reported that "nearly 50% of all those working in the United States would choose a new type of work if they had the chance." This *Wall Street Journal*/ABC News poll result hardly seemed to qualify as breaking news. The pollsters' explanation of the finding, however, was startling; they concluded that such apparently high levels of dissatisfaction with work are evidence that "we live in an age" in which work has become "more personal than ever—when who you are is what you do—a deeper source of personal satisfaction than ever." The authors of the summary brief offered a thankfully more cautious explanation, though one that sounded strangely like an admonition: "Many are reexamining their careers in light of the growing realization that work should be more than a job."

The proposition that Americans are seeking or should seek work that is "more than a job" implies that the work—more precisely, the waged labor—many, if not most, people already do is devoid of meaning and satisfaction beyond the wages earned; it is a simplistic proposition, one that silently privileges unspecified kinds of work. Likewise, the hidden suggestion that work that is more than a job subordinates or transcends its status as waged labor constitutes a bourgeois fantasy. But it appears positively surreal that the fact that 50 percent of the people working in the United States would choose a new type of work is interpreted as a sign of growing engagement with work, rather than alienation from it; that the statement "who you are is what you do" is delivered without irony in the context of an economy defined by the relentless creation of low-wage, dead-end jobs. These interpretations are like mantras: perhaps saying that work offers a deeper source of personal satisfaction than ever before will make it so.

Drawing on interviews with allied health care workers in New York City (nursing assistants, technicians, and other paraprofessional workers) and administrators in the training industry in which they participate, in what follows I examine how the imperative for work to be more than a job is created and deployed through training and education programs in the health care sector.[1] Surely there is no other kind of work more likely to be more than a job than that of providing care. Surely it is in providing care that the need to earn a wage can and should be transcended. But in the health care sector, the backbone of the service economy, workers who provide care are well aware of the latent function of the injunction that their work should be more than a job: the rationalization of their low wages. And even though they feel that their work is important, health care workers are nonetheless subjected, like the rest of us, to the creeping effects of the constant message that work should be more than a job. When Marie, a talented and compassionate nursing assistant, is asked by her neighbors what she does, she tells them she is a "professional butt cleaner" to—in her words—remind her of where she is at and where she hopes to be. "Don't get me wrong, I like my job," she added, "but it's just that it's the same thing repetitively, and I'm not growing." Juan, a registrar and physical therapy assistant, said about his work at a hospital: "I feel that I'm wasting here."

In the health care industry in New York City, such dissatisfaction with work has been channeled into a vast training and education apparatus. For many health care workers, continuing training and education is the most obvious way to satisfy their desire to grow, to change, to improve. Not surprisingly, the training industry in New York City that supports and fuels the ambitions of allied health care workers prospers in an era that invests great psychic, cultural, and material resources in the promise of work that is more than a job. In fact, federal and state governments have allotted hundreds of millions of dollars to hospitals and to training health care workers in New York State since the mid-1990s, on the premise that the workforce is woefully unprepared for the effects of competition and managed care in health care.[2] The influx of training funds into the health care sector in New York City spawned a cottage industry of health care workforce specialists, including individual entrepreneurs, consulting firms, community colleges, universities, and for-profit and not-for-profit vocational schools. These individuals and organizations often design and implement training in partnership with labor unions and employers. Leading the way is the City University of New York (CUNY)—the largest urban institution of higher education in the country, comprising seventeen public undergraduate institutions and enrolling more than 450,000 students—which has become a major developer of workforce training programs, including those in health care. The latest in a series of reports on the issue found that nearly half of CUNY's 2003 enrollment was in continuing education and work-force programming (adult education courses; employment and welfare-to-work programs; and business contract training).[3]

The interest in training health care workers is not surprising, given that the health care sector is New York City's single largest employer, employing nearly one out of eight workers in 2002.[4] Employment in the health care industry grew by 14.1 percent from 1990 to 2000 and is projected to continue to grow, making it a buffer against more volatile industries. The northeastern corridor stretching from Baltimore to Boston has become the "nation's health epicenter," adding 50,000 jobs between 2000 and 2002, while in the same period all other industries combined shed 220,000.[5] Training and educating health care workers constitutes yet another extension of the medical-pharmaceutical complex into the region's economy.

The possibility of such a large industry to train health care workers is based, in part, on the nature of the health care labor process and occupational structure: health care organizations continually tweak the division of labor in response to fiscal constraint and new technologies, often necessitating training. Regulatory agencies require training and continuing education as part of the licensing of professionals and organizations. In addition, while some corporations or public bureaucracies offer career ladders internal to the organization, the dominance of professions in the health care industry means that specific organizations can create only limited career ladders; career progression requires significant external education and often entails a switch in employer.

The training and education industry in this case, however, is also a specific product of the efforts of 1199 Service Employees International Union (SEIU), the largest health care workers' union in the country, which represents over 230,000 health care workers in New York State, to ensure its own institutional well-being, as well as that of the hospitals where the majority of its members are employed. The union's president, Dennis Rivera, was the mastermind behind the negotiation of a number of aid packages to New York's health care system, many of which specifically allocated funds for worker retraining. Most of these aid packages were negotiated in the mid-1990s, when New York City hospitals predicted they would undergo massive restructuring as a result of market-based reforms.

Here, I am focusing only on what the training and education industry has become, rather than whether it fulfills the expectations of the various stakeholders and powerbrokers who brought the industry into being. Regardless of the logic by which training funds were rationalized or the political interests served by them, the training and education industry for health care workers is something more and other than what an evaluation of its outcomes would reveal. The training industry contributes to the affect economy, an economy increasingly central to the production of value in a services-based, capitalist society. Focusing on the education and training industry in terms of its relation to affect necessitates a shift away from thinking about education and training in terms of its success at providing skills, knowledge, or upward mobility. Education and training are in fact valued and valuable apart from such traditional outcomes. Likewise, the nature and growth of this education and training industry cannot be solely explained by the individual's needs and the employer's demands which it supposedly fulfills. Instead, I am drawing attention to the unanticipated and less visible flows of value in the training and education industry for allied health care workers.

The concept of affect as I use it refers to a different register of phenomena than the concept of emotions, at least as the latter term is typically used in sociology. The necessity of holding to a distinction between emotions and affect is supported by research and thought in a number of fields such as philosophy, neuroscience, and communication studies. The neuroscientist Antonio Damasio recently proposed a distinction between emotions and feelings, though I propose to call the same distinction that between affect and emotions. For Damasio, when an organism encounters a stimulus capable of triggering an emotion, the emotion consists of the actual physical response of the organism as it is mapped and modified by the brain. This is a process that can become, but does not necessarily become, conscious. Emotionally competent stimuli in fact can be detected while bypassing attention and thought. Often—but again, not always—attention and thought are subsequently turned on these stimuli, but emotions are modifications of the body that are autonomous from conscious thought and attention. Feelings, on the other hand, are "largely constituted by the perception of a certain body state" or "the perception of the body state forms the essence of a feeling."[6] Feelings require a level of awareness and attention, awareness that is based on mental maps of the body's physical state. Emotions are changes in the state of the body, which the brain maps and which can then become the basis for feelings.

Damasio furthermore suggests that the relationship between an emotionally competent stimulus and the feeling that may emerge is not linear. The process encounters numerous types of interference. For instance, the physiological response of the body is not only a reaction to the stimulus but can also be informed by memories of the stimulus and prior reactions to it by oneself and others. Similarly the reaction to stimulus is by no means determined or hardwired into the brain; as a result of socialization the reaction to and selection of stimuli to which to react may change over time. In addition, there may be gaps in the brain's map of the body that forms the basis of feelings—the brain may not create a true "representation" of all physiological properties. Many of these relays between the body and the brain furthermore happen almost simultaneously.

The reason for using the term *affect* for the nonconscious aspect of emotion that Damasio describes is that in the social sciences, *emotion* is a term most often used as an equivalent of feelings. Literature on emotional labor and emotional management, in particular,[7] focuses on essentially cognitive adjustments—feelings—to the objects that cause emotions. In Arlie Hochschild's now classic work, flight attendants were asked in training seminars to manage their feelings so as to produce an experience airline passengers would want to buy. Damasio recognizes that we may consciously evaluate the objects that cause emotions: "One of the key purposes of our educational development is to interpose a nonautomatic evaluative step between causative objects and emotional responses."[8] We may attempt to consciously evaluate certain kinds of objects and produce socially acceptable (or even commercially acceptable) emotions about them. But I suggest that the training programs studied here are aimed in addition to intervene in affect, which shadows but is independent of consciously modified emotions or feelings. As such, the potential effects of the training considered here are rather different: automatic, noncognitive modulations of bodies in reaction to certain objects and environments. The concept of affect is not unknown to sociology, but it is relatively undertheorized as distinct from emotions or feelings since sociology is largely situated in the so-called action frame of reference, the level of expectations, motives, and decisions that has already been filtered out of affective potential.[9]

Instead I am engaging a concept of affect along the lines Brian Massumi has suggested. As he sees it, there are two levels at play in any event: that of intensity, a state of suspense, of potential disruption; and that of semantics and semiotics, of language, narrative, and expectations. These two levels resonate with one another; their vibrations are sometimes dissonant and at other times harmonious. Affect is "their point of emergence" and "their vanishing point," where the vibrations between the levels either emerge as something actual or fade into the virtual. Affect therefore shadows every event. It is the source of the unexpected, of the unmotivated, of surprise. The level of noncognitive intensity is autonomous from what emerges in consciousness, but it is nonetheless the realm of potential from which any cognitive realizations will be drawn. Cognition—the realm of language and decision making—reduces intensity, converting suspense into expectation.[10] To intervene in affect, therefore, is to attempt to control or regulate how intensity becomes expectation, action, and decision.

Substituting affect for Damasio's term *emotion* also seems appropriate since Damasio, like many theorists considered here, draws on Baruch Spinoza, in whose philosophical system affect also remained distinct from emotions. Antonio Negri, for one, elicits from Spinoza a simple definition of affect as the "power to act."[11] Accordingly, this essay examines how the training and education industry for health care workers attempts to direct the power to act (to engage, to actively participate), or to convert engagement into economic value. Training and education may also teach specific skills and knowledge— including those of emotion management—but these are of no value if they are not also enacted.

The analysis that follows furthermore posits that the power to act is not controllable because there is no linear path between a state of suspension or intensity and its actualization in specific feelings, expectations, or motives. The pressing explanatory gap in neuroscience is that of how the activity of neurons in the brain becomes the phenomenal experience of images, representations, and feelings. Some researchers have therefore turned to the nonlinear dynamics of self-organized systems, or chaos theory, for an answer. The dynamics of self-organized systems "can yield properties of the system that are qualitatively different from any linear combination of its variables."[12] Sociological studies of emotions acknowledge the neurological and physical bases of emotions, but they do not generally conceptualize the relation between them and experience,[13] let alone conceptualize those bases as a self-organizing system that cannot be linked to conscious emotions through linear series or correlations. Of course, none of this prevents those in the training and education industry from *attempting* to control the transformation of intensity into feelings, from making affect a valuable resource in the shifting economy.

This study is complicated by the fact that language only captures what has emerged from the level of intensity, that affect cannot be exposed through language. The conscious statements by people interviewed in this research are not representations of what has happened in affect, but, rather, indications of the significance for the organism or system of what has happened in affect. The discourse that emerged in these interviews as a particularly charged indication of changes in affect is that of "meaning." The sense that engagement or the power to act must be triggered or controlled, which underlies the injunction for work to be "more than a job," is often expressed as problems or questions of meaning, as the experience of Veronica shows.

Veronica, a nursing assistant,[14] spent two years from 1994 to 1996 in an 1199 GED program (run by its joint labor-management Training and Upgrading Fund), passed the exam on her third attempt, then enrolled in a union-run college preparatory course that helps participants acquire the language and math skills necessary to pass the entrance examination recently established for all four-year CUNY colleges. She passed the entrance exam and as of 2002 had completed four college courses at CUNY, paid for by the union. School had been an ongoing, concurrent activity to her work and home life for close to ten years. She hoped eventually to obtain an associate's degree in nursing.

> Yeah, I figured if you get into the hospital [and the union], I could become an LPN [licensed practical nurse] or something. I always wanted a job that means—you know, it's something, but as a nursing assistant you don't get no respect—I mean you get treated—it should be an important job, because you take care of people, you listen to their problems, you console them, and yet you get treated as if you're nobody. Especially by the nurses.

Veronica started to say that she had always wanted a job that means something, like an LPN. But she corrected herself, reminding herself that her job as a nursing assistant did, in fact, mean something, was an important job. Yet the problem was that it was not treated as an important job and that those who did it were not treated with respect. Nonetheless, she had begun to think of the work of licensed or registered nurses as meaningful in comparison to her own work. Veronica was aware that the way a job is perceived is not synonymous with its worth, but meaning was the discourse most ready to hand to explain her desire to have a job that would be valued and respected.

Hospitals and their management consultants also turn to this discourse of meaning when faced with the reality that many health care workers are unhappy and feel fundamentally unappreciated and underpaid. A recent report by the American Hospital Association (AHA) Commission on Workforce for Hospitals and Health Systems titled "In Our Hands: How Hospital Leaders

Can Build a Thriving Workforce" argued that fostering meaningful work is one of five keys to solving the "workforce crisis" in health care: "People enter health careers to make a difference in the lives of others. But hospital work is also demanding, hard, and exacting, requiring skill, focus, and attention to detail. As the demands on each caregiver and support workers have increased, the work has become less meaningful and more tedious."[15] The wish that hospital work would be once again meaningful is another expression of the imperative for work to be more than a job. This discourse of meaning is essential to understanding the investment in training and educating health care workers. However meaning is ascertained—as an objective measure of particular jobs or as a product of the way the jobs are socially regarded and valued—is increasingly not relevant except in relationship to the development of an affect economy, in relationship to the shift in capital accumulation to the domain of affect. The heath care industry and its training/education component is one important site for the development of techniques to intervene in affect and transform it into value. The search for meaning plays its part in the development of this economy: if meaningfulness is the measure of particular jobs, then the education and training industry, particularly in health care, creates credentials that confirm the presence of meaning and proceeds to credential people—for a fee. If the problem of meaning is that of how jobs are regarded, then education and training becomes a vehicle for elevating the status of some occupations or compensating for a lack that is ascribed to people in supposedly nonmeaningful jobs—for a fee.

Defining meaningful work only through implication, the AHA report is striking because it takes as given that health care work is not (or is no longer) meaningful. The link between meaning and caring is and can only be made by resorting to a romantic myth that one-on-one caring constitutes the true heart of hospital work: "Today, many in direct patient care feel tired and burned-out . . . with little or no time to experience the one-on-one caring that should be the heart of hospital employment."[16] One need only read a few histories of hospitals to come to the conclusion that one-on-one caring has never been the heart of hospital employment;[17] yet the report reinforces the notion that hospital work can and should transcend its status of wage labor, as does the statement that people enter health care work to make a difference in the lives of others. Both statements imply somehow that it is impossible to be a good caregiver and to be concerned about wages.[18] The fact that many of these workers do not have more lucrative options in the labor market, given their education and work histories, does not fully explain why people commit to the field of health care, particularly at entry-level, low-wage direct-care jobs. Many of the health care workers I have interviewed attested to their enjoyment in taking care of people, their sense of a calling to this kind of work and its rewards. But they were also concerned about their wages. Moreover, feelings of growth, of being challenged (intellectually, physically, or emotionally), and of autonomy do not automatically accompany the provision of care. Caring work is still work, and as such it has no intrinsic meaning, only the meaning that is assigned to it and represented in such things as wages and working conditions. Many nursing assistants are among those Americans who would choose a new type of work if they had the chance.

Meaning figures prominently in the discourses of health care workers, employers, trainers, and consultants, and the reason it is impossible to pin meaning down, to identify what constitutes meaningful work and declare when it is achieved, is because it is a free-floating engine of growth and production. The channeling and directing of the desire for meaning is the bread-and-butter business of an affect economy. The training and education industry can offer itself as a vehicle for achieving meaning while the industry's existence—in fact, its regeneration and growth—depends on the fact that meaning perpetually vanishes. The difficulty of Veronica's situation is that although she desires meaningful work, the desire for meaning is conditioned on the fact that meaning can never be found. Continual education and training is predicated on the limitless postponement of meaningful work. The education and training industry takes advantage of Veronica's desire for work that means something, but it does not provide such work. One can see how meaning might become perpetually deferred, but the engagement that the desire for meaning produces —affect—is continually reinforced.

Veronica expresses a desire for meaningful work and education and training takes advantage of this expressed desire, attempting to direct her engagement, her power to act, to direct affect. But it would be simplistic to interpret how Veronica describes her experience as evidence that the training and education industry is driven simply by the desires or needs of individual workers who demand it. Such an interpretation assumes that the power to act is located within individuals and outside history and society. Similarly, saying that workers have a growing realization that work should be more than a job fails to consider the political and economic conditions that make such a realization possible and probable. Wanda's experience, by contrast, shows that an individual's demand might not be necessary at all. In fact, the education and training industry is a productive apparatus that takes advantage of the desires it encounters, but it also modulates affect independent of the professed needs of individual workers or employers.

"I'm not comfortable just working like that. I wanted to be a nurse," Wanda said by way of explaining her most recent return to school to a registered nurse prep program at the age of forty-five. By "just working like that" she meant working without also going to school or pursuing other interests and passions. "I wanted to continue my education because I started it at home [Trinidad] . . . but I never finished. So I said, well, if I'm here, this is the place that they say is the land of opportunities, I'm going back to school." In Wanda's story, the way in which the education and training industry is organized has played a crucial role in coconstructing her pattern of mobility, as well as the relationship of that mobility to fulfillment and meaning. Wanda entered an industry with opportunities rare for a worker of her color and background,[19] and she gained access to an adjunct educational complex similarly uncommon in the world of low-wage service work. As soon as Wanda landed her first union (1199) job as a nursing assistant—a year after emigrating from Trinidad in 1987—she obtained her GED through a union-funded program. She obtained her LPN certificate in 1995 after attending a part-time, union-funded program for two years.

After obtaining her LPN certificate, she stopped going to school for a while, but said, "I shouldn't have done that because I got my [LPN] certificate in 1995, and if I had continued, I would have been finished by now [with the registered nurse, RN, degree]." I asked her why she took a break from school.

Well, at that time, when I graduated, they were not hiring RNs anymore. They were laying off the RNs. So I said, what's the point, you know? And I just kept on working as an LPN. And then the union also stopped giving the course, or paying for the course for RNs because it [the RN shortage] was not so extreme then. And until it was . . . we got some flyers saying that they had started paying for the RN course. So I said look, I'll take the opportunity.

Wanda said she would have continued with school without union support, but there is little doubt that the union education programs dictated, to a greater or lesser extent, the course of her career. The short-lived and ill-founded predictions of a registered nurse surplus in the mid-1990s eliminated nurse training programs so that health care workforce experts were caught off guard by the substantial, nationwide nursing shortage apparent only five years later. The joint labor-management Training and Upgrading Fund had only recently restarted several programs in response to the shortage, for which Wanda hoped to qualify.

But what is of particular interest about Wanda's story is not only that her career movements were not entirely a matter of individual choice but that they were also not dictated by a personal quest for meaning, respect, or fulfillment.

After obtaining her LPN certificate in 1995, she worked as a nursing assistant for three years, waiting for a job to open up at the hospital where she worked, from which she lived only one block in a hospital-owned apartment building. Our conversation shows how Wanda was taken up by, and asked to respond to, a process of perpetual modulation:

Ariel: *In that period when you were an LPN but you were still working as a nursing assistant, did that change how you did your job as a nursing assistant?*

Wanda: Well, I became an LPN while I was working in the OR [operating room]: I wasn't dealing with patients, I was dealing with the instruments. As the instruments came out from the OR, we had to wash them and we had to set them, set the trays. And then sometimes we had to sterilize them. So it was a different job altogether. I worked for three years in the OR.

Why did you first go to the OR?

They were downsizing one year, and they closed one of my floors, and I was floating, working different floors until I got the appointment in the OR.

How did you feel about that transition?

I felt good about it. Because I think I needed a change. Because I welcomed the change, the work was different. . . . Learning different—learning, learning, learning. I learned how to set the trays for the different operations. I did that until I got the appointment to be an LPN.

So you left the OR when you got the LPN position?

Yes. I went to the ER [emergency room] then. [laughs] That was another thing, whew!

How did you feel about that change?

I liked that change because it was something new. Remember, I was going as a nurse now. Then they said they did not want any more LPNs in the ER.

Why?

I don't know. We got new administrators; I don't know what took place. And that is how I came to be working in Peds [pediatrics]. The union took up the cause, because we would call that displacement, and then we had a meeting, and they asked me where I wanted to work, and I said I think I want to work in Peds, with the children. So that's where I went. It's nice working with the children.

Wanda found aspects of her work that engaged her and surprised her in the various jobs she has held. She became very animated when discussing her interactions with the mothers in the pediatrics unit in particular; but she also lit up when describing working with the operating room instruments. Wanda both sought out and was exposed to numerous training and education experiences. The course of her career had been steered by her personal and practical needs, but, just as importantly, by the availability of training and education, and the vicissitudes of the health care industry. A survey questionnaire might reveal that she was first a nursing assistant and then an LPN, *not* the variety of units on which she worked or the fact that she received two months training on the pediatrics floor, or that when she worked in the general medical/surgery unit on the fifth floor, the entire unit was sent to a mandatory communication class because of patient complaints, or that she took a computer class while working in the OR for her own edification. "Learning, learning, learning" animates her occupational history. Wanda did not embark on an explicit journey to track down meaningful work; she stepped into the circuits of an affect economy in which perpetual engagement is produced. For both Veronica and Wanda, the outcomes commonly attributed to education and training—a new job, better pay, knowledge—did not follow in an immediate or straightforward manner. Three years passed before Wanda put her LPN degree to use, and when she did, her eighteen-dollar-an-hour salary was only two dollars more than what she had been making on the evening shift as a nursing assistant. She waited to go on in school until industry predictions of a nurse surplus passed. She went into the OR and into pediatrics because of hospital downsizing and/or work reorganization. Wanda did not demand these changes, but she found that the learning each change entailed sustained her over the years in these jobs.

An affect economy cultivates engagement and generates energy, which are both before and other than meaning. Any technique for cultivating engagement and the power to act is potentially quite valuable economically. Antonio Negri goes so far as to argue that "*value* is now an *investment of desire.*"[20] One of the features of this affect economy is the struggle over this value: Who will benefit from its production? For many employers and trainers, the hope is that the training and education industry will channel engagement into hard work, into the attitude that "work is more than a job" and therefore requires commitment regardless of the conditions of that work.

For instance, one nonprofit organization dedicated to improving the quality of direct-care services has developed an initiative, in response to some of the new grants and funds available, to encourage workers (i.e., home care workers) to enroll in college courses. Participating workers can receive a nominal bonus and a specialized certificate after completing a noncredit college preparatory course and four specially designed for-credit college courses focusing on areas such as psychology, behavior management, disabilities, and therapeutic recreation. The mission of the organization is to improve the quality of care. Since one of the major barriers to quality care in settings such as home care is the substantial rate of worker turnover, due to the low wages, the organization's director hopes that increased worker training will serve not only to make these workers better caregivers but also as the grounds for negotiating better wages and working conditions. The organization's strategy recognizes that a central way to improve care is to improve the lives of those who provide it.

It seems possible, however, that training and educating direct-care workers will undermine the organization's goal of developing a more skilled, more committed workforce; after all, such workers are likely to leave their jobs as soon as they have enough education and credentials to do so. The certificate program had not yet translated into better wages, and the chances that the wages and working conditions of direct-care workers will soon improve enough to keep them in their jobs is slim. The director noted that this was a potential problem in principle more than in practice:

> It's true, you say, well, people become supervisors or push upward. On the other hand, a worker who's going to university, working and going to school taking one or two courses, it takes ten years. So if the turnover rate for direct-care workers is one and a half years or three years average and you had someone who was going to school, making their way, moving forward that way, and stayed for seven or eight years, that would be wonderful. A worker isn't necessarily going to college and getting a bachelor's degree, which opens up other doors.

There are, as the director reminded me, thousands of workers across the city pursuing college degrees this way—one course at a time, while working and, in most cases, managing a family. The certificate program the organization has developed, consisting of four courses, does not move these workers substantially toward a college degree. Nor is it a certificate that qualifies participants for a specific, better job. But, apparently, what it *can* do is engage the workers, give them a sense of accomplishment, and place the work within a context of more academic knowledge, all of which potentially improves the quality of care by improving the relations and exchanges between patients and caregivers. The director's implication is that workers in the certificate program might have a sense that they are moving forward and this may keep them in their jobs and improve their attitude and feelings about their jobs. Clearly the most direct way the training and education programs might improve care is to reduce turnover, regardless of any changes in the conditions and terms of work.

This is why education *and* training can be appropriately discussed as if they were synonymous. Doubtless there is a difference between in-service training for a new medical device and union-funded or bonus-carrying college courses. Presumably college credits establish a base for these health care workers to pursue an economically meaningful degree. Nonetheless, since it takes a working person—most of the health care workers I have interviewed—many years to prepare for college, let alone obtain a BA, employers and training program planners not only judge their programs in terms of traditional outcomes like a new job or significant wage increases but also consider how education and training affects the worker's relationship to his or her (con)current job. College credits are an important currency, but they do not show the dividends of a degree for many years, if ever. In the apparently widespread, but not surprising, situation that work fails to produce satisfaction and fulfillment, both training and education have been positioned as potential ways to compensate for that failure, in addition to (or rather than) serving to prepare workers for better work or to provide knowledge for its own sake. Most educational programs funded in this particular health care industry are furthermore a benefit of employment rather than a social right, so workers must continue to work while pursuing an education, extending the time it takes to earn a degree or credential.[21] While in some analytical contexts the difference between education and training is great, as is the difference between the potential earnings of a college graduate and a high school graduate, the reality for workers entangled in the education and training industry can be, and most likely will be, a matter of the perpetual deferment of typical outcomes.

Michel Foucault famously likened the school to the hospital to the prison to the factory as spaces of enclosure and discipline where bodies are classified and subjectivities molded to fit the needs of a modern society.[22] Gilles Deleuze has argued, however, that discipline, as a mode of arranging power, has given way to control (and that this is a transformation recognized and predicted by Foucault). In a control society, "just as the corporation replaces the factory, *perpetual training* tends to replace the *school*, and continuous control to replace the examination." In a control society, power is exercised through "limitless postponements" and continual modulations of life and relations that makes it increasingly less useful (in terms of politics or theory) to think of institutions (such as school, work, home) as distinct, with separate functions and distinct methods.[23] The attempt of hospital administrators and trainers to (re)claim work as the terrain of meaning, of subjective investment and fulfillment, betrays the impulse to control, as Deleuze has identified.

Phenomenological analyses, which suggest that interaction is performative and constructed, assume that no matter how fleeting, meaning construction is an act of consciousness, an activity that sets apart humans from other organisms and the inorganic. What the training and education industry allows us to see, what it exemplifies, is that the desire for meaning is immanent to an affect economy. The desire for meaning emerges from confluences of non-human (institutions, objects) and human actors, confluences not necessarily expressed in the motives or intentions of human actors. This immanent desire constitutes a protean bundle of energy, a force. While Veronica's story, her narrative, clearly shows how an individual's expressed desire for meaning might be taken up by the education and training industry, Wanda's story shows how the desire for meaning is constituted beside and beyond the conscious intentions and motives of actors. Learning is produced in surplus as Wanda moves through various jobs and training programs, and there are many directions in which such learning might be channeled.

Beyond phenomenological analysis lies an ontological revision of thought about the body, including the laboring/learning body. As Luciana Parisi and Tiziana Terranova have pointed out, bodies might best be viewed as compositions of fluids, forces, and affects preceding the phenomenological self.[24] A body, furthermore, is not synonymous with the human organism, but refers to material bits that can be drawn together or apart by forces, reorganized according to changes in these forces. A body, for Spinoza, is defined by its capacity of affecting and being affected. The education and training industry might be thought of as one system (among many) for controlling the flows of energy, in particular that generated by the desire for meaningful work. In so doing, it attempts to direct affect, the power to act. The training and education industry perpetuates the endless reconstruction of bodies and capacities, the limitless reconfiguration of desire and its investment. This is exemplified by Wanda's reaction to each of her job changes, that is, the way in which she ricochets between events that powerfully and momentarily engage her. It is also exemplified in the ways some trainers spoke about their programs.

At a large community-based training organization, I interviewed the former director of allied health programs. Her office was in the corner of a sunny warehouse loft, with windows facing a skyline recently emptied of the World Trade Center. She had just taken the newly created position overseeing workforce development projects, which had been implemented in the wake of the economic downturn exacerbated—but not caused—by the events of September 11, 2001. The loft had just been vacated by a dot.com gone bust, and the spatial transition from new media to training for entry-level health care jobs embodied the economic state of the city. Reflecting on her work as a trainer and, earlier, as a nurse, she said: "There has to be an administrative decision to constantly nurture the workforce. If I had my way, there would be all kinds of continuing opportunities for self-exploration and personal fulfillment. I think that those are linked to helping people to cope better with the kinds of jobs that they have in their lives, which are very rigorous and exhausting, emotionally and physically." In the particular setting of this interview, which pointed to a number of insecurities facing the city and its workers, it was not surprising that nurturance constituted the paramount concern of training. Moreover, it seemed politically and ethically important to demand nurturance, to expect it even from training courses on very narrow occupational and skill-based topics. This workforce expert went on to describe how nurturance could be implemented in short courses and in-services on topics like nutrition, stress reduction, body mechanics, and the health care worker's own health problems (which often stem from the physical demands of the work).

Like the credit-bearing certificate program described above, such courses would encourage workers to rearrange their relationship to their work. The implication is not that workers will be able to cope with their work and the brute necessity of waged labor because the experiences outside of work are richer, but because education and training will refashion work itself as an object or arena of stimulation and engagement. In this second case, the focus on the actual bodies and energies of the workforce proves significant; the trainer recognizes that the basic way in which workers are out of tune with their work is embodied, so that a more direct route to adjust their experience of work might be through their bodies, or through the noncognitive level that in fact conditions which emotions or attitudes can even be expressed.

Having identified this controlling impulse among trainers, as well as their incipient recognition that affect might be the source of economic value, one of the important features of affect to which it is necessary to return is its autonomy and its continual escape from capture by language or tools of assessment. There is indeterminacy in how affect is channeled into value and for whom. The trainers I have interviewed suggest that one of the potential benefits of their programs is that they take the desire to be engaged among health care workers and turn it into investment in, and identification with, the employing organization and/or the job, which could become measurable as (among other things) job satisfaction and lower turnover rates. Knowing that trainers harbor this hope, I asked Veronica during our interview several times whether "going to school has had any effect on how you feel or behave at work." Firmly, and without hesitation, she said no each time. Veronica said that she kept work and school separate; only one or two people at her place of employment even knew that she was trying to get a nursing degree. Veronica was concerned that if others at work found out, particularly supervisors and nurses, it would exacerbate their suspicions that she did not respect authority or defer to those above her.

Then, near the end of the interview, Veronica mentioned that she talked about the books she was reading in her classes with patients at her hospital (a private, nonprofit on the tony Upper East Side of Manhattan). Going over to a bookshelf, she pulled out a folder full of handwritten notes, essentially reading lists, from patients. One note included Howard Zinn's *People's History of the United States* and Noam Chomsky's *Understanding Power.Com.* Another note, written by a teacher, comprised three full pages of books. Veronica had read some of these books and referred to the lists when she was choosing what to read next. Employers who provide and fund training are banking on the fact that employees who are going to school make better workers—they bring what they are learning to the workplace, they are more engaged when they can see a future. Although Veronica told me that she did not see any connection between her work as a nursing assistant and the content of her college courses, the patients with whom she discussed books probably experienced a connection. Likewise, her employer, the hospital, benefited indirectly from what was undoubtedly a pleasurable interaction for both Veronica and her patients, even if none of her coworkers or supervisors knew she was going to school. Nonetheless the value of affect, the expression of Veronica's engagement, cannot be easily calculated by the hospital nor (so far) accounted for in its measures of productivity. It is as if Veronica's folder of notes from her patients forms the center of a body that holds Veronica together with her patients, the hospital, and her teacher—a more powerful body. This particular ripple in and between bodies coming together as organisms, individuals, forces, and institutions is potentially valuable.

Negri has argued that in the global market of postmodernity there is no possibility of measuring the value of labor and, furthermore, the "problem of measure itself cannot be located." Labor is neither outside capital (as it was under the conditions of primitive accumulation) nor is it inside capital, since money (exchange) no longer represents a specific quantity of labor nor does the reproduction of labor determine the value of goods. It follows that there can be no real correspondence between a wage and the value or productivity of work. Negri argues that "the more the measure of value becomes ineffectual, the more the value of labor-power becomes determinant in production. . . . In this paradoxical way, labor becomes affect, or better, labor finds its value in affect, if affect is defined as the 'power to act.' "[25] Accordingly, the value of Veronica's labor lies in those moments of engagement wherein her capacity for affecting others and being affected by others is expanded. And those moments of engagement are "determinant in production," in other words, they are necessary to the very functioning of the hospital.

What is being produced and traded in Veronica's encounter with education is not just technical skills per se, or knowledge, but affect. It sustains Veronica, personally, in a way the explicit tasks of her job do not, since in the immediate course of her daily life she uses her education to create interactions based on respect and sharing, in contrast to the disrespect she usually feels. But training and education cannot easily or solely funnel affect into the confines of waged labor—that is, these effects do not necessarily make her actual job more meaningful and more satisfying. Veronica did not, for instance, identify more closely with the hospital or become more satisfied with her job—her work did not become "more than a job"—but her education had overtones in her current job that were valuable—perhaps not capturable and measurable, but productive. And of course education is not without potential economic value to Veronica, who may in the long term acquire a college degree. The cumulative value of an economy of affect is considerable when we consider the vast size of this training industry and the fact that traditional ends of training and education—skills, a better job, more pay—may be perpetually delayed.

The affect economy in which the education and training industry for health care workers participates is embedded within capitalist relations of production. Such relations of production are directed toward the creation of a surplus of affective capacities via the promotion of the desire for meaningful work and in maintaining inequity in the distribution of the wealth created by these capacities. The desire of health care workers to change jobs is not so much a product of the fact that their work (waged labor) is or is not inherently meaningful, but a product of the fact that their jobs are undervalued compared to other kinds of technical and knowledge-based work that are consistently privileged, not least by social scientists when evaluating and ranking occupations. Health care workers, particularly those who do hands-on care work, know that it is so-called knowledge work or technical and creative occupations that are referenced in the notion that work should be more than a job. The cultivation of engagement in a capitalist economy is no doubt always oriented toward disguising these inequities in the value assigned to certain bodies and certain kinds of work while turning that engagement into even greater value, appropriated by a few.

Interventions in affect, which can bring some bodies together into more powerful and stable constellations than others, are not free from ethical and political implications. From a Deleuzian perspective on control, the training and education industry constitutes part of a historically specific formation of power that relates "to different levels of matter/energy through an intensification of perception and experimentation."[26] In the training and education industry there is an intensification of attention to meaning, in addition to skills, knowledge, or credentials. In these terms, the training and education programs might be understood as elements of a new system of domination—that of control—and therefore as experimental responses by capital to the problem of value creation. But the unpredictability that characterizes how the power to act is enacted means that education and training programs cannot guarantee that workers' engagement will emerge as the commitment to being more productive workers, at least by any traditional measure.[27] Because the education and training industry is to some extent self-perpetuating and capable of perpetually reconfiguring meaning, just as bodies and desires (e.g., for meaning) are capable of perpetual modulation, education and training are not merely or exactly tools of capitalist interests.

It is important to examine the specific ways in which the desire for fulfillment, satisfaction, and meaning gets taken up and channeled into productive, valuable circuits. The concept of an affect economy serves to identify and specify a register of production and exchange in which the political stakes of a control society may be rooted. The ways in which an affect economy is in fact consistent with a capitalist political economy, and therefore the extent to which transactions in the affect economy further specifically capitalist forms of domination and organizing work, are, however, unfolding. Power in an affect economy resonates as modulations and limitless postponements, but the question of the ability of capitalism to take advantage of that kind of power is not already foreclosed. Jonathan Beller has argued that "from here on, the development of capital will be unthinkable without the simultaneous development of technologies for the modulation of affect and the capturing of attention."[28] Doubtless this is true, but the case of the training and education industry for allied health care workers would suggest that affect is not subject to the usual forms of measurement and analysis, so that the political responses its modulation calls forth are emergent and unpredictable.

1. This essay is based on in-depth interviews and observations conducted as part of my dissertation research. I interviewed forty-four health care workers and trainers, educators, and planners participating in New York City health care training organizations and programs between 2000 and 2002. The health care workers interviewed were largely allied health care workers in the sub-baccalaureate labor market, where occupations require at least a high school degree and probably some sort of postsecondary training, credential, or degree, but not a baccalaureate degree. See W. Norton Grubb, *Working in the Middle* (San Francisco: Jossey-Bass, 1996). At least one third of those people working in health care in New York City are employed at this level. Some of the occupations that the people I interviewed held or were in training for included nuclear medicine technologists, licensed practical nurses, certified nursing assistants, respiratory therapists, and registrars or unit clerks. Most of the workers I interviewed were women, about half were black or Hispanic, and many were immigrants. The majority of health care workers I interviewed were 1199 members.

2. Barbara Benson, "Funds Aim to Retrain Health Workers: Union Gets Millions to Help Employees; Many Lack Basic Skills for New Jobs," *Crain's New York Business*, August 4, 1997, 1; Commission on the Public's Health System, "CHCCDP: Are We Getting Our Money's Worth?" April 2003, 1–63; Karen Pallarito, "Cashing in on Connections: N.Y.C. Hospitals' Funding Deal Angers Upstate Rivals," *Modern Healthcare*, August 4, 1997, 20; and from the three press releases from New York State, Office of the Governor, "Governor Opens Bronx Health Training and Childcare Center," October 22, 2002; "Governor Pataki Announces $250 Million in Aid for Hospitals," June 14, 1999; and "Governor: $80 Million for Health Care Workforce Training" October 25, 2001.

3. Center for an Urban Future, "CUNY on the Job: The City's New Workforce Workhorse," April 2004; "Putting CUNY to Work," June 1999; "Rebuilding Job Training from the Ground Up: Workforce System Reform after 9/11," August 2002.

4. Center for Health Workforce Studies, *The Health Care Workforce in New York City, 2002* (Albany: Center for Health Workforce Studies, School of Public Health, State University of New York at Albany, 2002).

5. David Leonhardt, "Growing Health Care Economy Gives Northeast a Needed Boost," *New York Times*, December 30, 2002.

6. Antonio Damasio, *Looking for Spinoza: Joy, Sorrow, and the Feeling Brain* (New York: Harcourt, 2003), 55, 89.

7. See, for example, Arlie Russell Hochschild, *The Managed Heart: Commercialization of Human Feeling* (Berkeley: University of California Press, 1983); John Van Maanen and Gideon Kunda, " 'Real Feelings': Emotional Expression and Organizational Culture," *Research in Organizational Behavior* 11 (1989): 43–103, esp. 53.

8. Damasio, *Looking for Spinoza*, 54.

9. A suggestive point of contact between sociological theory and the concept of affect is Randall Collins's formulation of "emotional energy." See his "Emotional Energy as the Common Denominator of Rational Action," *Rationality and Society* 5.2 (1993): 203–30; "On the Microfoundations of Macrosociology," *American Journal of Sociology* 86.5 (1981): 984–1014; and "Stratification, Emotional Energy, and the Transient Emo-

tions," in *Research Agendas in the Sociology of Emotions*, ed. Theodore Kemper (Albany: State University of New York Press, 1990), 27–57.

10. Brian Massumi, *Parables for the Virtual: Movement, Affect, Sensation* (Durham, NC: Duke University Press, 2002), 26–27, 32–33.

11. Antonio Negri, "Value and Affect," *Boundary 2* 26.2 (1999): 77–87.

12. Nicholas Georgalis, "Mind, Brain, and Chaos," in *The Caldron of Consciousness*, ed. Ralph D. Ellis and Natika Newton (Philadelphia: John Benjamins, 2000), 179–204.

13. For instance, Jonathan H. Turner, "Toward a General Sociological Theory of Emotions," *Journal for the Theory of Social Behavior*, 29.2 (1999): 133–61.

14. In the section that follows, readers unfamiliar with the world of health care work will find it useful to know that nursing work in most health care facilities is divided between several hierarchically arranged occupations: nursing assistants, registered nurses (RNs), and licensed practical nurses (LPNs). Nursing assistants (often called nurse aides) are the front-line workers responsible for the general physical and hands-on care of patients (washing and dressing them, feeding them). Their training ranges from a few weeks to a few months, although in New York most are now "certified" after completing a training program with at least one hundred hours of classroom instruction and a standard examination. Licensed practical nurses work under RNs and are permitted to carry out many of the same tasks as RNs (such as dispensing medication), though their clinical and legal responsibilities are much more limited. Licensed practical nurses are generally trained in one-year nondegree programs. Registered nurses are legally and ethically responsible for all nursing work in a unit. They also implement and delegate physicians' orders, though their autonomy and tasks vary greatly by setting and by their education. Registered nurses may have diplomas, but increasingly they have at least an associate's degree and frequently a bachelor's degree.

15. American Hospital Association, "In Our Hands: How Hospital Leaders Can Build a Thriving Workforce" (Report of the American Hospital Association Commission on Workforce for Hospitals and Health Systems), April 2002, 13.

16. Ibid., 8.

17. See, for example, Susan Reverby, *Ordered to Care: The Dilemma of American Nursing, 1850–1945* (Cambridge: Cambridge University Press, 1987); and David Rosner, *A Once Charitable Enterprise: Hospitals and Health Care in Brooklyn and New York, 1885–1915* (Cambridge: Cambridge University Press, 1982).

18. This is what Viviana A. Zelizer calls the oversimplified "hostile-worlds" view, in which commodified relations are seen as incompatible with intimate, caring relations. See her "Intimate Transactions," in *The New Economic Sociology: Developments in an Emerging Field*, ed. Mauro F. Guillén et al. (New York: Russell Sage Foundation, 2002), 274–300.

19. One of the most remarkable accomplishments of 1199, notwithstanding obtaining the legal right to organize health care in the first place, was its simultaneous commitment to workers' rights and civil rights during its organizing heyday in New York City (the 1960s and 1970s). See Leon Fink and Brian Greenberg, *Upheaval in the Quiet Zone: A History of Hospital Workers' Union, Local 1199* (Urbana: University of Illinois Press, 1989). Though I believe the problem of the devaluation of care work is fundamentally about gender inequality and the politics of how education is organized is fundamentally

about class inequality, in New York City, both are also shaped by racial inequality. Particularly in the health care world, occupational hierarchies sometimes align with racial and cultural difference (though hospitals do not make available the hard data to confirm this), exacerbating the experience of injustice. So when Veronica said that she was treated like a nobody by nurses, it was clear from our conversation that "nurses" sometimes meant "white nurses." The tendency for registered nurses to see nursing assistants as ancillary or nonprofessional personnel often dovetails with powerful cultural and racial prejudices. Therefore, while the Training and Upgrading Fund makes unparalleled opportunities available to allied health care workers and to women in health care, in New York City it also makes unparalleled opportunities available to immigrants and people of color who experience multiple forms of personal and institutional discrimination.

20. Negri, "Value and Affect," 87.

21. The question of release time—allowing workers to be released from work with pay while in a training or education program—makes for a contested issue between unions and employers. Those at the 1199 Training and Upgrading Fund have created more and more training programs offering release time, mostly because the training industry is currently so well funded and hospitals do not have to pay for training or replacement employees out of their bottom line. Nonetheless, as long as education remains an occupational benefit, both its content and form are largely shaped in response to the preferences of employers, not of employees.

22. Michel Foucault, *Discipline and Punish: the Birth of the Prison*, trans. Alana Sheridan (New York: Vintage, 1977).

23. Gilles Deleuze, "Postscript on the Societies of Control," *October* 59 (1992): 5.

24. Luciana Parisi and Tiziana Terranova, "Heat-Death: Emergence and Control in Genetic Engineering and Artificial Life," *CTheory* (2000), www.ctheory.net/text_file.asp?pick=127.

25. Negri, "Value and Affect," 78, 79.

26. Parisi and Terranova, "Heat-Death."

27. And it might make them less productive by traditional measures since talking to patients, as Veronica does, is an activity not included in the job description of nursing assistants and not usually counted as an essential part of their job. See Timothy Diamond, *Making Gray Gold: Narratives of Nursing Home Care* (Chicago: University of Chicago Press, 1992).

28. Jonathan Beller, "Capital/Cinema," in *Deleuze and Guattari: New Mappings in Politics, Philosophy, and Culture*, ed. Eleanor Kaufman and Kevin Jon Heller (Minneapolis: University of Minnesota Press, 1998), 91.

HAUNTING ORPHEUS:

PROBLEMS OF SPACE AND TIME IN THE DESERT

JONATHAN R. WYNN

> The two correspondences—that of rot and that of life and death—are aspects of the same phenomenon. In both cases, the meeting point of ideal and real space is a proscribed place; just as it is forbidden to experience pleasure while thinking about it, it is forbidden to look at the place where life touches death: Orpheus is not allowed to watch Eurydices' passage from death to life.
>
> —Bernard Tschumi, *Architecture and Disjunction*

> Autobiography has to do with time, with sequence and with what makes up the continuous flow of life. Here, I am talking of a space, of moments and discontinuities.
>
> —Walter Benjamin, "A Berlin Chronicle"

(. . .)

The following is a rotation between geographic places, Las Vegas and the ghost town of Rhyolite, not to reconcile the spaces of creation and decay, development and transgression, but to inhabit the spaces between them. To oscillate so wildly in between two distant towns is facilitated here through two forms: memory and fiction. The shifts between two real places occurs midsentence— where these two autoethnographics come close enough together that they collide. Through this relationship they become memories of one another, ghosts of each other's past and future. Segments from J. G. Ballard's *Crash* and Mark Z. Danielewski's *House of Leaves* offer a component of fiction to facilitate these transitions.[1]

These spaces are haunted by other moments as well—other voices, other texts, other subtexts—resulting in an ethnographic heteroglossia.[2] These outside voices cannot be fully connected, fully explained; they can only be woven together through the structure of the text. This is not a metaphorical trick, a stylistic farce. It is not a flight of fancy, but rather an attempted reconciliation of incongruous themes and stories. Such meaning making can be found in architectural projects such as Daniel Libeskind's Jewish Museum in Berlin today. Here the architect made three axes (representing continuity, exile, and the Holocaust) that cut across the site, creating cavities in the plan, some of which can be seen through slight windows, while others remain as enclosed and inaccessible as the moments of history and biography they are intended to represent. Libeskind's work intends to speak to the unspeakable and represent the unknowable.

There are spaces such as those within the present text as well. Each text here forms part of an axis, and the texts overlie and intersect with one another. The gaps here reveal holes in other texts as well, temporal as well as spatial, oral as well as written. This is a text that is as much about collisions and absences—and the haunting created by those collisions and gaps—as it is about presence. It is about what is on the page as well as what is not, about the author as well as about the reader. It is an autoethnography of two cities, one that is alive and thriving, and another that is almost a century gone. Another architect, Bernard Tschumi, sees a correspondence between life and death that meets in place.[3] This is a study *of* that place, as much as it *is* that place.

$$(\ldots)$$

The scars that are created from the overlapping and intersecting texts are clearly defined as the above brackets and ellipsis—the standard notation for an omission or signification of a sudden change in topic—cutting across the texts, fragmenting sections, in a way. This does not create disorder but a kind of emergence, a dissipated structure. A system does not necessarily mean equilibrium or consensus, but rather an organization of forces at play. At present, those forces include time and space, speed and memory, entropy and synergy. Like the automobile accidents in *Crash*, collisions between objects or forces may not be the sheer chance occurrences that they first appear to be. Ethnography, as a practice, never shies away from transcending the evident as evidence, but it has also increasingly come to value the personal experience of the ethnographer—from Elliot Liebow's appendix to *Tally's Corner* to such mainstream ethnographies as those by Mitchell Duneier, Loïc Wacquant, David Grazian, Philippe Bourgois, Elijah Anderson, and Sudhir Venkatesh.[4] The result is an open system wherein moments and fragments come together, one that is haunted by personal narratives and memories. For Jacques Derrida there is a close connection between structure and such troubling aspects of theory: "Contrary to what we might believe, the experience of ghosts is not tied to a bygone historical period, like the landscape of Scottish manors, etc., but on the contrary, is accentuated, accelerated by modern technologies like film, television, the telephone. These technologies inhabit, as it were, a phantom structure . . . . When the very first perception of an image is linked to a structure of reproduction, then we are dealing with the realm of phantoms."[5]

J. G. Ballard's character Vaughn sees the world as a series of such collisions, reminding us that we can all be connected depending on who (or what) metaphorically or literally crashes into whom. The scars from these collisions for Vaughn are new erogenous zones, new points to be explored. Or collected. Vaughn becomes the ever-loosening center of the story of *Crash*; the narrator of the text, James Ballard, is not the character in control. Vaughn is the one who reads the threads that connect the main characters, much as in the way he follows the scars on his own body. He sees more than felicitous happenstance; he fantasizes about endless variations of sexual experiences and prophesies as these couplings are brought together by the new technologies in automation. The scar represents a former connection and possible reconnection. Sexual or not, the significance has to do with absence—the missing past event and the possible future.

(. . .)

Javier Auyero's research on Argentine protest movements and Alessandro Portelli's work on oral history describe the complicated ways in which past and present are woven together, confusing as to which is the possible future.[6] Elizabeth Grosz's reading of Henri Bergson notes how the simultaneity of past and present is embodied in architecture as well.[7] These tensions of simultaneity found in spaces and stories are the points these concepts spin upon. Bernard Tschumi writes that architects turn away from traces of decay,[8] just as sociological texts turn away from the forces behind social investigations—the lapses, the darker moments of ethnographic tales and professional life. For Michael Bell, places are often haunted (or "personed—even when there is no one there") by ghosts in the sense of "a felt *presence*—an anima, *geist*, or genius—that possesses and gives a sense of social aliveness to a place."[9]

(. . .)

Route 95, a thin strand of road, connects two boomtowns of the American West. Looking at Rand McNally's *United States Road Atlas*, I see Las Vegas: in bold letters with its lively patchwork of colors, names, and lines of varying thickness. It has evidence of bustling civilization right there on the page. Tracing my finger northwest, up a thick red line toward Reno, I come across bone-thin font, Rhyolite, with two even smaller words in parentheses underneath it: (ghost town). The state of Nevada is scattered with towns that had at one point or another gambled for the future. For Las Vegas and Rhyolite, their boom days are separated by a century. There is little doubt that recent history has proven favorable to the southernmost tip of Nevada. The state even looks like a funnel, with all of its life draining south into the Colorado River and nearby Las Vegas.

More than rainwater flowed and was trapped in the part of the Great Basin I have found myself in. The flat belly of Nevada's midsection holds arid whispers and ghosts. The experiences of Las vegas and Rhyolite are tied together with more than a stretch of concrete.

(. . .)

> Mark Z. Danielewski's novel *House of Leaves* is, among other things, a story about a family that when measuring a room for bookshelves, realizes that the inner dimensions of their home are larger than its outer dimensions. The book is a fake "found" occult document partly about a found film short, called *The Navidson Record* after the filmmaker/owner of the house. It is a deft haunted house story dressed as an autodidactic investigation, with upside-down and see-through font and endless footnotes, complete with real citations (of Martin Heidegger, Gaston Bachelard, and Jacques Derrida) and fake ones (of Rosie O'Donnell commenting on the videotape of *Entertainment Tonight*). It is a summer reading book for eggheads, a more academic *Blair Witch Project*. *House of Leaves* is a series of documents that someone named Johnny Truant finds in a footlocker that was owned by a man named Zampanò who was apparently doing an investigation of a series of short films that Navidson made about his house, and the cultural uproar that the films created.*

---

*Half asleep, I lay in the dark of my bedroom. It's small, and the only window is through the pitch-black bath—placing a needle of light across my pillow. I wake because I feel a presence in the room. Drowsy, a movement in the corner catches my eye. There is a shadow of a man crouching there, at the foot of my bed. I sit up to see him quickly rise up and rush toward me with his arms outstretched. I swing out of the other side of the bed and turn on my light. I scurry for the walking stick leaning behind my door. It really is strange that I have even kept it for so long, but the stick is the first thing I think of. It's the only potential

On the border of California and the Death Valley, Rhyolite was founded in 1905. The promise of gold in the Ladd and Bonanza Mountains made this shallow pocket a boomtown. In August 1904, Frank "Shorty" Harris and Earnest Cross discovered gold in these ranges. As the news spread, prospectors flocked to the new town. Makeshift miners' tents quickly turned into makeshift hotels, saloons, and banks. A train station was built to ship in supplies. A jail was built for the drunks and thieves. Thousands traveled from as far as New Jersey to settle here. Soon whole families were coming, too, and civic-minded Rhyolitians raised enough money to build a school.

This boom growth occurred within five years. Eighty-five years later, I walk down the same strip that had once mixed parasols and perfume, homemade whiskey and horse dung. I am on a day trip, escaping Las Vegas with a quick two-hour drive northwest, away from my boomtown home with its own strip. These two streets are separated by 120 miles of thin black pavement. In Rhyolite, the roads smelled of gold; the Las Vegas Strip smells of green. These two elements configure Nevada's sacred cross—

(. . .)

Navidson's friend, Billy Reston, calls the house "a goddamn spatial rape."[10]

(. . .)

As the traditional way of the myth tells it, in a nutshell, Orpheus was a talented musician who married Eurydice, but on their wedding day, the latter was bit by a snake while frolicking in a field. Distraught over the loss of his wife, Orpheus descended into hell to save her. With only his music to barter, Orpheus managed to please Hades enough to be allowed to return with Eurydice on a single condition: that he not look back at her until they had arrived in the upper world. On that journey back to the land of the living, Orpheus struggled to hear her voice, an assurance of her presence. Going mad, barely able to wait another

---

weapon I own. I spin, and the room is completely empty. I rush into the bathroom, and then my living room, turning on lights to find nothing, no body. My heart thumping, I check all of the windows and doors. Cautiously. All of them are closed, locked. I stay up for the rest of the night, heart pumping, watching television with all the lights on. It was just a dream.

moment, he turned around at the mouth of the cave. Only it was a moment too soon, for she had yet to cross that crucial threshold, and so Eurydice descended back into Hades.

Given that Orpheus had broken their agreement, the gods could not let him return to hell a second time. Devastated, Orpheus wandered in solitude with only his instrument with no one as comfort, let alone another woman. This disinterest in others drove the women of Thrace into a frenzy and, in a fitful orgy, they tore Orpheus to pieces. His body was then buried at Mount Olympus and his head thrown into the river Hebrus. The Muses later found his head on the shores of the island of Lesbos and built the famous oracle at the site. A cult formed around the story of Orpheus, with its cycle of life and death and idea of the many folding into one.

(. . .)

—streets of Sahara Avenue and Las Vegas Boulevard, the so-called Strip. I had driven for four days across the country in a four-door, four-cylinder car with a small, misweighted U-Haul dragging behind me. I zipped across the plains of Iowa and Nebraska while the trailer felt like a car-sized bag of junk rolling and spinning and clamoring behind me. I slowly inched up the Rocky Mountains, and women in Jeeps honked at me as they sped past, laughing. As I inch up to the intersection I realized that crossing the six-lane monstrosity before me was one last big step.

The idea I had of riding triumphantly down the Strip to announce my arrival dissipated with the cars I saw fading off in both directions. Their red taillights stacked on one another formed a line that slowly blended into a cloud of neon and signage. Without a second look I raced straight up Sahara Avenue, away from the Strip as fast as I could. I parked in my mentor's parking lot two hours early and, while I waited, set radio stations on my car stereo and took a nap: breathing in strange new smells and feeling the asphalt radiate the day's heat back upward in my new city.

A few months later, I find myself walking down that famous street. Unlike the black street pavement two feet to the right, the gray concrete next to Las Vegas Boulevard has no apparent rules. Slower traffic, please stay to the right-hand lanes; red light, stop; green light, go. No, on the sidewalks of the Strip, there are only a few informal rules. The rush of people always seems to be where I am not. I see a flow moving forward and sidestep to it, and on cue they halt to pose for a picture. I stop, and since the people walking behind me had their eyes thirty feet above my head, I am pushed into the frame of the picture.

I think briefly about all the pictures that I will inadvertently be in the background of. Just by being here, I become international. I am Instamatically transported to a distant country without my knowledge, or my consent. I will be part of a memory, part of someone else's journey. In three days time, a picture with me in it will be shown to someone's uncle in Uruguay. In forty years time, I will still be in a Berlin photo album.

Locals stay away from here because it is exhausting to move from building to building. I still like it. The heads in front of me are speckled with colored light and a collective look of astonishment. I stop and look up at the nine-o'clock night, the lights blasting out fifty colors. It is a daylight more incredible than the real daylight. I walk under this strange—

(. . .)

twisted metal, crushed compression chambers, and gauges frozen in their precrash positions are the new elements of sexuality. . . . Vaughn sees an alternative to viewing the occurrences we see everyday . . . we are roadside rubberneckers and automotive actors, in every collision at every intersection.

(. . .)

There is a section of The Navidson Record called "The Five-and-a-Half-Minute Hallway." In House of Leaves, supposed bootleg copies float through the fictional cultural landscape, each, reputedly, with slightly different content.*

(. . .)

—desert sun, and my eyes are unable to fix on anything. The roadless expanse of scrub brush hides what lies only a few inches underneath it: the city of Rhyolite. It looks like the coarse landscape that a burlap sack would give if you

---

*I was spending a lot of time in my one-bedroom apartment at that point. It was what some people call a granny flat, a small apartment built onto the back of a nice six-room house on a quiet road. I had my own entrance, a nice window in the living room, a washer and dryer. I cooked dinners on a two-coil countertop range, and spent my afternoons watching rented movies as a break from writing. It was too hot to write in the middle of the day, and I could rent a movie for ninety-nine cents Tuesdays through Thursdays. I would pick a director and watch three of his films a week. It might have been Terrence Malick week when I started seeing the shadow in the corner of my bedroom, but I cannot be certain. I must admit that it is all a blur.

were to lay your head down against it, with its contents poking out at all angles, and little pockmarks. The brilliant sun bleaching out fine details, I find it hard to simply *see*. Even with my five-dollar sunglasses on, I am squinting.

I make a left at an otherworldly mining overspill area and park my car at the base of a small hill. I take a long pull of Coke so warm it burns my throat; staring through the plastic container, I look across the parking lot. Beyond the UPC code I make out a thirty-by-thirty plot of land, fenced off to corral a house made of bottles.

Tom Kelly built the Bottle House in 1906 with fifty thousand glass bottles. The walls are a honeycomb of green and blue bottle bottoms, some with a crack straight through the center, some with a circus mirrorlike tumor warping the outer edges. They are a network of tiny windows, each one producing a different opinion of the interior that, collectively, looks like the eye of a housefly. What does the desert look like from inside? A series of small eyes all blinking at you as leaves and clouds alter the light? What does it sound like when a dry desert breath blows over the empty lips of the bottles? A slow moan like you would hear in a movie?

I look down and see that the ten-foot fence with barbed wire that keeps me out is no more than a passing thought for the wave of broken glass and gravel that seeps well past the plot. The lawn furniture of the Bottle House, as well as the rest of Rhyolite I later found, is no more than a shadow, a space with a slightly lower temperature than the surrounding desert, hoping for a breeze. Cool blue fragments glisten in the sun; the walkway to the uneven wooden porch is lined with medicine, liquor, and Coke bottles. On the sloping post that supports the roof swing five misshapen, white numbers:

204

1 6

I walk a little north to where, I imagine, the rest of Rhyolite was.

(. . .)

Navidson's house is a psychological patient, a subject that its occupant's dreams and fears are placed on. Different explorations are more like therapy sessions, revealing inner depths and convolutions. The house changes repeatedly—expanding, contracting, shifting— which produces a low groan, a noise that could also be the sound of the monster at the unknown center of the labyrinth. There are tensions in the house that Navidson attempts to map, the house itself is a text that can be read—a structure. Later, it seems (to the "critics") that the house is the opposite—an object that changes depending on the psychology of those who enter it. The house becomes a part of the self, "in perfect relation to the mental state of the individual."[11]*

(. . .)

Libeskind's architecture is not the only example of these sorts of practices. Tim Etchells's theater group, Forced Entertainment, always included destruction and construction in their dramatic performances. Even the set was under a continual ebb and flow. The production shifted and rearranged its spatial fragments:

> We always loved the incomplete—from the building site to the demolition site, from the building that was used once and is no longer to the building that will be used. Did I tell that Steve Rogers and I used to talk about this? The fascination of ruined places, of incomplete places. It seems unethical to admit—the strange charge of buildings left to run down—but they always were the best places to play—stinking of previous use, ready for transgression. Every piss that you took in the corner and every window you broke and every game you played in the old factory, the old house was a writing over its everyday—a kind of accidental vandalism. And do you remember burying things in the foundations of new houses as they were being made? What a surprise for somebody—these traces of some inexplicable ritual? The cut-out pictures, the scribbled notes, the broken objects.[12]

(. . .)

At first there seems to be nothing more than desert flora, but slowly, like Robert Smithson's *Spiral Jetty* rising up out of the Salt Lake after thirty years of submersion, Rhyolite appears in the form of clusters of stone and lazy pathways. A whitewash in reverse. There are two dilapidated buildings—more like

---

*I was writing very little, but mostly on deserts and cities. For the most part, I was dreaming of moving out of town, so every time I bellied up to my computer, it was to browse the Internet for new cities, new places to work. As I moved off into other social circles away from friends and my mentor, Hilde—different places around town and different areas of interest—the gaps in my work grew wider, and interdisciplinary connections became more apparent. I stopped talking to friends out of guilt over the breakup with my girlfriend Annie. I'll tell you right now that this is a simplification of losing my girlfriend and distancing myself from my mentor simultaneously. I am telling you that I am not being completely honest here. There are gaps.

formations of broken walls—in the southeastern part of Rhyolite: the Bottle House and the jail. Amargosa Street connected both and was the main drag in this, the red light district of Rhyolite. More than a third of the working women in this boomtown lived here, now a collection of broken porcelain and rusted chains. Deep cavities are spaced evenly along Amargosa. I climb down into one of these and inspect the storage cans. They are not new, but they are not antique either—likely storage for someone passing through. Who knows. Who knows what is inside them.

As I walk up the hill on a street optimistically called Golden, six structures unfold like fingers through the scrub brush. Like the mountains around them, they are the color of dust. The golden strip tracks my eyesight; it takes a few deep breaths for me to accept the fact that people actually *lived* here. As if hidden in scrub and cracks of the surrounding mountains, it is only after thirty paces that I notice street signs to my right and left. I come to a full stop at one, Denver Avenue, and unsquint my eyes. The twenty-page guide that I bought for two dollars in a town twenty miles back states clearly that there is a road right here to my left, but it takes me a pause to notice the slight bulge in the gravel that is the centre of the road. I follow the meager line with my eyes up to the range beyond and find what looks like a small gopher hole in it. The gap is one of a handful of mines that pock the faces of the otherwise characterless mountain facades. The Denver and Gibraltar mine shafts are the only indication of depth; they seem to be propped up like a movie set for *The Outlaw Josey Wales.* But maybe it has to do with the buildings that stand before me. Window frames without windows show the blue sky beyond. The buildings seem to have the frailty of cellophane yet have still lasted almost a century. I feel that if I walk ten more feet, I will see a film crew and the two-by-fours that support—

(. . .)

Vaughn pours over accident photographs, piecing together a grand narrative with which he could understand humanity differently. A collage of snapshots spread across a table overlap, and can be rearranged into new collisions and new stories not a part of how we have looked at human experience before . . . .

(. . .)

In *House of Leaves*, the real-life spatial critic Christian Norberg-Schulz is quoted as saying that "architectural space certainly exists independently of the causal perceiver, and has centres and directions of its own."[13] The nonfictional urbanist Kevin Lynch is also included:

"[Environmental image, a generalized mental picture of the exterior physical world] is the product both of immediate sensation and of the memory of past experience, and it is used to interpret information and to guide action."[14] The effects that the haunted house induces leave some of its explorers disoriented at best and, at worst, according to film records, it drives some mad.[15*]

(. . .)

—the fronts of the casinos. In the darkness of space just behind the Strip, the shiny scaffolding of future projects is the bastard twin of the main artery of Las Vegas. It is the backdrop that this Hollywood convincingly allows you to forget is there. The desert beyond these buildings is the sound stage where vacations are screened every second of every day. Lights, camera, family vacation! Countless additions and new projects become a black web against the night sky, high enough to catch a few stars and enslave them into a life of red beacon lights. The new wing of Caesars Palace, the Luxor's two new towers, a new parking garage, the new Bellagio megaresort, even the Imperial Palace has a monumental new addition. When was the last time you heard of the Imperial Palace? This other side of Las Vegas makes the front a stage. Backstage, fat construction workers weld through the cool night, while below the front-stage cocktail waitresses smile for tips.

I walk by Caesars and the black hole skeleton of its new tower that rises behind it. As if looking at clouds, I blur myself to see this not as growth, but disarray. I walk not through a bustling city, but a decaying one: its bulk falling slowly, back to the earth. I see the skin of these buildings being peeled away, brick by brick, room by room, cell by cell; the facade gives way to an endoskeleton. The tall cranes that lift I-beams and neon signs and arches turn into bony fingers picking at a cadaver. Exterior walls are all that are left; poker chips lie on the ground like blue and green broken glass. My lobotomized companions stagger around me from one scene to another with a glazed look. I come to the obviously counterfeit Statue of Liberty at the corner of Tropicana and the Strip—just like in the movie, only without all the sand and talking apes—and realize that before me stands a reminder of American civilization.

---

*After Annie and I stopped talking, it became a surprisingly small town. I found other places, and sat quietly at their edges. To tighten the circle, Annie used her parent's money to purchase a house three blocks away from my apartment with a nice lawn and lots of space. I would sink low in my seat when a car that looked like hers passed me on the road. I would drive a few blocks more to avoid passing near her house.

Is there a juncture where construction looks like deconstruction, an indeterminate point when decay appears as production, cancer as growth? I am not very sure that Las Vegas and southern Nevada have ever moved from this question. For every implosion of a reasonably functional building in Las Vegas there is another explosion of activity and growth, but there is no confusion about the fact that something has indeed come to a cinematic end. It is of no mischance that these points are recorded for the benefit of Hollywood cameras. The implosion of the Landmark Hotel was filmed for a movie about aliens that attack Las Vegas. The Sands Hotel implosion was filmed for a movie about escaped convicts flying a plane. I even helped an independent filmmaker with the implosion of the Aladdin Hotel. Hollywood film crews—

(. . .)

> *like tarot cards, the pictures rub up against each other. laid across one another, they are not interpreted as being static. Pictures and stories can be arranged and shifted depending on the narrative read and the narrator who . . .*

(. . .)

> There is no Minotaur at the center of the House of Leaves, for there is no center of the house. There is no orientation, no balance. The very structure of the house is a ruse; the House of Leaves is a system at once taken apart, at once put back together. A continual shift, a continual rift of spaces and times. An ontological and epistemological horror indeed. A Jacques Derrida quote is included to tell that "notions of a structure lacking any center represents the unthinkable itself."*

(. . .)

—visited Rhyolite in 1926, leaving a heavy fingerprint on one of its fading landmarks. The Cook Building was built in 1907 on the corner of Golden and Broadway—a three-story office building at the center of town and the Rhyolite

---

*I am never able to fix on much more than the spreading arms and vague movements. I never see a face, or hair color. Just a shadow. As for my ex, she was wearing more black despite the desert sun. Her hair started out as long and light, but she had been adding a dark reddish brown in small increments. Hilde's hair was becoming dark reddish brown too. Annie and Hilde's clothes seemed to mirror each other's. I was in another space. Those nights I would sleep-wake to see the man in the corner of my room every other week or so. I was sleeping about four hours a night—and believed that the shadow had everything to do with what was inside my head.

business community. In 1926, Hollywood filmmakers used it, as well as the Amargosa Street Bottle House, for a western. Filmmakers radically altered the frontispiece of the Cook Building, forcing arches and iron bars over the windows, leaving scars and a partial truth to the town. Historians today see it as an unfortunate occurrence, but apparently the fourteen people that still lived in Rhyolite at that point did not mind the attention. Today, the forty-two-foot ruin, featured in the 2005 futuristic flick *The Island*, stands as the landmark of the Rhyolite Preservation Society, the tallest structure left.

I continue up the slight incline of Golden to see the upraised hills of gravel that denote what was once the Rhyolite Stock Exchange, the Poodle Dog Cafe, and the Java Restaurant. This was no small cluster of miners' tents. In its most prosperous years, Rhyolite was an explosion: by 1907, just two and a half years after Frank "Shorty" Harris claimed gold, Rhyolite boasted an opera house, two newspapers, two electric plants, telephone service, a hospital, three water systems, and an extensive red light district. It is estimated that up to ten thousand people lived in Rhyolite.

Parts of the two-story, twenty thousand–dollar schoolhouse still stand. It was overbuilt in 1908 to symbolize the stature of the town's optimistic future, but it never reached more than half its capacity. Rhyolite was already on the decline at its completion, and town bankers were getting nervous. On my walk, I have yet to see one of the most significant points in Rhyolite's brief history. One of the grandest moments of fanfare came when the first train rolled into town. The regular flow of—

(. . .)

> The multiple layers in the book are dizzying: it is a story written by Mark Z. Danielewski, the author, about a mysterious text that the seminarrator, Johnny Truant, finds in an empty apartment, which seems to be an investigation written by someone named Zampanò, which is about the video record of an investigation of a haunted house by Navidson. The text is a dizzying set of layers, a labyrinth. It is like a stack of transparencies with multiple codes, keys, and orders. Through Tschumi, the philosopher Mark C. Taylor writes that a pyramid—the image of transcendence, permanence, and singularity —is the antithesis of the labyrinth.[16]*

---

*Shortly thereafter, the people who lived in the front of the house told me that they were moving out. I thought of my old mentor, who I had heard was looking for a place to live with her new boyfriend. I think I left a yellow sticky note with my landlord's phone number

—tourists pump through this main artery of Las Vegas. I feel alone bumping haphazardly into other bodies, lackadaisically flowing with the current. I come back to the Mirage Hotel and look up at its magnificent golden skin from across the street. At the stoplight my toes curl over the curb, and my eyes barely notice the side-view mirrors that zip a foot and a half from my midsection. To be inside those hotel windows looking out must be dazzling. Do they look down at the line of cars and bodies through a golden hue? The Mirage was the first megaresort, the start of the third Las Vegas building and population boom after its beginnings around Fremont Street and the Rat Pack–fueled 1950s.

I do not have to look up at the light for a beckoning white walking man—I am pushed into the crosswalk, safe within the herd of tourists and bucket-clutchers. I still look up unabashedly across the street despite an anxious honk, and halfheartedly skip up the opposite curb.

In front of this Mirage monstrosity is a faux oasis, complete with a volcano that erupts on cue every fifteen minutes after sunset. I do not need a watch—the gathering crowd signals the quarter mark for me, and I push to the front. Like a rubbernecker, I want to see the carnage of the explosion and fire, the spectacle. A rumble fills my chest, and I can see members of the crowd raise their cameras. Golden red water flies from the man-made volcano, fire spouts from hidden flamethrowers. The rumbling mixes with the gasps from the crowd, the explosions of water and fire mix with the electrophosphorescent flashes from cameras. In the bushes around the volcano, dozens of burning red eyes/on lights sway in homage to the gambling god. I feel as if I am in a jungle, traveling deeper and deeper with only the repetitive square blocks of concrete as a guide.

The chant makes me nervous, camcorders humming as their wheels turn in plastic casings. Hundreds of tourists stand hypnotized by the staged exhibition. With one eye wide open, they bury the other deep within their prosthesis Sony Handycams. Playing a part in the ritual, our necks crane up at each plume. Fire races along the surface of the surrounding lake, appearing to float toward us. At its conclusion, an expected grand finale. The ceremony complete, our homage fulfilled, we are reassured that good fortune will follow us and that more tourists will come. With one more show of force, like a horror movie last grasp of the dead, the volcano lashes out one final mocking—

---

for her. Hilde and her partner moved in quickly. Sometimes I would hear music from our shared wall. Sometimes I would be embarrassed that my car often was just sitting out front.

(. . .)

Within *House of Leaves*, there is a section wherein Anne Rice, Stephen King, Camille Paglia, Stanley Kubrick, David Copperfield, Jacques Derrida, and Hunter S. Thompson comment on the videotape, which was fictionally released by Miramax films.*

(. . .)

—explosion that jars me out of the amnesia the desert inserts in the brain. Walking back down the hill to my car, I lose my train of thought to spin around and attempt to locate the noise that ripped across the desert valley. I feel the haze one feels after being jolted awake from a falling dream, and for a second I think perhaps it was an aberration, a mental joke. But surveying Ladd Mountain to the east, I see a cloud of sand and dirt float toward me in a breeze. The plume must be at least a hundred feet high. I never get to know what the explosion was, relegated in my head to just a part of scattered desert activity.

The wind has constantly blown against my ears like the *wrrrrrrrrrr* that you can pick up in the final scenes of *The Good, the Bad, and the Ugly*. Instead of giving me a keen awareness, with my gun unsheathed and ready, the wind pulls something from me. Carrying away my alertness like the dust from the explosion settling, the wind fills my head as I walk back to my car.

I head back to the red light district where my maroon car has been quietly baking in the sun, just like another colored piece of broken glass on the desert floor. I roll down the windows and sit for a full minute eating melted peanut M&M's before speeding back to Las Vegas.

Leaving, I breathe the arid air and feel the gravel in my sandals. The road far ahead of me quakes with heat, turning into a blur with indeterminate points of reference. Road. Sky. Desert. Like an aberration, I am floating between, I—

(. . .)

---

*Despite our thin relationship, Hilde asked me to take in her cat because her cat started fighting with her boyfriend's cat once they moved in. The cat was large and liked me well enough, so I relented. It was nice to have a roommate, but she never really cared for my apartment. She immediately began spraying the corner of my bedroom where the shadow appeared. I tried everything, but the carpet grew darker, and the smell became unbearable. I kept asking Hilde to take the cat back, or find her another home. Eventually, without response, I had to have the cat put down. I sat and played with her all day before she was picked up. For some reason, Hilde's boyfriend-turned-fiancé brought home another cat shortly thereafter.

two folds of flesh, separate prior, are fused through the automotive colli-
sion. the deep scar of new flesh for Vaughn is a new erogenous zone,
a new vertex of technology and sexuality. this also paints a new body
landscape . . . the body is reconfigured, molded, and forced into new
positions, new skin. new bodies that . . .

(. . .)

Parts of the Danielewski's text are cut out, missing, torn, and crossed
out (possibly by Zampanò, possibly by an editor from Pantheon) with
what looks like tar and black crayon. The gaps and obliterated sections are missing sections of the architecture.*

(. . .)

—haunt the Strip of Las Vegas, my head is emptied and vaporous. Inside, I am
intoxicated with the smell of a mob and the rush of delirious floodlights. I get
disoriented and think that this is what a seizure must feel like. It makes little
difference that there are no clocks because everyone is rushing to go nowhere,
and the spaces are all doubled and tripled by walls and walls of mirrors; and all
the time in the world is lost. The wave of people dies down on the weekdays,
but on a weekend, there seems to be only flow without ebb long into the
morning. A mislaid cocktail glass on the curb interrogates the march, the
parade of white sneakers and black socks, wondering which right foot will
knock it off into oncoming traffic. It teeters on the threshold, red swizzle stick
jutting out, as it is soon to be scattered into the gutter. In the melted ice the
lights swirl. By the frayed slice of lime, I gather that it was a rum and Coke.

---

*I moved out of town a few months later. All said, it was a nice space: cheap, separate access,
fireplace, washer-dryer, air conditioner, safe, and solitary. I offered the apartment to one of
my best friends, Liz, without thinking twice. When she visited, she had always commented
on my place, and she now jumped at the opportunity. I forgot about it all entirely, and
loved my new apartment in Brooklyn, despite its lack of hot water and a functional
bathroom or kitchen. Sleep returned to me. But before I left, my mentor gave me a book of
postcards, already stamped and addressed to her. Twelve postcards, one a month. And she
asked me in a note to "meet her halfway" from New York after having lived twelve feet from
her front door. She told me that I was going on a hegira, and told me that that meant an
"epic journey." The postcards seemed like a nice gesture until I thought about the framework of the communication. I know that Derrida's postcards are "the remainders of a
recently destroyed correspondence" to be resequenced, retransmitted, and redirected, but
these postcards with faces and bodies on them had no place for a return address. Still, I sent
twelve. I also looked up the definition of *hegira*.

I wander back again to the Luxor—a gigantic, black pyramid. Its windows reflect the black desert night all around it, and it is a mysterious form against the night sky that takes some adjusting to even see. Atop, there is a light that can be seen from 250 miles away on a good night, a beacon. Inside, there is the largest atrium in the world, at one point holding an inexplicable model skyline of New York City. Douglas Trumbell, who did the special effects for *2001: A Space Odyssey*, *Close Encounters of the Third Kind*, and *Blade Runner*, says of the cinematic experience he was attempting to achieve when he made a semi-historical film for the casino was the feeling that you are "not just looking at the movie, you're in the movie; you become a character."[17] One film, the *Secrets of the Luxor Pyramid*, weaves together past, present, and future into a seamless narrative. The audience is "always searching for the past that was never present, which forever approaches a future that never arrives."[18] In another myth structure, the pyramid served as the gateway between borders, as a sign of transgression, the in-between looking back.

(. . .)

Rainer Maria Rilke retells a different version of the Orpheus myth in his sonnets to Orpheus.[19] In them, Eurydice is happy to be free from human trappings in the underworld, and unwilling to leave with her husband. Lucky, she finds herself to be finally complete in the underworld and, rather than a potential savior, Orpheus plays the spoiler. When he turns around to see her on the edge of the land of the living, Eurydice is not damned, but saved. The twenty-ninth sonnet reads: "Silent friend of many distances, feel how / your breath enlarges all of space. / Let your presence ring out like a bell into the night . . . / Move through transformation, out and in."[20]*

(. . .)

---

*After leaving Las Vegas, the spaces I haunted and the work I did come back to me. Months later, Liz called me up asking if I had had any problems with the apartment. Not giving it much thought, I said no, and we moved on to exchanging our bad jokes and talking about books we were reading. One of which was a book a friend bought for me called *The House of Leaves*. Not a great summer reading idea after moving out of my old apartment, but it proved worthwhile. A few weeks later, Liz called and again asked me if I had had any problems with the apartment. Finally, she asked if I had seen a shadow in the bedroom. She admitted that she'd seen a shadow standing over her bed, and that her furniture would move. She said something happened about three times a week. Slowly, I began to tell her my story for the first time.

The artwork of Robert Smithson is a series of new monuments. They do not remind us of the past exactly, and they seem to make us forget the future.[21] There are empty spaces like these that make up a territory of forgetting.[22] According to the Guggenheim Web site, the Smithson piece *A Tour of the Monuments of Passaic, New Jersey* (1967) describes tangible manifestations of entropic states—industrial structures that were already deteriorating at the time of their construction. His piece, *Hotel Palenque*—in which he photographed an old, eccentrically constructed hotel undergoing a cycle of simultaneous decay and renovation during his trip to Mexico in 1969—embodies the artist's notion of a "ruin in reverse."[23]

Smithson writes about what he calls the "non-site," those places that blur the line between the interior and exterior:

> Between the *actual site* in the Pine Barrens and *The Non-Site* itself exists a space of metaphoric significance. It could be that "travel" in this space is a vast metaphor. Everything between the two sites could become physical metaphorical material devoid of natural meanings and realistic assumptions. Let us say that one goes on a fictitious trip if one decides to go to the site of the *Non-Site*. The "trip" becomes invented, devised, artificial; therefore, one might call it a non-trip to a site from a Non-site. Once one arrives at the "airfield," one discovers that it is man-made in the shape of a hexagon, and that I mapped this site in terms of esthetic boundaries rather than political or economic boundaries.[24]

Smithson's work indicates a connection between memory, space, and moments. He breaks down barriers of presence and coherence to create an object rich in informational and cultural content, moments that themselves then become the product of a new kind of labor, what Maurizio Lazzarato calls "immaterial."[25] This shift in the definition of work directs the careful reader toward open systems of networks and flows. As everyday life becomes increasingly inseparable from work, the issues of memory and narrative, as part and parcel of affect, gain prominence, and the resulting interpenetration of these texts and flows, stories and affects, is a heteroglossia.

(...)

Vaughn studies the automobile accidents of the rich and famous and calls himself a "TV scientist". . . . Ballard—the character, not the author— follows him toward his own accident—an intentional crash with a faux Elizabeth Taylor. . . . wounds, for Vaughn, were the way to "celebrate the dead"; they mimicked the scars of those who had died, and provided the imaginary ones for those who would . . . .

(. . .)

In one stunted blow of dry wind, within six years a town had come and gone. On April 30, 1910, the streetlights were turned off and the county commissioners informed the water companies that they could not pay. April 8, 1911, the last issue of the *Rhyolite Herald* was printed. In a reversal of flows, the Rhyolite train station that had been the conduit for incoming mail and goods became the fastest way to get out of town. The printing press used to announce the arrival of good fortune on the flatbed of the train was loaded onto the same flatbed three years later and shipped out.

Frank "Shorty" Harris, the man who started the penultimate boomtown in Nevada, died in poverty on November 10, 1934. Buried deep in the Death Valley, the epitaph on his headstone reads: "Here lies Shorty Harris, a single blanket jackass prospector."

(. . .)

There are moments that exist, between history and future, flesh and technology, decay and construction. There are moments in which reality bends a little and the points of history and time fuse together to form a historical loop, or better yet, an Escherian Möbius strip. Linear thought is problematized in culture, and we do not need to just look at cyberspace, where the historical and the spatial are collapsed. Jorge Luis Borge's "Aleph" is less fictional than we are willing to admit.

For Patricia Clough, the autoethnographic form "remains unexamined as to its relationship to changed relations of time and space or the shift in aesthetic concerns of narrativity to the speeds of territorialization and reterritorialization, along with the adjustment to the vulnerabilities of exposure to media event-ness."[26] It is not imperative that we report what lies directly in front of us; we often mistake its meaning anyway. It is nearly too obvious that what social actors see as the present mixes past memories and current experiences continually. Often a current event fits so well into a primary framework that there is little cognitive dissonance, often with the past fading into the gray spaces of our mind.[27] But there are other times when the present moment shocks us into someplace else we have been, switches us into another emotion and space altogether.

Some spaces deliberately create these affects, triggering memory or belonging,[28] and no place blurs the connections between spaces and times better and more deliberately than Las Vegas. Within minutes you can move from Greenwich Village to King Arthur's Court to the pyramids of Egypt to Paris. You hear the canned voice of Bono over the speaker system singing that it is "even better than the real thing," and you start to believe that it just might be. Everyone is friendly, and there is no French-Spanish-English dictionary needed to get the alcoholic beverage of your choosing.

(. . .)

As stated above, this is the collision between multiple sets, a collision between multiple spaces, multiple times, ethnographies, voices, and experiences. The suturing together of these moments leaves scars that need to have our fingers trace over them; they need to be explored as a new ethnographic site. Mark C. Taylor's *Hiding* investigates the skin as a border of spaces and times, a "skinscape." For Taylor, death, "like life, is not a momentary event but is an ongoing process whose traces line the body. At the point where I make contact with the world, I am always already dead."[29]

By naming the character with an acute lack of agency after himself, J. G. Ballard hints that there are other forces at work beyond his own control. Just as Orpheus and Eurydice are situated on the borders of life and death, and between coming and going, through blurring the lines between real and illusion, fiction and history, theory and narrative—in both *House of Leaves* and *Hiding*—the authors take a backseat to the spatial and temporal investigations in the text. The point of contact with the world, the text, is both dead and alive. There is a multiplicity of texts, but the collisions here create gaps that allow for the reader to enter into, to create. The present site before you is filled by the reader, just as Smithson's so-called non-sites are. The reader haunts the text, just as in the *House of Leaves*. The text bends and changes based on the self of the reader. The author is always lurking somewhere, however, in the corners.

(. . .)

NOTES

1. J. G. Ballard, *Crash* (New York: Noonday, 1979; Mark Z. Danielewski, *House of Leaves* (New York: Pantheon, 2000).

2. Mikhail M. Bakhtin, *The Dialogic Imagination: Four Essays*, trans. Caryl Emerson and Michael Holquist, ed. Holquist (Austin: University of Texas Press, 1981).

3. See also Edward S. Casey, *The Fate of Place* (Berkeley: University of California

Press, 1999); and Christine Boyer, *The City of Collective Memory* (Cambridge, MA: MIT Press, 1994).

4. Elliot Liebow, *Tally's Corner: A Study of Negro Streetcorner Men* (Boston: Back Bay Books, 1967); Mitchell Duneier, *Sidewalk* (New York: Farrar, Straus and Giroux, 2001); Loïc Wacquant, *Body and Soul* (New York: Oxford University Press, 2003); David Grazian, *Blue Chicago* (Chicago: University of Chicago Press, 2003); Philippe Bourgois, *In Search of Respect* (Cambridge: Cambridge University Press, 1995); Elijah Anderson, *Streetwise: Race, Class, and Change in an Urban Community* (Chicago: University of Chicago Press, 1990); and Sudhir Venkatesh, "Doin' the Hustle: Constructing the Ethnographer in the American Ghetto," *Ethnography* 3.1 (2001): 91–111.

5. Qtd. in Mark Wigley, *The Architecture of Deconstruction: Derrida's Haunt* (Cambridge, MA: MIT Press, 1995), 16.

6. Javier Auyero, *Contentious Lives: Two Argentine Women, Two Protests, and the Quest for Recognition* (Durham, NC: Duke University Press, 2003); Alessandro Portelli, *The Battle of Valle Giulia: Oral History and the Art of Dialogue* (Madison: University of Wisconsin Press, 1997).

7. Elizabeth Grosz, *Architecture from the Outside: Essays on Virtual and Real Space* (Cambridge, MA: MIT Press, 2001), 112.

8. Bernard Tschumi, *Architecture and Disjunction* (Cambridge, MA: MIT Press, 1997), 77.

9. Michael M. Bell, "The Ghosts of Place," *Theory and Society* 26 (1997): 813, 815; emphasis in original.

10. Danielewski, *House of Leaves*, 55.

11. Danielewski, *House of Leaves*, 165.

12. Tim Etchells, *Certain Fragments: Contemporary Performance and Forced Entertainment* (London: Routledge, 1999), 78.

13. Danielewski, *House of Leaves*, 171.

14. Ibid., 176.

15. Ibid., 278–79.

16. Mark C. Taylor, *Hiding* (Chicago: University of Chicago Press, 1997).

17. Qtd. in Taylor, *Hiding*, 243.

18. Qtd, in ibid., 245.

19. Rainer M. Rilke, *The Selected Poetry of Rainer Maria Rilke*, trans. S. Mitchell (New York: Vintage, 1989), 227–57.

20. Ibid., 255.

21. Robert Smithson, *Robert Smithson: The Collected Writings* (Berkeley: University of California Press, 1996).

22. Francesco Careri, *Walkscapes: El andar como práctica estética—Walking as an Aesthetic Practice*, trans. Maurici Pla, Steve Piccolo, and Paul Hammond (Barcelona: Editorial Gustavo Gili, 2002), 166.

23. http://www.guggenheimcollection.org/site/artist_work_md_146E_1.html.

24. Smithson, *Robert Smithson*.

25. Maurizio Lazzarato, "Immaterial Labor," in *Radical Thought in Italy: A Potential Politics*, ed. Paolo Virno and Michael Hardt (Minneapolis: University of Minneapolis Press, 1996), 133.

26. Patricia Ticineto Clough, *Autoaffection: Unconscious Thought in the Age of Tele-technology* (Minneapolis: University of Minnesota Press), 179.

27. Erving Goffman, *Frame Analysis* (Boston: Northeastern University Press, 1974), 450.

28. Dolores Hayden, *The Power of Place: Urban Landscapes as Public History* (Cambridge, MA: MIT Press, 1995).

29. Taylor, *Hiding*, 13.

ELIZABETH WISSINGER

While the heyday of postmodern criticism has passed, its challenge to rethink the body continues to demand attention in theorizing the social. Feminist theorists especially have led the way in destabilizing philosophical notions of the body as inert matter that acts as the ground for rational thought. Taken together, the works of feminist theorists such as Judith Butler, Elizabeth Grosz, and Donna Haraway offer an understanding of the body as continuous with its environment, rather than as a discrete entity with a fixed essence or an organism contained and bound by the skin. This move to think the body as continuous with the environment—as thoroughly social yet stubbornly material—has led to conceptualizing the fluidity of embodiment, rethinking the matter of the body as dynamic.[1] This is a move beyond a strictly social constructionist account of the body toward a "mattering" of the body,[2] where agency arises not only from subjectivity but from other forms of energy, coursing below the level of conscious subject identity. These forces move bodies and constitute bodies in this movement.[3]

To move beyond the closure of the organism, bodies must be reconceived as open to a dynamic interaction with technologies—scientific, laboring, information, or entertainment technologies. In this way, it is possible to think a body—uncontained and fluid—as being open to investment with technical capacities that further control, amplify, or channel bodily forces, temporarily giving a body a "whatever" identity in the body's function as a node in a network of preindividual forces.[4] This essay focuses on fashion models precisely because the labor of fashion modeling involves the model's body being (and being assisted to be) able to move and move with preindividual forces of energy or affectivity. Fashion modeling is the work of being (and being assisted to be) open to interaction with technologies, such as photography, that channel attention. Further, the fashion modeling industry offers a good look at the interrelationship of bodies and technologies for modulating bodily capacities in what has been referred to as an *affect economy*.

THE MOVE TOWARD AFFECT

The concept of affect resolves some of the difficulties of treating forces that may only be observable in the interstices between bodies, between bodies and technologies, or between bodily forces and conscious knowledge. In the analysis of the body, affect allows more than an analysis of discourses, meaning systems, and the social construction of the body; it also allows for an analysis of the dynamism of the body's matter, such that the body is thought as a center of action and reaction, a site of energy flows and changes in intensity.

Recently, theorists have engaged affect in rethinking relations between bodies and images in a media-saturated age,[5] in exploring new ways to grasp interrelationships between information machines and living organisms,[6] or to understand new forms of capitalist accumulation typical of an affect economy.[7] All of these theorists have shifted the notion of sociality by recognizing how affect "troubles the very distinction between self and others." After all, affects are not "within or without" the body; rather, they create "the very effect of the surfaces or boundaries of bodies and worlds."[8] Affectivity occurs between bodies, between physiological arousal and the conscious realization of it by bodies. Affect is social in that it constitutes a contagious energy, an energy that can be whipped up or dampened in the course of interaction.

While affect has been used by psychologists and sociologists differently to refer to demeanor, the external expression of emotion, or emotions more generally,[9] the way in which I use affect comes closer to the work of Silvan Tomkins, recently revisited by Eve Sedgwick and Adam Frank. Tomkins understood affect in terms of specific physiological responses that then give rise to various effects, which may or may not translate into emotions. Affect therefore precedes emotions; affect is not conscious, but it has a dynamism, a sociality or social productivity. The effects of affect, however, are not predictable; affective change from passivity to activity, from inertia to motivation, for example, is not reducible to a single stimulus.[10] In fact, a "circus of affective responses" can result from a single stimulus and differ in any one body at different times.[11]

It is no wonder that the study of bodily affectivity facilitates an understanding of bodies in interaction with recently developed technologies that calibrate bodily energies or capacities and feed them into economically productive flows. Here, bodies become "bodies of information" and "bodies as information,"[12] as two domains of affective production and modulation meet: on the one hand, there is the biomedical imaging of the body and the mass production of genetic materials outside the organism; and on the other, we have the production of images for circulation by communications technologies such as television, film, and the Internet. Clough argues that these technologies are changing: they are losing their orientation toward "representation and the narrative construction of subject identities" as they move toward "affecting bodies directly, human and non-human bodies."[13]

THE FASHION MODEL AND THE AFFECT ECONOMY

Fashion models are workers whose bodies have been ineluctably caught up in the latest developments in imaging technologies.[14] Over the years in which imaging technology has developed—from photography to film to television to the Internet—there has been an increased investment in the modeling industry, as well as a fragmentation of the work of modeling into ever finer divisions, each to be mined for value. The model emerged, for instance, in the mid- to late 1800s alongside new developments in commercial photography; at the dawn of the cinematic age in the 1920s, the first modeling agency was incorporated in the United States. Post World War II, amid massive changes in the relations among consumption, production, and the ubiquitous images that linked them, some models became photographic stars, some conquered the couture houses, and even the lowliest models began to make a decent wage as modeling became a professional career. The penetration of television into everyday life from the 1960s onward brought radical changes to the industry as models became three-dimensional personalities, called on to create images in motion in keeping with the new imaging norms. The jump in scale of televisual images to worldwide accessibility via satellite and the rise of global networks such as MTV and CNN in the 1980s provided fertile ground for the emergence of the supermodel, another revolutionary moment in the world of modeling. Finally, the global expansion of information technology in the 1990s via the Internet and other developments in telecommunications technologies brought with it a global expansion of the modeling industry as agencies opened new offices in dozens of cities and began to conduct searches for models in every corner of the globe.[15] As I will discuss below, part of the work of fashion modeling is to offer up the body to these types of networks, to produce images as content to feed the endless demand for images for use in circulating affective energy in an affect economy. Fashion models, therefore, are key players in the expansion of an affective economy, including its global expansion.

The affect economy developed out of the rise of the service sector and the shift to a consumer economy that has characterized postindustrial capitalism. But the affect economy is also characterized by a tendency to what Karl Marx referred to as "real subsumption," where capital shifts its domain of accumulation to bodily preindividual forces such that value is produced through enlivening, capacitating, and modulating affect, as Clough suggests.[16] She describes how value is sought in the expansion and contraction of affective capacity, and the resulting investments in affective flows are aimed at keeping the flows moving at different speeds. In this scenario, Clough's affective economy is one in which the human body and its preindividual capacities are made the site of capital investment for the realization of profit. These structural economic shifts also have been accompanied by increased investment in the means of technological amplification and modulation of affective flow.

This understanding of an affect economy recognizes the insights gained from Marxist feminists' studies of women's unwaged domestic labor as a contribution to the family wage.[17] But it also recognizes how social reproduction has been subsumed by capital, made a force of production, as socialization, therapeutic interaction, cooking, cleaning, child care, health care, and the like have been increasingly pulled into the domain of capital.[18] Within this tendency, all of social life can become a force of production, as all kinds of activities formerly coded as gendered and private, and lying outside of the domain of capitalist investment, are increasingly pulled into its domain.

Thus the tendency toward the subsumption of reproductive labor by capital brings with it the possibility for an affective economy. This tendency has also been understood in terms of the shift to a consumer society, the growth of the service sector, and the appearance of new forms of investment in information and intellectual production that some theorists have referred to as immaterial labor.[19] Immaterial labor has become more prominent in the transition from an industrial to a postindustrial society, in the move toward informational or communication-based economies.[20] It is most evident in the informatization of production,[21] the increase in the importance and number of jobs in "symbolic analytic services,"[22] and the rise of the service sector as an economic force. The immaterial labor that produces affects, in particular, plays a "certain role throughout the service industries, from fast-food servers to providers of financial services, embedded in the moments of human interaction and communication."[23]

Put another way, affective labor is the labor of interaction and human contact that can elicit "intangible feelings of ease, excitement, or passion."[24] Workers in health services and the entertainment industry, for example, produce feelings of ease or excitement. These industries are dependant on outputs of affective labor such as caring and emoting. These types of services usually constitute in-person services, but the production and manipulation of affect or feeling can also be achieved through human contact that is virtual (such as the work of an actor appearing in a movie, or the work of a model appearing in a photograph).[25] In this case, technology aids the circulation of affective flows.

Modeling work is also a good example of labor typical of an affect economy. As I will discuss below, models manipulate affect or feeling by acting, engaging, and connecting with themselves and others, with the goal of stimulating and projecting a feeling of vitality or aliveness, which, as Clough suggests earlier in this volume, constitutes the essence of autoaffection. Modeling may also be understood as work to capture and channel attention; models' work takes place in an area of the affective economy that can also be thought of as "an attention economy,"[26] in which an infinite expansion of images is met with a finite capacity for human attention. Since affect is connected to attention (insofar as it directs and channels it),[27] in an economy in which the control of attention has value, the control of affective flow has value as well. Within an attention economy, units of time spent attending to images are bought and sold in a "flattening out" of affective intensities into calculated units of "audiences" slated into "demographic boxes."[28] Similarly, modeling work produces value in the form of the accumulation and distribution of attention to images—a body's image and the image of bodies.[29] Models' work is to produce content for attention-gathering and -calibrating technologies such as photography, television, and the Internet.

FASHION MODELING AND FASHIONING AFFECT

If, as I am suggesting, the work of models is not so much aimed at the "narrative construction of subject identities" as it is oriented toward "affecting bodies directly," it is because in my interviews both with fashion models and those who work with them, I found less evidence of their effort to construct the fashion model as a particular cultural ideal, with a culturally assigned and subjectively interpretable meaning, and more evidence that their effort was focused on the model's capacity to constantly change appearance and personality, an effort, I would argue, aimed at modulating the affective flow—to be activated by the model's presence in person, or by his or her virtual presence in photographs.[30] In other words, while some of the activities involved in modeling work may be oriented toward creating meaningful representations to stimulate a specific consumer desire for a specific product, many of the activities I learned about in my research are better explained as working to activate affective flow and to put it into circulation within the networks of affective production that characterize contemporary capitalism.

If modeling work were primarily or solely oriented toward creating gendered ideals of femininity, masculinity, sexiness, or beauty, for example, it would stand to reason that my respondents would have talked more about giving their efforts to making models sexy, or womanly, or beautiful. I found, instead, that in their discussions of how and why they modify their appearance, the models I interviewed, and those who worked with them, were more oriented toward achieving a level of variability, a chameleon-like look that can be made to change at will. Contrary to the common assumption that all models conform to some strict standards of appearance, workers in the industry describe a world of shifting standards in which their work becomes a "guessing game" of who will succeed in a business where there is "not that much logic."

The idea, for instance, that there is an ideal beauty that will always sell seemed preposterous to some of my respondents. As Diane, an agent, mused, "They're always talking about the new this or the new that, like, the new wave of ugly models! I'm like, wait a minute. When Lauren Hutton was modeling, they thought she was ugly! And when Twiggy was modeling, they thought she was ugly. . . . There's always gonna be—it goes around and comes around again and again. There is no such thing as ideal beauty."

I spoke to a group of new models about the conventional understanding that all models are pretty, and most of them did not agree with this idea. Several of them said that it was more about having the right look, while one of them, Meg, went on to say, "I look in magazines and I don't think that any of the girls who are popular right now are pretty." Another, Dawn, was quick to point out that there are many models who do not look like a model per se, but that something about their look that gets them into magazines anyway. She sees herself as an example: "That's happened to me, where I think, I don't know what they see, but whatever."

Arguably, those working with this model had an affective response to her image; they might not have been able to describe to her in words what her look did for them, but they knew the feeling when her particular look provoked a visceral response. The idea that an appearance can have an effect that may be felt but not easily explained, is advanced by the theorist Brian Massumi in his work on affect and images. He postulates the "*primacy of the affective* in image reception" and splits off an image's content from its effect.[31] By this he means to indicate a split between the qualities of the image and the intensity of the image, such that the image's content, its conventional meaning, does not necessarily correspond with its impact. Thus an image can have an effect that does not necessarily correspond to its meaning, or without meaning anything in *particular* to the viewing subject that it *affects*.

The concept of the split between an image's content and its effect occurs during what Massumi calls the "event of image reception" (24). He breaks down the moment into two levels, intensity and qualification. The intensity of the image corresponds to the "strength or duration" of its effect. The qualities of the image are fixed by the indexing to meaning by the viewing subject; this indexing involves some conscious involvement, as it might put the image into narrative, associating it with "expectations which depend on consciously positioning oneself in a line of narrative continuity" (25).

Understood in this way, then, affective response takes place below the level of awareness; consequently, in makes sense that even those who are supposed to know what it is that makes a model command attention (e.g., the people who represent and manage models, such as model agents, or those who hire models, such as magazine editors) often remain unable to exactly explain a model's success. When they describe what it is that gets a model work, the agents and other modeling professionals I spoke to remained characteristically vague, referring to it in general terms as something that sparked their interest or caught their eye. They often described the gut reaction involved in making choices about whether to hire a model. Cameron, an agent in New York, explained how he decided if someone was worth the trouble to sign at the agency: "You try and look for the elements, the fundamentals, if someone has the right body to do shows, or they have the right body to do fashion—which is like a size 6, a size 4 to 6, really skinny, you know, that's what the designers want, 5′10″ to 5′11″, those are the girls that do well on the runway, so they have to have that body, and a face that isn't boring." Note how this agent qualified his statement of weights and measurements with reference to a much less easily quantified idea, a "face that isn't boring." It seems that even the most basic description of how a fashion model's body and face should look had to be immediately qualified with an addition of a requirement not exactly measurable, an x-factor that is in some ways immeasurable, but constitutes a necessary ingredient nonetheless. This x-factor, although indefinable and immeasurable, might be cultivated by the model, or it might be something that the model has without realizing it, so that the collaboration with other affective laborers brings it out. For example, models who are discovered (i.e., found on the street and recruited for modeling) might not know they have an affective quality to their look, but an agent or scout searching for a certain level of affectivity will respond to a prospective model's looks.

Recall Massumi's proposition that the qualification of an image is the process by which it is put into language and meaning, through its narrativization, in which an "intimation of what comes next" is interpreted by the observer (26). To qualify the image that a model might potentially present would be to assign it a meaning—for example, that the model looks all American, or like the girl next door. Intensity, on the other hand, is associated with nonlinear processes, such as resonance and feedback. The intensity of an image is measurable by its impact. If an image is hard to ignore, catches one's eye, is upsetting or exciting, its intensity is affecting. Intensity is "qualifiable as an emotional state" (26), but only when qualified as emotion (that is, assigned a meaning).

Before that, the movement of intensity is simply "motion, vibratory motion, resonation . . . it is not yet activity, because the motion is not of the kind that can be directed (if only symbolically) toward practical ends in a world of constituted objects and aims (if only on screen)" (26). Affective flow, if one reads it as intensity (as Massumi eventually does), is a reaction that occurs before the direction of aims and objects, that is, before there is individual desire or interpretation, before the affective flow is narrated as an affective state in a particular body. Intensity is felt in the moment of energy flow between bodies. It is not an energy directed toward anything in particular; it is the source of actions, although the effect of affective flow is always indeterminate until after it is registered and narrated as a physical state.

Thus to work with affect is to work with something volatile and difficult to control. There is a certain "irrationality to affective investment,"[32] and yet, in an affective economy, value is produced through enlivening, capacitating, and modulating affect. In such an economy, a primary goal of production is to stimulate attention and motivate interest by whatever means are possible, to produce affect in a volatile or turbulent situation. In this scenario, adhering to a fixed standard of appearance proves counterproductive. Value lies in producing variations within the standards that tend to govern a model's appearance. Thus while the reigning ideas of what a model could and should look like seem to be very stringent and uniform, in practice, they incorporate a variability of elements into the process to stimulate attention in the volatile world of affect production.

While there seems to be a hard-and-fast rule that women should be at least five foot, seven inches, and men should be six feet, for instance, these seem to be rules of thumb, rather than an actual barrier to entry. Most respondents cited some versions of these statistics; a model agent who worked with both male and female models, Ron, rattled his take on them for me: "Women have to be five feet, nine inches or taller, and men have to be at least six feet tall." Some, like Lewis, a male model in the business for seventeen years, believed there were practical reasons for the height requirements:

> Girls have to be at least 5′9″. And no more than 5′11″. Six feet is too tall for a girl, and 6′3″ and above is too tall for a boy. And you can't be too short, neither. When you have those elements, that's why everybody fits the same clothes, because no one is over 6′3″, and no one is under 5′10″. Because if it is, he is not going to fit the clothes. Ideal length is 34. So you've got to be the right height. That's why all the models can fit the clothes.

Yet in interviews, some reported a variation in standards that arguably had more to do with models' affective capacities than their height. That is to say, a model's power to create an affective image could override these strict standards. My respondents reported several examples of a tendency to relax those rules if a model was judged to have the x-factor that might translate into an image that will sell. Take, for example, the case of Kate Moss, who, in spite of her five-foot-seven frame, became a supermodel; she was the shortest one in the business until her success paved the way for others like her. Nea, a model I interviewed, also found she had a quality or power strong enough to override her lack of height:

> If they like you, they can do anything for you. . . . They'll say, you're too short, and then the next time, they're like, we're making you clothes. And I'm thinking, interesting. . . . Like this catalog, for example. I went to a casting the first time, and they're calling the agency saying, "Oh, we really liked her, but she's really too short, and you shouldn't send her over anymore," and I was like, oh, great. But at least they are honest. So I did ten campaigns in that one season, and they called back and said, "We don't care, we want her, we will make the clothes." Ever since, they've booked me every season, and they are making me clothes. I get paid an extra day just so they can make them for me.

If affect is only "produced as an effect of its circulation,"[33] then, as an object or sign circulates in an affective economy, affective value accrues to an image as it moves in circulation. Arguably, then, this model's appearance or exposure in certain circuits of value made her image more valuable, increasing in value as it increased in circulation. Each successive campaign accrued affectivity to this model's image with every successive layer of association that each campaign brought with it. Consequently, her affective capacity increased in accordance with the number and places her image appeared.

Reportedly, a model who has achieved this level of affectivity can then dictate the shape and style of a whole fashion show. That is to say, the affective capacity of a single model might be valued so highly that a designer might go to extraordinary measures to use him or her. For example, a model who had done a good deal of runway work, Stephanie, exclaimed, "If you are five foot, two inches and the designer likes you, they are going to think of something to make it work!" The flexibility with regard to standards of height extends to standards of appearance as well. To be affective, the model must not be married to a particular look, but rather must seek variation, to offer up a malleable body that can shift and change in a constant rhythm, in order to attract attention, hold interest, or create a reaction.

In my interviews, I found that several of the models were motivated to modulate their bodies in ways that produced subtle variations in appearance, in an ongoing effort to be constantly changeable. They did not talk about having to achieve a sexy appearance, or a feminine look, or even an attractive one; they were not seeking a meaningful body or appearance as such. Several of the models, for instance, spoke of the importance of being able to change their body and look for different markets and different times of year. Noting the difference between the New York and Paris markets, a female model, Brittany, claimed, "The Paris markets are tough, you have to be skinny, skinny, skinny." Another, Dawn, explained that a good model has to be ready to do anything, to take on whatever changes might come her way.

> This job has made me completely separate, psychologically, who I am from my looks. Like, I'll go to a casting, and they'll say, "Are you willing to cut your hair," and I'll be like, sure; "Are you willing to blah blah blah," sure, because I just don't hold it so tightly; I think this is my commodity, my looks are my commodity. I'm just like an architect, his building is his commodity, and he has to be willing to work with it, you know what I'm saying?

The female models talked predominantly about slimming their bodies, changing their hair, or being willing to wear different styles of clothing. The male models discussed altering their appearance primarily in terms of going to the gym. Many took an instrumental approach to their bodies, beefing up for some markets, slimming down for others, according to subtle distinctions between a fit or unstudied look. Stuart, a nineteen-year-old model relatively new to the business, noted that "I like to work out, but right now I haven't worked out in five weeks because I've been in Europe. Some guys I know, they do slim down for Europe, they don't lift any more when they go to Europe, because they like smaller guys over there." Lewis, a veteran of the industry, took a similar approach, referring to his body as his "tool," an instrument to produce whatever the market demanded at the time: "My body is my tool, and so that's why we go to the gym . . . it's very important to have a nice body; if you want to do underwear and do things that are revealing your body, then you're going to have to work out because they're going to pick the person with the nicest body. Or at least the more natural looking body, or a body that is suited to what they are looking for." Note how he qualifies the idea of the nicest or the best body, since he cannot clearly define what it is his body should look like: "Sometimes they don't want beefcake bodies, because that's not what they are looking for. They don't want all the muscles, they want just a natural look. But even within a natural look, you still have to have some sort of fitness." Lewis is talking about a standard without being able to pinpoint exactly what the standard is. Arguably, the lack of any real standard speaks to the idea that in the realm of affective production, it is often the unexpected or unassimilable that proves productive. The qualities in the model's image that push beyond the borders of conventional interpretation toward a direct, nonsubjective impact on the body are qualities that are valued and value producing.

ELICITING AFFECT: FROM THE PHOTO SHOOT TO WORKING 24/7

I am arguing that the stimulation of affective energy is the goal of much modeling work. This premise certainly helps to explain some of the observations models and their coworkers made about working at a photo shoot. The expectation that a model is the clay shaped by the photographer's directives was not borne out by the stories that models related about their work. Instead, they talked about efforts to stir up the energy in a photo session without being told what it is, exactly, that they were supposed to do in front of the camera. Kay, a makeup artist, for example, describes how it is the model's job to "get into the flow" without being told what to do. From her perspective, it is the model's job to get into the moment, to react in an uninhibited and variable manner:

> Some girls will get on the set, and they'll just have a fabulous flow and variety and movement, and they get it, and they look at the outfit before, and they look at the hair and the makeup before, and they'll get on the set

and they'll just . . . it's almost like watching an actress where there's no direction required; they're just flowing with it, they get it, and they've paid attention, and the photographer can take pictures for over an hour and not have to say one word because everything is just wonderful.

Getting into the flow appears to be the model's job insofar as he or she does the affective labor of opening up to the mood and environment the photographer and his or her team try to create. A model, Bitou, describes how she handles it when the clients and photographer are not "directive":

Sometimes they just want to let you do it. The photographers and clients aren't always so directive, they want to let you be yourself. So you have to be able to define your own way that you look better. You learn from seeing pictures of yourself. . . . Because often you have to smile and you have to find the right smile that is not too fake, and not too much at the same time. For me it's a feeling. You cannot smile when they tell you to smile. I'm, like, make me laugh, and I will smile. So they will bring somebody to make me laugh. I cannot put it on.

In this case, the labor to produce an affective response is collaborative, using "affect contagion,"[34] in which affect is communicated via facial expression. Pounding music, lavish food, or the creation of certain types of situations may also be employed at a photo shoot to create a mood, to get the models to relax and open up. If the model is not successful at getting into the flow, the members of the team assembled to create the image—the photographer, assistant, stylist, makeup artist, hairstylist, and so on—will try to help things along. In a sense, it is part of their job to create a context for or environment of affective amplification. Assistants at shoots use food and words of encouragement to elicit that "certain something" the photographer may be looking for, but perhaps is unable to articulate. Sometimes it just takes talking to the model; sometimes more drastic techniques are required. As the makeup artist Kay put it:

Once you've invested in the day, you do have to try to make it work. So sometimes it's about coddling the models, sometimes it's a lot about coaxing them. The hairstylist and I tend to be a little more of the support system for the model. Help her through the day emotionally; help her feel cared about and cared for. If it's cold, to bring her a cup of tea, or if her energy is sagging, or if she's not feeling, like, a good connection with the photographer, I might go over to her and say, you know, "Do you want some chocolate?" In a devilish tone. Whatever it takes. You know, stand on the side of the set and talk to them, so that their face looks a little bit more animated. Maybe they want me to get them to laugh, when the model can't do it themselves, because some people can't laugh on a dime; you need to talk to them to keep them awake looking.

The need to keep them "awake looking" also includes a need, at least on the part of some photographers, to shock an unexpected look from the model by using directions that might surprise or make the model uncomfortable, or at least not as studied. The former supermodel Cindy Crawford once described how an up-and-coming fashion photographer asked her to act like a small rodent in order for him to get the shot he was looking for:

> The first time I worked with him, he'd want you to do things like, you know, like, can you be a rat? And then he would take pictures. This was in my big cover heyday, and I was like, oh my God, what if he runs this picture? I'm still not sure why he made us do that. I think it was just to break the . . . so he got something different out of you. Because when you went from doing this (*she mimics being a rat by wriggling her nose and baring her teeth*), at least you've broken the mood and when you went back to your more normal modeling, it kind of worked itself out.[35]

This effort to create something unexpected, something extra or unplanned, points toward the goal of producing an affective response by creating an image that is unassimilable, that pushes beyond the borders of conventional interpretation. In this sense, models' work with affect is twofold. On the level of their own person and presence, they work to be sensitive to the flow of affect by broadening their affective capacity so that stimulus easily produces affects in their bodies that might then translate into an external change in demeanor, appearance, or attitude, becoming affective bodies. On the level of social interaction, these externalizations of affective flow can then be used to transmit energy and activate affective flow through others, which might perhaps then be captured as affects, and so on. Models' work with affective flow takes place both in person, when they are working with teams assembled to create images, or via the virtual human contact they establish in and through the images they produce. The job of a model is to be as open as possible to that flow, to keep it moving, without capping it off and defining it as any particular affect. As one of the model agents, Cameron, put it, models are "just conduits most of the time." Their work can be understood as the effort to amplify and modulate the flow of affect by embodying an image or stimulating an energy not immediately assimilable to consciousness.

I am arguing then, that the idea behind producing an affective image is to try to transmit a "force of potential,"[36] to use Massumi's phrase, that will counteract the limiting abilities of consciousness, which will explode the containment performed by actualization. The act of actualization is to assign meaning to an image, to delimit it, to bring it to the conscious plane of interpretation, as, for example, when affects are narrated as emotions, among other things. Understanding images merely in terms of their meaning misses a good portion of the force of their potential. If an image succeeds beyond its containment of actualization, to communicate that force, it "cannot but be felt" as it enables and simultaneously counteracts the limiting power of selection through which its effects come to consciousness (42).[37] Massumi claims we must think of images as "the conveyors of forces of emergence, as vehicles for existential potentialization and transfer" (43), which means to say that images transfer energy. They create potentialities—they create the potential for reception of the vitality that the image conveys.

A good model, then, is someone who has that x-factor, who has the ability to play on the energy that flows between us, to resonate with the virtual tendrils that form potential paths into our mutual futures and pasts. A good image is not just meaningful; some of its power lies in its lack of precise meaning. A good image conjures forth the sensation of as many of these possibilities in as many directions as possible. The best kind of image cannot be closed off; instead, it must offer possibilities, even after the most thorough of interpretations. It is for this reason that the model must get into a flow with the goal of bringing something unpredictable or unexplainable to him- or herself and the image. A model's job, in some sense, is to present these potentialities in the flesh—to be everything to everyone, or to be something in the extreme without being anything in particular. Models do their work at the "edge of the virtual, where it leaks into the actual" (43).

FASHIONING AFFECT AND THE INVESTED BODY

It is at the edge of virtuality that the bodies of the fashion industry become sites of investment. While some bodies are exploited at the very lowest end of the fashion industry—the sweatshop workers, for example, who produce the clothes models wear—the fashion model's body is marked to collect the surplus value produced by these workers. So marked, the fashion model's body becomes the site of further investment. Thus the highly paid supermodel has teams of professionals assigned to work on every detail of her or his appearance, investing time and energy into hair, skin, fitness, nutrition, personality, style, and overall image. This attention to the fashion model becomes an investment in bodily capacities, in body parts. In this way, the fashion modeling industry "modularizes" the body, such that the body is treated as a machinic assemblage with parts that are "micro-dissectable,"[38] replaceable, duplicable, or generally manageable.[39] The modularization of the body may be linked both to processes of removal or addition via medical technological intervention, as well as to the process of inscribing the body with cultural objects/signs, applied to the surface of the body.[40] This conceptual link between medical interaction with the body and the idea of cultural intervention dovetails with the idea that affective labor works with the body's capacities in general, through all kinds of interactions with various technologies, as the body increasingly becomes a space of technological intervention and investment.

While the models in my study did not narrativize their labor in terms of the process of making their bodies available as sites of investment, they did describe intense interest in and attention paid to details of their appearance, details that demanded a great deal of time and energy from them, as well as from the teams of professionals who worked with them. A modeling agent, Genevieve, described the intense scrutiny and interest with which the agency treated the models she worked with:

> We tell them how to dress, show them how to walk, show them how to put their hair [*sic*], we send them to the dermatologist if they don't have very good skin. . . . We tell them what to eat. I can see on the face what they eat; I can see whether they drink. I can see it. I know that you eat chocolate. They say, no! but I say, yes, I can see it in your face. I know if they eat fat, or if they are lying about their height.

The intense interest in modulating the inputs into and appearance of the model's body provides an example of how the model's body becomes invested by the professionals who work with them. It is also expected that the models will invest in their own appearance, as this makeup artist Kay explains:

> I say this is your product, and you are going to invest in it (and it *is* an investment), or you're not. Either you are going to find the right dermatologist, a good facialist if that's what you need, or you're not going to apply yourself. Either you're going to go to a gym and you're going to tone your body the right way—you may be as skinny as a pole, but that doesn't mean that you're in the right shape. Or, you might not. . . . I'll ask if they are eating right. I'll talk to them about going to a nutritionist. Finding out what works well with their body. What they should and shouldn't be eating, and that's

going to react to their energy level, how they feel emotionally, their hair and skin quality, as well as their weight.

Not only are the models working to produce images that mobilize bodily economies of dieting, skin care, and beauty products but they are also encouraged to engage in those economies themselves, to invest in those aspects of their appearance as part of their jobs.

Sometimes a professional who manages a model may get caught up in the finer details of managing the model's appearance to an extreme degree. The smallest details can seem crucially important in a market in which large sums may be made or lost depending on a model's hair length and color, breast size and shape, overall body type, or the quality of their skin. The investment of energy in and attention to the minutest detail of appearance is evident in this story a model, Stephanie, told me:

> I used to have bangs, but I didn't really like them, so I was always pulling them back with clips when I didn't have anything going on. I had to go into the agency, and my booker was, like, "Ahhhh! Bangs bangs!" gesturing toward his forehead saying, "You can't wear them like that!" And I was, like, "I'm not even doing anything. I came from home, I'm going to pick something up, and then I'm going back to my apartment. Leave me alone!" Everybody was looking at me and the booker, like, what's going on? He was yelling it out! I was, like, what's wrong with you? He didn't like it pinned back because it was uncool, it wasn't stylish. It was so annoying. Even when they see you in the street, they say, "You can't do this! You have to blah blah blah," you know? Like you are supposed to be on your job 100 percent of the time!

From this perspective, it is possible to think about how parts of model's bodies fluctuate in size and importance according to the imperatives of modulating affective flow. Models strive (and also suggest) to follow the trends in bodily fashions that fixate on one body part or another in a modulation of bodily shape that is constantly changing. Although there are norms governing those fashions, these are increasingly directed at body parts. Jenna, a veteran model who had worked through several decades of designer fads, had seen breasts go in and out of fashion, alternately taping hers down and letting them out: "Well, there was a whole rage [of plastic surgery] at one point. All these girls were getting boobs. I was going to work and was, like, oh my God. You know, and I remember strapping mine down, and nobody wanted to see them, and then all of a sudden, boom, they're in. And I was like, wow, I can breathe again! But then they went away again." Another model, Stephanie, noted variations on several levels at once: "Well . . . it doesn't matter—I've seen flat girls who are totally no hips with short hair—and then next season it's really curvy girls with hips."

The need to constantly stimulate attention and motivate interest in the appearance of models leads to pendulum swings in the variations within the standards that govern models' appearances. These observations point toward the idea that in an affective economy, it is not just the whole body that is used for marketing and creating images but parts of bodies become valuable as well—hair, shape and style, whether or not the model wears makeup, has clear skin, smiles or not, wears high heels, has large breasts or small ones, a cut stomach or not—all of these details can activate and circulate affect in their own right and so become the objects of intense scrutiny and control by those whose job it is to market a model's image.

FASHIONING AFFECT: THE NODAL BODY AND
THE TECHNOLOGIES OF CIRCULATION

I have been discussing how models work with teams of other artistic, affective laborers to construct flows of affective exchange, via images, or to create the contexts of affective amplification or modulation, which might then be captured in images. Massumi points out that to feel the flow of affect, or rather, the affect that escapes capture by our cognition, one feels the sense of "one's own vitality, one's sense of aliveness, of changeability."[41] Within the networks of affective production, the model's job is to be open to a free play of affective flow and to allow the capture of that flow as affect. In this way, the model acts as a node in those networks. In addition to cultivating and modulating affective flow in person, the networks of affective production include the fashion system of images, in which affective images are produced and distributed via the distribution channels of magazines, film, and television.

Massumi would call these outlets for image exposure the "apparatuses of actualization" (44). For those affective stirrings to have an effect, even a multiplicity of effects, there must be some determination of that flow into a direction by the "apparatuses of actualization and implantation that plug into them and transformatively relay what they give rise to" (44). Here Massumi refers to school, family, and church, "to name but a few" (44). In that group I would include the networks of the affective economy, of consumerism, branding, fashion, and more generally, culture, that direct affective flow toward points of receptivity on the receiving end in the form of audiences, who actualize and implant affective energy and relay it along a chain of action and reaction that may translate into profit somewhere along the line, if not all away along the line. In other words, affective flow is productive in the sense that it is vitality stimulated and then captured for release in networks of images, circulated for capitalist investment and realization of profit without a clear beginning and without a certain end.

Affective workers, then, make themselves available to the nodes of affective production; it is part of their labor to expose themselves to the apparatuses of actualization that determine the flow of affect, channeling it in various directions. These networks of affective modulation exist, for example, in the photographic apparatus of fashion photography and in the production of images to sell products. Insofar as the model's job is to expose him- or herself to the means of making images, it consists, of course, in posing for the camera to make fashion images. What is interesting about my findings, however, is how many of the models claimed that their jobs encompassed far more time and energy than such a narrow definition of their work implies. Increasingly, there appear to be neither time nor place for the model to be free of work opportunities. One model, Kate, referred to her job as being "24/7," saying, "You're always on display; you have to put on that show twenty-four hours a day. It's not as though you can go to the office and then go home and relax. You're always watching what you eat. You're always worrying about how you're coming across, always worried about being seen at the right places at the right times. It's just never ending." Part of the work of putting on "that show twenty-four hours a day" consists of making oneself available for the production and circulation of different kinds of fashion-related images, images that can be productive on many levels. Take, for example, the productivity of the social circuit of the modeling world. This circuit consists of industry parties, events sponsored by fashion companies, and the kinds of socializing that provide fodder for entertainment news and gossip columns. Models form an integral part of these circuits, and in fact are encouraged to participate in them. Hence "being seen at the right places at the right times" is part of a model's job.

The productivity of circulating models in a publicized social circuit may be interpreted in several ways. As the models tell it, socializing serves the functions of self-promotion and making contacts to get jobs. One model, Svetlana, who was careful to attend "model parties" told me that during fashion show weeks in the various cities of the fashion circuit of Paris, Milan, London, and New York, she thought of those events "as an 'evening casting.'" Other models agreed that even though they might be doing two fashion shows a day, and up to ten shows in a week (with fittings in between, on a hectic schedule), "you have to go to the parties, because a photographer might see you there and think you're cool, or be inspired by you," as Mika put it, which offers a quick route to getting hired.

Although they may seem to be mere social events, parties serve a very clear purpose for the models. Jody, a model who has "been on so many runways in one and a half years, I've lost count," was explicit about it: "Fashion parties are about meeting people, not about having fun." An American model, Suzie, who proudly reported working in twenty-five different cities in Spain for the Chanel tour, explained "I get jobs when I go out into the nightlife. It's un-believable who you can meet." She went out seven nights a week when she was "younger" because she found she made "so many connections," but now, having achieved some measure of success, is more "moderate—I go out about two to three nights per week." Going out is ostensibly a model's choice, but a young girl from Slovenia, Mika, who has been in the industry for about a year, said, "Sometimes even the bookers tell you, you have to go out, this night, because this photographer might be there. Certain parties at a studio you'll have to go to too." As these models attest to, circulating in the social scene frequently proves a job requirement.

This circulation is potentially lucrative not only for the models but also for the places they frequent. From the point of view of the bars and restaurants favored by models and their associates, the social circuit is productive in terms of self-promotion and building a clientele. The networking and schmoozing that is part and parcel of the business appears attractive to bars, clubs, restau-rants, hotels, gyms, and other urban gathering places, in which style, status, hotness, or coolness are circulated in the affective economy of city life and the media's portrayal of it. "There is a circuit of 'scenes' or power centers; it's very organic, and sometimes it *makes* a place or a company," observed Raul, a creative director at a fashion advertising agency. He explained that hip hotels and restaurants use the attention generated in the networks of affective pro-duction by models' socializing to make themselves more valuable in terms of building a reputation for being the "place to be."

An example of such a scene is a so-called model party. Model parties— events at a club or a bar hosted either by a modeling agency or a club promoter who invites models—provide a source of publicity for the clubs that host them; if a model gets into the gossip pages due to his or her activities at a party, it will generate press not only for the model but also for the agency that manages him or her, as well as the restaurant that hosts the party. Industry parties make for a lucrative and mutually beneficial business for all involved. A young female booker, Megan, laid out the logic—female models attract men with money, which brings in a higher bar tab: "They'll use any excuse—a model's birthday, a stupid holiday." The agency benefits from these parties because photographers who attend the party meet the agency's models who get exposure, getting their names out there and making contacts. If the press comes, all the better; the model's notoriety is built, which produces publicity for all involved.

These parties mutually benefit designers (their names get into the press), photographers (they may meet the "it" girl or boy, befriend them, and ultimately arrange to photograph him or her), and agencies (their models gain exposure). "Deals go down in bars frequently," Megan, the model agent, asserted; "brands of alcohol throw these parties too . . . to get the 'right' people there drinking their product to create the right image."

This type of promotion and image production is productive at a more abstract level as well. The publicized social circuit helps build the image of the industry overall, and helps promote interest in and attention to fashion. This attention and energy is focused by the television coverage of modeling and fashion events and extends into the realm of the Internet as well. Web sites devoted to the modeling industry (such as tearsheet.com and modelswire.com) serve both to distribute information about the industry and to pique interest in models and modeling by profiling models, following their careers, and publishing human interest pieces about them. Others exist solely for the purpose of publicizing parties and the models and fashion types who attend them. Sites such as wireimage.com, a sort of gossip column coupled with a fashion calendar detailing the shows around the world, and FTV.com, named for the twenty-four-hour cable channel called Fashion Television, provide endless options for cruising through images of fashion parties and following party schedules. The FTV.com site even allows subscribers to step through the frame and obtain invitations to parties in places as disparate as China, Nigeria, or New York, to name but a few.

The idea of focusing and channeling attention connects to one of the prime activities of affective production, in which images are circulated and, in circulation, attract attention and modulate affect as a result. Here, television and teletechnologies are engaged and become further invested. If televisual imaging is the form in which images may achieve direct impact without necessarily having to pass through the subjective circuit of meaning, they may be freed from the "perspective of an idea of meaning production tied to the logic of the body."[42] In this environment, images of fashion models are not necessarily called upon to produce meaning-driven consumption or subjective identities, to idealize and mimic exactly. Rather, images are circulated in order to produce attention, to make an impact, however ill defined or diffuse. As the modulation of attention to images has become a profitable enterprise, the speed and quantity of images in circulation has become more important than their ability to produce subjective meanings. Impact is the name of the game as developments in imaging technologies of computerization and television lead to an almost infinite expansion of images on view that exceed the human capacity for attention.

The developments in imaging technology that attract or focus attention have had a profound effect on the modeling industry. The introduction of cable and satellite television proved a major factor in the mainstreaming of fashion and the consequent skyrocketing of fees paid for models' work. As it became prohibitively expensive to produce narrative content, endless repetition on cable television turned into the norm in repeating loops of news, weather, talk, shopping, sports, and fashion.[43] Fashion proved a particularly appealing form of content, with its constant iteration of slightly different themes and its steady stream of young and beautiful people. As one model, Nathan, put it, "the supermodels of the late 80s and early 90s created an appetite for models in a more mainstream market" and therefore created new audiences for fashion content. As another model, Teri, put it in the late 1990s, "modeling is so Middle America now, people in Iowa know who Marc Jacobs is."

These images of the modeling industry, picked up by new developments in imaging technology and circulated within the context of fashion considered more generally, stimulated attention to Fashion with a capital *F*, so to speak. In this environment, modeling work produced value in the form of attention not only to models in fashion photographs but also to images of models in other settings: on the runway, backstage, socializing at parties, shopping, or going about their daily lives. Nicholas, a PR agent for a model agency, saw it this way: "There's a hunger for content because there are more outlets. The number of magazine titles in the past ten years has something like tripled. So you need more content, so you search for more subject matter. And in that search, the media writes about the lives of models, which I don't think twenty years ago anyone would have given a damn about."

Cameron, a model agent, felt the same way, saying, "there are now large channels of information looking for content, and models are a great thing to fill empty hours on the television." The increase in the number of media outlets (cable's growth to hundreds of channels, the Internet's expansion, and even the attention grabs on television news shows to compete for viewers with fluff items that have to do with sex or beautiful people) created a content vacuum of sorts, and among other forms of entertainment news, the appeal of fashion images made them particularly well suited to fill the gap.

From the 1980s onward, as the demand for model's images grew, so did their pay rates. The rise of the supermodels may be attributed at least in part to the increased avenues for models' affective production, particularly in the expansion of the autoaffective circuit of television to twenty-four hours in the 1980s in the form of channels such as CNN and MTV. In this time frame, top models began to make millions of dollars per year. Since the 1960s, models have been relatively well paid; but the $12 an hour and $60 a commercial made by the 1960s superstar model Penelope Tree was proportionately much less than the $50,000 a day models of that caliber were making by the late 1990s.[44] In 1994, the supermodel Cindy Crawford's gross yearly earnings were estimated at $6.5 million.[45] By 1998, they reportedly reached $8 million; that same year, Claudia Schiffer's income reached $10.5 million.[46] This was the era of the supermodel Linda Evangelista's comment that "we won't wake up for less than $10,000." As Carolyn, a veteran agent at an elite agency described it: "So from the mid-eighties into the early nineties it just kept snowballing, and got bigger and bigger, and that's when you may have heard Linda Evangelista and Naomi Campbell say 'I won't get out of bed for anything less than $10,000 a day'—and they were right, they didn't have to. It was a true statement: these girls were making from $10 to $25,000 to $50 to $150,000 dollars a *day* for certain jobs."

The lives of the supermodels became fodder for the entertainment mill, to the point where anything models did—from the very public, such as walking the runway, to the semiprivate, such as shopping, to the details of their private lives—became worthy of exposure as the need for more and more exposure extended further into model's lives. This work of televisual imaging, in which images of models are exposed in more places and in increasingly varied ways, extends (and is fed by) the work done by the model parties discussed above. Both exposure to potential clients at parties and exposure of a model's life as infotainment hook the model up with potential revenue streams. The proliferating images of models at work and living their lives also produces them as revenue streams in an environment in which there is a circuit of exchange from image to life to image, in a network the velocity of whose exchanges make it hard to distinguish between the two.[47]

Some of this interest in models' personal lives was, of course, part and parcel of the process of making celebrity. What is unique about the flows of affect this exposure activated, however, is that long after the supermodels ended their uncontested reign in the industry, average models stepped in to take their place, appearing on infotainment shows that depict models going to work, shopping, or playing with their dogs. A PR agent for a modeling agency,

Nicholas, pointed out that although the supermodels were a unique phenomenon, like lightning that does not strike twice, they created new income streams for the average model:

> Lightning does not strike twice. But it affects what happens now. [The supermodels] made it possible for girls to earn that much money. Even though the "quote" supermodels *now* aren't super in the way those girls were, they make just as much money. Look at what Michael Jordan did for athletes; it's the same thing. He paved the way for them to get a lot of money for endorsement deals, way more than anybody before that. He was the first athlete brand.

After the supermodels' earnings had reached the stratosphere, back down on earth, the value of models' image production had increased so much that even an untried fourteen-year-old might be paid a starting salary of $70,000 and within a few years could command as much as $100,000 to half a million dollars.[48] In other words, following the trails blazed by the supermodels, the affective production system developed to such a point that the affective energies of even average models could be picked up by the system, in a diffuse modulation that is characteristic of the affective economy.

CONCLUSION

In my analysis, I have sought to illustrate how the concept of affect resolves some of the difficulties encountered when contemplating complexities of the postmodern body. Viewed as an affective system, the body is understood as more than a mere product of meaning systems or of how it is represented; the concept of affect also encompasses the flows of energies that move in and through bodies, creating surfaces and moving bodies as they pass in and through them. I have been particularly concerned with how adopting this new perspective affords a view of how the energies that flow between bodies, released in social interaction, are being picked up and circulated in processes of capitalist production.

This type of circulation has been understood in terms of the subsumption of reproductive labor by capital, and I discussed how this shift in relations between bodies, labor, and capital brings with it the possibility for an affective economy. In such an economy, value is produced by "the augmentation or diminution of a body's capacity to act, to engage, to connect,"[49] usually by means of technoscientific or entertainment technologies. To flesh out this concept I briefly outlined how modeling, as a profession, has changed and developed in tandem with changes and developments in entertainment technologies such as photography, film, and television.

I chose the labor of fashion models as an example of affective production for two reasons. First, looking at the current specifics of modeling work as described in interviews with modeling professionals allowed me to detail how modeling work involves acting, engaging, and connecting with oneself and others with the goal of stimulating and projecting a feeling of vitality or aliveness. Second, modeling work is intimately involved with imaging technologies insofar as the work is the labor to offer up the body to various types of imaging networks and to produce images as content to feed the endless demand for images for use in circulating affective energy. As my data bear out, being a model entails acting as a conduit for bodily energy or vitality, to facilitate its capture and extension by means of technologies that create and distribute images used to gather and calibrate attention.

I also sought to illustrate how fashion modeling work is not primarily aimed at the narrative construction of subject identities, as it is conventionally understood, but rather is oriented toward affecting bodies directly. Specifically, the workers I spoke to in the modeling industry were not motivated by the need to create meaningful or even interpretable images, but rather sought to construct malleable images aimed more at the modulation of affect than the creation of specific consumer desires. By looking at examples of how models were judged as suitable for work, how they and their handlers worked with them to elicit the affective flow at a photo shoot, and the levels of intense scrutiny leveled at their bodies and overall appearance, I was able to think through the various ways in which models' bodies are made productive by exposure to imaging systems. In light of these findings, I concluded that certain types of affective labor involve the labor of exposing the body to imaging machines, making it available for imaging and thereby augmenting that body's ability to act, engage, or connect far beyond the range of mere physical presence.

Affective labor is not only accomplished by extension of the body's capacities but also by their intensification as well. My respondents' discussions of how they treat their bodies and how their bodies are treated as spaces of investment afforded some insights into the modularization of the body that is typical of an affective economy. In particular, I touched on ways in which attention to the fashion model becomes an investment in bodily capacities, or body parts, and how the fashion modeling industry modularizes the body into a space of technological intervention and investment.

In the modularization of the body, various technologies—biotechnology, surveillance, information, and entertainment technologies—come together and pick up energies from bodies and between bodies, circulating them for profit. These flows are sometimes actualized, transformed into desires or acts of consumption, but the aim of these technologies is to produce a constant flow that prevents finding a clear stoppage along the line that might enable us to stop and say that here is the point of application for politics of the body. The concept of affect, as I have argued, allows for the complexity of the intricate interdependencies of bodies and technologies that presently govern our lives. I propose that attention to the study of affect and bodies, particularly in relation to developments in imaging technology, constitutes an important supplement to the usual gender politics, consumer critiques, and body politics. To think beyond subjective identity to preindividual forces of affectivity and bodily energies is to gain a new angle on how media technologies and other imaging technologies of a scientific, information, or even warlike nature intersect and constitute bodies, demanding new conceptions of what it is to be a gendered body, or even a human body.

NOTES

1. As Karen Barad has observed, when speaking of the body, the dynamic body, or the cyborg body, there is agency in the matter of the body as much as there is agency in the delimiting of that body. As she put it, "Agency is about the possibilities and account-ability entailed in refiguring material-discursive apparatuses of bodily production, in-cluding the boundary articulations and exclusions that are marked by those practices" ("Agential Realism: Feminist Interventions in Understanding Scientific Practices," in *The Science Studies Reader*, ed. Mario Biagioli [New York: Routledge, 1999], 7). Al-though she was discussing scientific technology and its relations to the production of knowledge, I see in Barad's conception of agential realism a move away from pure social constructionist accounts of the body toward a "mattering" of the body (see Pheng Cheah, "Mattering," *Diacritics* 26.1 [1996]: 108–39) that parallels what I am seeking to conceptualize here. This line of thought in part grew out of Judith Butler's notion of bodies that matter (see her *Gender Trouble: Feminism and the Subversion of Identity* [New York: Routledge, 1990]), which claims that the body is the result not of a pregiven anatomy about which we have ideas, but rather of a tension between the psychic and the material in which an imaginary schema is laid over the material to make it available to our psyches. From this perspective, the body is a mode of appearance whose boundaries are conferred on it by psychic projections in a series of iterations, or repetitive instances. But since the body is iterated and reiterated, it is not fixed in form or meaning, and there are temporal gaps between the moments in which the structure that give it its meaning is instantiated.

Butler argues that these temporal gaps leave the body open to resignification, a repetition with a difference, since the body's anatomy always exceeds the terms with which it is given. Although she is not writing about affect, it is interesting to note that the idea of a body exceeding the terms in which it is given ties provocatively to the idea of a body always moving beyond, through, or around the schemas of discourse, meaning, or production into which it is put or within which it interacts. The body's affectivity, its reach into the virtual realm that surrounds it, may be thought in terms of excess. The body in a passional state is neither psychic nor material, but a mixture of both.

While Butler uses her concepts in the service of destabilizing received notions of gender, Elizabeth Grosz takes them a step further, employing them to destabilize the notion of the body itself. She claims that the body can be regarded as, in her words, a "hinge or threshold: it is placed between a psychic or lived interiority and a more sociopolitical exteriority through the inscription of the body's outer surface" (Elizabeth Grosz, *Space, Time, and Perversion: Essays on the Politics of Bodies* [New York: Routledge, 1995], 33). This is, as she puts it, a "power of inscription that knowledges, discourses, and representational systems impose on bodies to constitute them as such" (38). She defines inscription as the ways in which the subject is "marked, scarred, transformed, and written upon or constructed by the various regimes of institutional, discursive, and nondiscursive power as a particular kind of body" (33). From this perspective, it is possible to treat the idea of agency in a new register, and to think about the body as emerging through technologies that invest, channel, and direct it. In this process, the body is to the point that it becomes controlled, amplified, or channeled into a "whatever" identity, in which the body is a "material semiotic node" (Donna J. Haraway, "Biopolitics of Postmodern Bodies," in *Simians, Cyborgs, and Women: The Reinvention of Women* [New York: Routledge, 1991]). To think of the body as the "sum total of intensive affects" that it is "capable of at a given power or degree of potential" (Tiziana Terranova, "Cybernetics Surplus Value: Embodiment and Perception in Informational Captalism," unpublished manuscript, 2001, 17) is a move away from the idea of the body as organism, complete and distinct from technologies through which and in which it exists. In this scenario, relations between work, technology, and the body must be rethought in terms of the flows of energy through bodies and images as calibrated by imaging machines. As such, the body may be conceived as a machinic assemblage, in a move away from the epistemological question of "what is a body" toward the ontological question of "what is the being of a body."

2. Cheah, "Mattering."

3. Researchers have sought to observe these "material-discursive apparatuses of bodily production" (Barad, "Agential Realism," 7) in various ways. Some have sought to interrogate their own productions, to investigate how their methods are implicit in scientific findings about the social world. See Pierre Bourdieu, *In Other Words: Essays toward a Reflexive Sociology*, trans. Matthew Adamson (Oxford: Polity, 1990), on reflexivity; Sandra Harding, *The Science Question In Feminism* (Ithaca, NY: Cornell University Press, 1986), on the science question in feminism; Nancy C. M. Hartsock, "The Feminist Standpoint: Toward a Specifically Feminist Historical Materialism," in *Money, Sex, and Power: Toward a Feminist Historical Materialism* (Boston: Northeastern University Press, 1983), on the view from below; and Patricia Ticineto Clough, *The End(s) of Ethnography: From Realism to Social Criticism*, 2d ed. (New York: Peter Lang, 1998), on

rethinking ethnographic practice in sociology. Others have sought to investigate the scientific apparatuses that define life itself. See, for example, Barad, "Agential Realism," on techno-material agency; and Bruno Latour and Steve Woolgar, *Laboratory Life: The Construction of Scientific Facts* (Princeton, NJ: Princeton University Press, 1986), on scientific practices in the lab. Another approach has been to look into the powers of discourse, the shaping of the world by words, that may be summed up by the idea of the postmodern turn toward language, discourse, and texts.

4. Michael Hardt, "Affective Labor," *boundary 2* 26.2 (1999): 89–100.

5. Anna Gibbs, "Disaffected," *Continuum* 16.3 (2002): 335–41.

6. Eve Kosofsky Sedgwick and Adam Frank, eds. *Shame and Its Sisters: A Silvan Tomkins Reader* (Durham, NC: Duke University Press, 1995).

7. Patricia Ticineto Clough, "The Shift from Discipline to Control: Reentry and Beyond Reentry, Criticism and Policy-Oriented Research" Center for the Study of Women and Society Symposium, March 2003; and Michael Hardt and Antonio Negri, *Empire* (Cambridge, MA: Harvard University Press, 2000).

8. Sara Ahmed, "The Politics of Fear in the Making of Worlds," *Qualitative Studies in Education* 16.3 (2003): 381.

9. In sociology, the term *affect* has been used as synonymous with *emotion*, although scholars who have turned to Émile Durkheim have found a more complex understanding. From this perspective, affectivity has been understood as the "physiological capacity to generate emotions," a perspective similar to that embraced by Silvan Tomkins. In this register, affective arousal is posited as the basis of social interaction such that the "strongest and most meaningful social bonds are based on intense affective arousal and people seek to construct social worlds facilitating this arousal." Michael Hammond, "The Sociology of Emotions and the History of Social Differentiation," *Sociological Theory* 1 (1983): 90, 91.

10. Think of what music does for or to us, for example. Music passes as sound waves through bodies, both human and otherwise. When it passes through a body, it may, in the case of a nonhuman body, excite a vibration or some other type of relatively predictable action. In a human body, however, there is no telling what that body might do—it might dance, fall asleep, become angry, tap a foot absentmindedly, or sing along.

11. Sedgwick and Frank, *Shame and Its Sisters*, 11.

12. Patricia Ticineto Clough, "Future Matters: Technoscience, Global Politics, and Cultural Criticism," *Social Text* 80 (2004): 3.

13. Clough and others have argued there has been a shift from the narrative construction of the subject in the cinematic norm of imaging to the "autoaffective circuit" (ibid.) of the televisual. In the cinematic norm, images are edited together seamlessly to construct a narrative with which the viewing subject identifies, finding his or her subject position within the narrative structure. See Kaja Silverman, *The Threshold of the Visible World* (New York: Routledge, 1996); and Laura Mulvey, *Visual and Other Pleasures* (Bloomington: Indiana University Press, 1989). In the televisual regime, "neither narrative nor stories are necessarily or primarily the way in which the viewer and television are attached to each other" (Patricia Ticineto Clough, *Autoaffection: Unconscious Thought in the Age of Teletechnology* [Minneapolis: University of Minnesota Press, 2000], 99). With the televisual, in particular, comes the notion of automatic time, photographic time in which duration is conceived as instantaneous, moving faster than the subject, and in which images are generated by imaging machines in an "autonomous series" that "requires no interval to pass through a subjective formation" (Richard Dienst, *Still Life in Real Time: Theory after Television* [Durham, NC: Duke University Press, 1994], 160). Rather, images affect viewers directly, making points of contact, leaving impulses, intensities, and perhaps actions in their wake.

14. According to chapter 668s. 7505-A of the 1992 New York Labor and Compensation Law, a professional model is someone who "performs modeling services for; or consents in writing to the transfer of his or her exclusive legal right to the use of his or her name, portrait, picture or image, for advertising purposes or for the purposes of trade." He or she will transfer the right to their image "directly to a retail store, manufacturer, an advertising agency, a photographer, or a publishing company." The "services" in question include "the appearance by a professional model in photographic sessions or the engagement of such model in live, filmed or taped modeling performance for remuneration." The definition of a model's job is to provide the use of their image for trade especially in terms of being photographed.

15. The number of modeling agencies has grown every year since the first firm was incorporated in the 1920s. The number of agencies listed in the Manhattan Yellow Pages business listings increased from 8 to 124 between 1935 and 2000, with dips only during World War II and the recession of the early 1990s. There were 143 modeling agencies listed in 2002. In terms of sheer numbers, accurate records are hard to come by. The industry's image may derive from whichever models are currently in the public eye, but in truth, the number of working models is far greater, though far less visible. For instance, the 1994 Bureau of Labor Statistics' Occupational Outlook Handbook reported 3,155 models working in New York City alone; this number is projected to rise to 4,000 by 2005, and is expected to increase by 21 to 35 percent through 2010, a rate faster than the average rate of occupational expansion. Moreover, these reported totals are lower than the actual numbers, as many models, like other global workers in tentative work situations, work off the books, travel frequently, and have a high attrition rate, making it difficult for statistical methods to accurately capture their number.

16. As per the ideas discussed in the introduction to this volume.

17. Maria Mies, *Patriarchy and Accumulation on a World Scale: Women in the International Division of Labour* (London: Zed, 1998); Nona Y. Glazer, *Women's Paid and Unpaid Labor: The Work Transfer in Health Care and Retailing* (Philadelphia: Temple University Press, 1993); Hartsock, "The Feminist Standpoint"; Heidi Hartmann, "The Unhappy Marriage of Marxism and Feminism," in *Women and Revolution*, ed. Lydia Sargent (London: Tavistock, 1981), 1–41; Sylvia Federici, "Wages against Housework," in *The Politics of Housework*, ed. Ellen Malos (New York: Clarion, 1975), 187–94.

18. In other words, these feminists pointed out how social reproduction was indeed part of the production process, and should be compensated. This discussion connects to the idea of real subsumption of labor by capital, in which there is a tendency for domestic labor, and reproductive labor in general, to be subsumed by capital, absorbed as a form of production. In a sense, feminists, in the struggle to free women workers from servitude in the home, helped bring about the development of an affective economy, in which the divides between private and public, production and reproduction, personal and commercial activity, must be thought more fluidly. With Gilles Deleuze, Clough thinks of these changes as an investment in affect and attention, in which the "production of normalization is no longer simply trusted to the family or kin groups supported by institutions of civic society; it has become rather a matter of the invest- ment in and the regulation of a market-driven circulation of affect and attention" (Clough, "The Shift from Discipline to Control").

19. Maurizio Lazzarato, "Immaterial Labor," in *Radical Thought in Italy: A Potential Politics*, ed. Paul Virno and Michael Hardt (Minneapolis: University of Minnesota Press, 1996), 133–47; Hardt and Negri, *Empire*.

20. Hardt and Negri, *Empire*; Manuel Castells, *The Rise of the Network Society* (Cam- bridge, MA: Blackwell, 1996); Robert B. Reich, *The Work of Nations: Preparing Ourselves for Twenty-First-Century Capitalism* (New York: Vintage, 1992); David Harvey, *The Condition of Postmodernity: An Enquiry into the Origins of Cultural Change* (Oxford: Blackwell, 1989); Daniel Bell, *The Cultural Contradictions of Capitalism* (New York: Basic Books, 1976).

21. Castells, *Rise of the Network Society*.

22. Reich, *Work of Nations*.

23. Hardt, "Affective Labor," 96.

24. Hardt and Negri, *Empire*, 293.

25. The use of the word *virtual* here refers to a technologically created stand-in for something else; this use of the word should not be confused with the Deleuzian sense of the word, in which the virtual refers to a mass of potentialities that may or may not be actualized.

26. Thomas Davenport, "eLearning and the Attention Economy: Here, There, and Everywhere?" *LiNE Zine*, 2001, 1–4.

27. Sedgwick and Frank, *Shame and Its Sisters*.

28. Antonio Negri, "Value and Affect," *Boundary 2* 26.2 (1999): 77–88.

29. I am working from the notion advanced by Deleuze (who is working from Henri Bergson) and an idea that Richard Dienst deemed a "scandalous premise": that there is no "radical disjuncture" between bodies and images, that, in fact, bodies are images existing on the same plane as images that we must think of as image-bodies. See Dienst, *Still Life in Real Time*, 148. There is only movement between images, exchanges of energy and force whose speed and contact are translated through various types of manufactured images (a riff on Dienst, who is in turn working from Deleuze's *Cinema 1: The Movement Image*, trans Hugh Tomlinson and Barbara Habberjam [Minneapolis: University of Minnesota Press, 1986], xi). According to this conceptualization, the body is an image in an environment of other images.

30. This study involves fifty-four interviews with models and those who work with them. Contacts were made using a snowball sample, in which each person interviewed was asked for two or more contacts to interview. My focus was specifically on fashion models (there are specialized models who do parts and hair modeling, or those who do specific ages, such as child models, but they fall beyond the scope of this study). I interviewed thirty-two models (twenty-four female and eight male), eleven modeling agents (or "bookers" as they are known in the industry), two photographers, two advertising executives, two art directors, one designer, one PR agent, one casting agent, one makeup artist, and one production assistant. Interviews were semi-structured, conducted in public places, and lasted between one to two hours. The interviews were taped with consent, transcribed, and manually coded. They were conducted between

1999 and 2004. The age range for the sample was from sixteen to twenty-eight years old for the models; the other workers tended to be slightly older, mostly in their thirties and forties. Fashion models are predominantly white. This fact is reflected in the composition of this sample: there was one female Asian model, two black female models, one black male model, and two Latin models.

31. Brian Massumi, *Parables for the Virtual: Movement, Affect, Sensation* (Durham, NC: Duke University Press, 2002), 24.

32. Silvan Tomkins, qtd. in Sedgwick and Frank, *Shame and Its Sisters*, 54.

33. Sara Ahmed, "Affective Economies." *Social Text* 79 (2004): 120.

34. Gibbs, "Disaffected," 337.

35. Ann Alvergue and Michael Isabel, *And Again* (Brooklyn: Eye Spy Films, 2002).

36. Massumi, *Parables for the Virtual*, 42.

37. Massumi is drawing on the Bergsonian conception of consciousness as a limiting function here.

38. Terranova, "Cybernetics Surplus Value," 11.

39. David Serlin, *Replaceable You: Engineering the Body in Postwar America* (Chicago: University of Chicago Press, 2004).

40. Grosz, *Space, Time, and Perversion*, 33–38.

41. Massumi, *Parables for the Virtual*, 36.

42. Jeremy Gilbert-Rolfe, *Beauty and the Contemporary Sublime* (New York: Allworth, 1999), 63. The logic of the body refers to the space and time of conscious subjective perception. In televisual imaging, that logic is put aside, as Clough explains: "Rather than calling for the subject's unconscious identification through a narrative representation, television hopes for a continuous body-machine attachment" (Clough, *Autoaffection*, 70). According to Clough, television mechanizes the autoaffective circuit in a way that makes it impossible to reduce its functioning to the level of human subjectivity, in which images may be understood only in terms of their subjective meaning or how they are interpreted or self-reflected.

43. Brian Winston, *Media Technology and Society: A History from the Telegraph to the Internet* (London: Routledge, 1998), 318.

44. David Bailey, *Models Close Up* (New York: Universe, 1999), 139.

45. Kristin Tillotson, "Supersaturated: Supermodels—They Strike a Pose and America Can't Resist," *Star Tribune* (Minneapolis), June 7, 1995, 1E.

46. Scott Woolley, "High-Class Lookers," *Forbes*, March 22, 1999, 236.

47. In this sense, the work of modeling is in some ways immeasurable, as there is little distinction between when models are at or off work. The more they present themselves, the more value accrues to their image, and this exposure produces value in the affective production system

48. Bailey, *Models Close Up*, 50.

49. Clough in this volume, 2.

JEAN HALLEY

Caught, you probably know, horses will fight to get free. I know, it sounds simple, silly, or, as an intellectual man I know said, redundant. You probably say, tell me something new. Of course they fight to get free. Still. Still, I find it touching. They will fight to get free, no matter what free means. When a horse gets its leg caught in wire, it will struggle, even as the skin on its leg is peeled all away, even as the wire grips tighter and tighter to its bare bone. It is the nature of a horse caught in wire to fight, much as it is the nature of wire caught around the leg of a horse to tighten and grip ever more closely, holding the horse for dear life, as though the wire, too, felt desire.

I know about this push, this push from inside, for freedom. Once I held a blade—sharp and even, slender and perfect in its capacity—over my skin. The veins under my freckled pale skin are like my father's. They push out, they push out ready to press on, against, the blade, ready to fight. They are big and bulging, dark blue. And they swirl and swim up and down my arms like ivy. When I was pregnant, the nurses loved me for my veins, with their ready ripeness. Blood comes easy from me. It comes so easy that one time, called from my veins, an inexperienced nurse found herself, and me too, covered in bright red freshness spurting, gushing from the puncture she had made.

Once, feeling the push, the push from inside of me, pressing hard and tight against my ribs and throat, once I held a blade over a deep blue vein in my arm. It was moments from entering, moments from freeing blood to pour, to flood like a Montana river in early spring, out of me. The blade would have let my blood go, finally, rushing free from the confines of my skin and bone around it. It would have filled the bath where I sat, pushed the warm water aside, insisting on its presence, bright and red and thick.

Twice my horse has been caught in wire. The first time he did what horses do. Simply, he fought. He fought and the wire tightened and held ever more closely to him. It gripped around his bone, ungiving. Bone offers a match for wire that skin cannot meet. Thick and tough as horsehide is, it yields to wire, opens soft and smooth like petals, ready. My beautiful red horse fought the wire, and it held tighter and tighter and sliced as deep, as far as it could. His bone offered real resistance. The wire began to work on the bone and my horse, wet and exhausted, struggled more. Given time, I am sure the wire would have won. In a sense at least, in a sense, the wire would have won. But then again, the tables would have turned had the wire had time to work its way slowly through the bone of my horse's leg. The tables would have turned because, once through, once through horsehide and bone, the wire would find only itself, again. And my horse, my horse would have been free.

Yet, it did not come to that. We found my horse, my horse caught in wire, his leg drenched in red. We found my horse before the wire had a chance to work its way back, through my horse, to itself. The vet said I had to put my horse down. But I didn't. I kept him still for days to see if the flesh could find *its* way back together, meeting, joining, lumpy and hard. The vet said it would not heal. But what is healing anyhow. The flesh did find its way to itself, and it covered the naked leg bone in an awkward sort of way. My horse limps still, as though the memory of that wire holds him, even now, tightly.

Somehow life pushes for itself. It demands. It demands freedom. I know, I know it pulsing inside of me. I know it pushing, up my throat like vomit, pushing, insisting, pressing the breath from me. I imagine the relief of that breath let go. I imagine the relief of red flooding everywhere, filling all that emptiness, pushing out under through emptiness to something else. I imagine myself melting body into body, rotting flesh and bone into soil and root and other flesh. Finally free.

My friend Shannon pushed herself, material into material. She set herself free to become into. Something else. My friend Shannon used to sit in the bath the door closed as tightly as doors will close, and you know nothing ever shuts anything out for good. Shannon used to sit in the bath and listen to her mother's husband talk to her through the door. His voice cut through to her. He wanted to see her, be her, feel her young girl body, naked in the bath.

One day Shannon told someone. And because she was causing a disruption, of course they removed her from the home. She lived in foster care for a year until her body learned to control itself. Until her body quit asking her step-father to stand outside the bathroom door. No one ever knew if removing the body worked to bring rest to the disruption. Finally Shannon's drunk mother got rid of her drunk husband, and they figured they might as well let Shannon go home. She could not cause any more trouble at that point anyhow.

Shannon did go home. She allowed herself to fall and fall and fall, until she came to earth. She came matter to matter, body to body. The impact was noisy, a smacking of flesh on flesh. Her body burst inside, not out. Somehow the skin held everything together. But the insides of Shannon burst, exploded, pushing, merging, changing everything forever. The skin held tight, firm, resolved. Not a bit of Shannon leaked anywhere. At least not then. Because, eventually, even skin, even wire has to let go.

Twice my horse caught his leg in wire and wire caught my horse. The second time, I was riding him. I felt his body go taut beneath me. And I held him back, vomit rising in my throat, I held my horse. Still, I said. He and I quivered there together. If my horse went wild, wild like letting go as I jumped down from him, if my horse went wild, he could throw me hard to the ground. Leaping thrashing for freedom, my horse could so easily push and tangle me under him amid wire and earth and hard, sharp horse hoof. Still, I said, shaking as my hand felt its way down the tense leg of my horse, felt its way down through deep winter coat, dusty and warm. My hand bumped, cold, thin human skin against even colder, even thinner, so hard wire in the midst of thick horse fur. I met the wire there.

I know desire. I know desire. I too want freedom. I feel its push inside of me, pushing out up my throat, pushing pulsing. I want. Relief.

Maybe it is in my blood this push to leave skin and bone behind, this particular push for freedom. This longing to die. My mother and her mother, too, seemed to long this way. My mother ate a thermometer when she was four. They had told her about the mercury inside, beautiful silver stuff, moving like magic through the thin glass stick. She knew that mercury was to be admired from behind the safety of glass. So longing, longing, she shattered the glass, setting mercury free. She called it inside herself, longing. It is a funny kind of push. It is a funny kind push, for life, for life.

And my grandmother stayed with my grandfather. She stayed tempting his desire. Maybe her staying was also this longing called into living, this longing to be free. Maybe staying she hoped that somehow, someday his beating would break through and release her.

Oh, how I long to be free. Let me go let me go let me go let me go let me go. I long to be free. I imagine. Falling, falling falling. Shannon's friend said she was laughing when she fell. She fell free. She fell. And I, too, long to be free.

GREG GOLDBERG AND CRAIG WILLSE

On February 15, 2004, the *New York Times Magazine* published "The Permanent Scars of Iraq," in which Sara Corbett details the injuries of the U.S. soldiers Robert Shrode and Brent Bricklin, both wounded in action in the war on Iraq. "Shrode lost most of his right arm," Corbett writes, "which was amputated just below the elbow in a Baghdad field hospital. Even healed, his face is pitted with purple shrapnel scars the size of raindrops. Bricklin, a broad-shouldered former competitive swimmer who came home honeycombed with shrapnel, bears larger raw-looking scars from his thigh to his neck."[1] Three weeks later, Dan Baum's "The Casualty" appeared in the *New Yorker* and similarly reported on the returned soldier Michael Cain's injuries: "Doctors had amputated his right leg below the knee. The condition of the left leg was uncertain. Cain also had a smashed jaw, a broken thumb, a broken arm, and a wound on the back of his head. He'd lost a lot of blood."[2]

At the time of these articles' publication, we had been collaborating on a project concerned with the phantom limb in trauma theory and popular culture. In our research, we had already noted the body of the war-damaged soldier haunting the texts we were reading. Still, the explicit arrival of newly amputated, blinded, mutilated, and paralyzed soldiers forced us to pause in our work, drawing us toward contemporary geopolitical crises and into a highly charged and mutable near future, one marked by the instability of the U.S. occupation of Iraq and the unpredictability of the resistances and insurgencies taking place there. Articles and photographs documenting returning soldiers inspired in us feelings of both urgency and uncertainty about how to proceed. Within a timescape that denies the familiar "peacetime-war-aftermath" and puts in its place the ongoing battles beyond the end of an undeclared war, we experienced the fragments of the aftermath looping back toward us, and we wondered how to most responsibly account for what these stories and photographs urged us to consider.

We approached these stories and photographs with a sense of caution, aware of their problematic production and circulation, but also suspicious of our own overdetermined and emotionally complex attraction to them; in choosing to write on this media, we knew that we had been seduced by it. We wondered with what agendas we might be complicit in engaging this documentation, given the phenomena of the embedded journalist and governmental control of war imagery. What were we doing taking these stories seriously when U.S. media had, in part, been so discredited that the *New York Times* apologized for some of its own coverage?[3]

The question for us became, then, not how to determine the accuracy of this coverage, but rather how to explore what forces it mobilizes, excites, provokes, draws together and makes possible; when focusing on the *effects* of this media, its truth becomes incidental. Given how deconstruction has seriously drawn into question the possibility of truth in representation and has displaced intellectuals from our presumed vantage point outside representation, it should not be so difficult to give up on truth claims. Nonetheless, academic scholarship continues to engage media objects as exterior, applying theory against them to interpret or reveal their meanings and truths. But understanding academic practice not only from within the logics of representation but also as intimately implicated with the dangerous stuff of flows of capital, governmentality, and transnational information networks means that we are and can only be caught in the intellectual production of war and death. These concerns exceed accountability, forcing us to ask how complicity can work or be worked. For us, this is to begin practicing methods of writing from within an undefined terrain of "no outside."

We intend working from no outside seriously as a methodological goal, not simply as a rhetorical device. For example, our method parallels one engineered by World War II lieutenant colonel S. L. A. Marshall. Interviewing soldiers after battle, Marshall found that no one soldier could offer a complete account of what had taken place; a coherent narrative could only be pieced together from the partial and imprecise recollections of the entire company. As we will discuss later, Marshall's research illuminated the traumatic experiences of soldiers in war, yet this information was used not to tend to their individual needs, but to develop more effective training procedures that could, for example, anticipate and resolve the fear of killing another human. Regardless of their uses within the military, for us Marshall's studies survive as fragments of a history of trauma, war, and bodies that might serve other ends.[4] Similarly, to produce our own account, we untangle and stretch articles, photographs, sound bites, and the theory we find through them as facets of a story the ultimate "truth value" of which may be less relevant or interesting than its utility in drawing together some of the contemporary tendencies in operations of power. Our writing aims to produce documentation of our assembling theoretical and historical essays with contemporary media. Our mediated distance from the soldiers storied in the articles is, for us, no more problematic than the distance between the soldiers themselves and their lost memories.

This claim of documentation and our complicity within it makes us vulnerable to the criticism that our project is merely descriptive with no politic of its own. Of course, a document that is merely descriptive is entirely impossible, a point that we think undoes this criticism and furthermore suggests a politic that cannot be mapped in advance but for which conditions of emergence could be fostered. Rather than ascribing politics to a plan or a set of theoretical or ideological allegiances, our politics might be found in the impulses that drive us, or the attractions that draw us to the documents we investigate. So we arrive at this project in part because of a shared opposition to the occupation of Iraq, a morbid fascination with damaged bodies, and an ambivalence about technoscience that vacillates between philic and phobic. Accounts of the wounded soldier and his medical rehabilitation call to us as they surround us,[5] and though our engagement itself may not be a political choice (it may only be a giving in), we hope that something in our process might spark us toward an other politics that could prove unexpectedly viable.

While we piece together fragments of stories about specific soldiers, those stories move us away from the individual or human subject to consider how the trauma of war operates on other levels. Situating trauma in theories of power draws our attention to how trauma organizes biological matter in excess of the individual. Following Michel Foucault's argument that techniques of discipline and control coexist and cooperate, we will entertain the thought that the injured soldier be considered an assemblage of capacities. From this viewpoint, the rehabilitation of wounded soldiers is not the first instance of modifying or directing the form and expression of their bodies, but rather constitutes a singular practice within networks of technoscience and capital that continually calculate, engineer, and mutate the matter of life itself. We thus suggest an alternative theory of trauma that does not perceive a soldier's body as being whole, then broken, and then finally put back together. Rather, the soldier can be perceived as a temporary composition of matter/energy flows that conducts the networks of technoscience and capital in which it is embedded, allowing those networks to adapt and survive. The so-called rehabilitation of the wounded soldier is therefore incidental before the constant rehabilitation of technologies of power. Trauma in this sense occasions unexpected productivity, for which narratives of loss cannot fully account.

In her treatment of trauma theory, Ruth Leys recounts the historical development of a general theory of trauma focusing on the work of Sigmund Freud, the so-called father of trauma studies, and his disciples Abram Kardiner and Sandor Ferenczi. Leys highlights the work of Kardiner, whose compelling case studies of returning soldiers helped catalyze a paradigm shift within psychology and what would be called trauma studies, from an explanatory emphasis on libidinal forces to what Freud termed the life and death instincts. Leys cites a series of documented symptoms that, while not unknown within medicine and psychiatry when Kardiner published his findings in 1932, were nonetheless provocative within psychoanalysis, where war neuroses still "occupied a peculiarly uncertain position."[6] Kardiner's list of symptoms would eventually occasion a new diagnosis, "post-traumatic stress disorder" (PTSD):

> Terrifying repetitive nightmares connected to the war, often of an annihilating or sadistic nature, or hallucinatory reenactments of the traumatic situation; motor disturbances, including tremors and convulsions or motor paralyses, such as loss of speech; sensory deficits, such as hysterical blindness and other anesthesias; fainting spells or fits of unconsciousness resembling epileptic fits; irritability, including startled reactions to sudden noise and other stimuli; uncontrollable aggressive outbursts; intense fear and anxiety; disturbances of the autonomic system; and amnesia for the traumatic event. Above all . . . a profound mental "paralysis."[7]

This description provokes a reconsideration of the relationship between the mind and material flesh, as the two fold together such that the emotional stress of war disorders the body's proper functioning, inducing loss of motor control and sensory failure. This embodiment of war trauma, in which the mental traces of war injure the body after its return, exposes a current running through the history of trauma studies, that is, how a certain historically situated understanding of biology and physics (theories of homeostasis and thermodynamics, respectively) underwrites the emergence of trauma theory, largely determining the forms such theory would assume through the twentieth century.

This current begins with early conceptions of trauma, which described "a surgical wound, conceived on the model of a rupture of the skin or protective envelope of the body resulting in a catastrophic global reaction in the entire organism."[8] As Freud's *Beyond the Pleasure Principle* evidences, doctors and psychologists appropriated this definition, interpreting and treating war neuroses as a biological disruption of the nervous system sustained during a traumatic event. Freud, however, influenced by Kardiner's case histories of soldiers who had not experienced "the intervention of any gross mechanical force" during the war but who experienced similar traumatic neuroses as soldiers who had,[9] insisted on a theory of trauma that separated, to some extent, the traumatized mind from the traumatized body. In this split, Freud nonetheless favored an account of biological wholeness and bodily trauma that could be extended to the workings of the mind. This is evident in his definition of trauma: "We describe as 'traumatic' any excitations from outside which are powerful enough to break though the protective shield. It seems to me that the concept of trauma necessarily implies a connection of this kind with a breach in an otherwise efficacious barrier against stimuli. Such an event as an external trauma is bound to provoke a disturbance on a large scale in the functioning of the organism's energy and to set in motion every possible defensive measure" (33). Freud's theory posits a self-contained biological organism whose interior is delimited by a protective shell and to which violence and trauma are external. Under a stable set of conditions the shell functions properly, regulating the movement of energy flowing into and out of the organism; this expresses what Freud referred to as "the dominating tendency of mental life, and perhaps of nervous life in general . . . to reduce, to keep constant or to remove internal tension due to stimuli" (67). Freud's account of the biological organism follows the psychophysicist G. T. Fechner's constancy principle, which ascribes biological organisms a tendency toward homeostasis or stability, an expression in part of the "inertia inherent in organic life" (43). The nontraumatized body is perceived as an order of biological organ relations (including Freud's "organ of the mind") and psychological systems that function cooperatively and self-calibrate, achieving a state that Ferenzci calls "unified."[10]

With this model of the regulation of energy, psychoanalytic theory articulates war trauma and neuroses as fragmentation, or a puncturing that disrupts the homeostatic unity of the organism's protective shell and produces "an anarchy of the organs, parts and elements of organs, whose reciprocal cooperation alone renders proper global functioning—that is to say life—possible."[11] In other words, trauma, understood as an excess of stimulation/energy, disrupts the organism's unified state, overwhelming the mind/body's capacity to effectively bind incoming energy and moving the organism far from equilibrium toward death. As Luciana Parisi and Tiziana Terranova state: "The [thermodynamic] organism must ward off death constantly by charging and releasing the energy thus accumulated; nothing must be dissipated, everything must be used up and discharged once it has exhausted its function."[12] According to a general theory of trauma, the traumatized organism can restore homeostasis and prevent imminent death by channeling excess energy to the unconscious. This energy later manifests through traumatic neuroses, which repeat the failure of the organism to effectively bind the energy, impairing the complete reunification of the organism until the repression of the initial trauma can be sorted out, presumably through psychoanalysis.

We read the description of such a traumatic split in Dan Baum's "The Price of Valor," in which he recounts the following conversation with Dan Knox, a Vietnam veteran: "On the day we were talking, the *Times* ran a page-one story on Army snipers in Baghdad. A sniper who had killed seven men in a day was quoted as saying that he felt no remorse. 'He's got the thousand-yard stare,' Knox said, tapping the accompanying photograph with his index finger. 'Go back and find him in fifteen years.' "[13] Knox describes his own experience in Vietnam as a constant double image, the superimposition of war imagery/ memory on the present: "I see you sitting in that chair, and I'm also watching this funeral party I gunned. In a few minutes, it will be a sampan I gunned on a river, with a woman and her babies falling out of it into the water and kicking around as I shoot them."[14] Referring to soldiers recently returned from Iraq, Sara Corbett describes this type of delay as "psychological afterburn."[15] She quotes the damaged soldier Robert Shrode: "My body's here, but my mind is there" (42). This separation is one of many disjunctions experienced by returning soldiers, including significant memory loss that soldiers must be convinced they have experienced. For example, Michael Cain remembers nothing from between the time he was injured and the time when he woke up in a hospital; his memory is later pieced together from other soldiers' accounts. Keeping in mind a homeostatic perception of life that locates traumatic neuroses in the organism's failure to bind energy, we read Corbett's description of soldiers' volatility as that of an energy crisis. She describes "a visceral undercurrent of anger that makes them walk around feeling ready to explode" (40). Corbett quotes the damaged soldier Brent Bricklin: "I can go from being happy-go-lucky and joking to having someone's throat in my hand, like that . . . . My fuse is short . . . it's real short" (40).

Psychoanalytic theories of trauma do not merely record manifestations of trauma in the mind or body but mobilize specific ways of addressing bodily matter, intensifying perceptions of the body as a systemic organization of capacities and energy that, like a steam engine, can be regulated, overwhelmed, or cease to function altogether. If this thermodynamic model underwrites psychoanalytic accounts of trauma, it is in part due to the connection between thermodynamic organizations of bodily matter and what Foucault called disciplinary mechanisms of power. As Parisi and Terranova write, "The disciplined body is the thermodynamic organism, the hierarchical organization of organs, bounded within a self, crossed by currents of energy tending towards entropy and death."[16] That is, disciplinary mechanisms direct a perception of the body as solid matter which, like a machine, conducts energy, "centralizes the blockages and segments of the body, [and] intensifies reactive forces and delimits its function to a molar order."[17] The perception of this enclosed, systemic body emerged alongside industrial capitalism, which looked toward a solid body that could be trained and worked, and toward a social body whose labor could be exploited en masse.[18]

Though other works by Foucault (*The History of Sexuality* and *Madness and Civilization* come to mind) explore the "political anatomy" of docility and discipline, the soldier of *Discipline and Punish* allows Foucault's argument about disciplining to crystallize, bringing together in his body economic, political, and social arrangements and practices that characterize a disciplinary society.[19] For Foucault, the disciplinary society is not born at once, nor does it mark a revolution or complete break with the past; rather, it collects itself over a span of both sudden and slow mutations, transformations, and exchanges: "The 'invention' of this new political anatomy must not be seen as a sudden discovery. It is rather a multiplicity of often minor processes, of different origin and scattered location, which overlap, repeat, or imitate one another, support one another, distinguish themselves from one another according to their domain of application, converge and gradually produce the blueprint of a general method" (138). At these "scattered locations," disciplinary mechanisms operate on two different levels: first, producing the organic body, organized as systems within fleshy contours that are set in line with the limits of the self/subject, as well as addressing compositional or preindividual levels below the body-form (as parts and movements); and second, arranging body-forms in compositions and collections, what Foucault calls "enclosures" (the hospital, barracks, family). Approaching the first set of disciplinary mechanisms, those that not only enclose the body as an organism but also manage and develop its bodily capacities, forces, and movements, Foucault explains that docility is a "question not of treating the body, *en masse*, 'wholesale,' as if it were an indissociable unity, but of working it 'retail,' individually; of exercising upon it a subtle coercion, of obtaining holds upon it at the level of the mechanism itself—movements, gestures, attitudes, rapidity; an infinitesimal power over the active body" (137). Practical manifestations of this making docile, which we see recapitulated in the U.S. military today, would include exercises in posture, comportment, and placement of feet when walking or standing; the regulation of waking, eating, and sleeping times; and repetitive drills toward exact and timed performance of specific tasks. Therefore the soldier's body becomes one "that is manipulated, shaped, trained, which obeys, responds, becomes skillful and increases its forces" (136).

Hence our interest in discipline is not in terms of the identity of the soldier as such, but rather in terms of his capacity to act. The breakdown of the body into capacities that can be minimized or maximized renders the soldier more docile, more effective, and more controlled. In "The Price of Valor," Baum offers what we take as contemporary examples of preindividual disciplinary techniques characterized by an Army trainer as follows: "We attempt to instill a reaction. Hear a pop, hit the ground, return fire. Act instinctually."[20] Such instinctual reactions are clearly described in the following rescue:

> Brown resisted the impulse to move straight to the glaring red wounds, and instead snapped into protocols. Doing his best to ignore Cain's shrieking, he did an ABC check on his friend—airway, breathing, and circulation. Then he, Blohm, and two other medics lifted Cain out of the shattered cab and laid him on a litter. Cain wasn't in danger of bleeding to death; the bubbly, malodorous burns caused by the blast had cauterized his arteries. Though the pain was obviously horrible, Brown gave Cain no morphine, because he knew that he would be heading for immediate surgery and wanted him lucid enough to sign surgical-consent papers.[21]

In addition, Baum explains how the Army developed techniques to "play down the fact that shooting equals killing" in order to maximize the number of soldiers who would fire their weapons at other human beings.[22] This was largely achieved by isolating and managing the technical ability to discharge weapons, and disaggregating these skills from their possible meanings, for example, that shooting equaled killing; shooting instead became an end in and of itself. Hence, as Baum points out, the word *kill* is almost never used in Army training, which instead uses *massing fire*, a term that signals a technological shift from single-fire weaponry aimed at a specific target toward automatic weaponry that discharges a field of bullets across an undistinguished and hostile terrain. Developing combat capacities through these technological innovations circumvents a limitation posed by single-fire weapons: "A soldier who has learned to squeeze off careful rounds at a target will take the time, in combat, to consider the humanity of the man he is about to shoot."[23]

The docility of the soldier's body not only describes its openness to manipulation and regulation. It also proposes that of the capacities harnessed by discipline, the most significant perhaps is the capacity for openness, to give up to or give into. Thus addressing the soldier's body in terms of its preindividual forces or capacities also facilitates an understanding of the way in which those forces can be set into relation with other forms—specifically here, tools and weaponry—a process Foucault describes as "body-object articulation."[24] Departing from a Marxist ontology in which capitalism separates the laborer from the machine and the product of labor given up, Foucault emphasizes the process of giving up itself, a matter of practices that are invested in and reconstitute subject-object relations.

For instance, the *manoeuvre* of eighteenth-century military theory elaborates a precise coordination between the soldier and his rifle, aligning the parts of his body with the parts of his weapon and specifying a succession of movements and relations between them. In an example cited by Foucault, the act of "bringing the rifle forward" requires three distinct stages outlined in detail. For example, in the third and final stage, the soldier is instructed: "Let go of the rifle with the left hand, which falls along the thigh, raising the rifle with the right hand, the lock outwards and opposite the chest, the right arm half flexed, the elbow close to the body, the thumb lying against the lock, resting against the first screw, the hammer resting on the first finger, the barrel perpendicular."[25] Foucault thus argues that disciplinary tactics produce a synthesis or "coercive link" between parts of bodies and machines that a Marxist analysis of alienation may not effectively account for. He writes that the military maneuver "constitutes a body-weapon, body-tool, body-machine complex."[26] For this reason, the term *soldier* seems inadequate, as it reifies a subject position that exists prior to its technological articulation. Rather, we propose the term *soldier-body* to focus a perception of what are commonly called soldiers as temporal, technical compositions of military and technoscientific intervention whose borders are open to continual renegotiation.

We see this sort of body-tool-weapon-machine articulation in the aforementioned description of mass-fire weaponry. In this case, the articulation releases what the military sees as a moral obstacle, rendering the soldier more effective. We also see this body-tool-weapon-machine articulation in descriptions of the use of armor worn by U.S. soldiers. Neela Banerjee reports in the *New York Times*, "Thanks to advances in everything from flak jackets to battlefield medical attention, many soldiers survive attacks that would have killed them a generation ago. But as more survive, more inevitably return from Iraq with grievous injuries, including amputations."[27] Baum writes, "The ratio of wounded soldiers to killed is higher in this war (a little more than five to one) than in the Second World War and Vietnam, probably because of body armor and advances in battlefield medicine."[28] He continues, "Rather than trying to pierce shielded torsos with bullets, the Iraqis increasingly rely on blowing off the Americans' unprotected arms and legs with explosives: car bombs, mines, rocket-propelled grenades, and 'improvised explosive devices.' "[29] The soldier-body's protective shell, under these circumstances, is not simply the skin, but the skin armor, a complex relation that extends the body and secures and exposes soldiers to different harms such as dismemberment, increasing its capacity to avoid death in what have, in other wars, been unbearable traumatic collisions.

The training that the injured soldier Robert Shrode receives to manipulate his $35,000 carbon-fiber prosthetic is therefore a retraining or a continuation of training that sees the arm and its replacement alike as an embodied value potential. Even before the soldier-body enters the military, the military invests in the arm's potential value. For example, "America's Army," a video-game recruiting tool, invites civilians to participate in a real-time networked simulation of battle that not only draws their interest toward a military career (information about which is a hyperlinked click away) but also affords an opportunity to develop hand-eye coordination in simulated missions; the trigger finger thus learns to fire at virtual suspected targets long before it fires at actual ones.

If, in battle, the trigger finger or arm is valued for making the soldier efficient, it is also valued in its destruction—exposing it to harm and then reconstructing it with prosthetics, therapy, and medication. As Shrode's case suggests, the soldier's arm thus offers an entry point for networks of technoscience and capital. "The Army had flown him several times to Walter Reed to work with its best occupational therapists," Corbett writes of Shrode, "training the tiny reflexive muscles in his elbow so that they eventually could control the carbon-fiber myoelectric hand that was being custom-built for him in Nashville."[30] If his new prosthetic does not "work out well," Shrode can choose to have his elbow amputated and be fit for a more effective prosthetic. He thus acquires an interest in the destruction of his organic flesh—an event no longer figured as traumatic, but rather as value producing insofar as it contributes to the health of biomedical institutions, and in the retraining of his muscles/ prosthesis. In this way, Shrode himself invests in a body-tool-weapon-machine articulation, one that renders the organic and technological indistinguishable. The violence of this indistinguishability is made starkly clear by the wounded soldier Ed Platt: "The signature moment of his calamity was when the medics used the ribbons of his leg—shattered by a rocket-propelled grenade—as its own tourniquet."[31]

As mentioned before, discipline does not only seek to develop capacities and organize them into a bodily form; it also seeks to arrange bodies within larger enclosures. Therefore, the soldier-body operates as part of greater entities. Not only is the arm of the soldier part of a body-tool-weapon-machine articulation, the soldier-body also forms part of the composition of other bodies. By the nineteenth century, the thermodynamics of discipline operated not only on the organism but also across organisms. The factory of thermodynamic industrial capitalism evidenced this organization of docile bodies in coordinated arrangements, as workers were dynamically placed within the enclosure of the factory toward a maximization of collective output and a minimization of energy lost to work. Similarly, military science takes the docile soldier-body and situates it dynamically into compositions with other docile bodies, drawing from and feeding into other enclosures such as primary and secondary schools, enclosures that over time together solidify a general and coordinated arrangement of bodies and spaces. The troop of infantry in battle demands a certain occupation and articulation of space, and the individual bodies of soldiers become calculated in terms of how their synthesis serves those needs—soldiers are allocated a volume to inhabit with their body parts and movements toward a total volume required by the troop. In this sense, the soldier-body "is constituted as a part of a multi-segmentary machine."[32]

Following Foucault's explication of how discipline operates on and below the level of the body as well as across groups of bodies, we can now see how the soldier-body is never whole and never wholly his own. It cannot be rendered incomplete (punctured, violated, fragmented) even if dramatically injured in battle. Rather, it must be constantly engaged in a process of completion that precedes injury, in fact precedes the organism itself, and goes on and on. This is what we mean when we describe the making docile or disciplining of the soldier-body. As Foucault writes, "If economic exploitation separates the force and product of labour, let us say that disciplinary coercion establishes in the body the constricting link between an increased aptitude and an increased domination."[33] We can thus better understand Foucault's argument that the invention of the military suggests not simply the development of armed forces by which a nation-state engaged the "economic and demographic forces" of external enemies; in the development of military institutions and military sciences, there was an invention of "tactics by which the control of bodies and individual forces was exercised within states."[34] Simultaneously serving external and internal needs, Foucault's military develops a soldier-body that regardless of what is intended of it in battle, is not the property of itself, but always very much belongs to the domestic enclosures that draw it through networks of energy and capital.

A BIOPOLITICS OF CONTROL

Foucault's analysis suggests that the soldier-body belongs to complexes, compositions, or assemblages, the nature or form of which may change through the course of the soldier-body's training, deployment, destruction, and rehabilitation. However, as our ability to delimit the enclosure of the military breaks down, or as this enclosure opens up and bleeds into other enclosures (ROTC [Reserve Officers' Training Corps] programs in schools; military hospitals; VA [Veterans Administration] offices and programs; and more recently, National Guard troops in city subway stations), discipline may not be the only arrangement of power worth considering.[35] The military institutions that inspired Foucault's analysis have changed dramatically since the latter half of the twentieth century, and this has necessitated changes in the nature of the soldier-body, and what can be done with it as well. While the rehabilitation of a wounded soldier-body can be understood as a process of making docile, its capacities restored, altered, or enhanced, here we want to move to an analysis of biopolitical control that encourages us to look to another level—not to the body of an individual soldier, but to the treatment of a *population* of soldiers. At this scale, we can consider the regularization of the health, energy, and productivity of populations of soldier-bodies. To consider biopolitical control requires examining techniques of power that extend or intensify discipline, but also understanding the application of power toward making live and letting die.

The current context of U.S. military action in Iraq demands such a move to theories of biopolitical control. When we consider the unprecedented role of reserve and privately contracted security troops that challenge distinctions between civilian and soldier; when we learn that the summer of 2004 witnessed the largest turnover of forces in U.S. military history, with two hundred thousand soldiers rotated out and another two hundred thousand moved in; when we grapple with the disappearance of a front line and a surprising mix of both long-distance, automated-weapon deployment (which characterized the first Gulf War as well as Kosovo) and so-called hand-to-hand combat (more reminiscent of Vietnam-era guerilla combat tactics);[36] when we make note of the reorganization of combat units to include formerly centralized roles such as medics—we can only but grasp at other ways of comprehending what is taking place and what becomes of the soldier-body and its training in this context.[37]

For Foucault, the distinction between what he calls the "anatomo-politics of discipline" and the "biopolitics of control" hinges on scale. The power of biopolitics, Foucault writes, is "not individualizing," as is disciplinary anatomo-politics, but rather "massifying," what he calls "a 'biopolitics' of the human race."[38] Whereas discipline operates on the body or its subunits (parts, movements, gestures), biopolitics operates on the population, larger in scale than and different in quality from the enclosure. Biopolitics seeks to regularize capacities, both below the human body and above the human subject, treating them as populations. Biopolitical control is "addressed to a multiplicity of men, not to the extent that they are nothing more than their individual bodies, but to the extent that they form, on the contrary, a global mass that is affected by overall processes characteristic of birth, death, production, illness, and so on" (242). This does not mean that the organism or body of discipline is erased in the population, but that the organism is opened up, its capacities freed to be administered as a population of capacities. As Foucault states, both anatomo-politics and biopolitics "are obviously technologies of the body, but one is a technology in which the body is individualized as an organism endowed with capacities, while the other is a technology in which bodies are replaced by general biological processes" (249). Biopolitics employs "forecasts, statistical estimates, and overall measures" (244) that operate through mechanisms of "insurance, individual and collective savings, safety measures, and so on" (246). Increasingly, these mechanisms are informed with the products of all sorts of biotechnologies that operate at genetic, biochemical, and cellular levels.

Though Foucault argues that, historically, anatomo-politics emerges prior to biopolitics, he writes, "they are not mutually exclusive and can be articulated with each other," citing examples in urban planning, sexuality, and medicine that demonstrate the coexistence of both (250). We understand the anatomo-politics of discipline and the biopolitics of control as both addressing preindividual capacities—energy, ability, attention, knowledge, skill. Through techniques of discipline, capacities are organized within an organism/subject (for the soldier-body, these include energy for fighting, talent and skill at military tasks, strategic faculties, capabilities to interact and coordinate within a troop); through control, capacities are disaggregated from the individual and addressed at a mass scale. While we may find that biopolitical techniques are coming to free themselves of disciplinary arrangements, it seems fruitful to think, at least for the United States during a time in which disciplinary enclosures are mutating but not disappearing, of how anatomo-politics offers a ground for the emergence and articulation of biopolitical technologies.[39] This is to think of how the making docile of bodies renders them available for mechanisms of control. Drawing from Foucault's own work for an example, we can see how the disciplining of the family arranges sexed relations between bodies toward reproduction, crystallizing sets of acts in terms of identity formations. This disciplining of sexual behavior within families, in turn, makes possible a broader and more general regulation of the birthrate, through natalist policies, across a mass of familial enclosures.[40]

We see many examples of this folding of discipline into control in the contemporary context. The work of biopolitics moves through familiar gendered arrangements of the family, and so the specificity of some biopolitical techniques may be difficult to recognize. For example, various writers note the role played by the wives and mothers of returning soldiers in helping them adjust to new bodies and cope with the emotional fallout of war. Typical photos of injured soldiers depict them in domestic settings: the youthful soldier, missing a limb, immobile on a made-up bed, held in a motherly manner by a wife or girlfriend: "At night, in the quiet of their rented farmhouse, Robert Shrode lets Debra pick the shrapnel out of his body. Over the last six months, she's tugged out 15 pieces as they have worked their way to the surface of his skin. She has picked them from his legs, from his neck, his face. Sometimes he will study them, these twisted aluminum chunks that have managed to escape while so many more will forever live inside him."[41] Predictably, this description offers up the effeminization of the wounded soldier, who, interrupted in his militarized socialization into manhood, becomes trapped in boyhood.[42] It also inscribes the dutiful work of the wife/mother, tending carefully and quietly. But we cannot stop at this familiar narrative. We must also take note of other labors performed by the mothers/wives, such as the navigation of military and medical bureaucracies and the calculation of insurance claims. This labor, though channeled through a gendered anatomo-politics, characterizes the work of biopolitics, the assessment of generalizations, norms, and statistical measures. We see this in the story of Charlene Cain, who herself goes on antidepressants during the time of her son's return: "At the kitchen table, she is often immersed in the maze of forms required for every treatment, trying to insure that care will be adequate and costs will be covered—complexities that sometimes take her hours a day to manage."[43] After using up all her allotted vacation and sick pay at her job to assist her son Michael, Charlene relied on her coworkers' collective donation of one hundred hours of their own paid time off so that she could continue to give care to her son. The demands of laboring with the technological apparatuses of biopolitics, this labor of care directed not at soothing the body but at calculating its costs and probabilities against population standards, exposes how biopolitics draws from disciplined familial arrangements. Thus, even as nuclear families erode and marriages fall apart, biopolitics nonetheless travels through the networked remains of this enclosure.

Similarly, therapy groups in veterans' hospitals can be said to play a disciplinary role by containing the emotional energy of trauma and directing it back toward productivity. But many soldiers also report on these groups as sites for trading information about insurance claims, benefits programs, and self-medication.

> A number of soldiers confess that they were initially put off by the concept of group therapy, figuring it was going to be "a bunch of guys crying and wiping snot on their sleeves." Most insist they attend not for emotional release but rather to receive information—about disability benefits or discharge procedures. The soldiers' questions often reflect a me-against-the-world mistrust of what's to come, an indistinct but entirely accurate perception that this country has failed veterans of past wars. The war will stay with them, they realize, but after a point the Army won't.[44]

The failure of the contemporary U.S. Army to maintain itself as an enclosure expels returning soldiers into an unpredictable and risky terrain of being home. Here we witness the pressures of biopolitical life mutate the therapeutic setting into a node for information exchange; emotional healing takes a backseat to biopolitical practicalities as the soldiers, too, mutate and modify, adapting new survival skills for navigating the vast accounting bureaucracies that characterize biopolitical societies.[45]

Again, the biopolitics that moves through and perhaps subsumes anatomo-politics seeks something other than docile bodies. As Foucault writes, the purpose of statistical measures such as a birthrate "is not to modify any given phenomenon as such, or to modify a given individual insofar as he is an individual, but, essentially, to intervene at the level at which these general phenomena are determined, to intervene at the level of their generality."[46] The forces that discipline makes docile—more useful and more dominated—are those which biopolitics regularizes, across bodies and toward a massification of populations. Of course, soldiers are addressed by biopolitics not only in the above examples of rehabilitation. Biopolitics in fact organizes soldier-bodies as a soldier population, a massified body set to statistical predictors, in all phases of its deployment. The work of S. L. A. Marshall alluded to earlier helps elucidate what we could think of as the statistical soldier of control. Marshall's study of soldiers' performance in battle led to the formulation of an "average firer," a type whose behavior could be predicted and calculated. His analysis of the fact that soldiers in battle were often incapable of firing their weapons due to a fear of killing that overwhelmed a fear of being killed provided military tacticians with information from which to develop new training procedures, such as the earlier example of massing fire. As a result of such innovations, the Army subsequently found an increase of up to 90 percent of soldiers shooting back.[47] Hence we have not only a disciplined soldier-body but also a biopolitical soldier-type, a population of likelihoods and percentages with, for example, a suicide rate calculated to be one third "higher than average."[48] The contemporary crises of insufficient fighting forces for the continued occupation of Iraq (resulting in a mass mobilization of reserve forces and extensions of tours of duty) and the disproportionate impact of military needs on poor and non-white populations points to other biopolitical management techniques. Army recruitment practices draw from already statistically organized biopolitical populations, targeting neighborhoods and schools with raced and classed populations marked by a likelihood of military labor. The obvious point that the majority of current recruits enter the military due to a lack of educational and employment opportunities must be understood as the quantification and maximization of availability for absorption into military service.

If indeed damaged soldier-bodies returning from Iraq are drawn from the statistical bodies of soldier-types and if, as such, they are moved through routes that feed off of discipline, what might this mean for these soldier-bodies? Current journalistic profiles, echoing early theories of trauma, depict the return of U.S. soldiers as the final stage of a movement from wholeness to fragmentation and back toward wholeness. As our discussion of discipline shows, an alternate account considers the returning soldier-body as already placed within a web of disciplinary anatomo-politics that constantly organizes its capacities and corporeal forms. Furthermore, an analysis of a biopolitics of control suggests that we not only consider the individualizing procedures of disciplinary treatment but also turn toward larger-scale procedures for measuring and assessing damage: "Whereas most soldiers without major injuries will touch down on American soil and undergo a relatively impersonal and perfunctory post-deployment medical screening before returning to duty, many of the injured soldiers have already spent months being routinely examined, assessed and questioned about their well-being—arguably making it easier to ask for help."[49] As the qualifier "arguably" implies, the connections between the quantification of illness and the methods for improving the health of injured soldiers remain dubious. The science of measuring the health of this population perhaps serves other biopolitical ends. Hence we can look at processes for medical discharge, for example, as a technique of control. As a *New York Times* article reports:

> In order to be medically discharged, soldiers must go before the Army Physical Evaluation Board, which assesses their injuries and then either approves or disapproves the discharge. Eventually they receive a "disability rating" from the Department of Veterans Affairs, which determines how much money they are eligible for. A soldier deemed "100 percent disabled" is granted a base payment of $2,239 monthly. (The payment can be supplemented depending on the severity of the injury.) Though the V.A. judges each case individually, an amputated arm generally gets you a 60 to 90 percent disability rating.[50]

The soldier-body that survives in Iraq does so to be absorbed into systems of calculating the value of illness against potential productivity loss. Though biopolitics might work toward an elimination of the accident or the biological anomaly, illness nonetheless proves useful, productive—an opportunity for shifting and reorganizing flows of capital and energy. Foucault writes: "The field of biopolitics also includes accidents, infirmities, and various anomalies. And it is in order to deal with these phenomena that this biopolitics will establish not only charitable institutions ... but also much more subtle mechanisms that were much more economically rational than an indiscriminate charity which was at once widespread and patchy. . . . We see the introduction of more subtle, more rational mechanisms: insurance, individual and collective savings, safety measures, and so on."[51] If illness threatens the effectiveness of anatomo-politics as a leaking of capacities, a loss of energy available for work, it registers differently for biopolitics. The giving of illness toward calculation and regulation is for biopolitics a capacity, organized by the Army as balanced data of capital and life chances.

The biopolitics of control therefore arranges time, capacities, and value on a common plane, such that units of each can be interchanged. For individual soldiers operating within this field, their ability to present illness to the Army Physical Evaluation Board is necessary to obtain access to medical and other state services.[52] Soldiers are thus embedded in a complex calculus of illness, in which the relationship between health and value cannot be predicted in advance, but rather must be continually negotiated, as when soldiers measure the benefits of a higher disability rating against potential earnings that could be greater than medical relief. Injured soldiers face impossible choices, knowing that requests for antidepressants from their military doctors will be recorded in their files, quite possibly jeopardizing future career advancement;[53] medical "help" from this perspective looks more like a loss of options than actual assistance or rehabilitation. For example, Jeremy Gilbert, an Army medic who survived with a leg so damaged it required four operations in six months, wrestled with how to move ahead in his Army career: "He was hoping to stay in the Army for a few more years after he recovered, but worried that if he 'toughed it out' for a while, the fact that he was able to perform his duties (though in pain) would lower his disability rating when he did leave the service—a difference of potentially thousands of dollars."[54] The shock of absorption into biopolitical insurance technologies, or the everyday experience of living as a soldier-type, characterizes return for the contemporary soldier.

What, then, do we make of trauma within a biopolitical field? As discussed earlier, trauma as formulated by Freud and his peers (and as reformulated by doctors and in the popular imagination) addresses the human body as a thermodynamic system and characterizes trauma as an event that disrupts homeostasis. We associate this model of trauma with disciplinary anatomo-politics. The biopolitics of control, on the other hand, addresses bodily matter not as a closed, homeostatic system, but rather as an open, turbulent system. As capacities are freed from bodily constraints to be massified across populations, their disordering within an individual body matters less. Biopolitics, in other words, does not require a reduction of traumatic interference; the *management* of trauma is itself an end for biopolitics. Biopolitics therefore requires moving away from a model of trauma that constrains or fragments the body, and toward an understanding of trauma as a condition of possibility for technological development; away from an analysis that imagines critically wounded soldiers as the loss of a fighting force, and toward an analysis that assesses traumatized soldier-bodies as productive—productive, that is, for capital, military, and technoscientific interventions. The trauma of the Iraq war, a form of biopolitical illness, offers unexpected returns: opportunities such as the financialization of health, illness, and injury discussed above, as well as the development of new rehabilitative technologies, all of which offer the possibility to modify and extend governmental management and the administration of mutations of life.

We anticipate these developments within the biopolitical trauma of control to be extended to populations beyond those of soldier-types, just as, according to Foucault, mechanisms of discipline developed in the military traveled to and were modified within other enclosures. Thus we cannot privilege a body's capacities before trauma, which would imagine them as untouched by or prior to power. In other words, we cannot, therefore, interpret the traumatic event as a loss. To argue that trauma takes away or reduces capacities is to miss how conditions of trauma within biopolitics facilitate, develop, submerge, or re-direct capacities. Of course we recognize that the body in trauma may experience itself as constrained and split, especially in a social order that privileges normative embodiments; we do not mean to dismiss self-narratives of traumatic experiences of war.[55] Nonetheless, taking seriously a Foucauldian theory that power does not repress, but incites, provokes, and creates suggests that traumatic occurrences mobilize productive networks that do not prevent an organism from moving forth, but rather undo the individual such that bodily matter adapts around networks of trauma and statistical health. No longer able to perceive an organic body that could be returned to wholeness, under bio-political trauma we might instead explore the uneven distribution of exposure to and security from trauma and the directions and intensities of violence within those distributions.

CODA: GHOSTS OF THE BIOPOLITICAL

A consideration of the returning soldier, soldier-bodies, or soldier-types should not only concern health and injury. Biopolitical forces urge us to rethink the very nature of life and death in a society of control. For us, this is not to contrast soldiers that return with those that do not, as this distinction breaks down at the level of energy or force, where the dead may become material, palpable, affective. We cannot say, as one reporter does, that "for whatever societal void the dead disappear into, it is the wounded who must live with the confounding mix of anonymity and exposure wrought by surviving a war."[56] For us, given the saturation of all matter with biopower and capital's investments at levels above and below that of the individual, there can be no societal void. Rather, the phrase *confounding mix* might better describe the collapse of multiple spatialities in the temporality of trauma: " 'My body's here but my mind is there' " (43). Who or what has returned in this case? *Confounding mix* may also describe the confusion of longing, mourning, and missing—not for home, but for battle: "It wasn't until the newcomer mentioned that he wished he were back in Iraq that anybody else chimed in. 'I miss it, too,' another soldier said. 'At least there was a purpose.' 'I wish I was in Iraq because my buddies are there,' Robert Shrode offered" (43). Finally, *confounding mix* might best describe the copresence of the dead among the living. Stories of the current war reveal, if not forge, an ontology of death: the dead bodies of soldiers return as a haunting presence in the minds of soldiers, in collective memory. About an injured soldier who returns but cannot shake her memories of Iraq, Corbett writes, "Then there is the dead marine who visits her as she tried to sleep. A young guy, he can be angry, accusative, and sometimes he just shows up quietly and stares at her until she's jarred awake, heart racing—another night's rest stolen away" (39). The much-discussed ban on photographing coffins should not mislead us into thinking death has been disappeared— conversation about that absence is itself a form of being there, an afterlife in consciousness. The materialization of ghosts as PTSD, uncontainable energies that flow from soldier to soldier, is another.

Foucault and other writers such as Giorgio Agamben have demonstrated how the biopolitical management and production of life represents the reversal of an earlier sovereign authority to put to death or allow to live. Biopolitics, rather, is said to make live or let die—calling to mind the productivity of insurance and health regulation, but also biomedical engineering, gene therapy, and experimental forms of life such as the prosthetic-organic hybrids of damaged soldier-bodies. This is why Agamben argues that biopolitics, or what Foucault calls the "bioregulation by the state,"[57] addresses bare life, or life itself.[58] The "man" located in biopolitics is not the autonomous human subject that lines up with an anthropological human form. It is man-as-species, a form of biological life shot through with potentiality that exceeds the individual of discipline; in such a context, to be alive describes a material state prior to humanist notions of experience or meaning.

The characterization of biopolitics as the power to make live or let die takes on a chilling tone when read alongside a VA administrator's invocation of "the price of surviving war" for U.S. soldiers coming back from Iraq. Making live here is not just productive, but is a forceful command—you *must* live. This is the power to disallow death. The haunting words of the returned soldier Jeremy Gilbert recall this command: "You're not healing the way you thought you would. You start thinking, I wish they'd cut my leg off. You think maybe I was supposed to die."[59] When life itself becomes valuable for capital, and not always for the living, death becomes for biopolitics a threat that must be held off. As Foucault states, "Death becomes, insofar as it is the end of life, the term, the limit, or the end of power too."[60] Hence biopolitics operates to draw life out through technoscience and techniques of regulation, processes that may have nothing to do with claims of returning wholeness to the wounded soldier, but rather concern the life, health, and longevity of biopolitical processes and arrangements themselves.

NOTES

1. Sara Corbett, "The Permanent Scars of Iraq," *New York Times Magazine*, February 15, 2004, 38–43.

2. Dan Baum, "The Casualty: An American Soldier Comes Home from Iraq," *New Yorker*, March 8, 2004, 66.

3. "The Times and Iraq," *New York Times*, May 26, 2004.

4. We were first made aware of Marshall's work by Dan Baum, "The Price of Valor," *New Yorker*, July 12 and 19, 2004, 44–52.

5. We use male-gendered pronouns to refer to a general soldier throughout this essay as an indicator of the gendering of war trauma in the articles we address. Because the storying of war trauma assumes and depends on a normatively male gender, to impose gender-neutral language would mask these complexities of gendering. Questions of how narratives and theories of trauma collude with systems of regulating gender warrants its own extended analysis.

6. Ruth Leys, "Death Masks: Kardiner and Ferenczi on Psychic Trauma," *Representations* 53 (1996): 49.

7. Ibid., 48.

8. Ruth Leys, *Trauma: A Genealogy* (Chicago: University of Chicago Press, 2000).

9. Sigmund Freud, *Beyond the Pleasure Principle*, trans. James Strachey (New York: Norton, 1961), 10.

10. Leys, "Death Masks," 59.

11. Ibid.

12. Luciana Parisi and Tiziana Terranova, "Heat-Death: Emergence and Control in Genetic Engineering and Artificial Life," *Ctheory*, May 10, 2000, www.ctheory.com/article/a84.html.

13. Baum, "The Price of Valor," 46.

14. Ibid.

15. Corbett, "The Permanent Scars of Iraq."

16. Parisi and Terranova, "Heat-Death."

17. Ibid.

18. Hence the various strands of revolutionary ideology that seek to restore to the body its wholeness, its humanity. This formation, as we see it, begins to dissolve as the disciplinary enclosures of industrial capitalism are opened up to the intensification of biopolitical control.

19. For Foucault, docility describes an apparently contradictory but actually reciprocal practice of making bodies more useful as they are more deeply and effectively controlled. He writes: "A body is docile that may be subjected, used, transformed, and improved" (Michel Foucault, *Discipline and Punish: The Birth of the Prison*, trans. Alan Sheridan [New York: Vintage, 1977], 138). Disciplines, then, are the methods of producing and securing docile bodies. Foucault is suggesting that power operates at the level of force or energy, and it is especially this aspect of discipline and its historical, theoretical

articulation that interests us—the articulation and direction of bodily energies, capacities, or forces. This is to say that the thermodynamic energy is not simply enclosed in discipline; it is actively incited, assembled.

20. Baum, "The Price of Valor," 51.

21. Baum, "The Casualty," 66.

22. Baum, "The Price of Valor," 45.

23. Ibid.

24. Foucault, *Discipline and Punish*, 152.

25. Ibid., 153.

26. Ibid.

27. Neela Banerjee, "The Struggle for Iraq: The Wounded; Rebuilding Bodies, and Lives, Maimed by War," *New York Times*, November 16, 2003.

28. Baum, "The Casualty," 67.

29. Ibid.

30. Corbett, "The Permanent Scars of Iraq," 40.

31. Baum, "The Casualty," 71.

32. Foucault, *Discipline and Punish*, 164.

33. Ibid., 134.

34. Ibid., 138.

35. Michael Hardt, ""The Withering of Civil Society," in *Deleuze and Guattari: New Mappings in Politics, Philosophy, and Culture*, eds. Eleanor Kaufman and Kevin Jon Heller (Minneapolis: University of Minnesota Press, 1998), 23–39.

36. See John Armitage, "Ctheory Interview with Paul Virilio: The Kosovo War Took Place in Orbital Space," trans. Patrice Riemens, *Ctheory*, October 18, 2000, www .ctheory.net/text_file.asp?pick=132. See also Jean Baudrillard, *The Gulf War Did Not Take Place*, trans. Paul Patton (Bloomington: Indiana University Press, 1995).

37. For an excellent and thought-provoking analysis of the contemporary context of the war on/occupation of Iraq in terms of (neo)colonialism, media and military technologies, adaptations in military strategy related to Israel's management of Palestinian territories, and what Giorgio Agamben calls the "state of exception," see Derek Gregory, *The Colonial Present: Afghanistan, Pakistan, Iraq* (Malden, MA: Blackwell, 2004).

38. Foucault, *Discipline and Punish*, 243.

39. The varied and specific histories of disciplinary and biopolitical power have been explored by a range of writers, most provocatively by those who seek to correct Foucault's omission of the centrality of imperialism and colonial regimes to the emergence of modern biopower. See Ann Laura Stoler, *Race and the Education of Desire: Foucault's "History of Sexuality" and the Colonial Order of Things* (Durham, NC: Duke University Press, 1995); Rey Chow, *The Protestant Ethnic and the Spirit of Capitalism* (New York: Columbia University Press, 2002); and, for an early insight into the topic, Gayatri Chakrabarty Spivak, "Can the Subaltern Speak?" in *Marxism and the Interpretation of Culture*, ed. Cary Nelson and Lawrence Grossberg (Urbana: University of Illinois Press, 1988), 271–313.

40. Michel Foucault, *The History of Sexuality*, vol. 1, trans. Robert Hurley (New York: Vintage, 1979).

41. Corbett, "The Permanent Scars of Iraq," 42.

42. Susan Jeffords critically explores this theme, a powerful trope in discourse around the United States and the Vietnam War, in *The Remasculinization of America: Gender and the Vietnam War* (Bloomington: Indiana University Press, 1989).

43. Baum, "The Casualty," 71.

44. Corbett, "The Permanent Scars of Iraq," 42.

45. The rise of modern accounting sciences and the subsequent diffusion of accounting practices and logics throughout social and economic life has been explored by a number of writers. For an interesting study of quantification in accounting, as well as government and science, see Theodore M. Porter, *Trust in Numbers: The Pursuit of Objectivity in Science and Public Life* (Princeton, NJ: Princeton University Press, 1996). For comments on the function of statistics more generally, and some suggestions about their relationship to biopolitical regimes, see Ian Hacking, "How Shall We Do the History of Statistics?" in *The Foucault Effect: Studies in Governmentality; with Two Lectures by and an Interview with Michel Foucault*, ed. Graham Burchell, Colin Gordon, and Peter Miller (Chicago: University of Chicago Press, 1991), 181–95.

46. Michel Foucault, *Society Must Be Defended: Lectures at the College de France, 1975–1976*, trans. David Macey (New York: Picador, 2003), 246.

47. Baum, "The Price of Valor," 48.

48. Ibid.

49. Corbett, "The Permanent Scars of Iraq."

50. Ibid.

51. Foucault, *Society Must Be Defended*, 244.

52. Adriana Petryna makes a similar argument about postsocialist citizenship in relation to the Chernobyl nuclear disaster, in which a biological status of illness serves to stake claims to state protection—economic and social entitlements. She writes, "Protection is a legal right no longer self-evidently emanating from the state, but whose existence is at least partially assured by citizens' everyday exercise of their democratic capacities to identify, balance, or neutralize opposing forces that give or take life." Her formulation in this insightful essay helped clarify our own understanding of biopolitical negotiations. See Adriana Petryna, "Science and Citizenship under Postsocialism," *Social Research* 70.2 (2003): 562.

53. Corbett, "The Permanent Scars of Iraq," 40.

54. Ibid.

55. Within an analysis of trauma in biopolitical control, further questions arise about the way in which soldiers' feelings and narratives of trauma are themselves captured and modulated, generating media coverage, mental health practices, and emotional flows that can be generalized and distributed.

56. Corbett, "The Permanent Scars of Iraq," 43.

57. Foucault, *Society Must Be Defended*, 250.

58. Giorgio Agamben, *Homo Sacer: Sovereign Power and Bare Life*, trans. Danielle Heller-Roazen (Stanford, CA: Stanford University Press, 1998).

59. Corbett, "The Permanent Scars of Iraq," 43.

60. Foucault, *Society Must Be Defended*, 248.

BIBLIOGRAPHY

Abraham, Nicolas, and Maria Torok. *The Shell and the Kernel: Renewals of Psycho-analysis*. Chicago: University of Chicago Press, 1994.

Agamben, Giorgio. *Homo Sacer: Sovereign Power and Bare Life*. Trans. Daniel Heller-Roazen. Stanford, CA: Stanford University Press, 1998.

Ahmed, Sara. "Affective Economies." *Social Text* 79 (2004): 117–39.

——. *The Cultural Politics of Emotion*. Edinburgh: Edinburgh University Press, 2004.

——. "The Politics of Fear in the Making of Worlds." *Qualitative Studies in Education* 16.3 (2003): 377–98.

"American Government and Politics." *American Political Science Review* 54.2 (1960): 529–43.

Anagnost, Ann. "The Corporeal Politics of Quality (Suzhi)," *Public Culture* 16.2 (2004): 189–208.

Anderson, Elijah. *Streetwise: Race, Class, and Change in an Urban Community*. Chicago: University of Chicago Press, 1990.

Armitage, John. "Ctheory Interview with Paul Virilio: The Kosovo War Took Place in Orbital Space." Trans. Patrice Riemens. *Ctheory*, October 18, 2000, www.ctheory.net/text_file.asp?pick=132.

Aronofsky, Darrin, dir. *Requiem for a Dream*. Artisan, 2000.

Auyero, Javier. *Contentious Lives: Two Argentine Women, Two Protests, and the Quest for Recognition*. Durham, NC: Duke University Press, 2003.

Bailey, David. *Models Close Up*. New York: Universe, 1999.

Bakhtin, Mikhail M. *The Dialogic Imagination: Four Essays*. Trans. Caryl Emerson and Michael Holquist. Ed. Holquist. Austin: University of Texas Press, 1981.

Balakrishnan, Radhika, ed. *The Hidden Global Assembly Line: Gender Dynamics of Subcontracted Work in a Global Economy*. Bloomfield, CT: Kumarian, 2002.

Ballard, J. G. *Crash*. New York: Noonday, 1973.

Banerjee, Neela. "The Struggle for Iraq: The Wounded; Rebuilding Bodies, and Lives, Maimed by War." *New York Times*, November 16, 2003, query.nytimes.com/gst/health/article-page.html?res=9D05E5DC1038F935A25752C1A9659C8B63.

Barad, Karen. "Agential Realism: Feminist Interventions in Understanding Scientific Practices." In *The Science Studies Reader*, ed. Mario Biagioli, 1–11. New York: Routledge, 1999.

Basso, Pietro. *Modern times, Ancient Hours: Working Lives in the Twenty-first Century*. Trans. and ed. Giacomo Donis. New York: Verso, 2003.

Bataille, Georges. *The Accursed Share*. Vol. 1. Trans. Robert Hurley. New York: Zone, 1991.

Baudrillard, Jean. *The Gulf War Did Not Take Place.* Trans. Paul Patton. Bloomington: Indiana University Press, 1995.

——. *Simulacra and Simulation.* Trans. Sheila Faria Glaser. Ann Arbor: University of Michigan Press, 1994.

Baudry, Jean-Louis. "Ideological Effects of the Cinematographic Apparatus." In *Film Criticism and Theory: Introductory Readings*, ed. Leo Braudy and Marshall Cohen, 355–65. 5th ed. New York: Oxford University Press, 1999.

Baum, Dan. "The Casualty: An American Soldier Comes Home from Iraq." *New Yorker*, March 8, 2004, 64–73.

——. "The Price of Valor." *New Yorker*, July 12, 2004, 44–52.

Bauman, Zygmunt. *Wasted Lives: Modernity and Its Outcasts.* London: Polity, 2004.

Bell, Daniel. *The Coming of Post-industrial Society: A Venture in Social Forecasting.* New York: Basic Books, 1973.

—— *The Cultural Contradictions of Capitalism.* New York: Basic Books, 1976.

Bell, Michael M. "The Ghosts of Place." *Theory and Society* 26 (1997): 813–36.

Beller, Jonathan. "Capital/Cinema." In *Deleuze and Guattari: New Mappings in Politics, Philosophy, and Culture*, ed. Eleanor Kaufman and Kevin Jon Heller, 76–95. Minneapolis: University of Minnesota Press, 1998.

Benjamin, Walter. "A Berlin Chronicle." In *Reflections: Essays, Aphorisms, Autobiographical Writings.* Trans. Edmund Jephcott. Ed. Peter Demetz. 3–60. New York: Harcourt Brace Jovanovich, 1978.

——. *Illuminations: Essays and Reflections.* Trans. Harry Zohn. Ed. Hannah Arendt. New York: Schocken, 1969.

——. "One-Way Street." In *Reflections: Essays, Aphorisms, Autobiographical Writings.* Trans. Edmund Jephcott. Ed Peter Demetz. 61–94. New York: Harcourt Brace Jovanovich, 1978.

Bergson, Henri. *Creative Evolution.* Trans. Arthur Mitchell. Lanham, MD: University Press of America, 1983.

——. *The Creative Mind.* Trans. Mabelle L. Andison. New York: Citadel, 1992.

——. *Matter and Memory.* Trans. N. M. Paul and W. S. Palmer. New York: Zone, 1991.

Berlant, Lauren, ed. *Compassion: The Culture and Politics of an Emotion.* New York: Routledge, 2004.

——. *Intimacy.* Chicago: University of Chicago Press, 2000.

Bianco, Jamie "Skye." "Fertility and the Quantum Matrix: Hacking Bodies; or, Death Is a Fashion Accessory in Chuck Palahniuk's *Survivor* and Richard Calder's *Dead Girls*." Unpublished manuscript, 2005.

——. "Techno-Cinema." *Comparative Literature Studies* 41.3 (2004): 337–403.

——. "Virtual Theories: Virtualities, Actualities, Affection, and Bodies of Information." Unpublished manuscript, 2005.

Biehl, João. "Vita: Life in Zone of Social Abandonment." *Social Text* 68 (2001): 131–149.

Bogue, Ronald. "Gilles Deleuze: The Aesthetics of Force." In *Deleuze: A Critical Reader*, ed. Paul Patton, 257–69. Oxford: Blackwell, 1996.

Borch-Jacobsen, Mikkel. *Lacan: The Absolute Master.* Trans. Douglas Brick. Stanford, CA: Stanford University Press, 1991.

Borges, Jorge Luis. *The Aleph and Other Stories*. Trans. Andrew Hurley. New York: Penguin Classics, 2001.

——. *Labyrinths: Selected Stories and Other Writings*. Ed. Donald A. Yates and James E. Irby. New York: New Directions, 1962.

Boris, Eileen, and Elisabeth Prügl, eds. *Homeworkers in Global Perspective: Invisible No More*. New York: Routledge, 1996.

Boundas, Constantin. "Exchange, Gift, Theft." *Angelaki* 6.2 (2001): 1–5.

Bourdieu, Pierre. *In Other Words: Essays toward a Reflexive Sociology*. Trans. Matthew Adamson. Oxford: Polity, 1990.

Bourgois, Philippe. *In Search of Respect: Selling Crack in El Barrio*. Cambridge: Cambridge University Press, 1996.

Boyer, Christine. *The City of Collective Memory*. Cambridge, MA: MIT Press, 1994.

Briggs, John, and David Peat. *Turbulent Mirror: An Illustrated Guide to Chaos Theory and the Science of Wholeness*. New York: Harper and Row, 1989.

Brooks, R. "Intelligence without Reason." In *IJCAI-91: Proceedings of the Twelfth International Conference on Artificial Intelligence*. San Mateo, CA: M. Kaufman, 1991.

Brown, Steven, and Rose Capdevila. "Perpetuum mobile." In *Actor Network Theory and After*, ed. John Law and John Hassard, 26–50. Boston: Blackwell, 1999.

Brussa, Licia, ed. *Health, Migration, and Sex Work: The Experience of TAMPEP*. Amsterdam: TAMPEP International, 1999.

Burkett, Paul. "Nature's 'Free Gifts' and the Ecological Significance of Value." *Capital and Class* 68 (1999): 89–110.

Butler, Judith. *Bodies That Matter: On the Discursive Limits of "Sex."* New York: Routledge, 1993.

——. *Gender Trouble: Feminism and the Subversion of Identity*. New York: Routledge, 1990.

——. *The Psychic Life of Power: Theories in Subjection*. Stanford, CA: Stanford University Press, 1997.

Cadbury, Deborah. *Altering Eden: The Feminization of Nature*. New York: St. Martin's, 1997.

Caffentzis, George. "On Africa and Self-Reproducing Automata." In *New Encounters*. Ed. Midnight Notes Collective, 35–41. Jamaica Plain, MA: Midnight Notes, 1990.

——. "The Work/Energy Crisis and the Apocalypse." In *Midnight Oil: Work, Energy, War, 1973–1992*. Ed. Midnight Notes Collective, 215–71. Brooklyn: Autonomedia, 1992.

Calasso, Roberto. *The Ruin of Kasch*. Cambridge, MA: Harvard University Press, 1994.

Careri, Francesco. *Walkscapes: El andar como práctica estética—Walking as an Aesthetic Practice*. Trans. Maurici Pla, Steve Piccolo, and Paul Hammond. Barcelona: Editorial Gustavo Gili, 2002.

Caruth, Cathy. *Unclaimed Experience: Trauma, Narrative, and History*. Baltimore, MD: Johns Hopkins University Press, 1996.

Casey, Edward S. *The Fate of Place*. Berkeley: University of California Press, 1999.

Castells, Manuel. *The Rise of the Network Society*. Cambridge, MA: Blackwell, 1996.

Cha, Theresa Hak Kyung. *Dictée*. New York: Tanam, 1982.

Chapkis, Wendy. *Live Sex Acts: Women Performing Erotic Labor*. New York: Routledge, 1997.

Cheah, Pheng. "Mattering." *Diacritics* 26.1 (1996): 108–39.

Cheng, Anne Anlin. *The Melancholy of Race: Psychoanalysis, Assimilation, and Hidden Grief*. Oxford: Oxford University Press, 2001.

Cho, Grace M. "Murmurs in the Storytelling Machine." *Cultural Studies–Critical Methodologies* 4.4 (2004): 426–32.

Cho, Grace M., and Hosu Kim. "Dreaming in Tongues." *Qualitative Inquiry* 11.3 (2005): 445–57.

Choi, Chungmoo. "Introduction: The Comfort Women; Colonialism, War, and Sex." *Positions* 5.1 (1997): v–xiv.

Chow, Rey. *The Protestant Ethnic and the Spirit of Capitalism*. New York: Columbia University Press, 2002.

Chung, Chin Sung. "Korean Women Drafted for Military Sexual Slavery by Japan." In *True Stories of the Korean Comfort Women: Testimonies Compiled by the Korean Council for Women Drafted for Military Sexual Slavery by Japan and the Research Association on the Women Drafted for Military Sexual Slavery by Japan*, trans. Young Joo Lee, ed. Keith Howard, 11–30. London: Cassell, 1995.

Chung, Hye-jean. "Two Films Shed Light on 1945 Ship Tragedy." *Korea Times*, September 17, 2001.

Clark, Andy. *Being There: Putting Brain, Body, and World Together Again*. Cambridge, MA: MIT Press, 1997.

Clough, Patricia Ticineto. "Affect and Control: Rethinking the Body 'Beyond Sex and Gender.'" *Feminist Theory* 4.3 (2003): 381–86.

——. *Autoaffection: Unconscious Thought in the Age of Teletechnology*. Minneapolis: University of Minnesota Press, 2000.

——. *The End(s) of Ethnography: From Realism to Social Criticism*. 2d ed. New York: Peter Lang, 1998.

——. *Feminist Thought: Desire, Power, and Academic Discourse*. Cambridge, MA: Blackwell, 1994.

——. "Future Matters: Technoscience, Global Politics, and Cultural Criticism." *Social Text* 80 (2004): 1–24.

——. "The Shift from Discipline to Control: Reentry and beyond Reentry, Criticism and Policy-Oriented Research." Center for the Study of Women and Society Symposium (New York, March 2003).

Clough, Patricia Ticineto, and Joseph Schneider. "Donna Haraway." In *Profiles in Contemporary Social Theory*, ed. Anthony Elliott and Bryan S. Turner, 338–48. London: Sage, 2001.

Collins, Randall. "Emotional Energy as the Common Denominator of Rational Action." *Rationality and Society* 5.2 (1993): 203–30.

——. "On the Microfoundations of Macrosociology." *American Journal of Sociology* 86.5 (1981): 984–1014.

——. "Stratification, Emotional Energy, and the Transient Emotions." In *Research Agendas in the Sociology of Emotions*, ed. Theodore D. Kemper, 27–57. Albany: State University of New York Press, 1990.

Corbett, Sara. "The Permanent Scars of Iraq." *New York Times Magazine*, February 15, 2004, 38–43.

Damasio, Antonio. *Looking for Spinoza: Joy, Sorrow, and the Feeling Brain*. New York: Harcourt, 2003.

Danielewski, Mark Z. *House of Leaves*. New York: Pantheon, 2000.

Davenport, Thomas H. "elearning and the Attention Economy: Here, There, and Everywhere?" *LiNE Zine*, 2001, 1–4.

DeLanda, Manuel. *Intensive Science and Virtual Philosophy*. New York: Continuum, 2002.

——. "Nonorganic Life." In *Incorporations*, ed. Jonathan Crary and Sanford Kwinter, 129–67. New York: Zone, 1992.

——. *A Thousand Years of Non-linear History*. New York: Swerve, 2000.

Deleuze, Gilles. *Bergsonism*. Trans. Hugh Tomlinson and Barbara Habberjam. New York: Zone, 1991.

——. *Cinema 1: The Movement Image*. Trans. Hugh Tomlinson and Barbara Habberjam. Minneapolis: University of Minnesota Press, 1986.

——. *Cinema 2: The Time-Image*. Trans. Hugh Tomlinson and Robert Galeta. Minneapolis: University of Minnesota Press, 1989.

——. *Difference and Repetition*. Trans. Paul Patton. New York: Columbia University Press, 1994.

——. *Expressionism in Philosophy: Spinoza*. Trans. Martin Joughin. New York: Zone, 1990.

——. *The Fold: Leibniz and the Baroque*. Trans. Tom Conley. Minneapolis: University of Minnesota Press, 1993.

——. *Foucault*. Trans. Sean Hand. Minneapolis: University of Minnesota Press, 1998.

——. *Francis Bacon: The Logic of Sensation*. Trans. Daniel W. Smith Minneapolis: University of Minnesota Press, 2003.

——. *The Logic of Sense*. Trans. Mark Lester with Charles Stivale. Ed. Constantin V. Boundas. New York: Columbia University Press, 1990.

——. "Postscript on the Societies of Control." *October* 59 (1991): 3–7.

——. *Proust and Signs*. Trans. Richard Howard. Minneapolis: University of Minnesota Press, 2000.

Deleuze, Gilles, and Claire Parnet. *Dialogues*. Trans. Hugh Tomlinson and Barbara Habberjam. New York: Columbia University Press, 1987.

Deleuze, Gilles, and Félix Guattari. *A Thousand Plateaus: Capitalism and Schizophrenia*. Trans. Brian Massumi. Minneapolis: University of Minnesota Press, 1987.

——. *What Is Philosophy?* Trans. Hugh Tomlinson and Graham Burchell. New York: Columbia University Press, 1994.

Deleuze, Gilles, and Gregory Flaxman. "The Brain Is the Screen: An Interview with Gilles Deleuze." Trans. Marie Therese Guirgis. In *The Brain Is the Screen: Deleuze and the Philosophy of Cinema*, ed. Flaxman, 365–74. Minneapolis: University of Minnesota Press, 2000.

Derrida, Jacques. "Différance." In *Margins of Philosophy*, 1–27. Trans. Alan Bass. Chicago: University of Chicago Press, 1982.

——. *Donner le temps*. Paris: Galilée, 1991.

——. *Given Time.* Trans. Peggy Kamuf. Chicago: University of Chicago Press, 1992.

——. *Of Grammatology.* Trans. Gayatri Chakravorty Spivak. Baltimore, MD: Johns Hopkins University Press, 1976.

——. *Writing and Difference.* Trans. Alan Bass. Chicago: University of Chicago Press, 1980.

De Santillana, Giorgio, and Hertha von Dechend. *Hamlet's Mill.* Boston: David Godine, 1969.

Diamond, Timothy. *Making Gray Gold: Narratives of Nursing Home Care.* Chicago: University of Chicago Press, 1992.

Dienst, Richard. *Still Life in Real Time: Theory after Television.* Durham, NC: Duke University Press: 1994.

Ditmore, Melissa. "Report from the USA: Do Prohibitory Laws Promote Risk?" *Research for Sex Work* 4 (2001): 13–14.

Donzelot, Jacques. *The Policing of Families.* Trans. Robert Hurley. Baltimore, MD: Johns Hopkins University Press, 1997.

DuBois, Ellen Carol, and Linda Gordon. "Seeking Ecstasy on the Battlefield: Danger and Pleasure in Nineteenth-Century Feminist Sexual Thought." In *Pleasure and Danger: Exploring Female Sexuality*, ed. Carole S. Vance, 31–49. Boston: Routledge and K. Paul, 1984.

Duneier, Mitchell. *Sidewalk.* New York: Farrar, Strauss and Giroux, 2001.

Dyer-Witheford, Nick. *Cyber-Marx: Cycles and Circuits of Struggle in High Technology Capitalism.* Urbana: University of Illinois Press, 2000.

Dyson, Freeman. *Origins of Life.* Cambridge: Cambridge University Press, 1985.

Dyson, George B. *Darwin among the Machines: The Evolution of Global Intelligence.* Reading, MA: Addison-Wesley, 1997.

Edelman, G. *Bright Air, Brilliant Fire: On the Matter of the Mind.* Middlesex, UL: Penguin, 1994.

Ehrenreich, Barbara, and Arlie Russell Hochschild, eds. *Global Woman: Nannies, Maids, and Sex Workers in the New Economy.* New York: Metropolitan Books, 2003.

Ehrenreich, Barbara, and Deirdre English. *For Her Own Good: One Hundred and Fifty Years of the Experts' Advice to Women.* Garden City, NJ: Anchor, 1978.

Empower Chiang Mai. "A Report by Empower Chiang Mai on the Human Rights Violations Women Are Subjected to When 'Rescued' by Anti-trafficking Groups Who Employ Methods Using Deception, Force, and Coercion." Chiang Mai, Thailand: Empower Chiang Mai, 2003.

——. "US Sponsored Entrapment." *Research for Sex Work* 8 (2005): 25–27.

Eng, David L. *Racial Castration: Managing Masculinity in Asian America.* Durham, NC: Duke University Press, 2001.

Eng, David L., and David Kazanjian. Introduction to *Loss: The Politics of Mourning*, ed. Eng and Kazanjian, Berkeley: University of California Press, 2003.

Etchells, Tim. *Certain Fragments: Contemporary Performance and Forced Entertainment.* London: Routledge, 1999.

Faulkner, William. *Requiem for a Nun.* 1951. New York: Vintage, 1975.

Federici, Sylvia. "Wages against Housework." In *The Politics of Housework*, ed. Ellen Malos, 187–94. New York: Clarion Press, 1975.

Feyerabend, Paul. *Against Method: Outline of an Anarchistic Theory of Knowledge*. New York: Verso, 1975.

Fink, Leon, and Brian Greenberg. *Upheaval in the Quiet Zone: A History of Hospital Workers' Union, Local 1199*. Urbana: University of Illinois Press, 1989.

Fortunati, Leopoldina. *The Arcane of Reproduction: Housework, Prostitution, Labor, and Capital*. Trans. Hilary Creek. Ed. Jim Fleming. Brooklyn, NY: Autonomedia, 1995.

Foucault, Michel. *Discipline and Punish: The Birth of the Prison*. Trans. Alan Sheridan. New York: Vintage, 1977.

———. "Governmentality." In *The Foucault Effect: Studies in Governmentality; with Two Lectures by and an Interview with Michel Foucault*, ed. Graham Burchell, Colin Gordon, and Peter Miller, 87–104. Chicago: University of Chicago Press, 1991.

———. *The History of Sexuality*. Vol. 1. Trans. Robert Hurley. New York: Vintage, 1979.

———. *Society Must Be Defended: Lectures at the Collège de France, 1975–1976*. Trans. David Macey. New York: Picador, 2003.

Fraad, Harriet, Stephen Resnick, and Richard Wolff, eds. *Bringing It All Back Home: Class, Gender, and Power in the Modern Household*. London: Pluto, 1994.

Freeman, W. J., and J. M. Barrie. "Chaotic Oscillations and the Genesis of Meaning in Cerebral Cortex." In *Temporal Coding in the Brain*, ed. G. Buzsáki et al., 13–37. Berlin: Springer-Verlag, 1994.

Freud, Sigmund. *Beyond the Pleasure Principle*. Trans. James Strachey. New York: Norton, 1961.

———. *Civilization and Its Discontents*. Trans. Peter Gay. New York: Norton, 1989.

Fröhlich, H. "The Biological Effects of Microwaves and Related Questions." *Advanced Electronics and Electronic Physics* 53 (1980): 85–152.

Geertz, Clifford. *The Interpretation of Culture*. New York: Basic Books, 1973.

Georgalis, Nicholas. "Mind, Brain, and Chaos." In *The Caldron of Consciousness*, ed. Ralph D. Ellis and Natika Newton, Philadelphia: John Benjamins, 2000.

Gibbs, Anna. "Disaffected." *Continuum* 16.3 (2002): 335–41.

Gilbert, Karen Wendy. "The Urban Cyborg Sha(wo)men Manifesto." *Found Object* 8 (2000): 96–123.

Gilbert-Rolfe, Jeremy. *Beauty and the Contemporary Sublime*. New York: Allworth, 1999.

Gilder, George. *Wealth and Poverty*. New York: Basic Books, 1981.

Glazer, Nona Y. *Women's Paid and Unpaid Labor: The Work Transfer in Health Care and Retailing*. Philadelphia: Temple University Press, 1993.

Godbout, Jacques T., with Alain Caillé. *The World of the Gift*. Trans. Donald Winkler. Montreal: McGill-Queen's University Press, 1998.

Godelier, Maurice. *The Enigma of the Gift*. Chicago: University of Chicago Press, 1999.

Goffman, Erving. *Frame Analysis*. Boston: Northeastern University Press, 1974.

Graeber, David. *Toward an Anthropological Theory of Value: The False Coin of Our Own Dreams*. New York: Palgrave, 2001.

Grazian, David. *Blue Chicago*. Chicago: University of Chicago Press, 2003.

Gregory, Derek. *The Colonial Present: Afghanistan, Pakistan, Iraq*. Malden, MA: Blackwell, 2004.

Grosz, Elizabeth. *Architecture from the Outside: Essays on Virtual and Real Space*. Cambridge, MA: MIT Press, 2001.

——. *Space, Time, and Perversion: Essays on the Politics of Bodies.* New York: Routledge, 1995.

——. "The *Time* of Violence: Deconstruction and Value." *College Literature* 26.1 (1999): 8–18.

——. *Volatile Bodies: Toward a Corporeal Feminism.* Bloomington: Indiana University Press, 1994.

Grubb, W. Norton. *Working in the Middle.* San Francisco: Jossey-Bass, 1996.

Hacking, Ian. "How Shall We Do the History of Statistics?" In *The Foucault Effect: Studies in Governmentality; with Two Lectures by and an Interview with Michel Foucault,* ed. Graham Burchell, Colin Gordon, and Peter Miller, 181–96. Chicago: University of Chicago Press, 1991.

Hameroff, Stuart. "The Debate on Decoherence: Biological Feasibility of Quantum States in the Brain," 2002, www.consciousness.arizona.edu/hameroff/papers/deco herence/ decoherence.html.

Hammond, Michael. "The Sociology of Emotions and the History of Social Differentia-tion." *Sociological Theory* 1 (1983): 90–119.

Hansen, Mark. "The Time of Affect; or, Bearing Witness to Life." *Critical Inquiry* 30.3 (2004): 584–626.

Haraway, Donna J. *Modest__Witness@second__Millennium. FemaleMan__Meets__Onco Mouse__.* New York: Routledge, 1997.

——. *Simians, Cyborgs, and Women: The Reinvention of Women.* New York: Routledge, 1991.

Harding, Sandra. *The Science Question in Feminism.* Ithaca, NY: Cornell University Press, 1986.

Hardt, Michael. "Affective Labor." *Boundary 2* 26.2 (1999): 89–100.

——. "The Withering of Civil Society." In *Deleuze and Guattari: New Mappings in Politics, Philosophy, and Culture,* eds. Eleanor Kaufman and Kevin Jon Heller, 23–39. Minneapolis: University of Minnesota Press, 1998.

Hardt, Michael, and Antonio Negri. *Empire.* Cambridge, MA: Harvard University Press, 2000.

——. *Multitude: War and Democracy in the Age of Empire.* New York: Penguin, 2004.

Hartmann, Heidi. "The Unhappy Marriage of Marxism and Feminism." In *Women and Revolution,* ed. Lydia Sargent, 1–41. London: Tavistock, 1981.

Hartsock, Nancy C. M. "The Feminist Standpoint: Toward a Specifically Feminist His-torical Materialism." In *Money, Sex, and Power: Toward a Feminist Historical Mate-rialism,* 231–51. Boston: Northeastern University Press, 1983.

Harvey, David. *The Condition of Postmodernity: An Enquiry into the Origins of Cultural Change.* Oxford: Blackwell, 1989.

Hayden, Dolores. *The Power of Place: Urban Landscapes as Public History.* Cambridge, MA: MIT Press, 1995.

——. *Redesigning the American Dream: The Future of Housing, Work, and Family Life.* New York: Norton, 1984.

Hayles, N. Katherine. *Chaos Bound: Orderly Disorder in Contemporary Literature and Science.* Ithaca, NY: Cornell University Press, 1999.

——. *How We Became Posthuman: Virtual Bodies in Cybernetics, Literature, and Informatics.* Chicago: University of Chicago Press, 1999.

——. *Writing Machines.* Cambridge, MA: MIT Press, 2002.

Heidegger, Martin. *The Question Concerning Technology and Other Essays.* Trans. William Lovitt. New York: Harper and Row, 1969.

Heisenberg, Werner. *Physics and Beyond: Encounters and Conversations.* New York: Harper and Row, 1971.

Herbert, Nick. *Elemental Mind.* New York: Penguin, 1994.

Ho, Mae-Wan. "Bioenergetics and the Coherence of Organisms," *Neuronetwork World* 5 (1995): 733–75.

——. "Quantum Coherence and Conscious Experience." *Kybernetes* 26 (1997): 265–76.

——. *The Rainbow and the Worm: The Physics of Organisms.* Singapore: World Scientific, 1993.

Hochschild, Arlie Russell. *The Managed Heart: Commercialization of Human Feeling.* Berkeley: University of California Press, 1983.

Hutnyk, John. *Bad Marxism: Capitalism and Cultural Studies.* London: Pluto, 2004.

Huws, Ursula. *The Making of a Cybertariat: Virtual Work in a Real World.* New York: Monthly Review Press, 2003.

Hwang, Jang-jin. "South Koreans Urge Japan to Take Full Responsibility for 1945 Ship Blast." *Korea Herald*, August 25, 2001, www.koreaherald.co.kr/servlet/kherald .article. view?id=200108250034&tpl=print.

Jacob, François. *The Logic of Living Systems: A History of Heredity.* Trans. Betty E. Spillmann. London: Allen Lane, 1974.

"Japan/Korea: Fifteen South Koreans Awarded 45 Million Yen over Ship Blast." *Japan Times*, August 24, 2001, www.archk.net/news/mainfile.php/ahrnews_200108/ 1818/?print=yes.

Jeffords, Susan. *The Remasculinization of America: Gender and the Vietnam War.* Bloomington: Indiana University Press, 1989.

Johnston, John. "Machinic Vision." *Critical Inquiry* 26.1 (1999): 27–48.

Kauffmann, S. A. *The Origins of Order: Self-Organization and Selections in Evolution.* New York: Oxford University Press, 1993.

Kelso, J. A. S. "Behavioral and Neural Pattern Generation: The Concept of Neurobehavioral Dynamical Systems." In *Cardiorespiratory and Motor Coordination*, ed. H.-P. Koepchen and T. Huopaniemi, 224–34. Berlin: Springer-Verlag, 1991.

Kennedy, Barbara. *Deleuze and Cinema: The Aesthetics of Sensation.* Edinburgh: Edinburgh University Press, 2000.

Kim, Kyung Hyun. "Post-trauma and Historical Remembrance in Recent South Korean Cinema: Reading Park Kwang-su's *A Single Spark* (1995) and Chang Son-u's *A Petal* (1996)." *Cinema Journal* 41.4 (2002): 94–115.

Knorr-Cetina, Karin. *Epistemic Cultures: How the Sciences Make Knowledge.* Cambridge, MA: Harvard University Press, 1999.

"Korean 'Titanic' Amazes Moscow and Hong Kong Audience: To Be Exported to West." *People's Korea*, July 25, 2001.

Kracauer, Siegfried. *Theory of Film: The Redemption of Physical Reality.* New York: Oxford University Press, 1960.

Kuczynski, Alex. "Trading on Hollywood Magic: Celebrities Push Models off Women's Magazine Covers." *New York Times*, January 30, 1999.

Lacan, Jacques. *The Four Fundamental Concepts of Psycho-analysis*. Trans. Alan Sheridan. Ed. Jacques-Alain Miller. New York: Norton, 1978.

Latour, Bruno, and Steve Woolgar. *Laboratory Life: The Construction of Scientific Facts*. Princeton, NJ: Princeton University Press, 1986.

Law, John. "After ANT." In *Actor Network Theory and After*, ed. Law and John Hassard, Malden, MA: Blackwell, 1999.

Lazzarato, Maurizio. "Immaterial Labor." In *Radical Thought in Italy: A Potential Politics*, ed. Paolo Virno and Michael Hardt, 133–47. Minneapolis: University of Minneapolis Press, 1996.

Lee, Sang Oak, et al. *Korean through English*. Seoul: Hollym Corporation, 1993.

Leidner, Robin. *Fast Food, Fast Talk: Service Word and the Routinization of Everyday Life*. Berkeley: University of California Press, 1993.

Leys, Ruth. "Death Masks: Kardiner and Ferenczi on Psychic Trauma." *Representations* 53 (1996): 44–73.

——. *Trauma: A Genealogy*. Chicago: University of Chicago Press, 2000.

Liebow, Elliot. *Tally's Corner: A Study of Negro Streetcorner Men*. Boston: Back Bay Books, 1967.

Liem, Ramsay. "History, Trauma, and Identity: The Legacy of the Korean War for Korean Americans." *Amerasia Journal* 29.3 (2004): 111–29.

Lin Lean, ed. *The Sex Sector: The Economic and Social Bases of Prostitution in Southeast Asia*. Geneva: International Labour Organization, 1998.

Lipschultz, David. "Solar Power Is Reaching Where Wires Can't." *New York Times*, September 9, 2001.

Lynch, Kevin. *The Image of the City*. Cambridge, MA: MIT Press, 1960.

MacLean, Norman. *Genes and Gene Regulation*. London: Edward Arnold, 1989.

Margulis, Lynn. *Symbiosis in Cell Evolution*. San Francisco: W. H. Freeman, 1981.

Margulis, Lynn, and Dorion Sagan. *Microcosmos: Four Billion Years of Evolution from Our Microbial Ancestors*. New York: Summit, 1986.

——. *What Is Life?* New York: Simon and Schuster, 1994.

——. *What Is Sex?* New York: Simon and Schuster, 1997.

Marx, Karl. *Capital: A Critique of Political Economy*, Vol. 1. New York: Vintage, 1977.

——. *Grundrisse*. Trans. Martin Nicolaus. New York: Vintage, 1973.

Massumi, Brian. "Translator's Foreword: Pleasures of Philosophy." In Gilles Deleuze and Felix Guattari, *A Thousand Plateaus, Capitalism & Schizophrenia*. Minneapolis: University of Minnesota Press, 1987.

——. *Parables for the Virtual: Movement, Affect, Sensation*. Durham, NC: Duke University Press, 2002.

——. "Requiem for Our Prospective Dead (Toward a Participatory Critique of Capitalist Power)." In *Deleuze and Guattari: New Mappings in Politics, Philosophy, and Culture*, ed. Eleanor Kaufman and Kevin Jon Heller, 40–64. Minneapolis: University of Minnesota Press, 1998.

Maturana, Humberto R., and Francisco G. Varela. *Autopoiesis and Cognition: The Realization of the Living*. Boston: D. Reidel, 1980.

——. *The Tree of Knowledge: The Biological Roots of Human Understanding*. Boston: Shambala, 1968.

Mauss, Marcel. *The Gift: Forms and Functions of Exchange in Archaic Societies*. Trans. Ian Cunnison. New York: Norton, 1967.

Mbembe, Achille. "Necropolitics." Trans. Libby Meintjes. *Public Culture* 15.1 (2003): 11–40.

McAllester Jones, Mary. *Gaston Bachelard, Subversive Humanist: Texts and Readings*. Madison: University of Wisconsin Press, 1991.

McCaffery, Larry. Introduction to *Storming the Reality Studio: A Casebook of Cyberpunk and Postmodern Fiction*, ed. McCaffery, 1–16. Durham, NC: Duke University Press, 1991.

McClare, C. W. F. "Chemical Machines, Maxwell's Demon, and Living Organisms." *Journal of Theoretical Biology* 30 (1971): 1–34.

McFaddan, Johnjoe. "Synchronous Firing and Its Influence on the Brain's Electromagnetic Field: Evidence for an Electromagnetic Field Theory of Consciousness." *Journal of Consciousness Studies* 9 (2002): 23–50.

Mies, Maria. *Patriarchy and Accumulation on a World Scale: Women in the International Division of Labour*. London: Zed, 1998.

Mills, C. Wright. *White Collar: The American Middle Classes*. New York: Oxford University Press, 1951.

Monod, Jacques. *Chance and Necessity: An Essay on the Natural Philosophy of Modern Biology*. Trans. Austryn Wainhouse. New York: Knopf, 1971.

——. *The Logic of Life*. Trans. Betty E. Spillmann. New York: Pantheon, 1973.

Moon, Katharine H. S. "South Korean Movements against Militarized Sexual Labor." *Asian Survey* 39.2 (1999): 310–25.

Moten, Fred, and Stefano Harney. "The University and the Undercommons: Seven Theses." *Social Text* 79 (2004): 101–15.

Mulvey, Laura. *Visual and Other Pleasures*. Bloomington: Indiana University Press, 1989.

Negri, Antonio. *Marx beyond Marx: Lessons on the "Grundrisse."* Trans. Harry Cleaver. Ed. Jim Fleming. Brooklyn, NY: Autonomedia, 1991.

——. *Revolution Retrieved: Selected Writings on Marx, Keynes, Capitalist Crisis, and New Social Subjects, 1967–83*. London: Red Notes, 1988.

——. *Time for Revolution*. New York: Continuum, 2003.

——. "Value and Affect." *Boundary 2* 26.2 (1999): 77–88.

Ngai, Sianne. *Ugly Feelings*. Cambridge, MA: Harvard University Press, 2005.

Nicolis, Grégoire, and Ilya Prigogine. *Exploring Complexity: An Introduction*. New York: W. H. Freeman, 1989.

Nolan, Christopher, dir. *Memento*. Columbia/Tri-Star, 2000.

Overs, Cheryl, and Paulo Longo. *Making Sex Work Safe*. London: Russell, 1997.

Pal, Minu, et al. "The Winds of Change Are Whispering at Your Door." In *Global Sex Workers: Rights, Resistance, and Redefinition*, ed. Kamala Kempadoo and Jo Doezema, 200–203. New York: Routledge, 1998.

Parisi, Luciana. "Information Trading and Symbiotic Micropolitics." In "Technoscience," ed. Patricia Ticineto Clough, special issue, *Social Text* 80 (2004): 25–50.

Parisi, Luciana, and Tiziana Terranova. "Heat-Death: Emergence and Control in Genetic Engineering and Artificial Life." *CTheory*: www.ctheory.com/article/a84.html.

Parreñas, Rhacel Salazar. *Servants of Globalization: Women, Migration, and Domestic Work*. Stanford, CA: Stanford University Press, 2001.

Parry, Richard Lloyd. "Korea Rallys Round Kim Jong Il's 'Titanic' Tale of Slave Ship," *Independent News*, August 24, 2001, news.independent.co.uk/world/asia_china/story.jsp?story=90376.

Pearson, Keith Ansell. *Germinal Life: The Difference and Repetition of Deleuze*. New York: Routledge, 1999.

——. *Philosophy and the Adventure of the Virtual: Bergson and the Time of Life*. New York: Routledge, 2002.

——. *Viroid Life: Perspectives on Nietzsche and the Transhuman Condition*. New York: Routledge, 1997.

Petryna, Adriana. "Science and Citizenship under Postsocialism." *Social Research* 70.2 (2003): 551–78.

Plotnitsky, Arkady. *Reconfigurations: Critical Theory and General Economy*. Gainesville: University Press of Florida, 1993.

Pollack, Gerald H. *Cells, Gels, and the Engines of Life: A New, Unifying Approach to Cell Function*. Seattle: Ebner and Sons, 2001.

Portelli, Alessandro. *The Battle of Valle Giulia: Oral History and the Art of Dialogue*. Madison: University of Wisconsin Press, 1997.

Porter, Theodore M. *Trust in Numbers: The Pursuit of Objectivity in Science and Public Life*. Princeton, NJ: Princeton University Press, 1996.

Prigogine, Ilya, and Isabelle Stengers. *Order Out of Chaos: Man's New Dialogue with Nature*. New York: Bantam, 1984.

Puar, Jasbir K. "Abu Ghraib: Arguing against Exceptionalism." *Feminist Studies* 30.2 (2004): 1–14.

Rabinbach, Anson. *The Human Motor: Energy, Fatigue, and the Origins of Modernity*. New York: Basic Books, 1990.

Ramadanovic, Petar. "When 'To Die in Freedom' Is Written in English." *Diacritics* 28.4 (1998): 54–67.

Reich, Robert B. *The Work of Nations: Preparing Ourselves for Twenty-First-Century Capitalism*. New York: Vintage, 1992.

Reverby, Susan. *Ordered to Care: The Dilemma of American Nursing, 1850–1945*. Cambridge: Cambridge University Press, 1987.

Richman, Michele. *Reading Georges Bataille: Beyond the Gift*. Baltimore, MD: Johns Hopkins University Press, 1982.

Rilke, Rainer M. *The Selected Poetry of Rainer Maria Rilke*. Trans. S. Mitchell. New York: Vintage, 1989.

Rose, Jacqueline. *States of Fantasy*. Oxford: Claredon, 1996.

Rosner, David. *A Once Charitable Enterprise: Hospitals and Health Care in Brooklyn and New York, 1885–1915*. Cambridge: Cambridge University Press, 1982.

Rubin, Gayle. "Thinking Sex." In *Pleasure and Danger: Exploring Female Sexuality*, ed. Carole S. Vance, 267–319. Boston: Routledge and K. Paul, 1984.

Sachs, Jeffrey. *The End of Poverty: Economic Possibilities for Our Time*. New York: Penguin, 2005.

Schor, Juliet. *Overworked American: The Unexpected Decline of Leisure*. New York: Basic Books, 1993.

Sedgwick, Eve Kosofsky. *Touching Feeling: Affect, Pedagogy, Performativity*. Durham, NC: Duke University Press, 2003.

Sedgwick, Eve Kosofsky, and Adam Frank, eds. *Shame and Its Sisters: A Silvan Tomkins Reader*. Durham, NC: Duke University Press, 1995.

Serlin, David. *Replaceable You: Engineering the Body in Postwar America*. Chicago: University of Chicago Press, 2004.

Serres, Michel. *The Birth of Physics*. Trans. Jack Hawkes. Manchester: Clinamen, 2000.

——. *Genesis*. Trans. Geneviève James and James Nielson. Ann Arbor: University of Michigan Press, 1995.

——. *The Parasite*. Trans. Lawrence Schehr. Baltimore, MD: Johns Hopkins University Press, 1982.

Shan Women's Action Network. "Report by the Shan Women's Action Network (SWAN) on Services Provided to Trafcord on May 3, 2003." Chiang Mai, Thailand: Empower Chiang Mai, 2003.

Shannon, Claude Elwood, and Warren Weaver. *The Mathematical Theory of Communication*. Urbana: University of Illinois Press, 1949.

Shepherdson, Charles. "The Intimate Alterity of the Real." *Postmodern Culture* 6.3 (1996): 2–35.

Silverman, Kaja. *The Threshold of the Visible World*. New York: Routledge, 1996.

Simondon, G. "The Genesis of the Individual." In *Incorporations*, ed. Jonathan Crary and Sanford Kwinter, 297–319. New York: Zone, 1992.

Smith, Neil. "Contours of a Spatialized Politics: Homeless Vehicles and the Production of Geographical Scale." *Social Text* 33 (1992): 54–81.

Smithson, Robert. *Robert Smithson: The Collected Writings*. Berkeley: University of California Press, 1996.

Spillers, Hortense J. "Mama's Baby, Papa's Maybe: An American Grammar Book." *Diacritics* (1987): 65–81.

Spinoza, Baruch. *Ethics*. In *Complete Works*, ed. Edwin Curley. Princeton, NJ: Princeton University Press, 1985.

Spivak, Gayatri Chakrabarty. "Can the Subaltern Speak?" In *Marxism and the Interpretation of Culture*, ed. Cary Nelson and Lawrence Grossberg, 271–313. Urbana: University of Illinois Press, 1988.

——. *A Critique of Postcolonial Reason*. Cambridge, MA: Harvard University Press, 1999.

——. "Ghostwriting." *Diacritics* 25.2 (1995): 65–84.

——. *In Other Worlds: Essays in Cultural Politics*. New York: Methuen Press, 1987.

——. *Outside in the Teaching Machine*. New York: Routledge, 1993.

——. Translator's preface to *Imaginary Maps: Three Stories*, by Mahasweta Devi, trans. Spivak, xxiii–xxix. New York: Routledge, 1995.

Staples, David. *No Place Like Home: Organizing Home-Based Labor in the Era of Structural Adjustment*. New York: Routledge, 2006.

Stoler, Ann Laura. *Race and the Education of Desire: Foucault's "History of Sexuality" and the Colonial Order of Things*. Durham, NC: Duke University Press, 1995.

Suh, Alexandra. "Military Prostitution in Asia and the United States." In *States of Confinement: Policing, Detention, and Prisons*, ed. Joy James, 144–57. New York: St. Martin's Press, 2000.

Tajiri, Rea, dir. *History and Memory*. Women Make Movies, 1991.

Taussig, Michael. *Law in a Lawless Land*. New York: New Press, 2003.

Taylor, Mark C. *Hiding*. Chicago: University of Chicago Press, 1997.

Terranova, Tiziana. "Cybernetics Surplus Value: Embodiment and Perception in Informational Capitalism." Unpublished manuscript, 2001.

——. *Network Culture: Politics for the Information Age*. London: Pluto, 2004.

Thacker, Eugene. *Biomedia*. Minneapolis: University of Minnesota Press, 2004.

——. *The Global Genome: Biotechnology, Politics, and Culture*. Cambridge, MA: MIT Press, 2005.

Thom, René. *Structural Stability and Morphogenesis*. Reading, MA: W. A. Benjamin, 1975.

Thukral, Juhu, and Melissa Ditmore. "Revolving Door: An Analysis of Street-Based Prostitution in New York City." New York: Urban Justice Center, 2003, www.sex workersproject.org.

Thukral, Juhu, Melissa Ditmore, and Alexandra Murphy. "Behind Closed Doors: An Analysis of Indoor Sex Work in New York City." New York: Urban Justice Center, 2005.

Tillotson, Kristin. "Supersaturated: Supermodels—They Strike a Pose and America Can't Resist." *Star Tribune* (Minneapolis) June 7, 1995.

"The Times and Iraq." *New York Times*, May 26, 2004.

Tronti, Mario. *Operao e Capitale*. Turin: Einaudi, 1966.

Tronto, Joan. *Moral Boundaries: A Political Argument for an Ethic of Care*. New York: Routledge, 1993.

Tschumi, Bernard. *Architecture and Disjunction*. Cambridge, MA: MIT Press, 1997.

Turner, Jonathan H. "Toward a General Sociology Theory of Emotions." *Journal for the Theory of Social Behavior* 29.2 (1999): 133–61.

Tykwer, Tom, dir. *Lola rennt* [*Run, Lola, Run*]. Columbia/Tri-Star, 1999.

Uexküll, Jakob Johann von. *Mondes animaux et monde humain, suivi de théorie de la signification*. Paris: Gonthier, 1956.

United Nations Supplementary Convention on the Abolition of Slavery, the Slave Trade, and Institutions and Practices Similar to Slavery (1956).

Van Maanen, John, and Gideon Kunda. " 'Real Feelings': Emotional Expression and Organizational Culture." *Research in Organizational Behavior* 11 (1989): 43–103.

Venkatesh, Sudhir. "Doin' the Hustle: Constructing the Ethnographer in the American Ghetto." *Ethnography*. 3.1 (2001): 91–111.

Vercellone, Carlo, ed. *Sommes-nous sortis du capitalisme industriel?* Paris: La Dispute, 2002.

Virilio, Paul. *The Information Bomb*. Trans. Chris Turner. New York: Verso, 2000.

——. *The Vision Machine*. Trans. Julie Rose. Bloomington: Indiana University Press, 1994.

Wacquant, Loïc. *Body and Soul.* New York: Oxford University Press, 2003.

Walkowitz, Judith R. *Prostitution and Victorian Society: Women, Class, and the State.* Cambridge: Cambridge University Press, 1980.

Wallerstein, Immanuel. *The Uncertainties of Knowledge.* Philadelphia: Temple University Press, 2004.

Weiner, Annette B. *Inalienable Possessions: The Paradox of Keeping-While-Giving.* Berkeley: University of California Press, 1992.

Whalen, Tom. "Run Lola Run." *Film Quarterly* 53.3 (2000): 33–40.

Wiener, Norbert. *The Human Use of Human Beings.* Boston: Houghton Mifflin, 1950.

Wigley, Mark. *The Architecture of Deconstruction: Derrida's Haunt.* Cambridge, MA: MIT Press, 1995.

Wilson, Elizabeth A. *Psychosomatic: Feminism and the Neurological Body.* Durham, NC: Duke University Press, 2004.

Winston, Brian. *Media Technology and Society: A History from the Telegraph to the Internet.* London: Routledge, 1998.

Wolffers, Ivan. "Empowerment of Sex Workers and HIV Prevention." *Research for Sex Work* 3 (2000): 1–3.

Woolley, Scott. "High-Class Lookers." *Forbes* March 22, 1999, 236.

Working Class Autonomy and the Crisis. London: Red Notes and CSE, 1979.

Yang, Mayfair Mei-hui. "Putting Capitalism in Its Place." *Current Anthropology* 41.4 (2000): 477–510.

Yi, Yongsuk. "I Will No Longer Harbor Resentment." In *True Stories of the Korean Comfort Women: Testimonies Compiled by the Korean Council for Women Drafted for Military Sexual Slavery by Japan and the Research Association on the Women Drafted for Military Sexual Slavery by Japan,* trans. Young Joo Lee, ed. Keith Howard, 50–57. London: Cassell, 1995.

Yuh, Ji-Yeon. *Beyond the Shadow of Camptown: Korean Military Brides in America.* New York: New York University Press, 2002.

Zelizer, Viviana A. "Intimate Transactions." In *The New Economic Sociology: Developments in an Emerging Field,* ed. Mauro F. Guillén et al., 274–300. New York: Russell Sage Foundation, 2002.

Zimmer, Carl. *Parasite Rex: Inside the Bizarre World of Nature's Most Dangerous Creatures.* New York: Free Press, 2000.

Žižek, Slavoj. " 'I Hear You with my Eyes'; or, The Invisible Master." In *Gaze and Voice as Love Objects,* ed. Renate Salecl and Žižek, 90–126. Durham, NC: Duke University Press, 1996.

JAMIE "SKYE" BIANCO is an assistant professor in English and the director of composition at Queens College. She also teaches in the women's studies program at the Graduate Center of the City University of New York. Her recent dissertation, *New Media and Technoscience Fictions: Affect, Speed, and Control* received the Irving Howe Dissertation Prize for outstanding writing in politics and literature. She is the author of several articles, including "Zones of Morbidity," "Techno-cinema," and "Composing, Compositing, and 'New Media': Toward a Theory of Integrated Digital Composition Pedagogy and Processes."

GRACE M. CHO is an assistant professor of sociology and women's studies at the City University of New York, Staten Island Campus. She is also a contributing performance artist for *Still Present Pasts: Korean Americans and "The Forgotten War,"* a collaborative art project based on oral histories with Korean War survivors.

PATRICIA TICINETO CLOUGH is a professor of sociology and women's studies at the Graduate Center and Queens College of the City University of New York. She is author of *Autoaffection: Unconscious Thought in the Age of Teletechnology*; *Feminist Thought: Desire, Power and Academic Discourse*; and *The End(s) of Ethnography: From Realism to Social Criticism*.

MELISSA DITMORE is a senior research fellow at the Center for the Study of Women and Society and the coordinator of the Global Network of Sex Work Projects. She is also the co-founder of a web-based resource for anti-trafficking advocates and activists.

ARIEL DUCEY is an assistant professor of sociology at the University of Calgary, where she teaches in the areas of medical sociology and social theory.

DEBORAH GAMBS teaches sociology and works with communication across the curriculum at the City University of New York. She is completing her dissertation, " 'Becoming Artistic': Gender, Race and Technoscience for the Post-Human Era" at the Graduate Center, CUNY.

KAREN WENDY GILBERT teaches in the Teacher Education Department of the Borough of Manhattan Community College of the City University of New York, and consults for the New York City Department of Education. She is the author of numerous papers, including "Locating Agency in the Oreo Subject: Ontological and Ethical Issues"; "The Strength of the Weak: Some Considerations on How Awareness Becomes Conscious"; "Affect: A Mode of Cyborg Communication"; and "The Distributed Mind."

GREG GOLDBERG is a doctoral candidate in sociology at the Graduate Center of the City University of New York. He is currently completing work on a dissertation that addresses the rise of digital audio technologies and peer-to-peer networks and their intersections with information theory and political economy. He also plays in a pop band with Craig Willse.

JEAN HALLEY is an assistant professor of sociology at Wagner College. She is the author of the forthcoming book *Boundaries of Touch: Parenting and Adult-Child Intimacy,* as well as numerous articles, including four in the journal *Qualitative Inquiry.* She is currently working on her second book, a social history of cattle ranching and the United States beef industry.

HOSU KIM is a doctoral candidate in sociology at the Graduate Center of the City University of New York. She is currently finishing her dissertation on the figure of Korean birthmothers in the history of Korean intercountry adoption.

DAVID STAPLES is a research fellow of the Women in and Beyond Global Prison Project at George Washington University. Prior to this he was the development director of Tenants and Workers United in Alexandria, Virginia. He is the author of *No Place Like Home: Organizing Home-based Labor in the Era of Structural Adjustment.*

CRAIG WILLSE is a doctoral candidate in sociology at the graduate center of the City University of New York. He is currently completing work on a dissertation that explores political economies of technology and race in contemporary mental health management. He also plays in a pop band with Greg Goldberg.

ELIZABETH WISSINGER is an assistant professor at the City University of New York. She is the author of several papers on fashion modeling, including "Keeping up Appearances: Aesthetic Labor and Identity in the Fashion Modeling Industries of London and New York" (with Joanne Entwistle) and "Entrepreneurial Labor among Cultural Producers: 'Cool' Jobs in 'Hot' Industries," (with Gina Neff and Sharon Zukin). She is currently working on a book that explores the cultural, economic, and theoretical ramifications of modeling work.

JONATHAN R. WYNN is a lecturer at Smith College. He recently completed his dissertation, *The Walking Tour Guide: Cultural Workers in the Disneyfied City.* His research has been published in *Qualitative Sociology, Qualitative Inquiry, Radical Society,* and *Contexts Magazine.*

Corbett, Sara, 264, 269, 273, 283
Corporeal reason, x
Crack in time, 13
Crash (Ballard), 209, 210, 211, 218, 224, 227
Cuvier, Georges, 88–89
Cyber-Marx (Dyer-Witheford), 145 n.4
Cybernetics, 79, 85, 134, 135, 136

Damasio, Antonio, 190–91, 192
Danielewski, Mark Z., 209, 212
Darwin, Charles, 12
Davy, Georges, 149 n.59
Death, 213, 223, 227, 270, 282–83
Death drive, 10, 11
Deindustrialization, 131
DeLanda, Manuel, 8, 60, 73 n.11
Deleuze, Gilles, xiii n.2, 1, 4, 9, 11–14, 50, 51–52, 59, 63, 65, 67, 69, 72, 77, 80, 81, 86, 87–89, 93, 94–96, 134, 157, 200–201
Deleuze and Cinema (Kennedy), 70–71
Department for International Development, 171
Derrida, Jacques, 148 n.45, 210–11, 212, 220, 224; *Given Time*, 141–42, 143–44
Developing countries, 117–18, 131–32, 134, 135, 137–38
Dialogic Imagination, The (Bakhtin), 228 n.2
Diaspora, Korean, 4, 7, 151–69
Différancial time, 95
Disciplinary societies vs. control societies. *See* Control societies vs. disciplinary societies
Discipline and Punish (Foucault), 270
Ditmore, Melissa, 22, 170–86
Donzelot, Jacques, 125
Drugs, drug abuse, 26, 60–62, 64–65
Ducey, Ariel, 22, 187–208
Duneier, Mitchell, 210
Durbar Mahila Samanwaya Committee (DMSC), 170, 171, 174–75; office, 176–77; organizing activities, 178–84; services, 177, 178
Durée, 78
Durkheim, Émile, 142

Dyer-Witheford, Nick, *Cyber-Marx*, 145 n.4
Dynamism, of matter, 10, 86; nonlinear, 74 n. 13

Economy: of developing nations, 117–18, 131–32, 134; general, 138–41; gift vs. capitalist, 78, 82, 82–84, 121–22, 138–44; global, 2–3, 123–24, 131–32, 135, 137–38; information, 131, 140; open vs. closed system, 136; postindustrial, 78–79, 122–24; restrictive, 138–41; and unpaid labor. *See* Capitalism; Labor, unpaid
Education, of healthcare workers, 188–208
Egg, kinematics of the, 94
Ehrenreich, Barbara, 147 nn.19, 22
Eliot, T. S., 48
Emotions, vs. affects and feelings, 2, 190–92, 232–33
Empire (Negri), 123
Empowerment, 174, 179, 184
End of Ethnography, The (Clough), 73 n.13
Energy crisis, of 1973, 20–21, 22–24, 129–34
Eng, David, 49
English, Deidre, 147 n.19
Entrepreneurialism, 172
Entropic labor, 129–34, 133–35
Entropy, 18, 81, 82, 85–86, 136, 137, 270
Equilibrium systems, 74 n. 13; 86, 210
Ethnographic writing, 6, 210; as personal story, 9–10, 227
Evolution, mechanisms of, 11–15, 87–89
Exchange economy. *See* Gift economy
Exercise, athletic, 106–8, 109, 110, 112, 117
Exploring Complexity (Prigogine), 74 n. 13

Far-from-equilibrium systems, 18–19, 74 n. 13, 86, 210–11. *See also* Open systems
Fast Food, Fast Talk (Leidner), xiii n.3
Fear, 114–15
Fechner, G. T., 267–68
Feedback loops, 3

United Nations Supplementary Convention on the Abolition of Slavery, 185 n.12

Varela, Francisco, 9, 11
Venezuela, Constitution of, 119, 120
Venkatesh, Sudhir, 210
Vercellone, Carlo, xiii n.4
Virilio, Paul, 74 n. 14
Virno, Paolo, xiii n.4
Virtual vs. actual, 12–13; transition, 92–94
Volatile Bodies (Grosz), xii n.1

Wacquant, Loic, 210
Walkowitz, Judith R., 186 n.17
Walkscapes (Careri), 229 n.22
Wall Street Journal, 187
War, 26–27, 275–83. *See also* Diaspora
Wealth and Poverty (Gilder), 140
Weiner, Annette B., *Inalienable Possessions*, 147 n.20
Weiner, Norbert, 17–18
What is Sex? (Sagan and Margulis), 78

White Collar (Mills), 187
Wigley, Mark, 229 n.5
Willse, Craig, 16, 264–86
Wissinger, Elizabeth, 22, 231–60
Wolff, Richard, 145 n.3
Wolffers, Ivan, 174
Women's work, 121, 123–26, 130–35, 144–45, 234, 277–78. *See also* Reproductive labor
Work satisfaction, 187–88, 193–94
Work, unpaid. *See* Labor, unpaid
World Bank, 132
World Trade Center attacks, 21, 201–2
World War II, 152–56
Worldview, and language, 90–91
Writing, autoethnographic, 6
Writing Machines (Hayles), 76 n.46
Wunderblock (Freud), 54

Yang, Mayfair Mei-hui, 149 n.48
Yates, Donald A., 74 n.13

Zero-work, 119, 123, 126
Žižek, Slavoj, 164

LIBRARY OF CONGRESS CATALOGING-IN-PUBLICATION

DATA

THE AFFECTIVE TURN : THEORIZING THE SOCIAL /

EDITED BY PATRICIA TICINETO CLOUGH, WITH JEAN

HALLEY ; FOREWORD BY MICHAEL HARDT.

P. CM.

INCLUDES BIBLIOGRAPHICAL REFERENCES AND INDEX.

ISBN-13: 978-0-8223-3911-3 (CLOTH : ALK. PAPER)

ISBN-13: 978-0-8223-3925-0 (PBK. : ALK. PAPER)

1. AFFECT (PSYCHOLOGY). 2. COGNITION AND

CULTURE. 3. EMOTIONS. 4. INTERPERSONAL

RELATIONS. 5. TRAUMATISM. I. CLOUGH, PATRICIA

TICINETO. II. HALLEY, JEAN.

BF175.5.A35A335 2007

302.'1—dc22

2006033409